ASIAN AMERICANS
AND POLITICS

Asian Americans and Politics

Perspectives, Experiences, Prospects

EDITED BY

GORDON H. CHANG

WOODROW WILSON CENTER PRESS
WASHINGTON, D.C.

STANFORD UNIVERSITY PRESS
STANFORD, CALIFORNIA

EDITORIAL OFFICES:

Woodrow Wilson Center Press
One Woodrow Wilson Plaza
1300 Pennsylvania Avenue, N.W.
Washington, D.C. 20004
Telephone 202-691-4029
www.wilsoncenter.org

ORDER FROM:

Stanford University Press
CUP Distribution Center
110 Midland Avenue
Port Chester, N.Y. 10573-4930
Telephone 1-800-872-7423

2 4 6 8 9 7 5 3 1

Library of Congress Cataloging-in-Publication Data

Asian Americans and politics : perspectives, experiences, prospects /
edited by Gordon H. Chang.
    p. cm.
Includes bibliographical references and index.
ISBN 0-8047-4051-8 (acid-free paper) — ISBN 0-8047-4201-4 (pbk. :
  acid-free paper)
1. Asian Americans—Politics and government. I. Chang, Gordon H.
E184.O6 A8427 2000
323.1'195073—dc21

        00-012465

ABOUT THE CENTER

The Center is the living memorial of the United States of America to the nation's twenty-eighth president, Woodrow Wilson. Congress established the Woodrow Wilson Center in 1968 as an international institute for advanced study, "symbolizing and strengthening the fruitful relationship between the world of learning and the world of public affairs." The Center opened in 1970 under its own board of trustees.

In all its activities the Woodrow Wilson Center is a nonprofit, nonpartisan organization, supported financially by annual appropriations from the Congress, and by the contributions of foundations, corporations, and individuals. Conclusions or opinions expressed in Center publications and programs are those of the authors and speakers and do not necessarily reflect the views of the Center staff, fellows, trustees, advisory groups, or any individuals or organizations that provide financial support to the Center.

CONTENTS

FIGURES

TABLES

PREFACE

The majority of the contributions to this volume emerged from a conference on "Asian Americans and Politics," sponsored by the Woodrow Wilson International Center for Scholars and held in Washington, D.C., in the spring of 1998. This scholarly gathering was perhaps the first devoted to a broad discussion about the emergence of Asian Americans as a significant factor in American politics. Specialists from around the country, with backgrounds in political science, history, sociology, urban studies, ethnic studies, and anthropology, among others, explored a variety of the subject's dimensions from diverse viewpoints. In addition to most of the authors in this volume, invited conference speakers and participants included Akhil Gupta, Juanita Tamayo Lott, Purnima Mankekar, Mari Matsuda, Franklin Odo, Lena Sun, and Carolyn Wong. Their comments, and those of other conference participants, significantly contributed to the discussions and the eventual papers. Participants also benefited from presentations made by Rep. Patsy T. Mink of Hawaii and journalist and social commentator Juan Williams of the *Washington Post*.

ACKNOWLEDGMENTS

The conference and these papers would not have been possible without the generous support of the Wilson Center, the India Abroad Center for Political Awareness, the Japan Foundation, and the Korea Foundation. Thanks to all of them, and to Wilson Center staff members Li Zhao, Beth Brimner, and Mary-Lea Cox, whose inestimably efficient and friendly administrative work made the conference productive and enjoyable. My last expression of gratitude is a special one for Warren I. Cohen, the former consulting director of the Asia Program at the Wilson Center and Distinguished University Professor of History at the University of Maryland, Baltimore County. Warren actually first proposed that the Wilson Center sponsor a conference on Asian Americans. During the actual planning for the conference, Warren, as co-convener and colleague, offered warm support and wisdom gathered through years of experience in encouraging intellectual exchange. This volume would not have been possible without his leadership.

It might seem ironic, even inappropriate, for the *Asia* Program of the Wilson Center to have sponsored and largely funded this conference on *Asian Americans*. Conference participants, all of whom commented frequently on how Asian Americans have been marginalized by their perceived foreignness and inassimilability, noted this uncomfortable juxtaposition as well. Concern about conflating Asia and Asian Americans is legitimate. But the conference, if anything, represented the intellectual vitality of the Wilson Center's Asia Program and its willingness to support discussion of a new topic a bit removed from its usual agenda. I appreciate the Wilson Center's willingness to do something new. I also wish to thank Joseph Brinley and Carol Belkin Walker at the Wilson Center Press, freelance editor Sabra Bissette Ledent, and Muriel Bell at Stanford University Press for their energy and professionalism in the production of this book.

Gordon H. Chang

INTRODUCTION

GORDON H. CHANG

In recent years Asian Americans have become increasingly visible in the political life of the country. Once relatively marginal in local and regional, let alone national, politics, they are quickly becoming elected officials, high-level political appointees, significant constituencies in elections, social and party activists, campaign contributors, and influential policy advisers. As of mid-2000, 300 Asian Pacific Americans had been elected to public office, including 2 U.S. senators, 5 U.S. representatives, 2 governors, 49 state representatives, 89 city council members, 26 city mayors, 133 school board or higher education board members, and 210 judges. (These figures, of course, do not reflect the even greater numbers of Asian Americans who came close but ultimately failed to win their races, such as the closely contested mayoral elections in Los Angeles in 1993 and Oakland in 1994 and the California senate race in 1998.) And more than two thousand appointed officials at the state, federal, and territorial levels also are of Asian Pacific background. Finally, in the closing months of the Clinton administration, the president appointed Norman Mineta secretary of commerce, making Mineta the first presidential cabinet member of Asian ancestry in U.S. history.

Along with these achievements, interest in the voting power of Asian Americans has become commonplace, and Asian American voices have become prominent in many important social and public policy controversies, including in education, immigration reform, race relations, social policy, and political and economic relations with Pacific Rim countries. On a negative and ominous note, a national controversy with racial overtones erupted in 1996–1997 over alleged illegal Asian and Asian American campaign contributions and an illicit foreign influence on American politics. In 1999 a similar shadow loomed over the highly publicized accusations that Wen Ho Lee, a Chinese American physicist, had passed weapons secrets to the Chinese government. Thus the growing visibility of Asian Americans throughout American life has produced a new set of problems, along with unprecedented political opportunities.

What accounts for the growing significance of Asian Americans in politics? For one thing, the Asian American population has grown dramatically in recent decades. In 1965, the year federal immigration law was changed to allow entry of significantly more immigrants, Asian Americans numbered approximately one million. Today, the number is eleven million. Asian Americans are the fastest-growing racial/ethnic group, increasing at a rate of 43 percent in the 1990s. Although the majority of this population is foreign-born, those with citizenship, either through nativity or naturalization, are becoming an influential voting force, especially in those areas of the country where they live in concentrated numbers—the western states and in many urban areas of other regions.

The class and social position of Asian Americans also have changed in recent years. The current Asian American population is much wealthier, better educated, and more diverse in occupation than before. Yet the number of Asian Americans in the lowest socioeconomic strata has grown as well. These demographic changes have expanded the possibilities for Asian American activism and influence, but also have contributed to the perception that they have distinct social identities and social problems.

Finally, American society, and its formal political processes in particular, has changed since the 1960s, offering new possibilities for Asian American involvement. Students of Asian ancestry populate the campuses of top American schools in numbers proportionately much higher than the Asian American presence in the country's population. They are a majority or near majority at several campuses of the University of California and make up between 12 and 25 percent of the student populations of most of the country's elite private institutions. Bilingual ballots, legislation outlawing racial discrimination, and wider acceptance of the value of social "diversity" have all helped to weaken the restrictions that limited Asian American activities in the past. Yet at the same time, social and cultural patterns in America's racial and ethnic relations, including racial prejudice, continue to affect its politics. Today's Asian Americans inherit a long and intense history of being the targets of racial injustice. They also find themselves in the midst of a rapidly evolving and complex contemporary racial environment. America today is no longer characterized by a division only between white and black. African Americans, Latinos, Native Americans, whites, and Asian Americans are negotiating new positions and relations among themselves.

ORGANIZATION OF THIS BOOK

Though there is little question that Asian Americans have emerged as highly visible participants in the political processes of the country, scholarly study of this development is only beginning and trails far behind actual events. This volume is among the first to offer a broad look at Asian Americans and politics. It asks such questions as: What historically has been the position of Asians in the political life of the country? How have Asian Americans emerged as an important political force? What are some of the specific features of the growing political activity of Asian Americans? What distinctive forms of behavior, activity, interests, or issues can be associated with Asian Americans? How has dominant society responded to the growing involvement of Asian Americans in politics? And what might the future hold for Asian Americans and politics?

This volume offers initial and partial responses to these and related questions. No claim is made here for narrow consistency in approach or opinion; in fact, a deliberate effort has been made to offer a variety of disciplinary vantage points, interpretations, and conclusions. The contributors themselves represent many different academic disciplines, including history, political science, sociology, and urban studies, joined by several from the practical political realm. Their collective aim is to contribute to a wide-ranging discussion of the topic and to help open the way to further study. This volume, then, offers what are called emerging perspectives, *emerging* both in the sense that the dimensions of Asian American involvement in American politics are still forming and in the sense that the systematic study of this phenomenon is relatively new, with little collected empirical information as well as analytical reflection.

The essays in this volume are grouped into four sections. Part I, "Framing the Discussion," offers historical context and conceptual ways for thinking broadly about the place of Asian Americans in American politics. Historian Gordon H. Chang's essay focuses on what American observers, beginning in the nineteenth century, have thought about the role of Asians in the political life of the country. The story that emerges is considerably more complex than what many may assume and suggests that contemporary commentators in academia and in journalism, as inheritors of these past attitudes, adopt caution and self-reflection as they try to make sense of developments today. Past observers held strong feelings about the involvement, imagined and real, of Asians in American politics and reviewing these attitudes offers historical context for understanding contemporary attitudes and perceptions. Welcomed and suspected, Asians have occupied an uneasy place in the political life of the country since their arrival in large numbers in the mid-nineteenth century. Despised as irredeemably alien and racially or culturally threatening to America, or dismissed as apathetic, disinterested, and marginal, Asians and their politics have had warped images in the dominant society. These hostile and narrow assumptions need to be left behind as serious study is undertaken today to understand the actual forms of past and present Asian political behavior.

As minorities who have suffered racial discrimination and marginalization, Asian Americans have frequently been compared with other racial groups, such as African Americans. Little attention, however, has been devoted to the related and intertwined racialization of blacks and Asians. An examination of the dynamics of the "racial politics" of dominant society brings into sharp relief the inherited racial landscape we inhabit today, a landscape that continues to form a context for Asian Americans and politics. Political scientist Claire Jean Kim studies the particular racial position of Asians between blacks and whites and argues that Asians have long occupied a particularly awkward position in the country's racial hierarchy. Both used and abused by powerful social forces, Asian Americans have made the journey from the margins of social importance, where they have often been placed, to the middle of the country's evolving racial landscape. The contemporary political relationships being forged among whites, blacks, and Asian Americans, Kim reveals, cannot be divorced from the experiences of the past.

Although the institutions and attitudes of dominant society in the past may have largely set the context for Asian Americans, they still exercised agency and voice within these structures of constraint. Studies published in recent years reveal a wide variety of ways in which Asians sought political recourse, challenged discriminatory legislation and practices, and explored ways to advance their social position through the courts, labor organizations, social activism, and even international politics, often connected to their lands of ancestry. These avenues widen the notion of "politics" beyond electoral activity. If American law and practice dramatically restricted citizenship rights for Asian immigrants, which they did, and closed many avenues for participation in the mainstream of American political life, then the "politics" of Asians, understood on their own terms, must be examined in an expanded way to include an array of organized activity aimed at affecting social position and power.

Taking this expanded approach to Asian American politics, Neil T. Gotanda illustrates the particular ways in which in the past Chinese immigrants challenged their racialized position through the courts. But, as Gotanda shows, the story does not end in the past. Today, the limitations and assumptions of American law and its practice continue to restrict, even inhibit, the emergence of a full political life and identity for Asian Americans. Political/legal structures and deeply imbedded assumptions of suspicion persist in plaguing an active and visible Asian American population that is emerging in a vigorously transnational world. Gotanda calls this barrier to Asian American politics "citizenship nullification."

Don T. Nakanishi also argues that an expanded notion of "politics" is necessary, not only in considering history but also in appreciating the current conditions of Asian Americans. He reviews key events in the political development of Asian Americans in the 1990s and urges consideration of a variety of dimensions of Asian American political activity. He also recommends adoption of new paradigms of thinking that would include an expanded notion of politics. One of the special features of Asian American politics, in fact, may be its variety and wide scope, a feature appreciated by many of the contributors to this volume.

This being said, electoral politics is an increasingly important dimension of Asian American politics. From their relatively small numbers before the 1970s, Asian American voters have become a force in U.S. politics because of their dramatically expanded population base. But what kind of political profile does this population have? To what extent do the past and present realities of discrimination affect voting behavior? How are Asians situated as a racial group within the electoral landscape today? The essays in Part II, "Voting Behavior," are based on empirical investigations of aspects of recent Asian American voting behavior. Using public opinion polls and voting analyses, the authors reach different interesting, and possibly highly significant, conclusions about Asian American political attitudes and activity.

Wendy K. Tam and Bruce E. Cain examine Asian American attitudes toward two controversial ballot measures introduced in California in the 1990s. Proposition 187, on the ballot in 1994, drastically restricted undocumented immigrant access to state services, and Proposition 209, placed before voters in 1996, was viewed as a referendum on affirmative action. The authors use opinion and voter survey data to study Asian American opinions toward other racial groups, illegal and legal immigration, and affirmative action, among other issues. Their findings contribute to efforts to discern the unique political profile of the Asian American electorate and suggest that Asian Americans, at least in California, may be shaping a political identity distinct from that of Euro-Americans and from those of other minority groups.

Using data different from that of Tam and Cain, Paul M. Ong and David E. Lee offer other perspectives on the profile of voters of Chinese ancestry in San Francisco and find that it is changing rapidly. Ong and Lee focus on the emerging tension between U.S.-born Asian American political activists, whose lives were largely shaped by their experiences in the turmoil of the 1960s and early 1970s, and a new generation of political voters and leaders who have immigrant backgrounds. The authors identify not only the different interests of the two groups but also the different political identities and styles that separate them. The new Chinese immigrant voters are not quiet and apathetic, as some have assumed, but are quickly acquiring political skills and identifying their interests, which might even conflict with those of their U.S.-born counterparts. The political identities of the immigrant generation, not just among the Chinese but also among other groups such as Koreans, South Asians, Vietnamese, and Filipinos, all of whom have a very high number of first-generation voters, are still emerging.

Pei-te Lien, using national census data, further disaggregates the Asian American electorate by examining gender differences. In exploring the relationship between gender and racial identities, she finds interesting interplays between these social categories, as well as class, and suggests that generalizations formed from the study of other American social groups may not apply to Asian Americans. Among other things, she asks: Which identities, race or gender, prevail in determining Asian women's likelihood of participation in electoral politics? How does their experience differ from those of other groups of men and women? Lien argues that race, more than gender, has a high level of salience among Asian American voters.

Part III considers the emerging identities of Asian Americans and the implications for politics and policy. The essays in this section highlight one of the distinctive features of the Asian American population, which is its tremendous heterogeneity in ethnic background, socioeconomic position, migration experience to America, and history in this country. The designation "Asian American" in many cases refers to little more than a diverse population whose ancestry is in some way linked to countries ranging from South Asia all the way to the western rim of the Pacific Ocean. The contributors to this volume use the term in this broad sense, without suggesting a coherent, internal pan-ethnic identity. Yet as immigrant peoples "from a different shore," as peoples who have suffered various forms of racial discrimination, and as peoples that society and government practices often perceive and treat in similar racial ways, Asian Americans do have some common social experiences. These tensions of similarity and difference among the ethnic groups that collectively make up the Asian American population, and within ethnic groups themselves, are a concern that runs throughout the essays in Part III of this volume.

Kenyon S. Chan examines the possible policy implications arising from differences among Asian American families. After showing that the U.S.-born, immigrant, refugee, and indigenous families within the Asian/Pacific population have considerable socioeconomic and cultural differences, he asks whether these groups should be understood as distinct "communities." Chan's comparisons raise serious questions about the salience of "the family," and even ethnicity, as assumed stable factors, to many discussions about Asian Americans.

Peter N. Kiang also looks within the Asian American population by examining the attitudes of Asian American youth in the Boston area toward political participation. Using data from focus groups and interviews in his case study, Kiang seeks to understand how youth make meaningful, concrete choices at a micro level about their political participation in their schools and communities. The voices he records reveal that young Asian Americans retain a high degree of self-consciousness about their racial and ethnic identities and seek their own paths to political participation, even as they face restrictions. One wonders about the future political activities of these young Asian Americans when they reach adulthood.

The essay by Sanjeev Khagram, Manish Desai, and Jason Varughese studies one of the most rapidly growing, yet poorly understood, segments of the Asian American population, Asian Indians. Though large in number and possessing significant socioeconomic resources, this population is just beginning to make an impact on American politics. Khagram and his colleagues explore issues of possible interest to Asian Indians, including those in the realm of foreign policy and certain areas of domestic economic and social policy. One purpose of the essay is to suggest ways in which Asian Indians might increase their political presence in the country.

While other essays examine socioeconomic, ethnic, gender, and generational differences among Asian Americans, Edward J. W. Park's work on Koreans in Los Angeles investigates the specific political/ideological differences within the Korean community that have emerged since the 1992 upheaval that devastated South Central Los Angeles. Koreans have responded in very different ways to two central questions: Who victimized us? How do we politically empower ourselves? Park's account also provides insights into a number of other critical issues, including partisan politics and the "racial vision" of the place Koreans hold in America.

Finally, Part IV, "Toward the Future," explores recent experiences and their implications for the future of Asian American politics. Frank H. Wu and Francey Lim Youngberg, writing from the vantage point of Washington, D.C., discuss the controversies surrounding the 1997 campaign finance scandals and assess the attitudes of the media and leading political figures that emerged during the unfolding of events. Even though mainstream commentators and political figures have often described Asian Americans as a "model minority" exhibiting exemplary social behavior, moments such as the campaign finance scandal reveal that Asian Americans also continue to be viewed in suspicious, negative ways. This treatment disturbed Asian Americans throughout the country and raised questions about the desirability, or even possibility, of Asian American involvement in politics at the national level.

On a more positive note, Judy Yu and Grace T. Yuan write from their experience as "insiders" in one of the most interesting and significant events of Asian American politics, the election of Gary Locke as governor of Washington State in 1996. Yu and Yuan describe how Asian Americans, although constituting only a relatively small share of the state's population, played a major role in Locke's campaign, especially in its early days. Their account suggests the possibilities that lie ahead for Asian Americans interested in electoral politics.

In his specific response to the 1997 campaign finance uproar, Paul Y. Watanabe also offers thoughts on how Asian Americans might develop their political viability and on what lies ahead for Asian Americans at the local political level. He sees many possibilities for—and important obstacles to—further Asian American political influence and raises questions about the direction Asian Americans might take in politics, which he suggests must be understood beyond voting and traditional activities.

Yet Asian American political activists at the local level face difficult questions when confronting the entrenched political structures that impede the expansion of Asian American empowerment. They also face the practical problems of building coalitions among local groups, including other ethnic communities. Indeed, defining their place in the political landscape is not easy, as other essays in this volume show. Leland T. Saito's study of redistricting efforts undertaken by Chinese American activists in New York City reveals the practical dilemmas encountered in trying to build a local power base, as Watanabe urges.

A FINAL THOUGHT

There is much that this volume does not address. Little attention is devoted to transnational, cultural, labor, radical, sexual, or other forms of politics. Certain subgroups, especially Southeast Asians and Filipino Americans, partisan party politics, and the experience of Asians in Hawaii politics are inadequately discussed. These issues will have to be addressed at another time.

What emerges from the very different studies in this volume is that Asian Americans are having a mounting impact on American politics in a variety of ways. They are becoming important as activists, as voters, as candidates, as political contributors, and as participants in the policy debates. They are not a silent or inactive minority; they express themselves in distinct ways. Perhaps most important, it is becoming clear that Asian Americans are developing a self-consciousness about their potential strength and their interests—that is, they are beginning to think of themselves as a political force. Yet the features of this force, including its identity, interests, and cohesiveness, are far from clear, and it is too early to draw many solid conclusions about the direction of this political development. In fact, the social heterogeneity of Asian American populations argues against easy generalizations. As for those hoping to build a coherent political pan-ethnic force, it will not likely happen easily, if ever. Dominant social attitudes and established political structures and practices will impede the emergence of new political forces.

But it is also becoming clear from the essays in this volume that Asian Americans at many different levels of society are accumulating political experience through their involvement in established political processes, be it at the high school, local, state, or national levels. These experiences, and the reflection on their meaning, will undoubtedly lead to greater sophistication and an awareness that, despite the many ethnic, generational, cultural, and class differences among Asian Americans, there also are incentives to think pan-ethnically—after all, numbers, in the form of votes or dollars, mean power in politics. The goal of transforming these and other resources of Asian Americans into actual influence is finding its way onto the personal agendas of the growing numbers of this population.

PART ONE

FRAMING THE DISCUSSION

CHAPTER ONE

ASIAN AMERICANS AND POLITICS: SOME PERSPECTIVES FROM HISTORY

GORDON H. CHANG

Asian Americans and politics—for many people today, these two notions seem incongruous, even contradictory. Popular belief has it that persons of Asian ancestry have not, until very recently, been generally interested in American politics. Indeed, many observers characterize Asian Americans[1] historically as laboring and economic beings, not political in any way; their alleged political disinterest stemmed from cultural differences or a conscious decision to remain inoffensive and obscure in a hostile land. Conservative economist Thomas Sowell, for example, argues that Chinese Americans "deliberately kept out of the courts and out of the political arena" and that perhaps they and Japanese Americans came to enjoy social and economic success because they, in fact, "studiously avoided political agitation." Sowell's interpretation of Chinese and Japanese American histories, however, reflects less of an interest in the experiences of these racial minorities than in constructing an argument against state efforts to remedy social and racial inequality.[2]

Another argument advanced for why Asian Americans supposedly eschewed politics, even refusing to exercise the franchise when they could, is that years of rejection and discrimination created deep distrust of the political process and pessimism about the possibility of effecting significant change.[3] Reflecting the assumption that Asians, either by "culture" or because of historical experience, have been unpolitical in America, commentators have described the increasing visibility of Asians in American politics as something of a novelty and break from an unassertive past. Titles of recent articles from across the political spectrum in the mainstream press express this attitude: "Overcome Distaste for Politics in Order to Get Their Views Heard: Asian-Americans Seek to Join Power Structure,"[4] "Have Asian Americans Arrived Politically? Not Quite,"[5] "Apathetic Asian Americans? Why Their Success Hasn't Spilled Over into Politics,"[6] "Voters of Asian Heritage Slow to Claim Voice,"[7] and "Asian Americans Head for Politics."[8]

These articles are not wrong in appreciating the emergence of Asian Americans as a political force, albeit still in its formative stages. This development is important and a turning point in the history of Asian Americans and American public life.[9] But the articles are misleading in the way they characterize this development. Suggesting a linear movement from inactivity to political involvement, from apathy to activism, from powerlessness and voicelessness to increasing influence, and even from inoffensiveness to a possible threat, may be a convenient way to view events today, but it is not a historically accurate one. Neither is it one that leads to an appreciation of the complexities of current Asian American political behavior and an understanding of its distinctive features.

This chapter does not examine the complexities of current Asian American politics—other contributions to this volume do that. Instead, it reviews how past observers have described the relationship between Asian Americans and politics. This chapter deals, therefore, with perceptions and interpretations. But it is also about the meaning of these views, since past attitudes, assumptions, and suspicions continue to affect the ways in which current events are understood. For example, inflammatory rhetoric around the presidential campaign finance controversy of the mid-1990s echoed the fears that many in America held in the 1880s about the corrupting influence of the Chinese in American politics. The mounting assertiveness of Asian Americans in local politics around the country has met with reactions like those seen when Japanese Americans entered Hawaiian politics in the mid-twentieth century. And many sensational comments made in 1999 about the alleged Chinese communist theft of American nuclear weapons technology fall within a tradition of questioning the loyalty of Asians to America. By contrast, the wide celebration of Asians as model and unassuming citizens also invokes another set of historically imbedded notions about the unpolitical and compliant Asian.

Understanding Asian American political activity on its own terms, without the baggage of the past, is not an easy or comfortable task for many

Americans. In seeking to lighten, or at least open up, the kinds of interpretive baggage that affect much of the discussion about Asian American
politics today, this chapter will examine a selection of scholarly and popular literature, principally about the relationship that Chinese and Japanese
Americans, the two large, early Asian groups, have had with American
politics. This literature is divided into three different periods—the mid-
nineteenth century to the mid-1920s, the mid-1920s to the late 1960s, and
the late 1960s to the 1990s. Changes in the social profile of the Asian American communities and in the perceptions of their relationship to politics
distinguish each period.

This review will reveal that interest in the relationship of Asians to
American politics is not something that emerged only toward the end of
the twentieth century; it is a discussion with a long history, beginning with
the arrival of significant numbers of Asians in the United States in the mid-
nineteenth century. Writers have asked: What kinds of political beings are
these persons of Asian ancestry? How will they participate in the political
life of the country? What particular political interests will they have? What
agendas will they pursue? In various forms, these questions have been
posed through the years. The resulting discussion has waxed and waned,
but it has always been marked by great emotion—and often by considerable prejudice. It also has been a discussion closely connected to other
prominent issues of the day, including race, war, and national identity.

MID-NINETEENTH CENTURY TO THE MID-1920S

In the years immediately after the immigration of large numbers of Chinese to America, many commentators wondered about the social and cultural makeup of the new arrivals and about their political relationship to
the Republic. At first, the Chinese were frequently welcomed as positive
additions to the country, and the pundits optimistically predicted that they
would soon join other immigrant groups as part of the American political
family. Indeed, during the grand San Francisco celebration of the admission of California to the Union in 1850, local judge Nathaniel Bennett
specifically acknowledged the presence of Chinese and other immigrants in
the audience: "Born and reared under different Governments and speaking different tongues, we nevertheless meet here today as brothers. . . . You
stand among us in all respects as equals."[10] The participation of large
numbers of Chinese in the 1852 Fourth of July festivities in San Francisco

prompted the city's main daily newspaper to predict with confidence that "the China Boys will yet vote at the same polls, study at the same schools, and bow at the same altar as our own countrymen." The same year, California governor John McDougal publicly characterized the Chinese as "one of the most worthy of our newly adopted citizens."[11]

Time has shown, however, that these early writers were far off the mark in their sanguine expectations that the Chinese would slide easily into American life and society. Indeed, mounting hostility soon overwhelmed their predictions of Chinese acceptance. The Chinese as citizens, many now concluded, would be a catastrophe.

The famous decision handed down by the California Supreme Court in *People v. Hall* (1854) expressed this dark vision, which became the popular view about the Chinese and the implications of their presence in America. A jury had convicted George Hall of the murder of a Chinese, in part on the basis of the testimony of Chinese witnesses. In overturning Hall's conviction, the California Supreme Court pointed out that existing statutes maintained that "no black or mulatto person, or Indian" was allowed "to give evidence in favor of, or against a white man" in court. Chief Justice Hugh C. Murray argued that testimony from "Asiatics" also must be prohibited because the clear intent of the statutes was to distinguish whites from all others.

Murray's argument is usually cited today to illustrate the relegation of Chinese into a formal inferior racial caste along with other persons of color in America, but it is also revealing of the attitudes that would have a direct bearing on the involvement of the Chinese in American politics. "The same rule which would admit them to testify," Murray wrote, "would admit them to all the equal rights of citizenship, and we might soon see them at the polls, in the jury box, upon the bench, and in our legislative halls." Such prospects clearly frightened the chief justice. The possibility of Chinese participation in American politics was, he argued, "not a speculation which exists in the excited and overheated imagination of the patriot and statesman, but it is an actual and present danger."[12] While Murray's own imagination may very well have been "overheated," his decision in the Hall case became a cornerstone of much subsequent California legislation and policy, and his comments were accepted as sober, judicious, and well founded.

The chief justice was not alone in his fear. Many other white Californians shared his alarm about Chinese interest in American political life. They believed the Chinese would be *hyperpolitical*—that is, inordinately, even fanatically, interested in seeking political power and influence to the detriment of established society and government. In their view, such political activity would harm, not benefit, America.

The threat of Chinese hyperpolitical activity was a common ingredient in the popular "yellow peril" literature of the last decades of the nineteenth century. Written in florid, provocative language, this literature reveals much about how the Chinese were perceived by many serious writers and a reading public.[13] One of the most well known of these polemics warned America of impending doom. Published in 1880, the future-as-history novel *Last Days of the Republic* by Pierton W. Dooner was a call to action.If the state did nothing to stop Chinese immigration, Dooner wrote, the Chinese would soon inundate California and the country as a whole. The author described a terrible future that would see nothing less than the very conquest and demise of America because of white political apathy and underappreciation of the Asian threat. The Chinese, according to Dooner, aspired to nothing less than the political conquest of America. The book ends with the Chinese seizing Washington, D.C.

Dooner was seeking to rally whites to support restrictions on Chinese immigration and Chinese access to the ballot box. His was not simple fiction, but a forecast based on evidence from real life. Dooner included, for example, long, verbatim quotes from Chief Justice Murray in the Hall murder case to remind Californians of earlier wisdom about the political dangers posed by the Chinese.[14]

Not long after publication of Dooner's book, explicit concerns about giving Chinese the right to vote were expressed throughout hearings on the federal Chinese Exclusion Act, passed by Congress in 1882. Among other things, the act made the Chinese "aliens ineligible to citizenship." This provision, more than any other single act or incident, would confirm the relegation of the Chinese in America to a political nether world and establish a precedent for the political and social marginalization of subsequent Asian immigrants. The last ethnic restrictions against Asians becoming American citizens would not be lifted until 1952.

The 1882 exclusion act was the first in a series of such acts, yet many Americans continued to express concern about the political ambitions and abilities of Chinese immigrants. In 1898, for example, the respected *North American Review* published the article "The Chinaman in American Politics," which alerted readers to the political savvy of the Chinese and the extraordinary and undesirable influence they were still having on American politics.[15] "It is the prevailing opinion that politics as a profession is unknown to the Chinese, but nothing could be farther from the truth," the article began. "As a race they are astute politicians, and, singularly, one of the most active fields for the demonstration of their skill is found, not in China, but on the American continent and among the American people." Although the Chinese were virtually without the power of the vote, the essay argued that they wielded political significance far beyond their numbers and were "more effective" than "the entire Afro-American contingent," which was many times larger in number. Blacks, it said, even with the help of "philanthropic whites," had obtained far less desired legislation than had the Chinese. As evidence, the essay pointed to the ability of the Chinese "political machine" to frustrate further legislative efforts to control their population. No one in America, it was claimed, had "ever fought a campaign with more diplomacy," "more astuteness," and more ruthless determination than had the Chinese.

But in contrast to these accounts which saw a racial conspiracy against America, considerable contemporary evidence points to a different interpretation of the political sentiments and behavior of the Chinese. Chinese leaders, writers, and organization officials regularly spoke out against the legislation that discriminated against them, but, in doing so, they argued that the Chinese had no special interests other than in seeking the rights and privileges enjoyed by others in the country. Thousands of individual Chinese turned to the courts to seek redress of grievances and to claim rights denied them. And contrary to the later notion that the Chinese were uninterested in political democracy, many Chinese in America, inspired by the universalist declarations of American democracy, actively supported republicanism in China. Ironically, seeking to realize democracy in their faraway land of ancestry seemed a more realistic political alternative than struggling for a consistent democracy in a hostile America.[16]

But it was not just the Chinese who were characterized as hyperpolitical. In the 1920s, after two decades of Japanese immigration to America, a prominent political commentator, Montaville Flowers, raised the specter of the Japanese. He maintained that Japanese immigrants wanted

> all the rights and privileges of the American-born white man—the right of free entrance for [Japanese] nationals into the United States; the right to vote; the right to own American land anywhere, in any quantity, for any purpose; the right to be legislators and governors of states; the right to go to Congress and make the laws; the right to sit upon our Supreme Courts of State and Nation, and there to determine the very genius of our future civilization.[17]

For Flowers and many others of his day, efforts by the Japanese to seek these basic political rights was not only impudent but also evidence of another racial conspiracy. He warned that if Japanese immigrants could become citizens, they would work to end the laws restricting their economic activities. They would then concentrate their population "in certain states and in special centres in those states, and waiting, waiting for more men, for all their 'picture brides,' and for their native born children, who are American citizens by right of birth; waiting until all these vote, he [sic] will have his representatives at the capitols, control the balance of power and be master of his destiny." The Japanese effort to seize power, Flowers concluded, would be "a master stroke."

In the early twentieth century Flowers was not alone in seeing the Japanese as an outspoken racial minority in the country. The respected social scientist Jesse F. Steiner expressed a similar opinion when he observed that the Japanese, "instead of acquiescing in the position assigned them, as, on the whole, the great mass of the Negroes seem disposed to do, have taken a bold stand for their rights and insist that there shall be no discrimination against them."[18] Steiner was not the racial extremist that Flowers was, but he too warned white Americans about the changing racial balance of power in the world. In his book *The Japanese Invasion: A Study in the Psychology of Inter-Racial Contacts,* he concludes, "We must bear in mind that the Orient will not always come to us in the attitude of a supplicant. The Orientals feel deeply that their cause is righteous, and their hands are strengthened by the consciousness of growing power." Steiner favored restrictions on immigration and other measures against the Japanese to preempt expanded racial conflict on the West Coast.

Steiner's comparison of the Japanese with African Americans may seem strange today when African American activism has set the standard for "minority politics." In the early twentieth century, however, African American leaders themselves often praised Japanese immigrants as a positive model of racial pride and political activism for the black masses. Although African American writers drew very different conclusions than Flowers and Steiner about Japanese immigrants, they too saw the Japanese as highly political people.

In those days, not just the immigrant but even the native born of Asian ancestry was suspect. In 1919, for example, influential publisher V. S. McClatchy warned California of the political danger posed by the Nisei (second-generation Japanese Americans).[19] He pointed to Hawaii where, he said, "Japanese born under the American Flag," and thus having citizenship, would soon be able to "outvote any other race; and in a generation they will probably out-vote all other races combined." If the government did not restrict their numbers and their political privileges, including naturalization, McClatchy warned, the Japanese would imperil American institutions. Echoing earlier views of the Chinese, McClatchy described the Japanese immigrants and their descendants not as unpolitical, but as hyperpolitical beings, unafraid of using their vote and public office to advance their own alleged racial agenda.

Upon their arrival in America in the early twentieth century, Asian Indians and Filipinos also encountered deep suspicions about their political loyalties. Because of their antipathy to the British colonization of their homeland, Indians, many Americans believed, were hostile not only to the British but also to the entire English-speaking world, which included America, of course. Allegedly, then, Indians would sympathize with the anti-white appeals of the Japanese and Chinese.[20] Filipino immigrants represented a different sort of problem in the eyes of commentators during the 1930s. It was feared that Filipinos, like other colonials, harbored resentments against the country that oppressed their homeland. However, unlike other Asians, many Filipinos actually seemed to embrace America. Yet this love also was threatening to some Americans. As a specialist on Filipino immigration noted in 1931, the educated "Filipino is, if anything, *too* assimilable to accept the limitations imposed upon him by public opinion."[21] The problem here was "not that of the stranger who cannot be Americanized, but rather that of the would-be American who refuses to remain a stranger." Asians, even as putative friends, were still seen as a problem because they would not accept their subordinate place.

Thus in the view of many Americans in the first decades of the twentieth century, Asians could never become good, active citizens and join the American political family. Whether it was their different standards of morality and truth, their clannishness or cliquishness, their venality and worship of the material over principle, or their ambition and drive, Asians could not appreciate, understand, or partake of modern democracy, the argument went. They were either hyperpolitical or, as some commentators saw it, apolitical, uninterested in participating in a democracy. Though apparently contradictory, these two popular perceptions shared the assumption that Asians threatened American values and political life and could not live constructively in the country. Moreover, the loyalty and value of the Asian immigrant were suspect, according to either view. Both apolitical and hyperpolitical Asians were devoted only to advancing their own narrow interests and were unable or unwilling to accept the rules of civic participation in America.[22]

To be sure, some early observers did not view Asians in such suspicious and exaggerated ways, but they did not represent majority opinion during the period of immigration exclusion. The defenders of the Chinese and Japanese typically presented Asians as being no different from other immigrant groups in both their political behavior and attachment to America. Sociologist Mary Roberts Coolidge tried to counter the virulent anti-Chinese prejudices of her day by offering sympathetic perspectives from her own social research. In her classic 1909 work, *Chinese Immigration,* she observed that the American-born Chinese were already assuming everyday civic responsibilities.[23] "There is abundant evidence," she wrote, "that the Chinese of the second generation mean to claim their citizenship. In the smaller towns of California and in some other states they show strong patriotism, marching in Fourth of July parades and even drilling and volunteering for the army." Even the parents of these native-born Chinese, she noted, although they could not vote, were proud of the rights enjoyed by their children.

Kiyoshi K. Kawakami, a prolific, vocal defender of the Japanese in America in the pre–World War II years, argued similarly about the Japanese and suggested that the accusations about the evils of Japanese immigrant influence in America were wildly exaggerated.[24] A future historian of America examining the passions of the times, he wrote, "would no doubt wonder why there was so much ado about the naturalization of the Japanese." In his view, ending the denial of citizenship to Japanese would produce no dire results, but would simply remove a major irritant in Tokyo-Washington relations. In the views of both Coolidge and Kawakami, Chinese and Japanese Americans were really very much like any other immigrant group, and their attitudes toward politics were not fundamentally different in any way. For many years afterward, other observers would continue to frame the discussion of Asian American political behavior in a similarly simplistic way—that is, whether Asian Americans were the same or radically different from other social groups.

MID-1920S TO THE LATE 1960S

After passage of the Chinese Exclusion Act, designation of the "Asiatic Barred Zone" in 1917, and enactment of the Immigration Act of 1924, the

United States effectively ended further immigration from Asia and classified all Asian immigrants already in America "aliens ineligible to citizenship." In view of the impossibility of naturalization and the small, slow-growing, native-born sector of the population that did enjoy citizenship rights, Americans perceived Asian American communities to be much less threatening to the dominant racial order than they had been previously. Because of harsh social discrimination, the Asian communities also were relatively isolated from the rest of society. In the end, then, the exclusion of Asians largely quieted, though did not entirely end, popular fears of the Asian presence in America and its political threat.

In fact, from the 1920s to the 1960s the perception of Asians as hyper-political largely disappeared. Asian Americans came to be seen as only marginal to American mainstream society and politics, and the stereotype of Asians as basically unpolitical became imbedded in America. Writings based on the "Survey of Race Relations," the first comprehensive study of racial attitudes and the living situation of Asians in the West, reflected this view. The investigation, which involved scores of researchers in the mid-1920s, devoted little attention to the political behavior of Asians in America. For example, Stanford University's Eliot Grinnell Mears, secretary of the project, barely mentions Asian American political activity in his 1928 work *Resident Orientals on the American Pacific Coast: Their Legal and Economic Status*.[25] About all he says on the subject is that both the Chinese and Japanese in America wanted citizenship, with the Japanese more eager than the Chinese and "probably more so than the general run of American immigrants." Of the second-generation Chinese and Japanese, Mears simply describes them as "worthy Americans."

Mears's colleague at Stanford, Yamato Ichihashi, the leading authority on the Japanese in America in the prewar years, also wrote little about their political behavior in his now-classic 1932 study of Japanese immigrants.[26] Ichihashi devotes over four hundred pages to discussing their migration history, social life, economic activity, and prospects for life in America, as well as anti-Japanese agitation; three chapters are devoted especially to the situation of the Nisei. Yet in all these pages he says little about Japanese Americans and politics.

Ichihashi argues that the Japanese were as fit for residence in America as European immigrants and that, as for politics, the Japanese represented no threat. They admired America, including its political institutions, and only wanted to be given a decent chance in the country. The Nisei, he maintains, were rapidly becoming Americanized and culturally distant from their parents. In his view, it was white prejudice that prevented the full social and political assimilation of the Nisei into American life, and such prejudice was responsible, therefore, for their lingering ethnic distinctiveness.

A very different view of the future role of Japanese Americans in American politics appeared ten years later during the federal government's internment of Japanese Americans in World War II. Some social scientists and government officials linked to internment offered enthusiastic predictions about the exemplary political role Japanese Americans might play in the postwar world. They would be neither hyperpolitical threats nor apathetic citizens, these scientists and public officials asserted. Instead, they described Japanese Americans as an especially malleable human clay that could be molded for proclaimed democratic purposes. With great optimism, internment administrators and teachers often wrote about the potential of the camps as an unprecedented social engineering project for their vision of American democracy. They rejected the prewar notion that blood rendered the Japanese racial threats to America; instead, they believed that enlightened administrators could shape the Japanese into ideal citizens. One teacher wrote positively of her efforts along these lines with students at the Topaz, Utah, camp and majestically described her project as "Developing World Citizens in a Japanese Relocation Center." A leading official at the camp in Poston, Arizona, saw the internees under him as similar in potential. His challenge, he believed, was to make the Poston internment camp "a source of rich production, a school for wise and energetic Americans in years to come." He wanted to achieve nothing less than the transformation of his wards into "projectiles of democracy" who would go forward constructively into the anticipated difficult postwar world.[27] These educators saw the Japanese as compliant, without their own political identity or interests. The social engineers could make them into whatever was wanted. The Japanese would become, in a very real sense, "models," anticipating the characterization of Asian Americans two decades later.

Despite these developments, the view that the Japanese still represented a hyperpolitical threat persisted. Internment itself was the culmination of decades of racial suspicion about the loyalty of Japanese Americans. Even after the Japanese were incarcerated, hostile commentators continued to warn that Japanese Americans were waiting to exploit the political system for their own self-serving purposes. What would happen in the postwar period when the government released the internees from these camps located in sparsely populated states? What would prevent the efficient and prolific Japanese from soon dominating the politics of Nevada or Wyoming? A 1943 article in *American Legion Magazine* raised these sensational questions and challenged readers to consider "How long would it take for this fast multiplying, unresting, far-scheming race to have two Senators in Washington?"[28] The author proposed shipping all the internees to distant islands in the Pacific where they would live under direct rule from Washington without benefit of the franchise.

This thinking aside, the most common view among specialists on Japanese Americans at this time was that they were far from being the hyperpolitical threat once feared and, indeed, were notably less political, with a weaker political identity, than other Americans. Forrest E. LaViolette, a social scientist who had studied Japanese American political behavior in the years immediately before the war, concluded that the Nisei in fact had not "participated in elections to the fullest extent."[29] Based on his own research and reports in Japanese community newspapers, LaViolette suggested that only about a third of the Nisei eligible to vote had actually registered. He characterized this behavior as "political indifference" arising from the "lack of political consciousness" among the Japanese. Continuing social segregation, isolation of the parent generation from the political arena, and the "conservative character of Japanese tradition" all contributed to this low level of political attention among young Japanese Americans. Although he pointed to developments such as the rise of the Japanese American Citizens League as evidence of changing attitudes, LaViolette saw nothing dramatic ahead. The Japanese in America, he noted, were rather conservative and few were attracted to communism or other radical politics. He predicted that neither the Chinese nor Japanese would be interested in "racial voting blocs."

Through the 1950s and into the 1960s, the view that Asians were inoffensive and without a well-formed political identity became well established in America. One of the leading scholars of the Chinese in America, sociologist Rose Hum Lee, claimed that Chinese Americans were "not politically astute, or active in American politics."[30] Critical of the perceived "apathy," Lee chastised Chinese Americans as "politically immature" and as even disdainful of politics, except for a handful of officials connected to the Chinese Nationalist Party, the Kuomintang. Lee attributed this Chinese American political indifference to influences from their immigrant parents, social isolation, or their traditional suspicion of government, and she found nothing admirable in their attitude.

Other important books published in the 1960s about Chinese Americans, such as that by S. W. Kung, *Chinese in American Life: Some Aspects of Their History, Status, Problems, and Contributions* (1962), and Betty Lee Sung's influential *Mountain of Gold: The Story of the Chinese in America* (1967), contained similar points of view. In his book, Kung devotes considerable attention to the achievements of prominent Chinese Americans, principally in the professions, but pays virtually no attention to politics, other than celebrating the election of Hiram Fong as Hawaii's U.S. senator in 1959.[31] He does acknowledge, however, that though the Chinese in America were victims of injustice that relegated them to second-class status, they "have gradually come to understand the true significance of their right to vote." Although he believes their "potential political power" was "rapidly enlarging," he ventures no prediction of how that influence might be used. Betty Lee Sung's explanation for why the "Chinese tended to shy away from American political activity or from exercising their right to vote" is that they believed their franchise was inconsequential.[32] They were, however, "gradually beginning to realize the fallacy of their thinking." In Sung's view, Chinese political inactivity was on the wane because of a decline in the sojourner mentality as well as falling social barriers and reduced discrimination. The result would be increased participation in "American life."

Authors such as Ichihashi, Lee, and Sung were highly sensitive to the past and continuing prejudices against Asians in America, and much of their writing constituted responses to the prejudiced assumptions that had dominated the discourse on Asian Americans. Indeed, their writing effectively responded to the past negative portrayals and helped introduce new, much more positive images. To counter the view that Asians represented a threat to America, these writers emphasized the inoffensiveness of Asians and focused on the developing Americanism of the Asian American communities. And to counter the view that Asian Americans were poor and unskilled and contributed little to mainstream American life, the authors offered a picture of hardworking communities that aspired to becoming assimilated and full members of middle America.

As salutary as these efforts were to ending the virulently racist views from the past, these writers helped to construct images that were one-sided in their own ways. Indeed, sometimes this was done deliberately. Yamato

Ichihashi, for example, virtually omitted any discussion of politics in his prewar writings about the Japanese in America, but he knew full well the deep interest of the Issei (first-generation Japanese immigrants) and many Nisei in the politics of Japan. This interest was understandable because of the limitations they faced in the United States. Nevertheless, Ichihashi clearly crafted his accounts to create a positive and congenial image of the Japanese for his mainly Euro American audiences.[33] The writers who focused on Chinese Americans also consciously presented accounts that elided aspects of the experience that did not well serve their effort to forge a new narrative. They minimized or even entirely omitted discussion of the strong diasporic consciousness of Chinese in America and the social and political disenchantment with America that was widespread among immigrant as well as native-born generations. This scholarship helped to create the basis for the dramatically new public attitude toward Asian Americans that had emerged by the late 1960s.[34]

Toward the end of that tumultuous decade, the periodical press featured prominent articles that consistently described Asian Americans in positive, even praiseworthy ways and endorsed the idea that Asian Americans had been and continued to be politically indifferent. Whether about Chinese or Japanese Americans, written by Asians or non-Asians, these essays presented a remarkably similar point of view, much like the "yellow peril" literature decades earlier. The 1960s literature, however, presented a triumphant story of minority immigrant communities overcoming adversity and achieving a high degree of social integration and economic success in American life. And in all these accounts, the authors suggested that Asians had eschewed political involvement, although they were beginning to show interest in electoral activity. Unlike some earlier characterizations, however, some observers now attributed *positive* qualities to this putative apoliticalness. Asian aloofness from politics was celebrated.

An example of this sort of praise appeared in the *New York Times Sunday Magazine* in 1966. In his article "Success Story, Japanese-American Style," sociologist William Petersen wrote admiringly of the ability of the Japanese, as a racial minority, to overcome social discrimination, official persecution, and economic deprivation to attain "a generally affluent and, for the most part, highly Americanized life." In venturing an explanation for their achievement, Petersen described a hardworking, frugal, unassuming people devoted to family and educational improvement. Nowhere does political activity seem to have a place in the picture; in fact, politics appears to be almost anathema to the people in Petersen's story. Petersen followed his article with a book entitled *Japanese Americans: Oppression and Success* that elaborates on the themes introduced in his article.[35] A major addition is a discussion of the Japanese experience in Hawaii, including a complimentary description of their political activity in the state. In his view, however, their new-found political visibility was an outgrowth of their social and economic success and not in any way connected to any pursuit of "ethnic politics."

One of the most widely consulted books on Japanese Americans, Bill Hosokawa's 1969 *Nisei: The Quiet Americans,* developed the success story interpretation, but paid considerable attention to the moderate political philosophy of the Japanese American Citizens League.[36] Unwavering faith in America's basic goodness, even in the most adverse of times during World War II, sacrifice in the pursuit of democratic ideals, and triumph in advancing toward greater equality are prominent themes in this work. The politics described, however, is largely the politics of the most traditional Americanism, of a creed virtually devoid of any particular ethnic content, unless one argues that the remarkable and singular pursuit of acceptance in mainstream America is itself the unique contribution of Japanese Americans to ethnic politics. The Japanese Americans described by Hosokawa indeed seem very much like those "projectiles of democracy" promoted by the staff members of the internment centers.

This "model minority" literature appeared during a time of sharp social and political divisions in America and the emergence of assertive minority politics, especially among African Americans. While the ethnic politics of European immigrant groups was not a new subject in American intellectual life, concern about the behavior of the increasingly active African American population was.[37] And the alleged political indifference or super-Americanism of Asian Americans seemed to offer a positive contrast for writers concerned with the African American challenge. Edwin O. Reischauer, in his foreword to *Nisei: The Quiet Americans,* urged readers to appreciate the implications and message of Hosokawa's book which was that the Japanese American story was not an isolated one that concerned just one ethnic group. "It has much broader significance," Reischauer pointed out, for it offered an inspiration and, very important, a contrasting example "to others" critical of America. The Nisei showed there was another way.[38]

It was not difficult to determine who the "others" were. "The history of Japanese Americans," William Petersen had written, "challenges every such generalization about ethnic minorities." *U.S. News and World Report* wrote in a similar, but even blunter, way about Chinese Americans in 1966.[39] In the face of demands advanced by racial minorities upon the government, the Chinese American community, the magazine proclaimed, was "winning wealth and respect by dint of its own hard work." It went on to say that "still being taught in Chinatown is the old idea that people should depend on their own efforts—not a welfare check—in order to reach America's 'promised land.' "

Such commentary obviously pitted Asians against African Americans, but it also set Asians against themselves. Some activist-inclined Asian American commentators expressed impatience with the alleged political reticence of Asians. Rather than models of behavior, they were seen as laggards in ethnic politics. In a pioneering commentary on pan-ethnic Asian political behavior written during these same years, Alfred Song, one of California's first political figures of Asian ancestry, maintained that the "evolution of noticeable political involvement by Orientals has been relatively slow compared to other minority groups."[40] He did not cite ethnic apathy or cultural difference to explain what he believed was Asian American political apathy. Rather he attributed it to Asians' pragmatic estimations of the limited significance of their vote and the continuing sensitivity to their own marginalization. But even with the passage of time, Song argued, an Asian American politics would be unlikely. "It is doubtful that there will develop any real or lasting group political solidarity among Orientals." The achievement of any future political significance by Asians in California, he predicted, would stem from individual efforts rather than from "Oriental group action." In other words, the future was unlikely to see any Asian American politics.

LATE 1960S TO THE 1990S

At the very moment that the "success" stories about Chinese and Japanese Americans appeared, important social, political, and intellectual developments were occurring that would transform Asian American communities and make Alfred Song's prediction short-lived. In 1965 the United States ended the last vestiges of discrimination against immigration from Asia. The immigration act passed that year placed Asian immigration on the same formal basis as European immigration and sparked an unprecedented migration of Asians to the United States. Since 1965, the Asian population has grown from one million to over ten million, making Asian Americans the fastest-growing population group in America. In 1965 the majority of Asian Americans were American-born; today more than half are foreign-born. Moreover, by nationality Asian Americans have become tremendously more diverse and now include representatives of a score of different ancestries. The class base has expanded considerably as well because of immigration. Professionals and technical personnel now form a major, visible part of the Asian American population.

These demographic changes have complicated understanding the Asian American experience and the politics of Asian Americans in particular, because certain assumptions and perceptions from the past have been reinforced. For example, because many of those who have recently arrived in the country have been understandably hesitant to speak out on politics, some commentators continue to emphasize the alleged cultural or historical aloofness of Asians from politics. Yet the ethnic and class diversification of Asian Americans has made generalizing about them even more difficult than before. The fact is that Asian Americans have become increasingly involved in a wide range of political issues, including immigration legislation, social welfare and education policy, crime, racial violence, and even campaign financing at the local as well as national levels.

In addition to demographic changes, the late 1960s and early 1970s also saw the emergence of a new assertiveness by Asian Americans, which included the development of a pan-ethnic identity. Asian American intellectuals coined the term *Asian American* to help declare the birth of this self-consciousness. The designation's significance lay both in its emphasis on the commonalities shared by the different Asian ancestry groups (racial appearance, interpretation of historical experiences in America, social stigmatization, and so forth) and in its *political* claim. More than an ethnic label, the term *Asian American* also was a statement about perceived social position and group interest. Today, the term is ubiquitous. While it no longer carries the radical connotations it once did when used exclusively by activists on college campuses in the late 1960s, the designation continues to suggest a consciousness about place in American society, past and present—a consciousness that appears to be growing, not diminishing.[41]

Much of the writing about Asian Americans, which has grown tremendously in recent decades, reflects this thinking. Whether fiction or nonfiction, about the past or the present, the contemporary literature on Asian

Americans largely responds to the past negative characterizations of foreignness, inferiority, danger, or marginality by casting Asian Americans as historical actors, with human agency and feeling, and as full participants in American and trans-Pacific narratives. The literature in recent decades also challenges the representations of docility, political indifference, and "success" that were constructed during the mid-twentieth century. The notions of Asians as hyperpolitical threats or apolitical exemplars, which remain deeply imbedded in American life and thinking, do not go unanswered.[42]

Researchers are also helping to construct an entirely new understanding of the Asian American experience—and Asian American politics in particular. For example, early work is under way on the important story of the political activity of Asians in Hawaii;[43] the rich history of Asian American legal and civil rights activism is attracting considerable attention;[44] and the historical involvement of Asian Americans in the politics of their ancestral homelands has caught the eye of the research community.[45] Other historical work is exploring Asian American involvement in radical and labor politics,[46] and the literature on Asian Americans and certain areas of social policy, such as education, is growing.[47]

As noted, many authors since the 1960s have sought to offer a corrective to the popular picture of the inoffensive and politically indifferent Asian. In the words of the author of a path-breaking study on the Chinese struggle against legal discrimination in the nineteenth century, the "conventional wisdom" about the supposed "political backwardness" of the Chinese simply needed to be "stood on its head."[48] Charles J. McClain's comment could speak for a generation of writers who have focused on the past and present activism of Asian Americans, the similarities of Asian American experiences with those of other minority groups, and Asian American challenges to the culture and politics of the dominant society. Constructing an assertive, even radical, Asian American identity has been prominent on the agenda. By contrast, relatively little attention has been devoted to topics such as political conservatism, the growth of professionalism among Asian Americans, or even partisan politics. Clearly, then, much of the work on Asian Americans in the past two decades has been as "ideological" as the earlier literature.[49]

Perhaps because of Asian Americans' interest in alternative politics and in establishing an activist identity for themselves, study of Asian American involvement in the more prosaic domain of electoral politics has been neglected until rather recently. In fact, it was not until the mid-1980s that any scholarly work that seriously explored contemporary Asian American political behavior began to appear. This scholarship is trying to define, characterize, and interpret Asian American politics, including voting patterns, ethnic interests, ideologies, specific policy concerns, and leadership approaches. Although schools of thought, controversies, and contending interpretations—a discourse—are only beginning to emerge, it might be said that the very appearance of this literature confirms intellectually the actual existence of something that can now be called Asian American politics.[50] The irony, however, is that despite the highly political circumstances under which the term *Asian American* emerged in the late 1960s and despite the politicized field of academic work known as Asian American studies, the work on Asian Americans and politics has attracted relatively little attention compared with the other fields of study about Asian Americans.[51] This will not likely continue.

CONCLUSION

Observations about Asian American politics have varied wildly over the past 150 years. The reasons for this have been many, including genuine clashes in culture, ignorance and fear, prejudice, political agendas, and even purposeful self-promotion on the part of some Asian Americans themselves. They have been held up as models for change as well as for moderation. They have been labeled hyperpolitical and apolitical, as well as super-threatening and super-loyal. Some commentators have branded them suspect; others have welcomed them to the body politic. Whatever the case, any discussion of Asian Americans and politics has always been highly ideological. Indeed, it has been difficult for many observers to develop a detached sense of Asian Americans and politics, because the topic is inextricably linked to sensitive and volatile experiences in race relations, in American interactions with Asia, and in conflicts over defining national identity and purpose.

One cannot transcend history and context, of course, but perhaps this review of past observations will help present-day writers avoid adopting facile, unthinking assumptions. Today's commentators are the inheritors of much intellectual and cultural baggage and would do well to leave as much of it behind as possible. Recent historical research on the past political activities of Asian Americans suggests that expanded definitions of politics and political activity are necessary to understand the past on its own terms. The same must be done today by those taking a closer look at current Asian American politics, including participation in the nation's formal political processes.

NOTES

1. For discussion purposes, this chapter assumes the existence of a social group called Asian Americans, but it makes no effort to define the group or to attribute particular characteristics to it. The term is used to refer to persons whose ancestry is in Asia.

2. Thomas Sowell, *Ethnic America: A History* (New York: Basic Books, 1981). More specifically, Sowell says that Chinese Americans were able to keep out of the courts and the political arena "because the Chinese in America lived in tight-knit communities of people from one district of one province in China. In those enclaves, they kept alive and intact a culture, a set of traditions and values, that was eroding in China itself" (p. 140). Finding praiseworthy similarities between the Chinese and Japanese American communities, Sowell concludes, "Despite the supposed prerequisite of political cohesion, some of the most remarkable advances in the face of adversity were made by groups that deliberately avoided politics—notably the Chinese and Japanese" (p. 274).

3. Betty Lee Sung, *Mountain of Gold: The Story of the Chinese in America* (New York: Macmillan, 1967), 278–280.

4. Lee May, "Overcome Distaste for Politics in Order to Get Their Views Heard: Asian-Americans Seek to Join Power Structure," *Los Angeles Times,* February 17, 1985, A15.

5. Bob Gurwitt, "Have Asian Americans Arrived Politically? Not Quite," *Governing* (November 1990): 32–38.

6. Stanley Karnow, "Apathetic Asian Americans? Why Their Success Hasn't Spilled Over into Politics," *Washington Post,* November 29, 1992, C1.

7. George Skelton, "Voters of Asian Heritage Slow to Claim Voice," *Los Angeles Times,* August 19, 1993, A3.

8. John J. Miller, "Asian Americans Head for Politics," *American Enterprise* 6 (March/April 1995): 56–58.

9. See, for example, the significance given to Asian Americans in Peter Beinart, "The Lee Rout," *New Republic,* January 5, 12, 1998, 11–12.

10. *Daily Alta* (San Francisco), October 31, 1850.

11. Mary Roberts Coolidge, *Chinese Immigration* (New York: Henry Holt, 1909), 22.

12. See *People v. Hall* in W. Cheng-tau, *"Chink!"* (New York: World Publishing, 1972), 36–43. On how the case is employed, see Ronald Takaki, *Strangers from a Different Shore* (Boston: Little, Brown, 1989), 102.

13. "Yellow peril" literature includes many obscure writers but also well-known authors such as Jack London and H. G. Wells.

14. P. W. Dooner, *Last Days of the Republic* (San Francisco: Alta California Publishing, 1880). The Hall case is discussed on pages 185–187.

15. Charles Frederick Holder, "The Chinaman in American Politics," *North American Review* (February 1898): 226–233.

16. See many of the fine essays in: Sucheng Chan, ed., *Entry Denied: Exclusion and the Chinese Community in America, 1882–1943* (Philadelphia: Temple University Press, 1991); and K. Scott Wong and Sucheng Chan, eds., *Claiming America: Constructing Chinese American Identities during the Exclusion Era* (Philadelphia: Temple University Press, 1998). Also see Charles J. McClain, *In Search of Equality: The Chinese Struggle against Discrimination in Nineteenth-Century America* (Berkeley: University of California Press, 1994); and Lucy E. Salyer, *Laws Harsh as Tigers: Chinese Immigrants and the Shaping of Modern Immigration Law* (Chapel Hill: University of North Carolina Press, 1995).

17. Montaville Flowers, *The Japanese Conquest of American Opinion* (New York: George H. Doran, 1917), 52–53.

18. Jesse Frederick Steiner, *The Japanese Invasion: A Study in the Psychology of Inter-Racial Contacts* (Chicago: A. C. McClurg, 1917), 184–185, 208–209.

19. V. S. McClatchy, *The Germany of Asia; Japan's Policy in the Far East, Her "Peaceful Penetration" of the United States, How American Commercial and National Interests Are Affected* (Sacramento: 1919), 26–28, 37–41.

20. See Kalyan Kumar Banerjee, "The U.S.A. and Indian Revolutionary Activity: Early Phase of the Gadar Movement," *Modern Review* 97 (February 1965): 97–101. Also see the work by the Anglophile Ernest H. Fitzpatrick, *The Coming Conflict of Nations; or, the Japanese-American War* (Springfield, Ill.: H. W. Rokker, 1909).

21. Bruno Lasker, citing the work of Emory S. Bogardus, *Filipino Immigration to Continental United States and to Hawaii* (Chicago: University of Chicago Press, 1931), 267, 331.

22. See Samuel Gompers and Herman Gutstadt, "Meat vs. Rice—American Manhood against Asiatic Coolieism: Which Shall Survive?" Reprinted, with an introduction by the Asiatic Exclusion League, San Francisco, 1908. For a recent and influential recapitulation of the view of Chinese as inassimilable and uninterested in American life, albeit without the overt racism, see Gunther Barth, *Bitter Strength: A History of the Chinese in the United States, 1850–1870* (Cambridge: Harvard University Press, 1964).

23. Coolidge, *Chinese Immigration*, 442–443. Also see Patrick J. Healy and Ng Poon Chew, *A Statement for Non-Exclusion* (San Francisco: 1905). The authors observed that during the anti-Chinese agitation of the 1870s in San Francisco "the Chinese by no means slept on their rights. They prepared abundant and cogent arguments to refute the lying charges made against them by the ignorance and viciousness of the self-seeking demagogues" (p. 75).

24. Kiyoshi K. Kawakami, *The Japanese Question* (San Francisco: Japanese-American News, n.d.), 2, 3.

25. Eliot Grinnell Mears, *Resident Orientals on the American Pacific Coast: Their Legal and Economic Status* (Chicago: University of Chicago Press, 1928), 104–106, 113, 117–118, 397.

26. Yamato Ichihashi, *Japanese in the United States: A Critical Study of the Problems of the Japanese Immigrants and Their Children* (Stanford: Stanford University Press, 1932), 319–363. Also see Gordon H. Chang, *Morning Glory, Evening Shadow: Yamato Ichihashi and His Wartime Writings, 1942–1945* (Stanford: Stanford University Press, 1997), 11–87.

27. Wanda Robertson, "Developing World Citizens in a Japanese Relocation Center," *Childhood Education* 20 (October 1943): 66–71; and John W. Powell, "Education through Relocation," *Adult Education Journal* 1 (October 1942): 154–157.

28. Frederick G. Murray, "Japs in Our Yard," *American Legion Magazine* 34 (June 1943): 12–13, 42, 46.

29. Forrest E. LaViolette, *Americans of Japanese Ancestry: A Study of Assimilation in the American Community* (Toronto: Canadian Institute of International Affairs, 1945), 148–161. Also see LaViolette's "Political Behavior of the American-Born Japanese," *Research Studies of the State College of Washington* 8 (March 1940): 11–17.

30. Rose Hum Lee, *The Chinese in the United States of America* (Hong Kong: Hong Kong University Press, 1960), 178–180.

31. S. W. Kung, *Chinese in American Life: Some Aspects of Their History, Status, Problems, and Contributions* (Seattle: University of Washington Press, 1962), 261–262.

32. Sung, *Mountain of Gold,* 278–285.

33. Chang, *Morning Glory,* 52–72; Yuji Ichioka, "Japanese Immigrant Nationalism: The Issei and the Sino-Japanese War, 1937–1941," *Pacific Historical Review* 46 (1977): 409–437; the entire issue of *Amerasia Journal* 23 (winter 1997–1998); and Brian Hayashi, *"For the Sake of Our Japanese Brethren": Assimilation, Nationalism, and Protestantism among the Japanese of Los Angeles, 1895–1942* (Stanford: Stanford University Press, 1995).

34. Contrast the perspectives in the following essays with those found in works on Chinese Americans produced in the 1950s and 1960s: Him Mark Lai, "Roles Played by Chinese in America during China's Resistance to Japanese Aggression and during World War II," *Chinese America: History and Perspectives* (1997): 75–125; Him Mark Lai, "China and the Chinese American Community: The Political Dimension," *Chinese America: History and Perspectives* (1999): 1– 32; Shih-shan Henry Tsai, *China and the Overseas Chinese in the United States, 1868–1911* (Fayetteville: University of Arkansas Press, 1983); and Renqiu Yu, *To Save China, To Save Ourselves: The Chinese Hand Laundry Alliance of New York* (Philadelphia: Temple University Press, 1992).

35. William Petersen, "Success Story, Japanese-American Style," *New York Times Sunday Magazine,* January 9, 1966, 20ff.; and William Petersen, *Japanese Americans: Oppression and Success* (New York: Random House, 1971).

36. Bill Hosokawa, *Nisei: The Quiet Americans* (New York: Morrow, 1969).

37. See the pioneering book edited by Lawrence H. Fuchs, *American Ethnic Politics* (New York: Harper and Row, 1968). No essay on any Asian group appears among the thirteen entries, although there are two on African Americans. In his useful bibliographic essay, Fuchs observes that little work had been done on Chinese and "Spanish-speaking Americans" (p. 288).

38. Edwin O. Reischauer, foreword to *Nisei: The Quiet Americans,* by Bill Hosokawa (New York: Morrow, 1969).

39. "Success Story of One Minority Group in U.S.," *U.S. News and World Report,* December 26, 1966, 73–76.

40. Alfred H. Song, "Politics and Policies of the Oriental Community," in *California Politics and Policies,* ed. Eugene P. Dvorin and Arthur J. Misner (Reading, Mass.: Addison-Wesley, 1966), 387–411.

41. "New Sense of Race Arises among Asian-Americans," *New York Times,* May 30, 1996; "Asian Americans Scarce in U.S. Corridors of Power," *Los Angeles Times,* October 21, 1997; and "Asian American Programs Are Flourishing at Colleges," *New York Times,* June 9, 1999.

42. Several general histories and anthologies contain considerable material about Asian Americans and politics that span categories. See Amy Tachiki et al., *Roots: An Asian American Reader* (Los Angeles: Asian American Studies Center, University of California, 1971); Emma Gee, ed., *Counterpoint* (Los Angeles: Asian American Studies Center, 1976); Sucheng Chan, *Asian Americans: An Interpretive History* (Boston: Twayne, 1991); Roger Daniels, *Asian America: Chinese and Japanese in the United States since 1850* (Seattle: University of Washington Press, 1988); Ronald Takaki, *Strangers from a Different Shore: A History of Asian Americans* (Boston: Little, Brown, 1989); Shih-shan Henry Tsai, *The Chinese Experience in America* (Bloomington: Indiana University Press, 1986); Yuji Ichioka, *The Issei: The World of the First Generation Japanese Immigrants* (New York: Free Press, 1988); and Gary Okihiro, *Margins and Mainstreams: Asians in American History and Culture* (Seattle: University of Washington Press, 1994). Many articles about Asian Americans and politics, broadly defined, appear in *Amerasia Journal,* published by the UCLA Asian American Studies Center and in the *Journal of Asian American Studies.*

43. Tom Coffman, *Catch a Wave: A Case Study of Hawaii's New Politics* (Honolulu: University of Hawaii Press, 1973); Ronald Takaki, *Pau Hana: Plantation Life and Labor in Hawaii* (Honolulu: University of Hawaii Press, 1983); and Vincent N. Parrillo, "Asian Americans in American Politics," in *America's Ethnic Politics,* ed. Joseph S. Roucek and Bernard Eisenberg (Westport, Conn.: Greenwood Press, 1982), 89–112.

44. Peter Irons, *Justice at War: The Story of the Japanese American Internment Cases* (New York: Oxford University Press, 1983); McClain, *In Search of Equality*; Salyer, *Laws Harsh as Tigers*; and Leslie Hatamiya, *Righting a Wrong: Japanese Americans and the Passage of the Civil Liberties Act of 1988* (Stanford: Stanford University Press, 1993). The literature on activism during internment is growing. For example, see Richard Nishimoto, *Inside an American Concentration Camp: Japanese American Resistance at Poston, Arizona,* ed. Lane Hirabayashi (Tucson: University of Arizona Press, 1995).

45. See, for example, Eve Armentrout Ma, *Revolutionaries, Monarchists, and Chinatowns: Chinese Politics in the Americas and the 1911 Revolution* (Honolulu: University of Hawaii Press, 1990); Yu, *To Save China, To Save Ourselves*; Joan Jensen, *Passage from India: Indian Pioneers in America* (New Haven: Yale University Press, 1988); Delber McKee, "The Chinese Boycott of 1905–1906 Reconsidered: The Role of Chinese Americans," *Pacific Historical Review* 55 (1986); and several essays in S. Chandrasekhar, *From India to America: A Brief History of Immigration; Problems of Discrimination; Admission and Assimilation* (La Jolla, Calif.: Population Review Publications, 1982). Many of the recent studies on Asian diasporas offer comparative perspectives on the activities and lives of Asians dispersed in various countries. See, for example, Hyung-chan Kim, ed. *The Korean Diaspora: Historical and Sociological Studies of Korean Immigration and Assimilation in North America* (Santa Barbara, Calif.: ABC-Clio, 1977); and Lynn Pan, *Sons of the Yellow Emperor: A History of the Chinese Diaspora* (New York: Kodansha International, 1994).

46. See, for example, Peter Kwong, *Chinatown, New York, Labor and Politics, 1930–1950* (New York: Monthly Review Press, 1979); Peter Kwong, *The New Chinatown* (New York: Hill and Wang, 1996); Robert G. Lee, "The Hidden World of Asian Immigrant Radicalism," in *The Immigrant Left in the United States,* ed. Paul Buhle and Dan Georgakas (Albany: State University of New York, 1996), 256–288; Karl Yoneda, *Ganbatte! Sixty Year Struggle of a Kibei Worker* (Los Angeles: UCLA Asian American Studies Center, 1983); Him Mark Lai, "A Historical Survey of Organizations of the Left among the Chinese in America," *Bulletin of Concerned Asian Scholars* 4 (fall 1972): 10–21; Him Mark Lai, "The Chinese Marxist Left in America to the 1960's," *Chinese America: History and Perspectives* (1992): 3–82; Karin Aguilar San-Juan, ed., *The State of Asian American: Activism and Resistance in the 1990s* (Boston: South End Press, 1994); Craig Scharlin and Lilia V. Villanueva, *Philip Vera Cruz: A Personal History of Filipino Immigrants and the Farmworkers Movement* (Los Angeles: UCLA Labor Center, 1992); and Chris Friday, *Organizing Asian American Labor: The Pacific Coast Canned-Salmon Industry, 1870–1942* (Philadelphia: Temple University Press, 1994).

47. See Victor Low, *The Unimpressible Race: A Century of Educational Struggle by the Chinese in San Francisco* (San Francisco: East/West Publishing Co., 1982); Don T. Nakanishi and Tina Yamano Nishida, eds., *The Asian American Educational Experience: A Source Book for Teachers and Students* (New York: Routledge, 1995); and

Dana Takagi, *The Retreat from Race: Asian-American Admissions and Racial Politics* (New Brunswick, N.J.: Rutgers University Press, 1992).

48. McClain, *In Search of Equality*, 3.

49. See, for example, the following which have implications for thinking about the politics of Asian American studies: Gary Okihiro's interpretive history in *Margins and Mainstreams*; Sylvia Yanagisako's critical essay, "Transforming Orientalism: Gender, Nationalilty, and Class in Asian American Studies," in *Naturalizing Power: Essays in Feminist Cultural Analysis*, ed. Sylvia Yanagisako and Carol Delany (New York: Routledge, 1995), 275–298; and Henry Yu's "The 'Oriental Problem' in America, 1920–1960: Linking the Identities of Chinese American and Japanese American Intellectuals," in *Claiming America: Constructing Chinese American Identities during the Exclusion Era*, ed. K. Scott Wong and Sucheng Chan (Philadelphia: Temple University Press, 1998), 191–214.

50. See, for example, Timothy P. Fong, *The First Suburban Chinatown: The Remaking of Monterey Park, California* (Philadelphia: Temple University Press, 1994), and Chapter 8 in Fong's *The Contemporary Asian American Experience: Beyond the Model Minority* (Upper Saddle River, N.J.: Prentice-Hall, 1997); John Horton, *The Politics of Diversity: Immigration, Resistance, and Change in Monterey Park, California* (Philadelphia: Temple University Press, 1995); Leland T. Saito, *Race and Politics: Asian Americans, Latinos, and Whites in a Los Angeles Suburb* (Urbana: University of Illinois Press, 1998); Stephen S. Fugita and David J. O'Brien, *Japanese American Ethnicity: The Persistence of Community* (Seattle: University of Washington Press, 1991), especially Chapter 9; Yung-Hwan Jo, "Problems and Strategies of Participation in American Politics," in *Koreans in Los Angeles: Prospects and Promises* (Los Angeles: Koryo Research Institute, 1982), 203–218; Angelo N. Ancheta, *Race, Rights, and the Asian American Experience* (New Brunswick, N.J.: Rutgers University Press, 1998); Jere Takahashi, *Nisei/Sansei: Shifting Japanese American Identities and Politics* (Philadephia: Temple University Press, 1997); Yung-Hwan Jo, ed., *Political Participation of Asian Americans: Problems and Strategies* (Chicago: Pacific/Asian American Mental Health Research Center, 1980); Moon H. Jo, "The Putative Political Complacency of Asian Americans," *Political Psychology* 5 (1984): 583–605; Don T. Nakanishi, "Asian American Politics: An Agenda for Research," *Amerasia Journal* 12 (1985–1986): 1–27; L. Ling-chi Wang, "The Politics of Ethnic Identity and Empowerment: The Asian American Community since the 1960s," *Asian American Policy Review* 2 (1991): 43–56; Bruce E. Cain, "Asian American Electoral Power: Imminent or Illusory?" *Election Politics* 9 (1988): 27–30; Wendy Tam, "Asians—A Monolithic Voting Bloc?" *Political Behavior* 17 (1995): 223–249; Pei-te Lien, *The Political Participation of Asian Americans: Voting Behavior in Southern California* (New York: Garland Publishing, 1997); and Yen Le Esperitu, *Asian American Panethnicity* (Philadelphia: Temple University Press, 1992). Also see the seven editions of the *National Asian Pacific American Political Almanac* (Los Angeles: UCLA Asian American Studies Center).

51. Important work on cultural politics and Asian Americans includes that by: Dorinne Kondo, *About Face: Performing Race in Fashion and Theater* (New York: Routledge, 1997); Robert G. Lee, *Orientals: Asian Americans in Popular Culture* (Philadelphia: Temple University Press, 1999); Lisa Lowe, *Immigrant Acts: On Asian American Cultural Politics* (Durham: Duke University Press, 1996); David Li, *Imagining the Nation: Asian American Literature and Cultural Consent* (Stanford: Stanford University Press, 1998); and David Palumbo-Liu, *Asian/American: Historical Crossings of a Racial Frontier* (Stanford: Stanford University Press, 1999).

CHAPTER TWO

THE RACIAL TRIANGULATION OF ASIAN AMERICANS

CLAIRE JEAN KIM

Recently, the call to go "beyond black and white" in discussions of race has become something of a mantra in scholarly circles.[1] The conventional trope of "two societies, black and white"—crafted and reproduced over the past half-century by Gunnar Myrdal, the Kerner Commission, Andrew Hacker, and others—seems increasingly outdated as unprecedented levels of Asian and Latin American immigration continue to diversify the U.S. population. While the multi-racial composition of the American populace has always given the lie to a bipolar racial framework, these post-1965 demographic changes have thrown the framework's shortcomings into especially bold relief. But what does it mean to go "beyond black and white" in thinking about race? As with most ritualistic exhortations, the need to do something is more apparent than how it is to be done.

Scholars have adopted two broad approaches to going "beyond black and white," both of which have certain shortcomings. The first approach, which I call the different trajectories approach, examines racialization (the creation and characterization of racial categories) as an open-ended, variable process that has played out differently for each subordinated group. Michael Omi and Howard Winant's discussion of distinct and indepen-

This article was originally published in *Politics and Society*, Vol. 27 No. 1, March 1999, 105–138. © 1999 Sage Publications, Inc. Reprinted with permission.

dent group trajectories—"Native Americans faced genocide, blacks were subjected to racial slavery, Mexicans were invaded and colonized, and Asians faced exclusion"—exemplifies this approach.[2] As David Theo Goldberg notes about this approach, "the presumption of a single monolithic racism is being displaced by a mapping of the multifarious historical formulations of racism."[3] The second approach, which I call the racial hierarchy approach, emphasizes ordering groups into a single scale of status and privilege with whites on the top, blacks on the bottom, and all other groups somewhere in between. Gary Okihiro's argument that Asian Americans have been rendered an intermediate group on America's bipolar racial scale and Mari Matsuda's claim that Asian Americans constitute a "racial bourgeoisie" imply such a hierarchy (although both authors are more concerned with the implications of Asian Americans' intermediate status than they are with the overall notion of hierarchy itself). These two broad approaches are not necessarily mutually exclusive: Tomás Almaguer, for example, addresses both the "differential racialization" of various groups and the single racial hierarchy that these processes produced in a particular time and place.[4]

The shortcomings of both approaches suggest that the mandate to go "beyond black and white" remains at least in part unfulfilled. The problem with the different trajectories approach is that it imputes mutual autonomy to respective racialization processes that are in fact mutually constitutive of one another. Asian Americans have not been racialized in a vacuum, isolated from other groups; to the contrary, they have been racialized relative to and through interaction with whites and blacks. As such, the respective racialization trajectories of these groups are profoundly interrelated.[5] The problem with the racial hierarchy approach, on the other hand, is that its notion of a single scale of status and privilege is belied by the fact that whites appear to have ordered other racial groups along at least two dimensions or axes historically.[6] For example, Angelo Ancheta points out that blacks have been denigrated as inferior while Asian Americans have been denigrated more often as outsiders or aliens.[7] The challenge, it seems, is to find a way to talk about what Neil Gotanda calls the "other nonwhites" in a way that appreciates both how racialization processes are mutually constitutive of one another and how they can unfold along more than one dimension or scale at a time.[8]

My purpose in this chapter is twofold. First, I propose using the notion of a "field of racial positions" in order to move the conceptualization of racial dynamics "beyond black and white." Second, I argue that Asian

Americans have been "racially triangulated" vis-à-vis whites and blacks in this field of racial positions for the past century and a half. These two points are discussed in turn.

According to Stephen Jay Gould, Americans' racial thinking, conditioned by European ethnological frameworks of centuries past, is "subject to visual representation, usually in clearly definable geometric terms."[9] My first claim is that public discourse about racial groups and their relative status generates a field of racial positions (or, to borrow Gould's phrase, a particular "racial geometry") in a given time and place. The chief architects of this field are major opinion makers: white elected officials, journalists, scholars, community leaders, business elites, and so on. Although the most powerful always have the most say in defining it, this field is continually contested and negotiated within and among racial groups, both at the elite level and at the level of popular culture and everyday life. Since the field of racial positions consists of a plane defined by at least two axes—superior/inferior and insider/foreigner—it emphasizes both that groups become racialized in comparison with one another and that they are racialized differently.[10] As a normative blueprint for who should get what, this field of racial positions profoundly shapes the opportunities, constraints, and possibilities with which subordinate groups must contend, ultimately serving to reinforce white dominance and privilege.[11]

My second argument is that Asian Americans have been racially triangulated vis-à-vis blacks and whites, or located in the field of racial positions with reference to these two other points.[12] Racial triangulation occurs by means of two types of simultaneous, linked processes: (1) processes of "relative valorization," whereby dominant group A (whites) valorizes subordinate group B (Asian Americans) relative to subordinate group C (blacks) on cultural and racial grounds in order to dominate both groups, but especially the latter, and (2) processes of "civic ostracism," whereby dominant group A (whites) constructs subordinate group B (Asian Americans) as immutably foreign and unassimilable with whites on cultural and racial grounds in order to ostracize them from the body politic and civic membership (see Figure 2.1).[13] Processes of relative valorization and civic ostracism are linked both analytically and functionally. They are joined analytically by an essentialized reading of Asian American/Asian culture that produces a double elision among Asian American subgroups, on one hand, and between Asian Americans and Asians, on the other. As Paul Gilroy notes in another context, "Culture is conceived . . . not as something intrinsically fluid, changing, unstable, and dynamic, but as a fixed property of social groups."[14] Functionally, the two types of processes work in a complementary fashion to maintain Asian Americans in a triangulated position vis-à-vis whites and blacks. As Figure 2.1 indicates, both processes are required to maintain Asian Americans in this equilibrated position; the abridgment of either would change the position of the group.

Perhaps the most striking feature of the racial triangulation of Asian Americans is its historical persistence. The racial triangulation of Asian Americans has persisted since its inception in the mid-1800s, and it has undergone only cosmetic changes in the post-1965 era in keeping with contemporary norms of colorblindness. Before the civil rights era, racial triangulation occurred openly, in cultural-racial terms; in the post–civil rights era racial triangulation has occurred in a coded fashion, in cultural terms decoupled from overtly racial claims. Yet in both periods, racial triangulation (and the field of racial positions, more generally) has functioned as a normative blueprint for which groups should get what, repro-

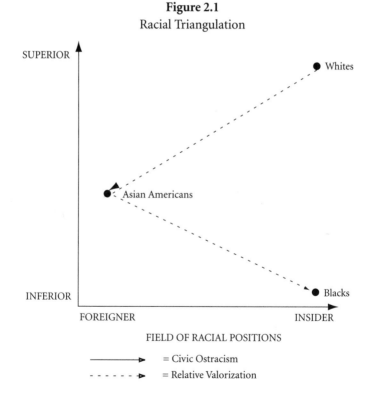

Figure 2.1
Racial Triangulation

ducing patterns of white power and privilege. As Omi and Winant note, racial categories and meanings may be social constructions, but they take on a life of their own over time, profoundly shaping the distribution of goods in society.[15] By illuminating the field of racial positions that lies just beneath the contemporary edifice of what appear to be racially neutral laws and policies, this chapter reveals how white racial power can continue to thrive in a formally colorblind society.

This chapter begins by examining open racial triangulation during the period 1850–1950. The second part examines coded racial triangulation from 1965 to the present.[16] The concluding section considers the implications of this analysis for future research on race and racialization.

OPEN RACIAL TRIANGULATION: 1850–1950

At the midpoint of the nineteenth century, white business and political elites in California faced a dilemma: they had voted to enter the Union as a "free" (nonslave) state just as booming regional economic growth intensified the need for cheap and plentiful labor.[17] Although Chinese immigrant labor promised to solve this dilemma, it raised the specter of a second form of slavery that would create yet another permanent class of degraded nonwhites. Racial triangulation reconciled the urgent need for labor with the imperative of continuing white dominance. By positioning Asian immigrants as superior to blacks yet permanently foreign and unassimilable with whites, racial triangulation processes fashioned a labor force that would fulfill a temporary economic purpose without making any enduring claims on the polity. Although Chinese immigrants often chose to be sojourners of their own accord, white elites embraced and reinforced this arrangement for their own purposes. Stuart Creighton Miller notes that even East Coast newspaper editors concurred during the mid-1800s "that while the Chinese were not biologically suited for America's melting pot, it would be foolish not to exploit their cheap labor before shipping them back to China."[18] Thus although white elites suffered the presence of other racial groups because they needed their services, the preference of white elites was clear: as one California newspaper put it, "We desire only a white population in California."[19] If the racial categories of black and white were historically constructed, as Barbara Fields argues, to reconcile the institution of slavery with the democratic ideals of freedom and equality, the third category of "Mongolian," "Asiatic," or "Oriental" was constructed to reconcile another labor system with the ideal of a pristine white polity.[20] With biological racism in its heyday, racial triangulation occurred quite openly during this period: elites overtly constructed each racial group as a fixed cultural-biological entity and justified its subordinated status accordingly.

Relative Valorization: 'One Chinaman Is Worth Two Negroes'

Entering the United States at mid-century during escalating national strife over slavery and black-white relations, Chinese immigrants were a racial wild card of sorts. They simply did not fit into the prevailing bipolar racial framework. Drawing on preexisting images of the Chinese as well as European ethnological research, white opinion makers began to triangulate Chinese immigrants vis-à-vis blacks and whites. As Miller points out, for decades before the first Chinese immigrants arrived on U.S. shores,[21] traders, missionaries, and diplomats had woven a largely negative image of China as alien, despotic and backward. In addition, the leading ethnologists of the time generally agreed on what Gould calls a "conventional racist ranking of Europeans first, Asians and Americans [Indians] in the middle, and Africans at the bottom."[22] Working with this raw material, white opinion makers constructed a "Mongolian" or "Asiatic" racial category and located it via triangulation (relative valorization and civic ostracism) in the field of racial positions.[23] In this way, they accorded Chinese immigrants as "Mongolians" highly conditional acceptance as laborers expected to fulfill only a narrow and temporary purpose.

Some scholars emphasize that Chinese immigrants were "negroized" or treated as "near Black" in racially polarized California.[24] Although white Californians rejected slavery and refrained from blocking free black inmigration to ensure prompt congressional approval of their admission into the Union, they unequivocally asserted their racial dominance over the few blacks living in the state. State legislation at mid-century prohibited blacks from becoming citizens, voting, holding public office, serving on juries, testifying against whites in court, attending public schools with whites, and homesteading public land. Whites indeed denigrated Chinese immigrants by associating them with blacks in various ways.[25] For example, the courts interpreted certain laws curtailing black civic rights as applying to the Chinese as well (see the discussion of *People v. George Hall* later in this chapter). The entrenched practice of calling Chinese immigrants "coolies" (despite the fact that they were not involuntary laborers) linked them with black slaves as part of a degraded, unfree caste that was anathema to "free labor" advocates.[26] White elites and workers alike worried openly that Chinese labor would lead to the resurrection of slavery in another form. Moreover, Chinese immigrants were sometimes seen as lazy, dishonest, irresponsible, docile, and thieving (vices persistently attributed to blacks); cartoons occasionally depicted the Chinese immigrant with "black" features: and the "heathen Chinee" character often appeared with the black "Sambo" character in Wild West minstrel shows.[27]

Yet the compelling fact remains that Chinese immigrants were not systematically lumped with blacks but instead often identified as a distinct racial group and lauded as superior to blacks on cultural-racial grounds. Relative valorization was neither universal nor constant; it sometimes occurred in a quite backhanded way. Indeed, according to Luther Spoehr, Chinese immigrants were simply demonized less uniformly and less insistently than blacks.[28] On balance, whites constructed the Chinese as bearers of a venerable (if now decrepit) culture while denigrating blacks as infantile, imitative, and cultureless. During the Joint Congressional Committee hearings on Chinese immigration held in 1879 in California, Charles Wolcott Brooks, the former U.S. consul to Japan, testified,

> I think the Chinese are a far superior race to the negro race physiologically and mentally. . . . I think that the Chinese have a great deal more brain power than the original negro. The negro['s] . . . mind is undisciplined and is not systematic as the Chinese mind. For that reason the negro is very easily taught; he assimilates more readily. . . . The Chinese are non-assimilative because their form of civilization has crystallized.[29]

Brooks's testimony, which attributes both Chinese superiority and Chinese permanent foreignness to a supposedly fixed Chinese cultural-racial essence, is a classic statement of racial triangulation. A clergyman writing that same year echoed Brooks's views on the immutability of Chinese culture: "There is nothing in human character, on the face of the whole earth so stable, so fixed, and so sure and changeless, as the character of a Chinaman."[30] Putative unassimilability (and actual disenfranchisement as "aliens ineligible to citizenship") actually made Chinese immigrants more attractive to employers, who presumed that it would make Chinese labor more docile and less demanding than black labor. For whites openly horrified by the imminent prospect of postbellum black political enfranchisement, the San Francisco *Daily Alta*'s 1869 description of the Chinese immigrant—"[he] knows and cares nothing more of the laws and language of the people among whom he lives than will suffice to keep him out of trouble and enable him to drive a thrifty trade"—was quite reassuring.[31] These sorts of calculations about labor efficiency and the preservation of white dominance moved one white Californian to expound, "One white man is worth two Chinamen; that one Chinaman is worth two negroes, and that one negro is worth two tramps."[32]

Reconstruction and the 'Apolitical, Noncitizen Coolie'

The mid-century mass media explosion and emergence of the penny press meant that official race talk during this period filtered both outward across regional lines and downward to the level of colloquial discussion. In other words, the field of racial positions within which Chinese immigrants were triangulated relative to blacks and whites was increasingly a national phenomenon, although its actual application saw some local and regional variation.[33] For this reason, when southern political and economic elites sought cheap labor to work their plantations and railroads and facilitate the reassertion of white dominance over blacks after the Civil War, they naturally turned to the newly triangulated "Mongolian" race. In 1869 leaders of the agricultural and railroad industries from throughout the South attended the Chinese Immigration Convention in Memphis, Tennessee, forming companies and hiring agents to contract Chinese workers from California, Cuba, and China and transport them to southern locales.[34]

Reputed to be hardworking and intelligent, known to be "aliens ineligible to citizenship" and thus politically powerless, and believed to be sojourners who would pose no long-term burden, Chinese immigrants seemed tailor-made for the needs of southern elites reeling from the black political and economic challenge posed by Reconstruction. Southern elites were not shy in discussing the motives behind their ambitious labor experiment. To begin with, in the words of one Georgian planter, Chinese immigrants were "said to be better laborers[,] more intelligent and can be had for $12 or $13 per month and rations."[35] Just as important, though, Chinese immigrants' civic disenfranchisement made them useful pawns in the game of reasserting white dominance over blacks. One southern journalist wrote in 1869, "We will state the problem for consideration. It is: To retain in the hands of the whites the control and direction of social and political action, without impairing the content of the labor capacity of the colored race."[36] That the importation of Chinese workers was meant as a retort to Reconstruction is clearly suggested by this journalist: "The tune . . . will not be 'forty acres and a mule,' but . . . 'work nigger or starve.' "[37] Overall, James Loewen notes, "The apolitical noncitizen coolie, it was thought, would be a step back toward the more docile labor conditions of slavery times."[38] The prospect of turning back the clock made some white southerners quite giddy; one planter's wife even exclaimed, "Give us five million of Chinese laborers in the valley of the Mississippi, and we can furnish the world with cotton and teach the negro his proper place."[39] As it turns out, her optimism was unfounded. The experiment with Chinese immigrant labor proved more costly, difficult, and cumbersome than southern planters had expected. It died out when the end of Reconstruction in 1877 heralded a return to antebellum racial dynamics.

During the late 1800s, after the last Chinese workers had vacated the plantations, several small Chinese American communities took root and flourished in some parts of the South such as the Mississippi Delta. The experiences of these Chinese Americans point up some interesting contrasts with the California story. On the one hand, the Chinese Americans living in Mississippi were also triangulated vis-à-vis black and white. Overwhelmingly concentrated in the grocery trade, they served a "middleman" economic function between blacks and whites much as Korean immigrant merchants in central cities do today. On the other hand, Chinese Americans in Mississippi moved from a near-black status in the late 1800s to a near-white status (still triangulated) by the 1920s and 1930s, while those living in California did not experience such a shift in position. As Loewen recounts, incremental white gestures of acceptance prompted Chinese Americans in Mississippi to dissociate from blacks over time.[40] Many Chinese Americans discouraged intermarriage with blacks, ostracized group members who interacted with blacks, gave their children white names, attended white churches, and made donations to white organizations in a deliberate bid to become white.[41] If the black struggle for advancement has historically rested on appeals to racial equality, the Asian American struggle has at times rested on appeals to be considered white (and to be granted the myriad privileges bundled with whiteness).[42] The relative location of the two groups within the field of racial positions accounts for this important difference. In any case, both the relative sizes of the white, black, and Chinese American populations in California and the South and the presence of a more rigid and established racial caste system (Jim Crow) in the South may explain why white southerners felt they had less to lose than white Californians in permitting a slight shift in the racial positioning of the intermediate group.

Civic Ostracism: 'A Viper Is Nonetheless a Viper'

While Chinese immigrants were often valorized relative to the most deni-grated laboring class, blacks, they were also constructed as immutably for-eign and ostracized from the body politic on these grounds. Asian immi-grants, seen as both unfit for and uninterested in the American way of life, were in fact the only group in American history to be legally rendered "aliens ineligible to citizenship."[43] Again, it was the conjunction of these two types of processes—relative valorization and civic ostracism, both grounded on essentializing cultural-racial claims—that triangulated Asian immigrants in the field of racial positions. When Chinese and other Asian immigrants challenged the bar on naturalization through litigation, law-makers and jurists at the national and state levels responded by fortifying the border between white and "Mongolian" and rigorously denying the latter the privileges of civic membership. White elites' selective and incon-sistent appeals to the authority of ethnological research and their vacilla-tion between classifying Asian immigrants as black and nonblack clearly demonstrate that they were less concerned with jurisprudential and statu-tory integrity than they were with keeping Asian immigrants in their place.

Antebellum legal rulings ostracized Chinese immigrants from the body politic by simply lumping them with blacks, whose thorough exclusion from civic life during this period has already been noted.[44] Although whites distinguished Chinese immigrants from (and valorized them relative to) blacks in certain contexts, they did not hesitate to render them black for the purposes of political disenfranchisement. Having recently rejected slavery and reluctantly accepted free black in-migration, the California state legis-lature in 1850 reasserted white dominance by passing a law stating that "no Black, or Mulatto person, or Indian shall be allowed to give evidence for, or against a White man" in criminal proceedings. A case addressing the loca-tion of Chinese immigrants in this racial schema quickly arose. In *People v. George Hall* (1854), California Supreme Court chief justice Hugh Murray ruled that Chinese testimony against a white man was inadmissible accord-ing to the 1850 law and reversed the murder conviction of George Hall, which had been obtained through reliance on such testimony.[45] Citing the alleged racial kinship between the Chinese and Indians as well as legislative intent, Murray argued that black meant not just "negroes" but all non-whites, including Chinese immigrants. As Murray explicitly noted, the 1850 law protected "the [white] citizen" from "the corrupting influences of the degraded castes" both in the courtroom and beyond:

The same rule which would admit them [the Chinese] to testify, would admit them to all the equal rights of citizenship and we might soon see them at the polls, in the jury box, upon the bench, and in our legislative halls. This . . . is an actual and present danger. The anomalous spectacle of a distinct people, living in our community, recognizing no laws of this State except through necessity . . . whose mendacity is proverbial; a race of people whom nature has marked as inferior, and who are incapable of progress or intellectual development beyond a certain point . . . between whom and ourselves nature has placed an impassable difference, is now presented . . . [the] privilege of participating with us in administering the affairs of Government.

People v. George Hall turned out to be a landmark case that paved the way for numerous anti-Chinese laws and ordinances in the period leading up to the exclusionary legislation of 1882.

The postbellum naturalization and (formal) enfranchisement of blacks prompted the generation of new strategies for ostracizing Chinese immigrants. In 1870 Congress amended the Naturalization Law of 1790 (which had granted the right to naturalize to "free Whites" only), extending this right for the first time to "aliens of African nativity or persons of African descent." Seeking to bring former slaves into the body politic, if only symbolically, Congress was just as determined that Chinese immigrants remain "aliens ineligible to citizenship." Although Sen. Charles Sumner of Massachusetts argued eloquently that Congress should delete the words "free Whites" from the statute so that Chinese immigrants might be permitted to naturalize, Congress refused to take this step. When an amended 1873 naturalization statute inadvertently omitted the words "free Whites," Congress hastened to reinsert them into a revised version. Congress's intent—to render Chinese immigrants "not black" for the purpose of civic ostracism—was clear, as the courts emphasized in subsequent rulings. The apparent paradox of inviting much-reviled blacks into the polity while excluding the less-reviled Chinese was not lost on Sen. Lyman Trumbull of Illinois, who reminded his colleagues that the Chinese immigrant was, after all, "infinitely above the African in intelligence, in manhood, and in every respect."[46] The material consequences of what Stanford Lyman calls the "civic stigmatization" of Chinese immigrants were tangible: laws discriminating against the Chinese (and later Japanese) as aliens disadvantaged them in mining, agriculture, and other types of work.[47]

Chinese and other Asian immigrants fought the bar on naturalization by arguing that they were in fact white and thus eligible for citizenship. This strategy for group advancement seemed efficient given their triangulated position and the persistent bundling of important privileges with whiteness. In response, the courts engaged in often tortured arguments to fortify the border between white and "Mongolian." In *In re Ah Yup* (1878), the circuit court in California ruled that Chinese-born Ah Yup could not naturalize because he was a member of the "Mongolian" race and therefore not Caucasian, which was the "well settled meaning [of white] in common popular speech." Citing the authority of Blumenbach, Linnaeus, and Cuvier, the court pointed out that all three leading ethnologists distinguished "Mongolians" or "Asiatics" from whites (even though they differed as to the actual number of human "races"). In *Takao Ozawa v. United States* (1922), U.S. Supreme Court justice George Sutherland, citing *In re Ah Yup*, ruled that Japanese-born Ozawa was a member of the "yellow" rather than Caucasian race and therefore was not white. Playing upon valorizing notions of Asian immigrants relative to blacks, Ozawa's counsel made the unsuccessful argument that white meant *not* black, or "a superior class as against a lower class." Just one year later, the same Court ruled in *United States v. Bhagat Singh Thind* (1923) that a Hindu, though considered Caucasian by ethnologists, was not white "in accordance with the understanding of the common man." In other words, the same Court barred Ozawa from citizenship because he was not Caucasian and therefore not white, while it barred Thind, a Caucasian, from citizenship because he was not white by common parlance. These jurisprudential contortions indicate that the courts were determined to use whatever arguments proved useful in maintaining the boundary between whites and Asian immigrants, regardless of how inconsistent or illogical their decisions may have appeared.[48]

Civic ostracism and relative valorization functioned together to triangulate Asian immigrants in the field of racial positions. This triangulated pattern, which secured a cheap and plentiful labor supply while hindering the permanent formation of a second degraded caste seeking inclusion in the polity, left Asian immigrants quite vulnerable to cycles of white aggression. Indeed, the anti-Chinese exclusion movement of the 1870s, the anti-Japanese exclusion movement of the early 1900s, and the internment of Japanese Americans during World War II were less aberrations from than extensions of an ostracizing and denigrating logic already in place. Conventionally, these three events are attributed to major economic or geopolitical shifts—for example, to California's economic depression during the 1870s, Japan's appearance on the world stage after the Russo-Japanese War of 1905, and Japan's aggression during World War II. What has been underemphasized is that the everyday, ongoing practices of racial triangulation laid an ideological foundation without which neither the exclusion movements nor the wartime internment would have occurred.

The road from racial triangulation (defining the alien) to exclusion (keeping the alien out) and internment (rounding up the alien within) turned out to be remarkably smooth. The same putative unassimilability that once endeared Chinese immigrants to white employers became, in the hands of anti-Chinese organizers, grounds for exclusionary legislation. After all, the "fixed" and "changeless" cultural-racial nature of Chinese immigrants meant not only that they constituted "an indigestible mass in the community" but also that they represented the front line of a threatened "Asiatic" economic and military takeover.[49] In 1869 *New York Tribune* writer Henry George warned, "The 60,000 or 100,000 Mongolians on our Western coast are the thin edge of the wedge which has for its base the 500,000,000 of Eastern Asia."[50] California senator Aaron Sargent, who chaired the 1879 Joint Congressional Committee hearings on Chinese immigration, sounded the same ominous note in his final report: "The Pacific Coast must in time become either American or Mongolian."[51] This strategy of exaggerating the threat posed by Chinese immigrants by linking them, via cultural essence, to the amassing "Mongolian" hordes was highly effective. The 1882 exclusionary act reiterated that Chinese immigrants were "aliens ineligible to citizenship" and banned further Chinese immigration for ten years. Legislation in 1888, 1892, 1902, and 1904 extended, expanded, and strengthened the original prohibition on Chinese immigration.

Japanese immigrants arriving after the act of 1882 also were classified as "Mongolians" and racially triangulated vis-à-vis blacks and whites.[52] This is not to say that whites could not or did not sometimes distinguish between Japanese and Chinese immigrants. In fact, the "Mongolian" category itself was at different times internally stratified: Japan's emergence as a major power during the early 1900s led some whites to valorize Japanese over Chinese immigrants, while China's alliance with the United States during World War II reversed this comparison. Still, both groups were, in turn, racialized as "Mongolian," triangulated vis-à-vis blacks and whites, and subjected to exclusionary movements and legislation. The anti-Japanese exclusion movement of the early 1900s modeled itself so closely after the earlier anti-Chinese movement in its personnel, organization, rhetoric, and agenda that Roger Daniels refers to it as "a tail to the anti-Chinese kite."[53]

Unappeased by the passage of the Immigration Act of 1924, which halted Japanese immigration to the United States, whites continued to view

Japanese immigrants and their descendants as the enemy within, harbingers of the "yellow peril" posed by Japan's steady ascendance during the prewar period.[54] Again, whites' essentialized reading of Asian American/Asian culture rested on a double elision—between Chinese and Japanese immigrants, on one hand, and Asian Americans and Asians, on the other. That many Japanese Americans were native-born citizens by the time of World War II made no difference to those sounding the "yellow peril" alarm: race to them was a matter of blood, not formal citizenship. In his final report on the wartime evacuation and internment of Japanese Americans, Gen. J. L. Dewitt stated, "Racial affinities are not severed by migration. The Japanese race is an enemy race and while many second and third generation Japanese born on United States soil, possessed of United States citizenship, have become 'Americanized,' the racial strains are undiluted."[55] Or, as the *Los Angeles Times* put it, "A viper is nonetheless a viper wherever the egg is hatched—so a Japanese American, born of Japanese parents, grows up to be a Japanese, not an American."[56] Although whites did view Chinese Americans more favorably than they did Japanese Americans during the war, this eleventh-hour effort at racial differentiation was rather ineffective, despite *Time* magazine's civic-minded gesture of publishing in December 1941 an article entitled "How to Tell Your Friends from the Japs."[57] There was indeed an "impassable difference" between whites and Asian Americans during the century of open racial triangulation, but it grew out of the former's exercise of racial power rather than the latter's blood.

CODED RACIAL TRIANGULATION: 1965 TO TODAY

Did the civil rights movement of the 1950s and 1960s usher America into a new era of colorblindness, or did it simply generate formal norms of colorblindness that mask ongoing racial domination? Many mainstream scholars contend that the civil rights legislation of the mid-1960s transformed the United States into a substantially colorblind society by removing discriminatory barriers to political participation and economic mobility.[58] Racial formation theorists and critical race scholars, on the other hand, argue that colorblindness is not a social fact but rather a formal ideology or set of norms that obscures continuing patterns of white dominance in the post–civil rights era.[59] My argument here—that the field of racial positions that emerged during the pre-1965 period to reinforce white privilege has proven remarkably stable and that it continues to function as a normative blueprint for who should get what in the contemporary era—clearly allies me with the latter perspective.

The field of racial positions has undergone one salient change in response to the post–civil rights context: it is now elaborated in nonracial terms. In the 1800s, white opinion makers spoke openly about the intrinsic superiority of certain biological "races" over others. Since culture was for them entirely derivative from biological race, their claims about Chinese cultural inferiority were meant and taken as a specification of the broader claim about the intrinsic racial inferiority of this group. It was not until the emergence of the Chicago School of sociology and assimilation theory in the early 1900s that scholars rejected biological determinism, made a clear analytical distinction between culture and biological race, and rendered culture a relatively autonomous essence of its own. As a result of this development, it became possible to talk about a group's culture while disavowing any claims about its intrinsic racial nature, although overtly racial claims certainly persisted, as the earlier discussion of civic ostracism demonstrated.

Since the norms of colorblindness have expurgated overtly racial claims from the "public transcript" during the post–civil rights era, talk about a group's culture often serves to disguise what are fundamentally racial claims.[60] The field of racial positions has now been rearticulated in cultural terms: rather than asserting the intrinsic racial superiority of certain groups over others, opinion makers now claim that certain group cultures are more conducive to success than others. Thus Asian American cultural values are seen as more conducive to success than (read: superior to) black cultural values. Since talk of cultural differences inevitably activates deeply entrenched views of racial differences, however, this field remains, at bottom, an ordering of racial groups qua racial groups. Culture has become code for the unspeakable in the contemporary era.

It is precisely because it has been revamped in nonracial language that the field of racial positions so effectively reinforces white privilege today. Representing a cultural explanation for group inequalities, the field of racial positions implies that American society is substantially colorblind and that the American Dream is still viable. If this message seems tailor-made for the conservative agenda of racial retrenchment, the persistent triangulation of Asian Americans in particular—now in cultural terms—generates an even more serviceable story.[61] The valorization of Asian Americans as a model minority who have made it on their own cultural steam only to be victimized by the "reverse discrimination" of race-conscious programs allows white opinion makers to lambast such programs without appearing racist—or to reassert their racial privileges while abiding by the norms of colorblindness.[62] It allows them to displace what is fundamentally a white–nonwhite conflict over resources (higher education, jobs, businesses, contracts) with a proxy skirmish between nonwhites, thus shifting attention away from the exercise of white racial power. We will see this type of displacement at work with regard to both affirmative action and black-Korean conflict. At the same time, the continuing civic ostracism of Asian Americans on the grounds that they are culturally foreign maintains the "impassable difference" between Asian Americans and whites. As before, ostracizing claims entail a double elision among Asian American subgroups, on one hand, and between Asian Americans and Asians, on the other—this notwithstanding the fantastic diversification and growth of the Asian American population following the implementation of the Immigration and Nationality Act of 1965.[63] Indeed, it is precisely the reality of this diversification that is effectively obscured through persistent patterns of triangulating discourse. In 1850 racial triangulation allowed whites to exploit Asian immigrants as workers while denying them civic membership; today it allows them to conscript Asian Americans into the war of racial retrenchment while denying them genuine equality with whites. Now, as then, racial triangulation enhances white dominance over Asian Americans and blacks alike.

Relative Valorization: The Good, the Bad, and the Colorblind

Since the mid-1960s, Asian Americans have been widely valorized relative to blacks via the model minority myth. Journalists, politicians, and scholars alike have constructed Asian Americans as a model minority whose cultural values of diligence, family solidarity, respect for education, and self-sufficiency have propelled it to notable success. The often explicit suggestion is that blacks have failed in American society because of their own deficiencies: after all, if Asian Americans can make it, why can't blacks?[64] Despite appearances, this myth represents a continuation of earlier constructions in a different guise. It is true that earlier constructions steadfastly held Asians to be culturally unassimilable into white society, whatever their virtues as laborers. Yet the model minority myth does not claim that Asian Americans are culturally assimilated into white society: instead, it posits their material success and attributes this to their ongoing cultural distinctiveness. It also suggests that Asian Americans are too busy getting ahead and making money to worry about politics, thus echoing the old trope of Asian American apoliticalness. Once again, relative valorization is inextricably linked to civic ostracism.

For over three decades, scholars in Asian American studies have generated powerful critiques of the model minority myth, pointing out that it exaggerates Asian American prosperity, homogenizes this extremely diverse population, and obscures discriminatory treatment against it.[65] The myth's stubborn survival suggests that its value lies less in truth telling than in erecting a racially coded good minority/bad minority opposition supportive of the conservative imperative to roll back minority gains while appearing nonracist. Indeed, the emergence of the model minority myth in two waves—the mid-1960s to early 1970s and the early 1980s onward— correlates with two important periods of racial change. During the first, conservatives embraced formal colorblindness in a strategic effort to delegitimate the emergent Black Power movement and arrest the growth of race-conscious social programs (read: "this far and no more"); during the second, they have attempted to roll back earlier minority gains, challenging affirmative action programs, redistricting plans, and so on. As in the South a century earlier, relative valorization continues to serve the cause of racial reaction against black political assertion. The model minority myth's suggestion that Asian Americans prosper despite (and in some cases because of) their apoliticalness not only disparages politically active blacks but also cautions Asian Americans against seeking greater political involvement.[66] The message is clear: Asian Americans have "much to lose if they decide to join other politically active minority groups."[67]

The model minority myth was first articulated in a magazine article in 1966, the very year that Stokely Carmichael popularized the phrase "Black Power" and nonviolent integrationism gave way to its more radical successor. The article, William Petersen's "Success Story, Japanese-American Style" published in the New York Times Magazine, explicitly valorizes Asian Americans relative to blacks on cultural (or racially coded) grounds.[68] According to Petersen, Japanese Americans have succeeded relative to problem minorities such as blacks because they hold "Tokugawa" values (diligence, frugality, and achievement orientation) that link them with the "alien" culture of Japan and serve the same motivating purpose as the Protestant ethic. Petersen indeed argues that Japanese Americans' self-generated success casts doubt on the effort to help blacks through social programs. The clear implication is that blacks would do well to dispense with political agitation and demand making and follow the example of the model minority. Though ostensibly laudatory, Petersen's essentializing description of Japanese American culture clearly suggests the immutable foreignness of this group. Why does Petersen assume that Japanese Americans are bearers of Japanese, not American, culture when in 1966 the Japanese American population consisted almost entirely of native-born U.S. citizens, Japanese immigration to the United States having been barred between 1924 and 1965? While Petersen avoids explicit mention of race, his implicit suggestion is that culture is a matter of blood or biological race—that those of Japanese descent are unalterably and essentially Japanese. Via the model minority myth, both blacks and Asian Americans are kept in their place in the field of racial positions without a single overtly racial claim having been uttered.

Later magazine articles from the mid-1960s to early 1970s echo Petersen's construction of Asian Americans as a model minority. One *U.S. News and World Report* article, entitled "Success Story of One Minority Group in the U.S.," praises Chinese Americans for their cultural values—their embrace of education, diligence, family solidarity, discipline, self-sufficiency, respect for authority, thriftiness, and morality.[69] Again, the author suggests that Chinese Americans' ability to move ahead on their own steam undermines the claims of other minorities to government aid. A few years later, *Newsweek* published an article—"Success Story: Outwhiting the Whites"—that attributes Japanese American success to the resilience of "traditional" Japanese values such as duty, restraint, and perseverance.[70] Again, the notion that Japanese Americans are culturally Japanese rather than American is so taken for granted that it is asserted without substantiation. The article suggests that Japanese American youth seeking a sense of cultural heritage find solace in watching Toshiro Mifune movies and contends that the internment experience motivated Japanese Americans to become better Americans. In other words, no amount of externally imposed hardship can keep a good minority down. The article closes with a quote from a Japanese American man who admits that he would prefer not to have black neighbors because they do not take care of their things and drive property values down, and who suggests that blacks have to work hard like the Nisei (second generation Japanese Americans) if they want to get ahead. By using Asian Americans as proxy whites or spokespersons for white views, the article indirectly conveys a denigrating image of blacks—that they are lazy, that they want something for nothing, that they bring chaos and crime with them wherever they go—while avoiding charges of racism.

The renaissance of the model minority myth in the early 1980s coincided with the start of a vigorous conservative campaign to turn the clock back on civil rights, affirmative action, redistricting, and social welfare programs. The Reagan administration pursued this racial retrenchment agenda—abandoning desegregation appeals, weakening affirmative action requirements in federal contracting, halting record-keeping procedures vital to civil rights and fair housing enforcement, and more—under the legitimating guise of promoting a colorblind society.[71] Once again, the model minority myth conscripted Asian Americans into the conservative war to protect (or, in this case, retrieve) white privileges from black encroachment. This time around, rather than focusing on Chinese Americans or Japanese Americans only, purveyors of the myth lumped all Asian Americans together, producing a double elision—of distinctions among Asian American subgroups as well as between Asian Americans and Asians. As Keith Osajima points out, however, opinion makers learned to pay lip service to intra-Asian diversity and anti-Asian discrimination even as they reiterated the same essentialized good minority/bad minority trope.[72]

Newsweek's 1982 article, "Asian-Americans: A 'Model Minority,' " for example, opens by juxtaposing images of Connie Chung, a successful Chinese American news anchor for CBS, and an unemployed Cambodian refugee who has just lost his welfare benefits.[73] Yet the article closes by concluding that Asian culture—in particular Asian "gung-ho"—accounts for the group's astonishing achievements. The author's scrupulous observation of intra-Asian diversity thus gives way, in the end, to a homogenized and essentialized view of Asian culture. In his book *Who Prospers? How Cultural Values Shape Economic and Political Success*, Lawrence Harrison also reproduces the double elision mentioned earlier, arguing that "Confucian-Americans" (Chinese Americans, Japanese Americans, and Korean Americans) "have imparted pro-work, pro-education, pro-merit values to the melting pot at a time when those values are much in need of revival."[74] That Harrison also opposes affirmative action and black nationalism while championing integrationist ideals should come as no surprise.

The model minority myth has always worked in tandem with explicit constructions of blacks as culturally deficient. From the publication of Daniel Patrick Moynihan's *The Negro Family* in 1965 to the explosion of works on the black "underclass" in the 1980s, white (and sometimes black) opinion makers have argued that black cultural pathology explains black "failure" in American society.[75] And while the term *underclass* is conspicuously nonracial or colorblind on the surface, it is the quintessential example of racial code, conjuring up images of blacks as reliably as references to the "ghetto" and "urban poverty." That the model minority myth and underclass myth are in fact precise mirror images highlights that they are constructions serving to affix the two groups in their respective places within the field of racial positions (see Table 2.1). By emphasizing internal sources of success or failure, both myths decisively shift attention away from structural determinants of group outcomes, including institutionalized white dominance.[76] Racial inequalities have nothing to do with politics or power, we are told, but only with differences in group values. Asian Americans are thus wise to ignore politics in their pursuit of prosperity, and blacks would do well to follow their example. Thus conservative author Thomas Sowell writes, "[T]hose minorities that have pinned their greatest hopes on political action have made some of the slower economic advances. This is in sharp contrast to the Japanese American, whose political powerlessness may have been a blessing in disguise, by preventing the expenditure of much energy in that direction."[77] "Apolitical, noncitizen coolies" are toasted once again as an alternative to politically assertive blacks.

Some conservatives have actually courted Asian American political participation on the assumption that Asian Americans would make a suitable model for other minorities in the political realm. In a 1985 *New Republic* article entitled "The Triumph of Asian Americans," David Bell notes approvingly that Asian Americans, unlike other minorities, do not pursue an Asian American agenda per se. William McGurn, in a 1991 *National Re-*

Table 2.1
Characteristics of the Model Minority versus the Underclass

Model Minority	Underclass
Diligence	Laziness
Discipline	Lack of discipline
Strong family values	Weak family values
Respect for authority	Criminal inclinations
Thriftiness	Inability to defer gratification
Morality	Deviance
Self-sufficiency	Dependency
Respect for education	Tendency to drop out

view article, "The Silent Minority: Asian Americans' Affinity with Republican Party Principles," echoes Bell, arguing that Asian Americans would be political paragons because they would quietly follow the Republican Party agenda rather than complaining and pressing for special advantages as blacks do.[78] In other words, Asian Americans could define a new mode of minority politics, one that involves not acting like a minority. McGurn's depiction of Asian Americans as docile and compliant is explicitly gendered. Thus he chooses to cite Nancy Kwan—who played the title character in *The World of Suzie Wong*, a film notorious for its portrayal of Asian women as exotic, submissive sexual objects—as a spokesperson for Asian Americans.[79] The implication is that Asian Americans would be the Suzie Wongs of American politics—sweet, docile, and eager to follow white directives. But even as it purports to usher Asian Americans into civic life, McGurn's article also ostracizes them. He asserts that the United States is the adoptive land of Asian Americans and celebrates Nancy Kwan's discussion of Asian Americans as "we" versus "them" (white Americans) in a way that powerfully reinscribes Asian American "otherness." As always, relative valorization implies civic ostracism. After a century of classifying Asian Americans as "aliens ineligible to citizenship," whites have invited them into the polity on the condition that they "honor" (Kwan's word) white prerogatives.

Affirmative Action: 'Asian Victims and Black Villains'

Valorizing Asian Americans relative to blacks via the model minority myth permits conservatives to pursue racial retrenchment without appearing racist. Yet when the two groups are juxtaposed not only in abstract comparisons but also in real-life conflicts, the ideological payoff is even greater. Opinion makers invariably interpret such conflicts as the bad minority victimizing the good minority, thus rendering each group's image more extreme: blacks become evil, Asian Americans saintly. When whites then side with Asian Americans in an effort to push back black political demands, they can come across as antiracist champions of the underdog rather than as acutely self-interested actors.[80] This payoff is so rich that conservatives have actually manufactured conflicts between blacks and Asian Americans in order to achieve it. Conservative discourse about affirmative action, the single most important target of racial retrenchment efforts, illustrates how the false construction of interminority conflict serves to protect white prerogatives from minority encroachment.

The first step in this construction process consists of redrawing the political lines of conflict about affirmative action. Most Asian American advocacy groups concur that Asian Americans, like blacks, have benefited from and continue to benefit from affirmative action programs in higher education, professional employment, public employment, contracting, and so on.[81] Affirmative action has helped, in other words, to level the playing field between the unfairly advantaged (whites) and the unfairly disadvantaged (nonwhites). Yet conservatives persistently argue that Asian Americans, the model minority, have "made it" by meritocratic standards and that they do not need "preferential treatment." Ronald Reagan's speech on February 23, 1984, congratulating Asian Americans for revitalizing the American Dream, conveyed this message. Indeed, Nathan Glazer expresses disbelief that "Oriental Americans" are included in affirmative action programs at all: "Having done passably well under discrimination, and much better since discrimination was radically reduced, it is not clear why the government came rushing in to include them.[82] In this way, conservatives represent Asian Americans as "near Whites" or honorary or proxy whites, recasting the opposition between whites and nonwhites over affirmative action into an opposition between whites and Asian Americans, on one hand, and blacks, on the other.[83] While whites and Asian Americans excel by meritocratic standards, we are told, blacks demand special treatment. This redrawing of group boundaries denies the ongoing discrimination suffered by both Asian Americans and blacks and weakens the overall justification for affirmative action.

Once conservatives set up Asian Americans and blacks on opposite sides of the fence, it is easy for them to paint Asian Americans as the hapless victims of "reverse discrimination" engendered by affirmative action. This is precisely what occurred during the Asian American admissions controversy of the 1980s. When Asian American student and community groups noticed that increasing Asian American application rates at several prestigious universities (Brown, Harvard, Princeton, Stanford, Yale, University of California Los Angeles [UCLA], University of California Berkeley) during the 1970s and 1980s failed to yield a comparable increase in admissions rates, they raised the possibility that these schools employed tacit racial quotas to keep Asian American admission rates low and preserve the whiteness of their student bodies.[84] As Dana Takagi argues, conservatives bent on eliminating affirmative action saw their chance and took it.[85] Deliberately and systematically, they shifted public debate from the real issue at hand—whether or not several leading universities imposed racial quotas on Asian American students to preserve the whiteness of their student bodies—to the false issue of whether affirmative action programs designed to benefit blacks and Latinos unfairly discriminated against Asian Americans. In doing so, they ignored the fact that affirmative action programs could not have depressed Asian American admission rates since they applied to only a tiny percentage of the slots in question.

With the use of smoke and mirrors, conservatives transformed an issue of white discrimination against Asian Americans into one of black "reverse discrimination" against the same. Under Reagan's instructions, the Office of Civil Rights of the Department of Education vigorously pursued Title VI antibias compliance investigations on behalf of Asian American applicants. Administration spokespersons repeatedly conflated anti-Asian racial quotas with affirmative action programs designed to increase diversity, denouncing both as racist and unfair. Columnist George Will wrote of the controversy, "Affirmative action discriminated against Asian Americans by restricting the social rewards to competition on the basis of merit. . . . [I]t is lunacy to punish Asian Americans—the nation's model minority—for their passion to excel."[86] Finally, Rep. Dana Rohrabacher introduced a bill that sought to undermine affirmative action under the guise of condemning anti-Asian racial quotas. Thus to further their war on affirmative action, conservatives literally manufactured this conflict between "Asian victims and black villains."[87] Although numerous Asian American advocacy groups and community organizations resisted conscription into this manufactured war, the mass media ignored their efforts, perhaps because they contradicted the reassuring myth of Asian American apoliticalness. The University of California Regents' decision of July 1995, the passage of Proposition 209 in California in 1996, and the proliferation of anti-affirmative action initiatives nationwide suggest that the conservative strategy of championing Asian Americans as proxy whites is having its desired effect.

Black-Korean Conflict: 'Hardworking Immigrants' versus 'Black Racial Agitators'

Since the late 1970s, conflicts between Korean immigrant merchants and the black communities within which they own and operate stores have become commonplace in many major U.S. cities. White racial power decisively shapes the backdrop to such conflict by slotting Korean immigrants and blacks into their respective places in the urban political economy through practices such as language and accent discrimination, redlining (denial of home loans in low-income black areas), residential segregation, and racial violence. Yet the mass media consistently interpret black-Korean conflict as a morality play—or as the bad minority's persecution of the good minority. By focusing on each group's putative characteristics and deflecting attention away from the architectonic exercise of white racial power, this interpretive move works to depoliticize the conflict and delegitimate black grievances about discrimination and racial inequality. Blacks come across as bullies picking on the little guy rather than as bona fide political actors challenging white dominance; whites once again come across as antiracist champions of the underdog even as they protect their own institutionalized privileges. If valorizing Asian Americans relative to blacks is primarily the work of conservatives regarding the affirmative action issue, it is a nearly universal practice when it comes to black-Korean conflict.

The mass media's interpretation of the Flatbush boycott of 1990—a purposive, highly organized, year-long retail boycott and picketing campaign led by black and Haitian activists against two Korean-owned grocery stores in central Brooklyn—was particularly revealing.[88] Precipitated by an altercation between a Korean-born store manager and a Haitian-born woman customer, the Flatbush boycott developed into a full-fledged social movement. More precisely, it became a movement within a movement, or part of a broader resurgence of the Black Power activism that took place in New York City during the 1980s. A revolutionary nationalist group born of this Black Power resurgence, the December 12th Movement, assumed leadership of the Flatbush boycott. Framing the merchant's alleged assault on the customer as symptomatic of antiblack racism in American society, the December 12th Movement exhorted blacks to mobilize in pursuit of community control, self-determination, and racial liberation. This group had led other boycotts against Korean-owned stores during the 1980s, but the Flatbush boycott achieved a singular magnitude because of its intersection with mayoral politics. David Dinkins, who had just been elected the first black mayor of New York City with the aid of many Black Power activists, had campaigned on a promise to protect the city's "gorgeous mosaic" of racial, ethnic, and religious groups. By treating the boycott as a test of Mayor Dinkins's campaign promise—would he be fair to Korean Americans or would he pander to his main constituency?—the mass media transformed the Flatbush boycott into a political crisis of historic proportions.

Yet even as the media politicized the boycott's connection to Mayor Dinkins, it depoliticized the event itself by casting it as a morality play between the bad minority and the good minority. The entire mainstream media—from the *New York Times* to the tabloids to television news programs—interpreted the boycott as greedy, demagogic blacks scapegoating the innocent, apolitical model minority.[89] Many journalists suggested that the boycotters were opportunists trying to advance their own interests or even that they had staged the merchant-customer altercation as part of an extortion scam. That such scapegoating constituted "reverse racism" was hardly in doubt: one *New York Post* editorial, entitled "Anti-Asian Bigotry," condemned the boycott as racist and suggested that blacks, who were the most dependent on welfare programs, would have the most to lose if taxpaying Korean merchants stopped subsidizing the city.[90] In its zealous effort to depoliticize the boycott, the media ignored the fact that the December 12th Movement was seeking to pose a fundamental, long-term challenge to white dominance rather than to extort short-term material concessions; indeed, the group rejected the Brooklyn borough president's offer of a new small business loan program as a palliative that did nothing to address systemic racial inequities.

By valorizing Korean immigrants and defending them against black "agitators," the media once again used Asian Americans and the norms of colorblindness to protect white privilege from a Black Power challenge. One journalist made the connection with the 1960s explicit, comparing the Flatbush boycott unfavorably with the integrationist boycotts of the civil rights movement.[91] Eventually, the media's misportrayal of this normative conflict about racial justice culminated in its comparisons of the boycotters with Nazis and Ku Klux Klan members. Having successfully manufactured public outrage over black "reverse racism," the media finally compelled Mayor Dinkins to intervene in the conflict. The image of the city's first black mayor crossing a black picket line to shop in the two Korean-owned stores at the insistence of the white-owned media says a great deal about racial politics in the post–civil rights era.

Civic Ostracism: 'Here a Nip, There a Nip, Everywhere a Nip, Nip'

The racial triangulation of Asian Americans continues to protect white privileges from both black and Asian American encroachment today—just as it did a century ago. Valorizing Asian Americans helps to deflect black demands for racial reform, and civic ostracism ensures that Asian Americans will not actually "outwhite" whites. Indeed, relative valorization not only implies civic ostracism—through its essentialized reading of Asian/Asian American culture—but creates a need for it. Although the bar on naturalization was lifted in 1952, white opinion makers continue to police the boundary between whites and Asian Americans by imputing permanent foreignness to the latter. They do not overtly deny civic membership to Asian Americans; yet their skepticism about the legitimacy of Asian American participation in public life and their readiness to see Asian American public figures as agents of a foreign power powerfully constrain what civic privileges Asian Americans do enjoy. Racially motivated violence against Asian Americans, which escalated during the 1980s, is only the most dramatic manifestation of persistent practices of civic ostracism. The model minority may prosper in American society because it has been culturally programmed to do so, but in the eyes of most whites it will never be truly American.

Civic ostracism need not be hateful or vicious to be effective. Media commentary on Japanese American Kristi Yamaguchi's 1992 Olympic figure skating contest with Japanese Midori Ito, for example, often suggested that the fourth-generation, native-born Yamaguchi was as much Japanese as she was American and hinted at the irony of her representing the United States in this international contest. In his *Newsweek* cover story on the subject, Frank Deford writes that Yamaguchi's and Ito's "bloodlines both stretch back, pure and simple, to the same soft, cherry-blossom days on the one bold little island of Honshu. . . . Certainly, deep within her, she [Yamaguchi] is still Japanese—some of her must be—and if she should win it's because, while others have the triple axel, only she has the best of both worlds."[92] The author's mention of bloodlines in this context is eerily reminiscent of General Dewitt's wartime commentary about Japanese Americans' "undiluted racial strains." Although the article appears to praise Yamaguchi's endowments, its ostracizing thrust is unmistakable: Kristi Yamaguchi is no Dorothy Hamill.[93]

Asian Americans who have achieved positions of authority or leadership routinely confront accusations that their foreignness makes them unfit for their jobs. Simply put, they are seen as outsiders without standing. When Sen. Daniel Inouye of Hawaii chaired the Iran-contra hearings in 1987, this decorated war hero who volunteered for the famous 442nd Regimental Combat Team in the midst of internment and lost an arm fighting in Italy received hundreds of letters saying that he had no right to question an American hero (Oliver North) and that he should "go back to Japan."[94]

When University of California, Berkeley, professor Elaine Kim wrote a *Newsweek* essay about how the media obscures the roots of black-Korean conflict, she received hundreds of letters with statements such as, "If you are so disenchanted, Korea is still there. Why did you ever leave it? Sayonara" and "If you cannot accept the fact that you are American, maybe you should be living your life in Korea."[95] In the mid-1990s, public commentary on the O. J. Simpson criminal trial demonstrated that the practice of ostracizing Asian Americans goes beyond hate letters and in fact permeates discourse at every level. Radio host Howard Stern sang a ditty about the trial to the tune of "Old McDonald" on the air in October 1994; one line, referring to Judge Lance Ito, was "here a Nip, there a Nip, everywhere a Nip, Nip." In April 1995, New York Sen. Alfonse D'Amato mimicked Judge Ito by speaking in a thick accent on a radio show (Ito, a native-born Japanese American, speaks without an accent).[96]

Tacit suspicions about Asian American participation in American politics broke out into the open during the campaign finance scandal surrounding President Bill Clinton's 1996 reelection campaign. Here the abiding assumption of Asian American foreignness segued rapidly into the accusation that Asian Americans were secret agents working for communist China. Once again, the resonance with the treatment of Japanese Americans during World War II is striking. During the scandal, opinion makers painted Democratic National Committee (DNC) fund raisers John Huang and Charlie Yah-lin Trie not just as shady businessmen engaged in allegedly illegal practices but specifically as "untrustworthy and unscrupulous aliens eager to buy influence into the Clinton administration and to subvert American democracy and national security."[97] Journalists fanned the flames of public anxiety with headlines such as "Bamboo Connection" and "American Guanxi." Aroused by the scent of a communist plot, Sen. Fred Thompson of Tennessee, chairman of the Senate Governmental Affairs Committee, led four months of hearings (July–October 1997) to investigate whether Huang and Trie had solicited donations from illegal Asian sources for Clinton's 1996 electoral campaign. Under pressure to act, the DNC initiated its own investigation in which it telephoned Asian American donors (identified by their Asian-sounding last names) and interrogated them as to their citizenship status, income level, credit history, and so on. The DNC also announced that it would accept donations from "citizens only" in the future. The point here is not that Huang and Trie were innocent scapegoats or that the influence of transnational capital was unworthy of examination, but rather that the readiness of opinion makers to view all Asian Americans as subversive foreign agents reflects and reinforces centuries-old practices of civic ostracism.

When white Americans closed ranks against the Japanese "threat" during the U.S.-Japan trade tensions of the 1980s and early 1990s, they once again identified Asian Americans with the foreign foe. Japan's emergence as a global economic power during this period prompted the revival of the "yellow peril" alarm: opinion makers warned that Japan was continuing World War II by other means, that it was carrying out an "economic Pearl Harbor," and that it planned to invade and take over the American economy.[98] From every mountaintop, the "yellow peril" alarm rang out. Academics and other writers produced an explosion of cautionary books about Japan's nefarious agenda,[99] and corporate elites, politicians, and populist groups alike encouraged participation in a "Buy American" consumer campaign.[100] The marking of the fiftieth anniversary of the bombing of Pearl Harbor in 1991 intensified these jingoistic appeals.

Asian Americans were symbolically rounded up and expelled from the body politic during this dramatic "call to [racial] arms."[101] At the time of the Pearl Harbor anniversary, the Japanese American Citizens League received a phone message saying, "I'll show you a year of remembrance, you dirty Japs. What we remember is Pearl Harbor. . . . We'll get you, you dirty pigs."[102] It also received mail that read, "Dear Jap Cocksuckers: All sneaky Yellow Beggars out of America. You Gook punks stink in the sight of honest people. Go back where you belong. You are not wanted." This note was signed, "Patriot."[103] Since civic ostracism has always entailed a double elision among Asian American subgroups as well as between Asian Americans and Asians, the anti-Japanese furor has in fact produced a climate of fear for all Asian Americans. The Vincent Chin case—in which two white autoworkers beat Chinese American Vincent Chin to death in Detroit in 1982 while calling him a "Jap"—is notorious but not atypical. Monitoring groups such as the National Asian Pacific American Legal Consortium, the Japanese American Citizens League, and the Los Angeles County Human Relations Commission report that racially motivated violence against all Asian Americans has increased dramatically during the past decade, in part because of the intensification of anti-Japanese sentiment.[104] Triangulated between black and white, Asian Americans have been granted provisional acceptance for specific purposes, but they have never been embraced as true Americans.

CONCLUSION

Going "beyond black and white" in a rigorous sense requires more than tracing separate racial trajectories or elaborating a single hierarchy defined by the black-white opposition. The notion of a field of racial positions helps us to grasp that group racialization processes are mutually constitutive and that they generate rankings along more than one dimension. Within this field, as we have seen, Asian Americans have been triangulated vis-à-vis blacks and whites through simultaneous valorization and civic ostracism since their first arrival in the United States. This triangulation pattern has proven remarkably robust over time, undergoing only cosmetic changes in the post–civil rights era. The field of racial positions generally—and the location of Asian Americans specifically—continues to reinforce white racial power, insulating it from minority encroachment or challenge.

This has been an admittedly one-sided story about the exercise of white racial power. My omission of Asian American and black agency has been a matter of economy rather than of principle, however, since I agree with Omi and Winant that subordinated groups continually contest imposed racial meanings through political struggle.[105] Racialization is clearly a reflexive as well as externally imposed process. In defense of the partial narrative offered here, I suggest that this study of racial triangulation serves as an important prelude to and backdrop for future research on racial resistance by both Asian Americans and blacks. White racial power may not tell the whole story, but it does generate a distinct structure of opportunities, constraints, and possibilities—parameters of resistance—with which groups of color must contend. Too often, scholars overlook these parameters and treat minority politics as though it occurred in a discursive and ideological vacuum and was entirely self-determining.

Contextualizing minority politics within the field of racial positions raises a bevy of interesting research questions. Rather than simply polling Asian Americans about affirmative action, we might explore whether relative valorization shapes their perspectives on the issue by encouraging them to publicly disidentify with blacks. Must Asian Americans still attempt to be white in order to get ahead?[106] Similarly, we might examine the degree to which Korean American responses to black grievances buy into relative valorization practices or black grievances against Korean merchants buy into ostracizing practices. In general, we can become more sensitive to the impact of each group's empowerment strategies on the relative positions of other subordinated groups and gain new insight into both the difficulty and promise of multiracial coalitions. We can also be in a position to speculate about what unified resistance to the field of racial positions might look like. Recognizing that this field constrains minority resistance does not mean surrendering to it, but rather exposing it once and for all to meaningful and effective challenge.

NOTES

1. I would like to thank the following for their comments on an earlier draft of this paper: Rogers Smith, Harry Eckstein, Helen Ingram, David Easton, Bernard Grofman, Akhil Gupta, and Sanjeev Khagram. Thanks to Cheryl Larsson for assistance with the figures.

2. Michael Omi and Howard Winant, *Racial Formation in the United States: From the 1960s to the 1980s*, 2d ed. (New York: Routledge Kegan Paul, 1994), 1. While I discuss Asian Americans generally and touch on the experiences of Chinese Americans, Japanese Americans, and Korean Americans in particular, my arguments are more or less applicable to the experiences of different Asian American subgroups.

3. David Theo Goldberg, ed., *Anatomy of Racism* (Minneapolis: University of Minnesota Press, 1990), xiii.

4. Gary Okihiro, *Margins and Mainstreams: Asians in American History and Culture* (Seattle: University of Washington Press, 1994); Mari Matsuda, "We Will Not Be Used," *UCLA Asian American Pacific Islands Law Journal* 1 (1993): 79–84; and Tomás Almaguer, *Racial Fault Lines: The Historical Origins of White Supremacy in California* (Berkeley: University of California Press, 1994).

5. Excellent studies of how whites and blacks or whites and Asian Americans have been racialized relative to one another are available. See, for example, David Roediger, *The Wages of Whiteness* (London: Verso, 1991); and Alexander Saxton, *The Indispensable Enemy: Labor and the Anti-Chinese Movement in California* (Berkeley: University of California Press, 1995). Apparently, few works go significantly beyond dyadic analysis.

6. In a single-scale hierarchy consisting of groups A, B, and C (from top to bottom), group B possesses all of the privileges that group C possesses and more; Asians living under South African apartheid were a classic group B. Racial ordering in the United States has been more complex: Asian Americans have been more privileged than blacks in certain ways and less privileged in others.

7. Angelo N. Ancheta, *Race, Rights and the Asian American Experience* (New Brunswick N.J.: Rutgers University Press, 1998).

8. Neil Gotanda, " 'Other Non-Whites' in *American Legal History: A Review of Justice at War*," *Columbia Law Review* 85 (June 1985): 1186–1192.

9. Stephen Jay Gould, *The Mismeasure of Man*, revised and expanded edition (New York: W. W. Norton, 1996), 403.

10. I discuss only two axes of racial domination, but I am open to the argument that there are in fact more. This is a matter to be investigated empirically rather than determined a priori. I do not discuss Native Americans or Chicanos/Latinos in this chapter, although both groups figured prominently in the history of the West generally and California in particular. This is primarily a decision of economy that is defensible insofar as Asian Americans were usually compared with blacks and whites rather than with these other two groups, who were less integrated into the expanding capitalist labor market. Still, a study of Native Americans and Chicanos/Latinos and their respective places in the field of racial positions would complement this paper nicely.

11. I argue throughout that the field of racial positions (and racial triangulation specifically) reinforces white dominance in various ways and that white opinion makers sometimes deploy it quite strategically in defense of their own group interests. However, I am not claiming that the field of racial positions is entirely instrumental or functional or that it arose for the sole purpose of abetting white racial power. It makes more sense to me to trace the emergence and development of this field empirically than to make this kind of a priori theoretical claim about it.

12. According to the *Merriam-Webster's Collegiate Dictionary* (tenth edition, 1996), "triangulation" is a way of "finding a position or location by means of bearings from two fixed points a known distance apart."

13. Figure 2.1 highlights only relative valorization and civic ostracism and omits numerous other practices (or arrows) by which whites assert dominance and Asian Americans and blacks respond to it.

14. Paul Gilroy, "One Nation under a Groove: The Cultural Politics of 'Race' and Racism in Britain," in *Anatomy of Racism*, ed. David Theo Goldberg (Minneapolis: University of Minnesota Press, 1990), 262–282, 266.

15. Omi and Winant, *Racial Formation*.

16. I do not discuss the civil rights era (1955–1965), during which blacks challenged white dominance in the South through collective action and the elaboration of an ideology of colorblindness. In the next section, however, I do focus on how this ideology has been appropriated by conservatives in the post–civil rights era.

17. During the 1850s, the black population in California was quite small—between one thousand and a few thousand; see Dan Caldwell, "The Negroization of the Chinese Stereotype in California," *Southern California Quarterly* 53 (June 1971): 123–131, 127. The Chinese immigrant population in California grew rapidly during this time, from approximately 3,000 in 1851 to over 20,000 in 1852 to just under 50,000 in 1870; see Almaguer, *Racial Fault Lines*, 156.

18. Stuart Creighton Miller, *The Unwelcome Immigrant: The American Image of the Chinese, 1785–1882* (Berkeley: University of California Press, 1969), 159.

19. Almaguer, *Racial Fault Lines*, 17.

20. Barbara Jeanne Fields, "Slavery, Race, and Ideology in the United States of America," *New Left Review* 181 (May/June 1990): 95–118. Although Filipinos were classified as "Malays" rather than as "Mongolians," they too were located between blacks and whites and outside of the body politic. According to European ethnology, both "Malays" and "Mongolians" occupied an intermediate status between blacks and whites.

21. Miller, *Unwelcome Immigrant.*

22. Gould, *Mismeasure of Man*, 405. The three most prominent ethnological frameworks of the time actually differed as to the precise number of human "races": Johann Friedrich Blumenbach's system included Caucasians, Mongolians, Ethiopians or Negroes, Reds, and Malays or Browns; Carolus Linnaeus's system included European/Whitish, American/Coppery, Asiatic/Tawny, and African/Black; and Baron Georges Cuvier's system included simply Caucasians, Mongolians, and Ethiopians. See Stanford Lyman, "The Chinese before the Courts: Ethnoracial Construction and Marginalization," *International Journal of Politics, Culture, and Society* 6 (1993): 443–462. Nevertheless, most ethnologists located "Mongolians" or "Asiatics" somewhere between blacks and whites in their rankings.

23. Congressional debates about the bar on naturalization and the exclusion of Chinese immigrants, as well as public hearings on the latter, are rich examples of racializing discourse from this period.

24. The first phrase is from Caldwell, "Negroization of the Chinese Stereotype"; the second is from Okihiro, *Margins and Mainstreams.*

25. The racialization of Asian immigrants as "Mongolians" unfit for various privileges and that of various European immigrants as whites entitled to those privileges were mutually constitutive processes. The presence of Chinese immigrant miners was "indispensable" to the construction of a white racial identity among Irish, German, English, Scotch, and Welsh immigrant miners in California. See Saxton, *Indispensable Enemy.*

26. See Almaguer, *Racial Fault Lines*, for a discussion of free labor ideology.

27. Caldwell, "Negroization of the Chinese Stereotype."

28. Luther Spoehr, "Sambo and the Heathen Chinee: Californians' Racial Stereotypes in the Late 1870s," *Pacific Historical Review* 43 (May 1973): 185–204.

29. Quoted in ibid., 198–199.

30. Lewis Carlson and George Colburn, *In Their Place: White America Defines Her Minorities, 1850–1950* (New York: Wiley, 1972), 177.

31. Charles McClain, Jr., "The Chinese Struggle for Civil Rights in Nineteenth Century America: The First Phase, 1850–1870," *California Law Review* 72 (1984): 529–568. McClain argues that Chinese immigrants were in fact remarkably politically adept. He examines their successful lobbying efforts against discriminatory taxation in 1870 and analyzes their contribution to the development of the equal protection doctrine in the courts.

32. Arnold Shankman, "Black on Yellow: Afro-Americans View Chinese-Americans, 1850–1935," *Phylon* 39 (spring 1978): 1–17.

33. During the 1870s, a few employers in Massachusetts and New Jersey imported Chinese immigrant workers as strikebreakers. These labor experiments received extensive press coverage and helped to nationalize awareness of the "Chinese problem."

34. Okihiro, *Margins and Mainstreams*, 47.

35. Ibid., 44.

36. James Loewen, *The Mississippi Chinese: Between Black and White* (Cambridge: Harvard University Press, 1971), 22.

37. Eric Foner, *Reconstruction: America's Unfinished Revolution, 1863–1877* (New York: Harper and Row, 1988), 419.

38. Loewen, *Mississippi Chinese*, 23.

39. Foner, *Reconstruction*, 420.

40. Loewen, *Mississippi Chinese*.

41. Jeannie Rhee, "In Black and White: Chinese in the Mississippi Delta," *Journal of Supreme Court History* (1994): 117–132.

42. Some blacks derided Asian Americans who were trying to be white as Uncle Toms. See Shankman, "Black on Yellow." Indeed, some black leaders bought into the ostracization of Asian Americans: Booker T. Washington, for example, remarked publicly about the foreignness and unassimilability of Chinese immigrants. On the other hand, many black public figures spoke out in behalf of Chinese immigrants as fellow victims of white racism. For example, Frederick Douglass denounced the Reconstruction experiment with Chinese labor as an effort to subjugate both black and Chinese workers and advocated Chinese naturalization rights during the 1870 debates, and Sen. Blanche Bruce from Mississippi spoke out against (and voted against) the exclusionary legislation of 1882.

43. Aside from some exceptions made during World War II, Asian Americans remained "aliens ineligible to citizenship" until the McCarran-Walter Act of 1952 lifted the bar on naturalization.

44. Although blacks have been excluded from meaningful civic participation for most of American history via a shifting combination of law, informal practice, and terror, they have not been ostracized in precisely the same way that Asian Americans have. For one thing, blacks were granted formal citizenship in 1870, but Chinese immigrants remained "aliens ineligible to citizenship." In addition, blacks have historically been deprived of civic privileges (formally or informally) on the grounds that they are racially inferior and unfit for participation—not on the grounds that they are foreign. Today many whites continue to see black immigrants as simply "black" even as they see native-born Asian Americans as foreign.

45. *People v. George Hall*, 4 Cal. 399 (1854).

46. Miller, *Unwelcome Immigrant*, 160.

47. Lyman, "Chinese before the Courts."

48. *In re Ah Yup*, 1 Fed. Cas. 223 (1878); *Takao Ozawa v. United States*, 260 U.S. 178 (1922); and *United States v. Bhagat Singh Thind*, 261 U.S. 204 (1923). Chinese Americans, who were lumped with blacks in *People v. George Hall* (1854) and distinguished from blacks in the 1870 Naturalization Act, were once again lumped with blacks in *Gong Lum et al. v. Rice et al.*, 275 U.S. 78 (1927). In this famous case, Chinese American Gong Lum challenged Mississippi's practice of placing Chinese American students in black schools (Mississippi law mandated the segregation of "colored" students from white students). Although Lum's attorney argued that Chinese American students were not "colored"—" 'Colored' describes only one race, and that is the negro"—and that they should be allowed to attend white schools in order to escape the degrading influence of black students, the U.S. Supreme Court ruled that Chinese American students such as native-born Martha Lum, as members of the "yellow race," were indeed "colored" and therefore properly placed in black schools. This is yet another example of the courts' willingness to sacrifice jurisprudential consistency in the name of protecting white privilege.

49. Spoehr, "Sambo and the Heathen Chinee," 191.

50. Quoted in Roger Daniels, *Asian America: Chinese and Japanese in the United States since 1850* (Seattle: University of Washington Press, 1988), 40.

51. Quoted in ibid., 53.

52. Between 1885 and 1924, approximately 180,000 Japanese immigrants entered the continental United States; see Ronald Takaki, *Strangers from a Different Shore* (Boston: Little, Brown, 1989), 45. That the 1930 census showed fewer than 140,000 Japanese immigrants living in the United States (and less than 100,000 in California) suggests significant rates of sojourning; see Roger Daniels, *The Politics of Prejudice* (Berkeley: University of California Press, 1977), 1.

53. Daniels, *Politics of Prejudice*, 21.

54. "Yellow peril" was a highly flexible term, used by white opinion makers to refer to the different kinds of threat (military, economic, demographic, social, or cultural) posed by China and/or Japan. See Richard Thompson, *The Yellow Peril, 1890–1924* (New York: Arno Press, 1978).

55. Susan Lee, "Racial Construction through Citizenship in the U.S.," *Asian American Policy Review* 4 (1996): 89–116.

56. Takaki, *Strangers from a Different Shore*, 388.

57. The article presents four pictures—two of Japanese men and two of Chinese men—for purposes of differentiation, once again eliding the distinction between Japanese and Japanese Americans, on one hand, and Chinese and Chinese Americans, on the other. The Chinese men have placid, pleasant expressions; their faces are illuminated by generous lighting. The Japanese men are frowning and serious; their pictures are darker and filled with shadows. Conceding that there is no "infallible way" of telling the two groups apart because they share certain "racial strains," the author nevertheless offers ten "rules of thumb" for differentiation

regarding height, weight, hip width, hirsuteness, eyewear preferences, width of space between the eyes, facial expression, facial structure, gait, and social skill. During the war, some Chinese Americans actively disidentified with Japanese Americans, featuring "I am not a Jap" signs on their businesses, homes, and, sometimes, even on their persons. Racialization, like other forms of politics, creates strange bedfellows.

58. See, for example, Thomas Sowell, *Ethnic America* (New York: Basic Books, 1981); William Julius Wilson, *The Truly Disadvantaged* (Chicago: University of Chicago Press, 1987); and Nathan Glazer, *Affirmative Discrimination: Ethnic Inequality and Public Policy* (Cambridge: Harvard University Press, 1987).

59. See, for example, Omi and Winant, *Racial Formation*; Derrick Bell, *Faces at the Bottom of the Well: The Permanence of Racism* (New York: Basic Books, 1992); and Neil Gotanda, "A Critique of 'Our Constitution Is Color-Blind,' " *Stanford Law Review* 44 (1991): 1–68.

60. For the concept of a "public transcript," see James C. Scott, *Domination and the Arts of Resistance: Hidden Transcripts* (New Haven: Yale University Press, 1990).

61. Blanket statements about white opinion makers are less tenable now than they were a century ago. When discussing contemporary events, therefore, I often distinguish certain white opinion makers from others (for example, conservatives from progressives regarding affirmative action). But such distinctions are not always necessary: for example, white opinion makers of all political persuasions talk about black-Korean conflict in a similar way. Also, I occasionally use "mass media" and "white opinion makers" as synonyms because the former continue to reproduce white racial power, regardless of the fact that today more journalists of color are in the newsroom.

62. See David Wellman, "The New Political Linguistics of Race," *Socialist Review* 16 (1986):43–62; and Frank H. Wu, "Neither Black nor White: Asian Americans and Affirmative Action," *Boston College Third World Law Journal* 15 (summer 1995): 225–284.

63. Although they constitute less than 4 percent of the U.S. population, Asian Americans are the fastest-growing minority group. Their total numbers went from 3.8 million in 1980 to over 7 million in 1990 and are projected to reach 20 million by 2020. The Asian American population, which is two-thirds foreign born, has diversified by national origin (and other measures) quite dramatically since 1965. Before 1965 Chinese Americans and Japanese Americans made up the majority of Asian Americans; since 1965 other East Asian groups, Southeast Asian groups, and Pacific Islanders have come in ever-increasing numbers. Today the largest five subgroups are, in descending order, Chinese Americans, Filipino Americans, Japanese Americans, Indian Americans, and Korean Americans. For discussion of the post-1965 diversification of the Asian American population by national origin, class, and other dimensions, see Paul Ong, Edna Bonacich, and Lucie Cheng, eds., *The New Asian Immigration in Los Angeles and Global Restructuring* (Philadelphia: Temple University Press, 1994).

64. See Keith Osajima, "Asian Americans as the Model Minority: An Analysis of the Popular Press Image in the 1960s and 1980s," in *Reflections on Shattered Windows: Promises and Prospects for Asian American Studies,* ed. Gary Okihiro, Shirley Hune, Arthur Hansen, and John Liu (Pullman: Washington State University Press, 1988), 165–174; Okihiro, *Margins and Mainstreams*; and Ki-Taek Chun, "The Myth of Asian American Success and Its Educational Ramifications," in *The Asian American Educational Experience,* ed. Don Nakanishi and Tina Yamano Nishida (New York: Routledge Kegan Paul, 1995),95–112.

65. See Chun, "Myth of Asian American Success"; Bob Suzuki, "Asian Americans as the 'Model Minority': Outdoing Whites? Or Media Hype?" *Change* (November/December 1989): 13–19; and Won Moo Hurh and Kwang-chung Kim, "The 'Success' Image of Asian Americans: Its Validity, and Its Practical and Theoretical Implications," *Ethnic and Racial Studies* 12 (October 1989): 512–533.

66. Opinion makers (including mainstream scholars) reinforce the myth of Asian American apoliticalness by consistently ignoring or downplaying evidence of Asian American political involvement. As a result, most people have no idea that there was an Asian American movement in the late 1960s—let alone that it contained a revolutionary wing or that it left a vital legacy in the form of Asian American Studies programs nationwide.

67. Moon Jo, "The Putative Political Complacency of Asian Americans," *Political Psychology* 5 (1984): 583–605, 594–595.

68. William Petersen, "Success Story, Japanese-American Style," *New York Times Magazine,* January 6, 1966, 20ff.

69. "Success Story of One Minority Group in America," *U.S. News and World Report,* December 26, 1966, 73ff.

70. "Success Story: Outwhiting the Whites," *Newsweek,* June 21, 1971, 24–25.

71. Omi and Winant, *Racial Formation.*

72. Osajima, "Asian Americans as the Model Minority."

73. Martin Kasindorf, "Asian-Americans: A 'Model Minority,' " *Newsweek,* December 6, 1982, 39ff.

74. Lawrence Harrison, *Who Prospers? How Cultural Values Shape Economic and Political Success* (New York: Basic Books, 1992).

75. For a critique of the underclass myth, see Adolph Reed Jr., "The Underclass as Myth and Symbol: The Poverty of Discourse about Poverty," *Radical America* 24 (January 1992): 21–40. Certain Asian American subgroups (especially Southeast Asian Americans) have been classified as part of the "underclass" when their behavior controverts the model minority myth. Consider the case of the four Vietnamese and Chinese Vietnamese youths who held up a Good Guys electronics store and seized hostages in Sacramento in April 1991. (Their demands included passage out of the country to fight communists in Southeast Asia.) The media and the police promptly characterized these youths as gang members even though they had no

evidence to substantiate this charge. See Michael Peter Smith and Bernadette Tarallo, "Who Are the 'Good Guys?' The Social Construction of the Vietnamese 'Other,' " in *The Bubbling Cauldron: Race, Ethnicity, and the Urban Crisis*, ed. Michael Peter Smith and Joe Feagin (Minneapolis: University of Minnesota Press, 1995), 50–76.

76. Although Wilson in *The Truly Disadvantaged* does attribute the formation of the black "underclass" at least in part to large-scale economic processes, he minimizes the continuing impact of institutionalized racism. Moreover, others have interpreted his underclass argument as a culture-of-poverty argument so relentlessly that he has called for the expurgation of the term *underclass* from discourse about poverty.

77. Thomas Sowell, *Race and Economics* (New York: McKay, 1975), 128.

78. David Bell, "The Triumph of Asian Americans," *New Republic* (July 1985): 24–31; and William McGurn, "The Silent Minority: Asian-Americans' Affinity with Republican Party Principles," *National Review* 43 (June 1991): 19ff.

79. In the film, Suzie is a hooker with a heart of gold who accepts her white boyfriend's violence against her as a sign of his love. Nancy Kwan has built her career on white fantasies about and distorted constructions of Asians and Asian Americans. During the 1980s she appeared in paid television commercials for "Oriental Pearl Creme," insisting that the product was the secret to the youthful appearance of "Oriental" women.

80. Do whites feel that affirmative action threatens their privileges? Consider the following *U.S. News and World Report* cover story from February 13, 1995: "Does Affirmative Action Mean . . . NO WHITE MEN NEED APPLY?"

81. See Japanese American Citizens League, *Why Asian Americans Should Oppose Proposition 209* (San Francisco); Chinese for Affirmative Action, *Asians and Affirmative Action* (San Francisco); and Leadership Education for Asian Pacifics (LEAP), *Perspectives on Affirmative Action* and *In Support of Civil Rights* (Los Angeles: LEAP Asian Pacific American Public Policy Institute, 1996). Although the leading Asian American advocacy groups support affirmative action, Asian Americans as a whole have shown marked ambivalence toward the issue, perhaps in part because they have been misled by conservative efforts at relative valorization. After all, there is no reason to think that Asian Americans are any less confused about affirmative action than whites. An April 1995 survey by Louis Harris and the Feminist Majority found that 81 percent of Californians claimed to support Proposition 209; this number dropped to 29 percent, however, when they were told that Proposition 209 would eliminate all affirmative action programs in the public sector. See Janine Jackson, "White Man's Burden: How the Press Frames Affirmative Action," *Extra!* (September/October 1995): 7–9.

82. Glazer, *Affirmative Discrimination*, 74. During the late 1990s, Glazer publicly reversed his position on affirmative action, declaring his qualified support for it.

83. The phrase "near white" is from Okihiro, *Margins and Mainstreams*.

84. Brown and Stanford admitted to irregularities of their own accord. Internal and external reviews of the other universities produced mixed results. The Office of Civil Rights cleared Harvard of wrongdoing but ordered UCLA's math department to admit certain graduate school applicants that it had rejected. Both the state auditor general and the California Senate subcommittee on higher education investigated UC Berkeley; in 1989 UC Berkeley's chancellor, Ira Michael Heyman, publicly apologized for "disadvantaging Asians" in the school's admissions process. See Dana Takagi, *The Retreat from Race: Asian American Admissions and Racial Politics* (New Brunswick, N.J.: Rutgers University Press, 1992).

85. Ibid.

86. Don Nakanishi, "A Quota on Excellence? The Asian American Admissions Debate," in *The Asian American Educational Experience*, ed. Don Nakanishi and Tina Yamano Nishida (New York: Routledge Kegan Paul, 1995), 273–284.

87. Takagi, *Retreat from Race,* 109.

88. This section on black-Korean conflict is based on *Bitter Fruit: The Politics of Black-Korean Conflict in New York City* (New Haven: Yale University Press, 2000).

89. On the whole, the black-oriented media (newspapers, television programs, radio shows) offered more balanced coverage of the Flatbush boycott, seriously addressing the black activists' political activity without attacking the Korean merchants and their advocates.

90. "Anti-Asian Bigotry" (editorial), *New York Post,* May 24, 1990.

91. Sheryl McCarthy,"When Boycotts Were for Just Causes," *New York Newsday,* February 4, 1991.

92. *Newsweek,* February 10, 1992, cited in Asian American Journalists Association, *Project Zinger: A Critical Look at News Media Coverage of Asian Pacific Americans* (Washington, D.C.: Center for Integration and Improvement of Journalism, 1992), 7–8.

93. In the next issue of *Newsweek,* a reader wrote in with the observation that no one ever implied that Dorothy Hamill felt some "deep allegiance" to the land of her forefathers. See ibid., 7–8.

94. Moon Jo and Daniel Mast, "Changing Images of Asian Americans," *International Journal of Politics, Culture, and Society* 6 (1993): 417–441.

95. Elaine Kim, "Home Is Where the Han Is: A Korean-American Perspective on the Los Angeles Upheavals," in *Reading Rodney King/Reading Urban Uprising,* ed. Robert Gooding-Williams (New York: Routledge Kegan Paul, 1993): 215–235.

96. Cynthia Kwei Yung Lee, "Beyond Black and White: Racializing Asian Americans in a Society Obsessed with O.J.," *Hastings Women's Law Journal* 6 (summer 1995): 165–207. Thanks to Katheryn Russell for bringing this article to my attention.

97. L. Ling-chi Wang, "Race, Class, Citizenship, and Extraterritoriality: Asian Americans and the 1996 Campaign Finance Scandal," *Amerasia Journal* 24 (1998): 1–21.

98. In 1991 a Fairfax, Virginia, organization called "Americans for Fair Play" sent out solicitation letters that read in part:

LET'S STOP JAPAN'S UNFAIR ECONOMIC WAR AGAINST AMERICA! . . . The Japanese are attempting to do economically what they could not do militarily—conquer America! . . . [I]t took an atomic bomb to knock some sense into the Japanese. . . . [Its leaders] conceived an incredibly bold plan to (1) take over the banking and financial systems of the West (2) buy huge amounts of American real estate (3) purchase entertainment and educational institutions to change Western public opinion to more favorable Japanese views (4) "buy" significant political power in the US Senate and House and (5) loot United States oil and gas industries, agriculture, and manufacturing through buyouts, acquisitions, and "third party" takeovers. In short, they prepared their detailed "war plan."

See Japanese American Citizens League, *The Impact of Japan-Bashing and the "Buy American" Movement on Japanese Americans: An Educational Workbook* (San Francisco, 1992).

99. Robert Reich has identified at least thirty-five such books written during the late 1980s and early 1990s, including Clyde Prestowitz Jr.'s *Trading Places* (1988), Daniel Burstein's *Yen! Japan's New Financial Empire and Its Threat to America* (1988), Karel Van Wolferen's *The Enigma of Japanese Power* (1989), Pat Choate's *Agents of Influence* (1990), William Holstein's *Japanese Power Game* (1990), and William Dietrich's *In the Shadow of the Rising Sun* (1991). See Robert Reich, "Is Japan Really Out to Get Us?" *New York Times Book Review*, February 9, 1992, 1ff.

100. The "Buy American" movement ignored the glaring if inconvenient fact that American cars are increasingly difficult to distinguish from Japanese cars. Many American brand-name cars are made in Japan, and many Japanese brand-name cars are made in the United States. Moreover, Detroit's Big Three automakers all own stock in Japanese auto companies: General Motors owns 38 percent of Isuzu, Ford owns 25 percent of Mazda, and Chrysler owns 6 percent of Mitsubishi. See Japanese American Citizens League, *Impact of Japan-Bashing*, 4.

101. In "Is Japan Really Out to Get Us?" Robert Reich suggests that the anti-Japanese furor of the late 1980s and early 1990s was a national "call to arms"—a call for Americans to come together against what they perceived as a common threat in order to strengthen their sense of identity in the post–cold war world. What Reich fails to note is the degree to which this was in fact a "call to [racial] arms," an exhortation to an imagined community that has always been exclusively white.

102. Masako Iino, "Asian Americans under the Influence of 'Japan Bashing,'" *American Studies International* 32 (April 1994): 17–30.

103. Japanese American Citizens League, *Impact of Japan Bashing*, 9.

104. Hate crime statistics are notoriously unreliable since most state and local law enforcement agencies do not collect and record the relevant data. Indeed, police de-

partments are often reluctant to classify hate crimes as such because they want to avoid unwanted publicity (or because one of their own members is the perpetrator). The Hate Crimes Statistics Act of 1990 mandates the collection of data at the federal level, but it still relies on the data collection efforts of lower-level agencies.

105. Omi and Winant, *Racial Formation.*

106. My thanks to Helen Ingram and Rogers Smith for posing this question to me. I have referred to conservatives' "conscription" of Asian Americans into the racial retrenchment war, yet not all Asian Americans have resisted the draft. In this context, Mari Matsuda urges all Asian Americans to proclaim "We Will Not Be Used" (1993).

CHAPTER THREE

CITIZENSHIP NULLIFICATION: THE IMPOSSIBILITY OF ASIAN AMERICAN POLITICS

NEIL T. GOTANDA

In the late 1990s anti-immigrant sentiment in the U.S. news media took a distinctly anti-Chinese turn. Diverted from California's Proposition 187 and its focus on a Mexican or Latin invasion, the public swung its attention to Chinese subversion. Specifically, beginning in 1996 a steady series of charges were directed toward China revolving around a presidential campaign finance scandal and accusations of Chinese spying in American nuclear weapons laboratories.

Allegations of corrupt campaign donations by Chinese officials continued through never-ending congressional investigations, which were accompanied by occasional low-level indictments. These investigations hinted that the suspect Chinese donations would somehow undermine the American political system. As for Chinese spying, hysterical headlines proclaimed that Chinese intelligence, operating through spies of Chinese ancestry, had stolen crucial nuclear weapons secrets.

After several years of investigation and debate, no major figures were indicted on campaign finance violations and no criminal charges of spying were filed. Throughout this period, even as the investigators were finding little evidence of Chinese American wrong-doing, the Chinese continued to serve as targets of public and media suspicion. In the absence of high-profile defendants, Chinese and Chinese Americans became the medium by which allegations of espionage and corruption were conveyed.

The media campaigns were conducted across the confusing terrain of citizenship, race, ethnicity, and claims to the American national identity. Existing conceptions of race only partially describe this complex set of considerations. This chapter theorizes an alternative mode of racialization that offers new perspectives on race, ethnicity, and citizenship. These new viewpoints will provide a context in which the media fixation with China and the Chinese might be better understood. This chapter also will reveal that a group of related yet distinct ideas—Asiatic inassimilability, the conflation of Asian Americans with Asian citizens, and the perception of Asians as a threat to the American nation—are more than misunderstandings and stereotypes. They describe a distinct mode of racialization of Americans of Asian ancestry—labeled here *Asiatic racialization.*

Asiatic racialization developed in the late nineteenth century during campaigns for Chinese exclusion from the United States. It did not portray the Oriental or Asian as inherently inferior. Instead, it linked the idea of permanent foreignness—inassimilability to America—with national or ethnic categories such as Chinese, Japanese, or Korean. Asiatic racialization is thus characterized by a distinctive form of racial category linked to the idea that those so categorized are permanently foreign and inassimilable.

The term *citizenship nullification* is used in this chapter to describe the act of stopping the exercise of a person's citizenship rights through the use of the implicit link between an Asiatic racial category and foreignness. In political terms, Asiatic racialization and citizenship nullification have rendered genuine Asian American citizenship an impossibility today because race continues to thwart America's promise of full citizenship rights. This is likely to remain true so long as race occupies a significant place in American life.

In presenting Asiatic racialization as an alternative to traditional understandings of race, this chapter is not suggesting that it has replaced or supplanted present understandings. Rather, it is an additional description of the complex American processes of racialization.[1]

ASIATIC RACIALIZATION: RACIALIZED CITIZENSHIP

The terms *racialized* and *racialization* capture the idea that race is often a process. The now frequently expressed notion that "race is socially constructed" similarly emphasizes the historical and social contexts in which various ideas of race have developed.

As it developed in the latter half of the nineteenth century, Asiatic racialization was the process whereby first the "Chinese race" and then other Asian national/ethnic "races" became known. Americans of Asian ancestry were normalized into commonsense social categories with understandable social meanings. An integral part of this development was the linkage of inassimilable "foreignness" with these Asiatic racial categories. Thus these Asiatic "races"—the Chinese, Japanese, Korean, Hindu, and others—were ultimately inassimilable to American society.

In its considerations of race in the nineteenth century, the U.S. Supreme Court couched the notion of assimilability to America in the language of citizenship. In other words, in many of the Court's published opinions, citizenship became the preferred form of expressing who could or could not participate in America. The clearest statement of this linkage of race, citizenship, and participation in America came in 1857 in the well-known *Dred Scott v. Sandford* decision.[2] In that opinion Chief Justice Roger Taney made Dred Scott's citizenship a crucial issue. Taney redefined a technical legal question—citizenship for purposes of jurisdiction—into a sweeping inquiry into the basic national rights of an American:

> The question is simply this: Can a negro, whose ancestors were imported into this country and sold as slaves, become a member of the political community formed and brought into existence by the Constitution of the United States, and as such become entitled to all the rights, and privileges, and immunities, guarantied [sic] by that instrument to the citizen. One of which rights is the privilege of suing in a court of the United States in the cases specified in the Constitution.[3]

Taney's answer to that question—a resounding no—attempted to exclude forever any possible participation by the "negro" in American society.

This portrayal of citizenship as the basis for participation in American society, and therefore for becoming a true American, continued to play a role in the Supreme Court's decisions about the Chinese. In this racialized context, citizenship was far more than a description of a simple legal status. Instead, citizenship was the sum total of being an American.

At the end of the nineteenth century an important example of this linkage appeared in Justice John Marshall Harlan's celebrated dissenting opinion in *Plessy v. Ferguson* (1896).[4] In objecting to the majority decision which upheld a Louisiana state law requiring racial segregation in railroad cars, Harlan couched his dissent almost entirely in the language of citizenship. It is citizens—white and Negro—whose rights are in dispute, he asserts in his dissent. The implications of his use of "citizen" become clear in his short discussion of the "Chinese."

> There is a race so different from our own that we do not permit those belonging to it to become citizens of the United States. Persons belonging to it are, with few exceptions, absolutely excluded from our country. I allude to the Chinese race. But, by the statute in question, a Chinaman can ride in the same passenger coach with white citizens of the United States, while citizens of the black race in Louisiana, many of whom, perhaps, risked their lives for the preservation of the Union, who are entitled, by law, to participate in the political control of the state and nation, who are not excluded, by law or by reason of their race, from public stations of any kind, and who have all the legal rights that belong to white citizens, are yet declared to be criminals, liable to imprisonment, if they ride in a public coach occupied by citizens of the white race.[5]

In Harlan's view, the Chinese were properly excluded from citizenship. They were "so different" that they were properly barred from ever becoming Americans. In 1896 when Harlan was writing, Chinese were barred from becoming citizens both by Chinese exclusion laws and the general limitation of U.S. naturalization to "white persons."[6] For the Chinese, being a member of the "Chinese race" was an explicit barrier to citizenship.

Even though the racial barrier to naturalization has been abolished, the linkage of citizenship and race remains intact today. In commentaries on citizenship, legal scholars and social scientists continue to use a broad understanding of American citizenship as the context for any analysis of the place of "minorities." Citizenship remains one of the crucial legal and political categories around which the exercise or denial of democratic rights turns.

In his influential book *Democracy and Distrust: A Theory of Judicial Review,* published in 1980, John Hart Ely discusses the peculiar and proper place of Supreme Court review in the U.S. political system.[7] As a context for his justification of the Court's actions, Ely outlines a general theory of constitutional politics. For Ely, the U.S. Constitution provides a process of representative democracy to allocate costs and benefits. This process includes the kind of pluralist wheeling and dealing by which the various minorities that make up U.S. society typically interact to protect their interests.[8]

Ely's pluralist wheeling and dealing are not limited to electoral politics. Citizenship rights should include general participation in all aspects of the modern life of a civil society, including commerce and civic life. Consider the comments of philosophers Will Kymlicka and Wayne Norman:

> At the level of theory, [examining citizenship] is a natural evolution in political discourse because the concept of citizenship seems to integrate the demands of justice and community membership. . . . Citizenship is intimately linked to ideas of individual entitlement on the one hand and of attachment to particular community on the other.[9]

Citizenship remains the necessary condition for full participation in American society and politics.

The Supreme Court's decisions on race thus reflect a substantial history linking race to a broad concept of citizenship. For Americans of Asian ancestry, this has meant that simply attaining the legal status of citizen has been insufficient to guarantee full citizenship rights. The former explicit statutory barrier to becoming a U.S. citizen has, for the Chinese, been replaced by an indirect barrier. The linkage of race and citizenship has meant that the "foreignness" attached to the Chinese—an Asiatic racial category—can prevent them from obtaining full citizenship rights.

This remains true even for those persons of Asian ancestry who are legal U.S. citizens. Because racial identification—membership in an Asiatic racial category—is separated from the technical legal status of being a U.S. citizen, this racial barrier to full citizenship participation is insulated from legal status. An assumed aspect of the social and political identity of any American of Asian ancestry is that foreignness can be invoked at any time by any person. Citizenship nullification, then, is the ability to invoke "foreignness" to deny full political participation to any person of Asian ancestry.

THE CHINESE RACIAL CATEGORY

The racial categories that emerged for Asiatic racialization differed from the existing black and white racial categories. In African American racialization, the Negro and white racial categories emerged in the North American colonies with the rise of slavery in the 1600s. In the seventeenth century, a description of origin—African—was displaced by the social category Negro or black. Earlier identities—Yoruba, Hausa, Fula—were eradicated. Similarly, English was supplanted by a generic racial category:

white. The category of Negro or black functioned as a classification for enslaveability. It emerged as a clear marker of the inferior—that is, the enslaveable—within a black-white racial dialectic. The intertwined understandings of Negro inferiority and white superiority embodied in the black and white racial categories[10] continued to develop in the formative years of the Republic. In the 1850s, in the midst of the continuing struggles and divisions growing out of slavery, the Supreme Court would issue what would become one of its most famous pronouncements on race and inferiority. Chief Justice Roger Taney's 1857 *Dred Scott* opinion stated:

> They [Negroes] had for more than a century before been regarded as beings of an inferior order, and altogether unfit to associate with the white race, either in social or political relations; and so far inferior, that they had no rights which the white man was bound to respect; and that the negro might justly and lawfully be reduced to slavery for his benefit.[11]

At the mid-nineteenth century, then, the Supreme Court provided a clear statement in which the Negro racial category was unambiguous. Attached to that racial category was a forceful claim of the inferiority of the Negro.

By contrast, when Asiatic racial categories took root, the racialization did not coalesce around an "Oriental" or "yellow" racial category. Those terms were widely used, yet they did not occupy a significant place in the race language of the Supreme Court. Instead, the idea of Chinese or Japanese became themselves racialized categories. As Asiatic racialization developed, a reference to Chinese was not a reference to a person with Chinese citizenship, or a person born in China. Instead, it was a reference to any person of Chinese descent. All persons from a mythic China—not necessarily the historical China—and the descendants of these persons were considered "Chinese."

An additional understanding developed alongside the inferiority of the nonwhite. Sometimes as an alternative and sometimes as a supplement, the social characteristic "permanent foreignness" was attributed to the Chinese—that is, the Chinese were inassimilable to American society. This Asiatic racialization was subsequently transferred to members of other Asian groups—the Japanese, the Hindu, the Korean, the Filipino.

In contrast to the certitude over the Negro that marked the language in the 1857 *Dred Scott* decision, an 1854 California Supreme Court opinion in *People v. George Hall* suggested an era in which the racialization of Chinese was ambiguous and incomplete.[12] The case involved a homicide in which a white defendant had been convicted of the murder of a Chinese on the testimony of a Chinese witness. As in many states, California maintained a statutory prohibition of Negro or Indian testimony against white defendants. The California Supreme Court faced the issue of how to classify a Chinese witness.

The court did not seriously consider whether Chinese should be allowed to testify against white defendants. Instead, it preoccupied itself with how to fit Chinese within the categories of Negro, colored, or Indian. In a remarkable commentary, the court first examined how explorer Christopher Columbus had mistakenly adopted the name "Indian." The court then speculated on how Indians may have crossed the Bering Strait given the physical similarities of Mongolians, "Esquimaux," and American Indians and concluded that "the name of Indian, from the time of Columbus to the present day, has been used to designate, not alone the North American Indian, but the whole of the Mongolian race."[13] Thus including Chinese within the statutory category of Indian would have excluded Chinese testimony. That was not enough, however. The court went on to hold that

> the words "White," "Negro," "Mulatto," "Indian" and "Black person" wherever they occur in our Constitution and laws, must be taken in their generic sense, and that, even admitting the Indian of this Continent is not of the Mongolian type, that the words "Black person" must be taken as contradistinguished from White, and necessarily excludes [from testifying against a white person] all races other than the Caucasian.[14]

These speculations are notable for their lack of focus and consistency. Although anti-Chinese agitation was already well under way in the 1850s, the California court in 1854 in this case of first impression found certainty only in the conclusion that the Chinese were not white.

The campaigns against the Chinese grew in volume and violence over the next three decades. The hesitancies found in *People v. George Hall* are no longer present in federal legal documents from the late 1800s. Laws passed by Congress and federal court decisions provide evidence of the consolidation of the Chinese racial category and the explicit articulation of the Chinese racial category as marked permanently by foreignness. The federal courts, together with Congress through the passage of legislation, developed the racialized meaning of "Chinese."

After decades of agitation from the Pacific coast and a presidential veto of Chinese exclusion legislation in 1879, a renegotiated treaty with China set the scene for congressional passage of the first Chinese exclusion law in 1882. The act was intended to exclude Chinese workers without interfering with treaty provisions guaranteeing reciprocal freedoms for merchants and traders. The specific exclusionary phrase was "Chinese laborers." By contrast, language elsewhere in the 1882 legislation prohibited naturalization to citizenship for "Chinese."[15]

The next year, 1883, the meaning of the phrase "Chinese laborer" was interpreted by a Massachusetts federal court. A carpenter of Chinese ancestry had shipped from Manila aboard a British ship and then stayed in Boston. The local U.S. attorney charged the carpenter with violation of the 1882 exclusion law. The court found, however, that since he had been born in Hong Kong and was a British subject, he was not a Chinese laborer under the statute. The court reasoned that the statute was implementation of a treaty with China and that the statutory term *Chinese laborer* therefore referred to Chinese subjects and did not apply to British subjects, regardless of their ancestry. Shortly thereafter, a federal court in San Francisco came to the opposite conclusion and found such Chinese covered by the exclusion act.[16]

Within the statute, the difference of interpretation involved whether "Chinese laborer" was to be interpreted as a racial term. If Chinese was a racial category, the statutory phrase included all persons of "Chinese blood." The Massachusetts court, however, found "Chinese laborer" to be a political term, limited to Chinese subjects or to those whose "national origin" was Chinese territory, not British territorial lands. In 1884 this issue was resolved by Congress which stated in legislation that the act applied to "all subjects of China or and Chinese, whether subjects of China or any other foreign power." The ban on naturalization of Chinese was apparently subject to no such ambiguity and was applied on a racial basis.

The conflict among the federal courts was not resolved by an appeal to the U.S. Supreme Court. The "Chinese laborer" language was reformulated by Congress in the 1892 Geary Act, which continued exclusion and added a system of mandatory resident certification. The operative language in the Geary Act was "Chinese person or person of Chinese descent."[17] The new language made the statutory category a racialized category.

This use of Chinese as a racialized category in immigration legislation was applied to all subsequent major immigration legislation. In the 1944 legislation repealing the Chinese Exclusion Act, Congress provided Chinese with a national origins quota, thus placing China on an equal footing with other nations. The quota, however, was extended to all persons of Chinese ancestry, regardless of place of birth and point of origin before coming to the United States. The Chinese national origins quota was thus a Chinese race quota. This pattern of racialized categories for Asian nationalities continued through the repeal of the Chinese Exclusion Act in 1944 and persisted until the abolition in 1965 of the national origins quota system.[18]

In summary, the Chinese racial category conflates several different aspects of "Chineseness." First, as applied to the Chinese nation-state, it follows international law practice and includes as "Chinese" the many national and ethnic minorities who live within the Chinese nation-state. Second, as applied to U.S. national origin immigration laws, the immigration category "Chinese" includes a woman of Chinese ancestry who might carry a British passport if born in Hong Kong. Third, as applied today within the United States, the term *Chinese* could apply equally to a fifth-generation, Harvard Law School–trained U.S. citizen and to an immigrant only recently arrived from Beijing. These conflations within the Chinese racial category include an implicit assumption that the "Chinese" share more in common with each other than with "Americans." As such, the category includes the premise that "true" assimilation is an impossibility.

Similarly, when this attribution of "foreignness" is present, the Chinese are not "ethnic" Americans in the European immigrant tradition of successful assimilation into American life. Asian immigrant success stories have been told, but they should be examined to see if the story encompasses Asiatic racialization or a more traditional racial and ethnic narrative.

FOREIGNNESS AND THE CHINESE RACIAL CATEGORY

In the late nineteenth century the U.S. Supreme Court chose to review the constitutionality of Chinese exclusion legislation. The Court's language illustrates the consolidation of foreignness as an attribute of being Chinese. Taken together, the Chinese exclusion cases describe the evolution of a particular kind of "Chineseness"—permanent foreignness—that coincided with the development of the Chinese racial category. The two developments should be seen as part of the same process—the development of a distinctive Asiatic racialization.

Chew Heong v. United States (1884)

The first Supreme Court opinion to address Chinese exclusion was *Chew Heong v. United States* in 1884.[19] Passed initially in 1882 and amended in 1884, the Chinese exclusion acts "temporarily suspended" the immigration of Chinese laborers for ten years. These acts were intended to respect, however, the basic provisions of the Burlingame Treaty of 1868 which established the freedom of both Chinese and Americans to travel and work in the United States and China. The acts included certification procedures for Chinese already resident in the United States who wished to travel. Under the acts, before any departure from the United States Chinese residents had to obtain certificates that would prove their U.S. residency upon their return. Chew Heong, a Chinese laborer, left the United States before passage of the first exclusion act in 1882. Upon his return he was barred from admission, and that act was upheld by a state court. After agreeing to review the case, the Supreme Court reversed the lower court and held that Chew Heong had properly been allowed to present evidence other than the certificate to prove he had been resident of the United States before passage of the exclusion acts. Justice Stephen J. Field, who had written the decision against Chew Heong while assigned to the lower court, dissented from the majority. His comments were typical of sentiments against the Chinese:

> But notwithstanding these favorable provisions [of the Burlingame Treaty of 1868] . . . they have remained among us a separate people, retaining their original peculiarities of dress, manners, habits and modes of living, which are as marked as their complexion and language. They live by themselves; they constitute a distinct organization with the laws and customs which they brought from China. Our institutions have made no impression on them during the more than thirty years they have been in the country. They have their own tribunals to which they voluntarily submit, and seek to live in a manner similar to that of China. They do not and will not assimilate with our people; and their dying wish is that their bodies may be taken to China for burial.[20]

In his opinion, Field essentially characterizes the Chinese as inassimilable. He asserts that besides the basic social and cultural considerations—dress, manners, language—the Chinese do not accept the basic American civic institutions. In fact, they are so divorced from America that they are unwilling even to have their bodies buried here, apparently preferring a heathen ritual in China to a proper Christian burial in America.

Chae Chan Ping v. United States (The Chinese Exclusion Case, 1889)

Agitation against the Chinese continued through the 1880s, accompanied by the passage of ever-more restrictive immigration legislation by Congress. In 1888, after further negotiations with China, the Scott Act was enacted to bar all entry of Chinese laborers into the United States. The act was passed by Congress even though China had failed to ratify the new treaty arrangements.

Besides extending the "temporary suspension" of immigration, the Scott Act prohibited all reentry of Chinese laborers and rescinded all earlier certificates of reentry. Chae Chan Ping, a Chinese worker who had properly obtained a certificate for reentry, was barred from reentry even though he arrived only days after passage of the act. An estimated 30,000 Chinese residents were similarly outside of the United States. The Supreme Court upheld Congress's right to unilaterally abrogate treaties and declared that, as an aspect of national sovereignty, Congress had complete constitutional authority to admit or exclude immigrants at U.S. borders. The constitutionality of this legislation was reviewed in the so-called Chinese Exclusion Case.[21]

Justice Field, this time writing for the majority, found that:

> The competition steadily increased as the laborers came in crowds on each steamer that arrived from China, or Hong Kong, an adjacent English port. They were generally industrious and frugal. Not being accompanied by their families, except in rare instances, their expenses were small; and they were content with the simplest fare, such as would not suffice for our laborers and artisans. The competition between them and our people was for this reason altogether in their favor, and the consequent irritation, proportionately deep and bitter, was followed, in many cases, by open conflicts, to the great disturbance of the public peace.
>
> The differences of race added greatly to the difficulties of the situation. Notwithstanding the favorable provisions of the new articles of the treaty of 1868, by which all the privileges, immunities, and exemptions were extended to subjects of China in the United States which were accorded to citizens or subjects of the most favored nation, they remained strangers in the land, residing apart by themselves, and adhering to the customs and usages of their own country. It seemed impossible for them to assimilate with our people or to make any change in their habits or modes of living. As they grew in numbers each year the people of the coast saw, or believed they saw, in the facility of immigration, and in the crowded millions of China, where population presses upon the means of subsistence, great danger that at no distant day that portion of our country would be overrun by them unless prompt action was taken to restrict their immigration. The people there accordingly petitioned earnestly for protective legislation.
>
> In December, 1878, the [California constitutional] convention . . . memorialized Congress upon it, setting forth . . . that the presence of Chinese laborers had a baneful effect upon the material interests of the State, and upon public morals; that their immigration was in numbers approaching the character of

an Oriental invasion, and was a menace to our civilization; that the discontent from this cause was not confined to any political party, or to any class or nationality, but was well-nigh universal; that they retained the habits and customs of their own country, and in fact constituted a Chinese settlement within the State, without any interest in our country or its institutions; and praying congress to take measures to prevent their further immigration.[22]

By 1888 the Supreme Court was willing to accept the California constitutional convention's anti-Chinese rhetoric from a decade earlier. Besides reemphasizing the inassimilability of Chinese, the Court accepted the image of the massed hordes of Chinese laborers who threatened not only the good working people of California, but also American society itself through the Chinese cultural disloyalty of refusing to accept American life and ways.

Fong Yue Ting v. United States (1892)

The most restrictive Chinese exclusion legislation was the 1892 Geary Act.[23] The earlier Chinese exclusion laws, in deference to China, had been limited to ten-year terms. The Geary Act made permanent both the ban on Chinese immigration and the prohibition on Chinese becoming naturalized citizens. In 1892 the act was upheld by the U.S. Supreme Court by a 6–3 vote. Justice Horace Gray wrote for the majority:

> After some years experience under that treaty, the government of the United States was brought to the opinion that the presence within our territory of large numbers of Chinese laborers, of a distinct race and religion, remaining strangers in the land, residing apart by themselves, tenaciously adhering to the customs and usages of their own country, unfamiliar with our institutions, and apparently incapable of assimilating with our people, might endanger good order, and be injurious to the public interests.[24]

This 1892 statement succinctly summarizes the attitude of the day toward the Chinese: inassimilable, non-Christian laborers who are disloyal to the basic American interest in public law and order.

ANALYZING FOREIGNNESS

Since the 1997 Democratic Party campaign finance scandal, a steady stream of popular press articles have denounced China for its purported efforts to interfere in American politics. The campaign finance matter was followed in 1999 by charges that Chinese spies had stolen plans for U.S. nuclear weapons. An important question is why the campaign finance violations took on media life as a political scandal. During the same period there were other significant violations of campaign finance laws not involving Asians, but they did not reach the level of a major national scandal.[25]

The extraordinary level of media attention to China did not spring forth in a vacuum. Criticism of China had been high since 1989 when the Chinese government violently suppressed student demonstrators in Beijing's Tiananmen Square. But as long as the issues were international—human rights violations by the Chinese government and United States–China trade competition—the media attention was episodic and limited.

Chinese issues leapt into the popular headlines when China was linked to a domestic issue: campaign donations to President Bill Clinton and the Democratic Party. Chinese Americans were the nexus of the campaign finance and nuclear weapons spying charges and provided the crucial link between the international and domestic contexts. The initial round of charges centered on campaign finance law violations by Chinese Americans. The nuclear weapons spy charges focused on Chinese American research scientist Wen Ho Lee and other nuclear weapons researchers of Chinese ancestry.[26] Thus the charges of improper Chinese interference in U.S. politics became headline news through the Chinese American presence. The link to Chinese Americans provided two dimensions that gave breadth and power to the charges against China. First, the allegation of Chinese machinations and spying provided a mythic depth to the charges, a call to deep, popular cultural suspicions of the foreign and inassimilable Chinese. Furthermore, the link to Chinese Americans provided a domestic group who could be labeled as potential traitors. The presence of large numbers of Chinese in America qualitatively expanded the purported threat to national security. Instead of an individual misfit betraying America, a large, well-placed group presented a far greater and more ominous danger.

In response to the charges, Chinese Americans accused politicians and the news media of racism.[27] Their allegations took on a "two nations" flavor. Many studies of U.S. black-white racial relations have observed a sharp gap in black versus white perceptions and understandings.[28] That pattern was reproduced in these exchanges to such an extent that even the Chinese government felt free to associate itself with diasporic Chinese and accuse American officials of racism. U.S. House member Christopher Cox of Orange County, California, principal author of a widely publicized congressional report accusing China of the theft of U.S. nuclear secrets, was specifically charged with racism in a Chinese press conference held in Beijing.[29] In response to those charges and others by Chinese Americans, Cox joined a congressional resolution sponsored by Rep. David Wu, the House's first Chinese American, saying it was wrong for Congress and Americans to stereotype people.[30]

The notion of misleading stereotypes was found widely in Chinese American and Asian American responses to the media campaigns.[31] The responses focused on the idea that images of foreignness are "false" stereotypes that grow out of old misunderstandings and prejudices. While important, the idea of stereotype inadequately describes the processes at work in these campaigns. The concept of a "false" stereotype situates the problem in the consciousness of the individuals harboring the "false" stereotype. Such a stereotype suggests that if such individuals were educated, a "true" understanding would emerge and the "false" stereotype would simply disappear. While current images of foreignness are excessive generalizations properly called stereotypes, the notion of a "false" stereotype seriously underestimates the depth and significance of these representations of Asians. The manner in which Chinese Americans—Democratic Party fund-raisers and nuclear research scientists—were used as the bridge and nexus was an invocation of a racial practice particular to persons of Asian ancestry—Asiatic racialization.

A closer look at the historical depth and social breadth of Asiatic racialization will illustrate the inadequacies of the notion of the "false" stereotype. It does not describe the many aspects of foreignness that have been a part of Asiatic racialization since the 1890s. Instead of individual prejudice or error, the images of foreignness are deeply embedded, historically established racial understandings. They have been remarkably stable, remaining largely unchanged for over a hundred years.

The varied aspects of foreignness also have great range, encompassing a wide variety of social relations. An examination of the images, stereotypes, and caricatures of Asians that have emerged over the past century reveals certain distinct themes: (1) political foreignness, (2) social and cultural foreignness, and (3) foreignness in labor and economics. These themes all date from the beginnings of anti-Chinese agitation on the Pacific coast and continue today. Only one significant image has fallen aside. The early Chinese immigrants were quickly characterized as the first wave of an invasion by the massed hordes of Asia. During World War II, the threat of invasion was directly cited by all government authorities as justification for the detention and evacuation of Japanese Americans. And as recently as the American military intervention in Vietnam, the metaphor of "falling dominoes" suggested that Asian communists would overwhelm the Pacific region, leading directly to American shores. Since then, however, the image of invading Asian hordes has abated. The idea of an alien invasion, however, has not disappeared, merely changed characters. In the current popular imagination, the Mexican has displaced the Asian in depictions of a foreign invasion of America.

The other themes of Asiatic foreignness remain active in the American imagination. Aspects of political foreignness are the related ideas of political disloyalty and a preference for despotic, antidemocratic rule. Asians, both in the United States and in Asia, are seen as naturally averse to democracy and likely to betray American democracy. Asiatic inassimilability also dominates social and cultural foreignness. In addition to its recurrent generalization in descriptions of the Asian from the nineteenth century through current writings, two specific forms are notable: language and religion. Language inassimilability has been the target of "English only" campaigns, including several municipal ordinances in California aimed at prohibiting Asian language business and street signs. As for religion, an important nineteenth-century theme was converting the heathen Asian. Recently, however, the exotic and inassimilable nature of Asiatic religions has stolen the spotlight. For example, the media repeatedly emphasized that a Buddhist temple was the site of Vice President Al Gore's alleged unlawful fund-raising. Finally, there is a labor and economic dimension to foreignness. "Coolieism"—the doctrine that the Asian laborer will endure conditions and salaries unacceptable to American workers—has played an important part in economic history. The recent media fascination with Asian "slave labor" in garment sweatshops continues this tradition. Directly related to coolieism is the industrial corollary of unfair industrial competition. It goes something like this: because Asian coolie labor is willing to accept so much less in pay and working conditions than Americans, Asia possesses an unfair competitive advantage in the world market.

ASIATIC RACIALIZATION: THREE EXAMPLES

In the three recent examples of citizenship nullification described in this section, Chinese Americans were attributed with foreignness. As a direct result of this attribution, Chinese Americans and other Asians were blocked or limited in their participation as citizens. The first example, the campaign finance controversy, involved public sphere issues: voting, campaign finance, and individual participation in electoral politics. The second example came to light during the campaign finance scandal and involved a cartoon used on the cover of *National Review*. The third incident was a battle waged entirely in the private sphere: a hostile corporate takeover attempt by Charles Wang, head of Computer Associates, the second largest computer software company in the United States. In that takeover fight, the Asiatic foreignness of Wang played a significant role.

The Campaign Finance Scandal

The difference between lawful and unlawful campaign donations often turns on technical definitions. The essential practice of campaign donations remains the same whether the donation is lawful or unlawful. Donors give money to a political candidate or a political party in the hope and expectation that later they will be treated favorably. If a direct connection between money and reward is eventually revealed, the donation becomes a bribe and is a serious criminal offense. The starting point of the 1996 campaign finance controversy was campaign donations to the Democratic Party and various political campaigns. In relation to this core aspect of the scandal, few serious criminal charges were filed.

It has been reported that in most of the negotiated pleas of Asian campaign donors, the charges admitted did not constitute bribery but rather violations that were technical in nature—that is, the donors were either foreign nationals or the donated amounts exceeded certain limits. In contrast to the limited nature of the actual crimes, the media reports suggested that the donations in question were bribes by Asians who did not understand the democratic process. The mere existence of campaign donations from Asian sources was treated as conclusive evidence of the antidemocratic practices of Asian donors.[32]

In accounts of the Asiatic dimensions of the controversy, there was only peripheral mention of campaign finance reform. When the topic was the Asian connection, the issue was not how money corrupts the political process, but whether the Clinton Democrats sold out to the Chinese. The underlying political practice of donating campaign money for political influence went unquestioned when Chinese foreignness dominated the discussion; campaign finance reform was hidden from view by charges of unscrupulous Asiatic bribery. For Asian Americans, the issue was thus transformed into a challenge to their personal loyalty to America. They were accused of being antidemocratic and unable to assimilate to Western political practices. Instead of joining the American system of campaign donations, they had attempted bribery to achieve their anti-American ends.

During the campaign controversy, the incident best illustrating this attribution of Asiatic foreignness to Asian American donors occurred as the controversy began to attract national attention. Officials of the Democratic Party compiled a list of all donors with Asian-sounding surnames and then began to call them, interrogating them about their citizenship status. The recipients of the telephone calls were outraged at being singled out for interrogation based solely on their surnames. The reaction among Asian Americans was immediate and vocal, and the telephone calls themselves became an issue. The Democratic Party soon apologized.[33]

The actions of Democratic Party officials encompassed several aspects of Asian foreignness. First, using surnames as a marker, they presumed that each Asian donor was in violation of campaign finance laws. Second, they assumed that each person with such a surname was a noncitizen and unassimilated to American political culture. Furthermore, the suspicion motivating the telephone calls was that the donations by Asian Americans constituted undemocratic or disloyal bribes on behalf of a foreign power rather than the exercise of a citizen's right to participate in electoral politics.

National Review Magazine Cover

Another incident in the campaign finance controversy came in the form of a cartoon that appeared on the cover of *National Review* magazine. Al Gore, Hillary Rodham Clinton, and Bill Clinton were portrayed in various kinds of Oriental garb: Al Gore in a monk's robe; Hillary Clinton in a Red Guard–era army jacket and cap; and Bill Clinton in a peasant outfit with a conical straw cap. Clinton also sports a wispy Fu Manchu moustache, a braided queue, large teeth protruding from a narrow smile, and slit-like eyes. In addition, Gore is carrying a tin cup with dollars protruding, Hillary Clinton holds Mao's little red book, and Bill Clinton bears a tray with tea or coffee.[34] Besides the various political inferences, the clear physical intention of the cartoon was to portray the three as having "gone over" to the other side. The cover generated substantial debate, and while *National Review* never relented in its presentation, its editor in chief reportedly was forced by demonstrators at Yale University to leave a speech before its completion.[35]

Around 1900 a similar cartoon appeared aimed at criticizing politicians who favored trade with China. In the cartoon President William McKinley and other white political figures are shown dressed in Chinese robes, wearing long pigtail queues, burning incense, and ringing a gong. They are also bowing to an obese, smug, smiling Chinese man.[36] The similarities in visual images and themes of the two cartoons are striking, even though they were drawn nearly a century apart. The central theme is ridicule of politicians who would curry favor with China. In both cartoons, a foreign policy tie to China is portrayed as offerings to the Chinese—coffee or tea from Bill Clinton; the bowing and burning of incense in the earlier cartoon. The cultural references are to alien ideologies and religions, signified in the *National Review* cartoon by a Buddhist robe and in the 1900s cartoon by incense and a gong. In both cartoons, the Asiatic male appearance is characterized by facial hair—thin moustache and pigtail hair—as well as narrow eyes and buck teeth for Bill Clinton.

The ultimate ridicule is to link, through costume and physical appearance, white politicians with Asiatic foreignness. The themes of heathenism, antidemocratic despotism, and inassimilability are all ironically ascribed to white politicians. That the cartoons should be so similar in form and theme illustrates the stability and continuity of perceived Asiatic foreignness over the past century.

Charles Wang of Computer Associates

Another contemporary example of how foreignness can be used to block citizenship participation involved a major hostile corporate takeover, far removed from the realm of electoral politics. Notwithstanding the distance from Washington to Wall Street, the attributions of foreignness imposed on Charles Wang of Computer Associates were remarkably similar to those imposed in the campaign finance controversies. The events are best described in excerpts from two *Washington Post* news stories. On February 26, 1998, the paper reported:

> Lawyers for Computer Sciences Corporation are combing through public records around the world for information on Computer Associates International Inc., a software firm that has launched a $9.8 billion offer to buy CSC. . . .

Sources close to CSC—which has a work force in [the Washington] region of 7,300 people, many of whom perform extremely classified computer integration work for agencies such as the National Security Agency and the CIA—said the company plans to raise questions about Computer Associates ties to foreigners, its lack of classified experience and its track record [in acquisitions].

The foreign ties include aggressive efforts by Computer Associates' chief executive, Charles B. Wang, to not only nurture business in China but also help Chinese enterprises develop their software industries.

A U.S. citizen who was born in Shanghai and emigrated to this country at age 8, Wang said in an interview this week that "it's almost a racist attitude" for someone to question his Chinese business dealings.[37]

Two weeks later Wang abandoned his takeover attempt. On March 16, 1998, the *Post* reported:

In announcing the decision, CA Chairman and Chief Executive Charles Wang accused Computer Sciences of waging "a campaign of unlawful roadblocks and baseless, outrageous lawsuits," and of "mudslinging" that he said included racial slurs.

Wang said during a teleconference with reporters this morning that CSC had raised questions about CA's suitability to undertake contracts for the U.S. government, based on the fact that he was born in China (he became a U.S. citizen 45 years ago) and that Sanjay Kumar, CA's president and chief operating officer, is of Sri Lankan origin.

"This kind of mudslinging, the ugliness, the racial stuff . . . is just plain ugly and that is the wrong thing to do," Wang said.[38]

While the story of a hostile corporate takeover is undoubtedly complex, all of the various newspaper accounts noted that charges of foreign ties were an important roadblock in the takeover attempt. According to the news reports, the charge that Asian ancestry raised national security questions was a genuine issue within the financial circles where multibillion-dollar takeovers are approved or denied. Wang was victimized by allegations that he was still insufficiently assimilated to be trusted to have contacts with China. Even after decades of U.S. residency and citizenship, his Asiatic inassimilability led directly to questions about his political loyalty. Furthermore, questions about Wang's loyalty transformed his sales and investments forays into China into improper collaboration with an unfair competitor—China. Thus a Chinese American's search for new markets was transformed from competition among domestic rivals into unfair Asiatic subversion of "true" Americans.

CONCLUSION

Asiatic racialization provides a framework for examining recent attacks on China as drawing on a particular racial tradition. These attacks—in connection with charges of campaign finance and nuclear weapons research improprieties—grew into headline news when there was both an international and a domestic context for the controversies. Thus the linkage of China to partisan Republican and Democratic Party politics propelled what otherwise might have been a limited issue to the forefront of national controversy. The racialized Chinese connection tied the international context to the domestic context, and the notion of citizenship nullification captures the manner in which Chinese Americans were used as a racial nexus between China and domestic politics.

The attribution of foreignness to Chinese Americans is a racial practice—a practice that is clearly racist when used to attack individual Chinese Americans and create mass guilt by association. Those seeking to develop a politics of opposition have been hindered by their failure to appreciate that Asiatic-white racialization has diverged historically from black-white racialization. Because citizenship nullification is not invoked against a pan-Asian category such as Oriental or Asian but against a particular racialized Asian ethnicity/nationality category, pan-ethnic coalitions opposing these racial practices should be aware of the overlapping but distinct practices. Failure to appreciate the historical complexity of Asiatic racialization may well undermine oppositional politics.

One means of effective democratic participation in American civil life is normalization—that is, a citizen becomes invisible through ordinariness. When campaign contributions, standing for public office, or involvement in corporate America pass as commonplace and unworthy of special note, the very ordinariness of the action will demonstrate that special racial barriers and considerations are no longer significant. When Chinese and other Asian Americans can participate without comment in all aspects of democratic life, private and public, an important barrier will have been overcome.

The idea that Americans of Asian ancestry are "foreign" is an ordinary, commonsense understanding which, upon examination, has significant racial implications. Contesting this kind of everyday practice of race has proven enormously difficult in American society. Americans continue to engage in bitter debates over completely discredited ideas such as the biological inferiority of the African race. Those experiences suggest that efforts to contest the foreignness of Asiatic racialization will be at least as difficult. Asian Americans will continue to face challenges to the legitimacy of their participation in American democratic life. Because of those barriers, a racially uncontested Asian American citizenship will be impossible for the foreseeable future.

NOTES

1. Examples of racialization within the white–black or white–nonwhite paradigm are anti-Asian violence and Asians as a "model minority." Freedom to inflict violence is a clear assertion of inferiority. For the Asian "model minority," the Asian is inserted between black and white, thereby creating an expanded white–nonwhite paradigm.

2. *Dred Scott v. Sandford,* 60 U.S. 393 (1857).

3. *Dred Scott v. Sandford,* 403.

4. *Plessy v. Ferguson,* 163 U.S. 537 (1896).

5. *Plessy v. Ferguson,* 561.

6. See Ian Haney Lopez, *White by Law: The Legal Construction of Race* (New York: New York University Press, 1996).

7. John Hart Ely, *Democracy and Distrust: A Theory of Judicial Review* (Cambridge: Harvard University Press, 1980).

8. Gregory R. Stone, Louis M. Seidman, Cass R. Sunstein, and Mark V. Tushnet, *Constitutional Law,* 3d ed. (Boston: Little, Brown, 1996), 604; and Ely, *Democracy and Distrust,* 151.

9. Will Kymlicka and Wayne Norman, "Return of the Citizen: A Survey of Recent Work on Citizenship Theory," *Ethics* 104 (1994): 352, 354, as quoted in Ibrahim J. Gassama et al., "Citizenship and Its Discontents: Centering the Immigrant in the Inter/National Imagination," *Oregon Law Review* 76 (1997): 207, 213.

10. This interpretation is argued in Neil T. Gotanda, "A Critique of Our Constitution Is Color-Blind," *Stanford Law Review* 1 (1991): 23–36.

11. *Dred Scott v. Sandford,* 403.

12. *People v. George Hall,* 4 Cal. 399 (1854).

13. *People v. George Hall,* 402.

14. *People v. George Hall,* 404.

15. Charles McClain, *In Search of Equality: The Chinese Struggle against Discrimination in Nineteenth Century America* (Berkeley: University of California Press, 1966), 147–155.

16. Ibid., 155–160.

17. This section of the Geary Act is reprinted in Hyung Chan Kim, ed., *Asian Americans and Congress* (Westport, Conn.: Greenwood Press, 1996), 138–139.

18. Neil T. Gotanda, "Towards Repeal of Chinese Exclusion," in *Asian Americans and Congress,* ed. Hyung Chan-Kim (Westwood, Conn.: Greenwood Press, 1996).

19. *Chew Heong v. United States,* 112 U.S. 536 (1884).

20. *Chew Heong v. United States,* 566–567.

21. *Chae Chan Ping v. United States,* 130 U.S. 581 (1889).

22. *Chae Chan Ping v. United States,* 595–596.

23. The Geary Act is included in *Fong Yue Ting v. United States,* 149 U.S. 698, 699 (1893), fn. 1.

24. *Fong Yue Ting v. United States,* 717.

25. Robert L. Jackson, "German Given Record Fine in Campaign Donations Case," *Los Angeles Times,* July 19, 1997, A16.

26. The media coverage has been overwhelming. See, for example, the *Newsweek* discussion of the Cox House Committee report on alleged Chinese espionage and the Wen Ho Lee case: Daniel Klaidman and Mark Hosenball, "The Chinese Puzzle," *Newsweek,* June 6, 1999.

27. Michelle Locke, "Chinese American Scientists Fear Backlash," Associated Press, May 25, 1999; and William Foreman, "Chinese Fear Spy Report Could Mean Anti-Chinese Backlash," Associated Press, May 27, 1999.

28. This is a now commonplace observation. See, for example, Andrew Hacker, *Two Nations: Black and White* (New York: Scribners, 1992).

29. Michael Laris, "To Make a Point, China Downloads U.S. Arms Data: Attack on Spy Report Grows," *Washington Post* Foreign Service, June 1, 1999, A10.

30. Jim Abrams, "Lawmakers Warn against Stereotyping Asian-Americans," Associated Press, May 27, 1999; and Michelle Locke, "Asian Scientists Fear Backlash from Chinese Spy Scandal," Associated Press, May 28, 1999.

31. "Lawmakers Urge People Not to Stereotype Asians," *Las Vegas Review-Journal,* May 28, 1999; and Jim Abrams, "Lawmakers Warn against Stereotyping Asian-Americans," Associated Press, May 27, 1999.

32. George Archibald, "China's Gifts Part of Espionage: United States Agencies Lack Evidence but Are Certain," *Washington Times,* March 17, 1997, A1.

33. K. Connie Kang, "Asian Americans Bristle at Democrats' 'Interrogation' Fund-raising: In Aftermath of Scandal, Many Feel Stigmatized by Party's Queries about Their Donations," *Los Angeles Times,* February 27, 1997, A1.

34. *National Review,* March 24, 1997. See generally, Robert G. Lee, *Orientals: Asian Americans in Popular Culture* (Philadelphia: Temple University Press, 1999), which discusses the *National Review* cover on pages 1–14.

35. John O'Sullivan, "A Yale Colloquy on Race," *Wall Street Journal,* April 17, 1997, A22.

36. Philip P. Choy and Lorraine Dong, eds. *The Coming Man: Nineteenth Century American Perceptions of the Chinese* (Seattle: University of Washington Press, 1995), 154.

37. John Mintz and Mark Leibovich, "CSC May Fight Takeover by Citing Classified Work, Company Could Point to Suitor's Foreign Links," *Washington Post,* February 26, 1998, E01.

38. Mark Leibovich, "Wang Blames Racism for an Ugly Experience," *Washington Post,* March 16, 1998, G01.

CHAPTER FOUR

BEYOND ELECTORAL POLITICS: RENEWING A SEARCH FOR A PARADIGM OF ASIAN PACIFIC AMERICAN POLITICS

DON T. NAKANISHI

The November 1996 presidential and local elections were major milestones in the ever-increasing participation and visibility of Asian Pacific Americans in the grand theater of American electoral politics. In the months before and after President Bill Clinton's reelection victory, however, the enormous attention Asian Pacific Americans received from the mass media, Senate and House committees, and federal agencies did not focus on their many noteworthy achievements. Instead, the spotlight shone brightly on the damaging, and often invidious, allegations and innuendoes of improper or illegal campaign finance activities by some Asian and Asian Pacific American donors and fund-raisers. Actors like John Huang and places like the Hsi Lai Temple in Hacienda Heights, California, dominated this controversial political drama, which likely will become the most significant legacy of the 1996 elections for Asian Pacific Americans.

WHEN THE SPIN IS OUT OF CONTROL

For many Asian Pacific American leaders, the November 1996 elections were supposed to produce a far different result: an uplifting, efficacious, and indeed well-managed spin. They were supposed to be, for example, a celebration of the highly successful, first-ever, nationwide voter registration movement that targeted the Asian Pacific American population. The effort produced a reported 75,000 new Asian Pacific American voters, who were added to the approximately 1.2 million Asian Pacific American registered voters across the country.[1] In California, where the over 3 million Asian Pacific Americans represent one in ten residents, the hope that the state's electorate might someday reflect this demographic profile and Asian Pacific Americans would become an important swing vote no longer seemed visionary and unrealistic.[2]

The November 1996 elections also were historically significant because of the number of Asian Pacific Americans elected to public office throughout the country. The most notable was Gary Locke, who was elected governor of the state of Washington. He became the first Chinese American to successfully capture a state's top post, as well as the first Asian Pacific American elected governor outside of Hawaii. In California, the election of Mike Honda of San Jose to the California Assembly was hailed as a major political achievement, because he became only the second Asian Pacific American in the 120-member California legislature. Similarly, the elections of Leland Yee and Michael Yaki to the San Francisco Board of Supervisors and Martha Choe to the Seattle City Council lent further credence to the view that the November 1996 elections were pathbreaking for Asian Pacific American electoral empowerment.

Expectations also ran high, especially among Asian Pacific American Democrats, when exit polls such as those conducted by the *Los Angeles Times* and the National Asian Pacific American Legal Consortium (NAPALC) showed that Asian Pacific American voters, many of whom were voting for the first time, strongly favored Democratic president Bill Clinton over his challengers, Republican Bob Dole and independent Ross Perot. The exit polls in California also revealed that Asian Pacific American voters, despite their portrayal by conservative pundits and politicians as being just like the majority of white voters in the state in opposing affirmative action, went to the polls and voted against the anti–affirmative action Proposition 209 ballot initiative by a very substantial margin—61 percent according to the *Los Angeles Times* exit polls and over 75 percent according to the NAPALC polls—levels nearly comparable to those of other voters of color.[3] Indeed, there was anxious speculation by many Asian Pacific American community leaders that the Democratic Party might now become the party of choice for Asian Pacific Americans, who usually registered in nearly equal proportions as Democrats, Republicans, and independents.[4]

And, just as for every presidential election held in the past two decades, new campaign fund-raising records were expected to be set by both political parties in Asian Pacific American communities, especially by the Democrats, who seemed delighted with the attractiveness of Clinton's incumbency and the strong lead in voter polls he enjoyed throughout the campaign. In the early 1970s, when I first undertook research on Asian Pacific American political participation, I interviewed an elderly leader in Los Angeles's Japanese American community, who expressed great pride in having convinced nine other Japanese Americans to contribute $100 each so they together could purchase a $1,000 table at a fund-raiser for incumbent president Richard Nixon.[5] By contrast, at one memorable fund-raising gala in the Century City district of Los Angeles in July 1996 organized by John Huang and attended by James Riady, Maria Hsia, Ted Sioeng, and others who gained notoriety in the postelection campaign finance controversy, nearly one thousand Asian Pacific Americans contributed $1,000 each to hear President Clinton speak. The event raised almost $1 million.

Finally, Asian Pacific Americans hoped that this time around, President Clinton, in assembling a cabinet that "looks like America," would appoint at least one of their own. University of California Berkeley chancellor Chang-lin Tien and former Democratic member of Congress Norman Mineta of California were prominently mentioned almost immediately after the November 1996 elections as serious and viable contenders for the positions of secretaries of energy and transportation, respectively. Given the decisive electoral and financial support Clinton received from Asian Pacific Americans during the elections, a first-ever Asian Pacific American cabinet-level appointment seemed almost assured.

That, then, is how Asian Pacific American leaders wanted the momentous November 1996 elections to be portrayed. Events over the next two years, however, followed a much different and unexpected script, and the seemingly positive trends in Asian Pacific American electoral participation came crashing to a halt in the face of the rough and tumble world of partisan politics and the relentless news media. Moreover, the anticipated nominations of Tien and Mineta did not materialize, and the president once again constructed a cabinet that did not include any Asian Pacific Americans. Some Asian Pacific American leaders felt that the unprecedented media and partisan focus on campaign violations by a few Asian and Asian Pacific Americans would have a "chilling effect" on the involvement of Asian Pacific Americans in electoral politics.[6] Several asserted that the "Asian-bashing" controversy was the worst thing that had happened to

Asian Pacific Americans since the incarceration of 120,000 Japanese Americans during World War II.

Regardless of the spin or counter-spin that one might offer for the November 1996 elections, there is little question but that the issues of electoral political access, representation, and influence have become increasingly salient and compelling for the Asian Pacific American population. The San Francisco-based *Asianweek,* which might be dubbed the semiofficial newspaper of Asian Pacific American electoral politics, is filled weekly with stories and editorials about the personalities, aspirations, and controversies of Asian Pacific Americans in local and national politics. At the same time, the scholarly and policy-relevant literature on Asian Pacific American electoral politics continues to grow, especially with the contributions of a new generation of political and other social scientists, who are breaking new theoretical and empirical ground in their analyses of an array of topics ranging from individual-level voting behavior to group-level conflict and coalition building in redistricting and reapportionment processes.[7]

It is during this period of heightened attention to the electoral participation of Asian Pacific Americans by the mass media, politicians, government agencies, scholars, and community leaders that it is perhaps most appropriate to pause and consider a host of fundamental issues about the conceptual and paradigmatic parameters of a field of inquiry into Asian Pacific American politics. What political phenomena, for example, would be the most significant and compelling for empirical and theoretical investigations, and how should scholars go about trying to understand those phenomena? By not doing so, they may inadvertently and uncritically accept the long-standing paradigm in political science of defining minority politics almost exclusively in electoral terms and, by extension, giving greater normative legitimacy and scholarly attention to electoral-oriented processes, participants, leaders, and issues than to other forms of political activity among the Asian Pacific American population.

Electoral politics is, of course, a vital part of the political experiences of Asian Pacific America, and there is no question but that the electoral system has had an enormous impact, sometimes quite devastating, on the quality of life and societal opportunities and status of Asian Pacific Americans. At the same time, Asian Pacific American communities across the nation have engaged in a host of activities such as voter registration campaigns in order to further develop a viable electorate and an effective political infrastructure. Yet the significance of electoral politics for Asian Pacific Americans, and indeed its preeminence, should be carefully weighed in terms of a wide array of political activities and relationships that go beyond domestic electoral politics and that have greatly influenced or have been pursued by large sectors of the Asian Pacific American population. By not investigating these activities and relationships, scholars may provide electoral politics with a symbolic mandate that it neither deserves nor has gained, especially in the context of the historic (and, some would argue, continuing) exclusion or underrepresentation of Asian Pacific Americans in the most significant arenas of electoral power and decision making.

The discussion that follows represents a renewed personal search for a paradigm of minority and immigrant politics, based in large part on the Asian Pacific American political experience.[8] It begins with an empirical and analytical assessment of the major characteristics and trends of Asian Pacific American electoral participation, which in recent years have been distorted by the media and partisan spins and interpretations that accompanied the campaign finance scandal. It also provides a baseline of national, state, and local data and insights for understanding the longitudinal growth and the as-yet-unrealized potential of Asian Pacific American electoral politics, especially in relation to the critical dimension of voting. Special attention is given to the challenges of increasing the electoral involvement and accelerating the political acculturation of Asian Pacific immigrants and refugees, who represent the majority of the Asian Pacific American population.

The discussion then goes in a far more theoretical direction and considers the electoral participation of Asian Pacific Americans within a broader framework of minority and immigrant politics, which includes nonelectoral and nondomestic political experiences and relationships. Nonelectoral political activities include social movements, labor organizing efforts, and the often unexplored dimensions of internal ethnic community politics, which are largely pursued and thrive outside of the formal processes and institutions of the American electoral political system. Nondomestic political experiences and relationships include the transnational political activities of Asian Pacific Americans in relation to Asia, particularly their homelands; the transnational political involvement of Asian homeland governments and quasi-governmental institutions in Asian Pacific American community affairs; and the impacts of bilateral and multilateral relations between the United States and Asian nation-states on the political, economic, and social status of Asian Pacific Americans. Nondomestic also includes efforts by Asian Pacific Americans to influence U.S.-Asia relations, especially in advocating changes in American foreign policy toward their countries of origin; the ways in which international processes and policies related to the flow of people, money, goods, and ideas impinge on the political behavior and status of Asian Pacific Americans; and the impact of international political conflicts and domestic political crises involving Asian homelands on interethnic and intracommunity political relations involving Asian Pacific American communities.

This broad, multifaceted conceptualization is intended to encourage scholars to be inclusive rather than unnecessarily exclusive in establishing their paradigmatic priorities for the study of Asian Pacific American politics. It also seeks to steer them toward examining potential intersections among these different forms of political relationships and experiences, which have been significant for Asian Pacific Americans in the past and most likely will be in the future. For example, the decades-long movement by the Japanese American community to seek redress and reparations for the removal and imprisonment of 120,000 Japanese Americans during World War II can only be fully documented and analyzed through use of an integrated analytical framework that takes into account both the electoral and nonelectoral dimensions of the movement.[9] Likewise, the vigorous protests by anticommunist community groups against city councilman Tony Lam of Westminster, California, the first Vietnamese American ever elected to public office, for not actively mobilizing city resources and personnel or introducing a council motion to close down a video store displaying a flag of Vietnam would require multiple lenses of analysis, be they in terms of ethnic community politics or transnational political activities.[10]

DEVELOPMENT OF THE ASIAN PACIFIC AMERICAN POLITICAL INFRASTRUCTURE: FROM VOTERS TO ELECTED OFFICIALS

Large-scale immigration from Asia since enactment of the Immigration and Nationality Act Amendments of 1965 has had a dramatic impact on many states and regions across the nation, as well as on the contemporary Asian Pacific American population. From a largely U.S.-born group of 1.5 million in 1970, Asian Pacific Americans had become a predominantly immigrant population of 3.5 million by 1980. By 1990, the population had doubled again to 7.2 million nationwide, of which 66 percent were foreign-born. According to recent projections, the Asian Pacific American population will continue to increase—to nearly 12 million in 2000 and nearly 20 million by 2020. The foreign-born sector is expected to remain in the majority until 2020 and probably beyond.[11]

In recent years some political commentators and scholars have speculated about whether Asian Pacific Americans will become a major new force in American electoral politics, perhaps akin to American Jews, because of their dramatic demographic growth and concentration in certain key electoral states such as California, New York, and Texas.[12] Many believe that if Asian Pacific Americans, like American Jewish voters, come to represent a proportion of the electorate that is comparable to, if not greater than, their share of the total population, then they could become a highly influential swing vote in critical local, state, and national elections. California, for example, controls the nation's largest number of congressional seats and electoral college votes. If Asian Pacific Americans, who are one out of every ten residents of the state, also became one out of every ten voters, they could play a strategically important role in local and national elections. Indeed, their voting potential coupled with other attractive dimensions of their political infrastructure—such as their proven record of campaign fund-raising—could elevate Asian Pacific Americans to the status of important new actors in American electoral politics.[13]

During the past two decades, there has been an unmistakable increase in the representation of Asian Pacific Americans in electoral politics. In 1978, for example, when the first edition of the *National Asian Pacific American Political Almanac* was published, it listed several hundred elected officials, who held offices primarily in Hawaii, California, and Washington.[14] Almost all were second- and third-generation Asian Pacific Americans, the vast majority being Japanese Americans. By contrast, the eighth edition of the political almanac, published in 1998, lists over two thousand Asian Pacific American elected and major appointed officials in thirty-three states and the federal government.[15] Although most continue to be second or third generation, a growing number of recently elected politicians have been immigrants—among others, Jay Kim of Walnut, California, the first Korean American elected to Congress; David Valderrama, the first Filipino American elected as a delegate to the Maryland legislature; and city councilman Tony Lam of Westminster, California. Other Asian Pacific American candidates have run well-financed, professional campaigns for mayor in some of the nation's largest cities, including Los Angeles, San Francisco, and Oakland. And Ben Cayetano and Gary Locke are the governors of Hawaii and Washington, respectively.

Yet despite these electoral achievements, the reality is that this immigrant-dominant population has yet to reach its full electoral potential, especially in transforming its extraordinary population growth into comparable proportions of individuals who register to vote and then actually go to the polls during elections. In California, for example, Asian Pacific Americans may represent one of every ten residents, but, according to estimates by one of the state's major public opinion polling organizations, they are no more than one in twenty of the state's registered voters and three in every hundred of those who actually vote.[16]

The analysis that follows compares the levels and determinants of voter registration and voting for naturalized Asian immigrants ages eighteen and over with those of U.S.-born Asian Pacific Americans and other racial and ethnic populations. It is based on the 1990, 1992, and 1994 Current Population Surveys (CPS) conducted by the U.S. Census Bureau, which include information on voter registration and voting for Asian Pacific Americans. The 1994 CPS data, which are the primary focus of the analysis, were particularly useful because they provided detailed information on the citizenship status of individuals similar to that obtained through the decennial census. It was therefore possible to differentiate not only between Asian Pacific Americans who were foreign-born and U.S.-born, but also between immigrants and refugees who were naturalized and those who were not. This data source does not, however, allow any analysis of the differences in electoral participation among the array of Asian ethnic communities. Nevertheless, previous studies have found that rates of voter registration vary markedly, with Japanese Americans having the highest proportion of registered voters and Southeast Asians having the lowest percentage.[17] Although the CPS data do have their limitations, they do allow study of both national and regional trends with a sufficiently large sample of Asian Pacific Americans,[18] and they allow analysis of the potential differences in registration and voting rates among U.S.-born and naturalized citizens—something very seldom examined rigorously.[19]

An analysis of the CPS data reveals that citizens who are Asian immigrants and refugees have lower rates of voter registration than U.S.-born citizens. However, Asian naturalized citizens who have been in the United States for over twenty years have rates of registration that are comparable to or exceed those of U.S.-borns, while those who arrived over thirty years ago have higher rates of both registration and voting. Just as in a separate analysis of naturalization rates,[20] multiple regression analysis found that year of entry was the single most important factor in determining voter registration rates. In terms of actual voting, year of entry, educational attainment, and age were found to be the best predictors. Finally, the characteristics of Asian Pacific American voters as a whole, or those of U.S.-born and foreign-born taken separately, reflect an ethnic electorate that is far from monolithic in its political party affiliations, ideological preferences, and voting preferences. Rather, it has many dimensions, which are influencing its continued development.

The Asian Pacific population in the United States is characterized by the largest proportion of individuals ages eighteen and over (hereafter, adult) who cannot take the first step toward participating in American electoral politics because they are not citizens. In 1994, 55 percent of adult Asians were not citizens compared with 44 percent of Latinos, 5 percent of African Americans, and 2 percent of non-Hispanic whites. The proportion of noncitizens varied by geographic region, with Honolulu having the lowest percentage of noncitizens among its adult Asian Pacific population (21 percent), and New York having the highest (73 percent). Sixty-three percent of adult Asians in Los Angeles County and 52 percent of those in the Oakland–San Francisco region also were not citizens.

Nationwide in 1994, some 1,165,900 Asian Pacific Americans were registered voters. Of those, 58 percent (680,190) were U.S.-born and 42 percent (485,710) were foreign-born (Table 4.1). California's Asian Pacific American electorate, which in 1994 accounted for 40 percent of the country's Asian Pacific American registered voters, mirrored the nation's composition of U.S.-born (58 percent) to foreign-born (42 percent) voters. Hawaii, by contrast, which has witnessed far less immigration than many mainland states, had an overwhelmingly U.S.-born Asian Pacific American

Table 4.1
Distribution of U.S.-Born and Naturalized
Asian Pacific American Registered Voters, 1994

	California	Hawaii	Rest of Nation	National
U.S. born	271,820 (58%)	218,580 (88%)	189,790 (42%)	680,190 (58%)
Naturalized	194,840 (42%)	29,190 (12%)	261,680 (58%)	485,710 (42%)
Total	466,660	247,770	451,470	1,165,900
Percent of national total	40	21	39	100

Source: Current Population Survey, 1994.

electorate (88 percent) in 1994. Hawaii's Asian Pacific American voter profile was similar to those of other racial and ethnic populations, which had substantially higher proportions of U.S.-born voters: Latinos, 87 percent; African Americans, 99 percent; and non-Hispanic whites, 98 percent.

As for rates of voter registration, Asian Pacific American citizens (by birth or naturalization) have exhibited very low ones overall. According to the 1994 CPS census data, nationwide 53 percent of all Asian Pacific American citizens were registered compared with 61 percent of African Americans and 69 percent of non-Hispanic whites (Table 4.2). Latino citizens and Asian Pacific Americans had the same voter registration rates—53 percent. In 1992 similar patterns were observed for these population groups in Los Angeles, Oakland–San Francisco, New York, and Honolulu. Indeed, in some regions the differences in voter registration rates between Asian Pacific Americans and non-Hispanic whites, who usually have the highest rates of registration, were quite substantial. For example, in 1992 in the Oakland–San Francisco region 56 percent of all adult Asian Pacific Ameri-

Table 4.2
Voter Registration and Turnout Rates, United States, 1994

	Percent Registered to Vote	Percent Voted in 1994 Elections
Asian Pacific Americans		
U.S.-born	56	78
Foreign-born	49	74
Overall	53	76
Latinos		
U.S.-born	53	62
Foreign-born	53	74
Overall	53	64
African Americans		
U.S.-born	61	63
Foreign-born	58	78
Overall	61	63
Non-Hispanic Whites		
U.S.-born	69	73
Foreign-born	68	78
Overall	69	73

Source: Current Population Survey, 1994.

can citizens were registered to vote compared with 86 percent of non-Hispanic whites, 73 percent of African Americans, and 63 percent of Latinos. At the same time, there were differences in voter registration rates for different Asian Pacific American communities, with Los Angeles having the highest (64 percent) and New York having the lowest (54 percent). Many previous studies had found that Asian Pacific Americans had lower rates of voter registration than African Americans and non-Hispanic whites and usually the same or somewhat lower rates than Latinos. Although this is a consistent finding, it is nonetheless an extremely puzzling one because of the relatively high group-level attainment levels of Asian Pacific Americans in education and the other socioeconomic variables that political scientists have long associated with active electoral participation.[21]

Among Asian Pacific American citizens, those who were born in the United States have a higher overall rate of voter registration than those who were born abroad and have become naturalized. In 1994, 56 percent of all U.S.-born Asian Pacific Americans were registered compared with 49 percent of those who were naturalized (Table 4.2). Indeed, foreign-born Asian Pacific American citizens had among the lowest rates of any group, including Latino naturalized citizens (53 percent). In terms of electoral participation beyond registration, however, both Asian Pacific American naturalized and U.S.-born voters had among the highest rates of voting in the 1994 elections. Therefore, Asian immigrants appear to exhibit a provocative series of discrete, nonlinear trends from becoming citizens to becoming registered voters and then to becoming actual voters: they have one of the highest rates of naturalization after immigrating, but one of the lowest rates of voter registration after becoming citizens. Once registered, however, Asian Pacific American naturalized citizens have among the highest voting rates of any group.[22]

A more detailed examination of Asian naturalized citizens indicates that those who immigrated over twenty years ago, prior to 1975, have rates of voter registration comparable to, if not greater than, those who were U.S.-born (Table 4.3). Indeed, this was the case for practically all age groups and educational attainment levels and for women (Table 4.4). By contrast, Asian Pacific naturalized citizens who immigrated within the past twenty years have registration rates that are, for the most part, substantially lower than those of U.S.-born and naturalized citizens who arrived before 1975. This finding was consistent for practically all age and educational attainment levels, as well as for men and women. Just as in the case of naturalization, multiple regression analysis revealed that year of entry was the best

Table 4.3

National Registration and Voting by Year of Immigration,
U.S.-Born and Naturalized Citizens, United States, 1994

	Percent Registered to Vote	Percent Voted in 1994 Elections
U.S.-born	56	78
Naturalized citizens		
(by year of immigration)		
Pre-1965	77	92
1965–1974	57	66
1975–1985	43	71
1986–1994	26	81
Overall	49	74

Source: Current Population Survey, 1994.

predictor of voter registration for Asian naturalized citizens. For voting, year of entry, educational attainment, and age were the strongest explanatory variables for Asian naturalized registered voters.

The importance of time-dependent variables for electoral participation is consistent with the view that immigrants and refugees often must undergo a prolonged and multifaceted process of social adaptation and learning before fully participating in their newly adopted country. The process of becoming actively involved in American electoral politics and politically acculturated may be one of the most complex, lengthiest, and least-understood learning experiences. Adult Asian immigrants and refugees, like other groups of immigrants,[23] largely acquired their core political values, attitudes, and behavioral orientations in sociopolitical systems that were different in a variety of ways from that of the United States. Some of their countries of origin did not have universal suffrage, others were dominated by a single political party (which made voting nearly inconsequential), and still others were undergoing extreme political upheaval stemming from civil war or international conflict. Indeed, one major reason many Asian refugees left their homelands in the first place was to escape horrendous political situations such as the killing fields of Cambodia. As a result, previously learned lessons and orientations toward government and political activities may not be easily supplanted or supplemented. For example, the adult education classes in American civics and government that immigrants

Table 4.4

Profile of Registered Voters, Asian Pacific American Naturalized and
U.S.-Born Citizens Eighteen Years and Older, United States, 1994
(percent)

| | Number of Years in United States (naturalized citizens) | | | | | |
	0–5	6–10	11–14	15–19	20+	U.S.-Born
By age						
18–24	0	0	20	15	10	26
25–29	0	13	16	0	31	25
30–39	0	3	15	4	40	31
40–49	0	8	37	42	20	24
50–59	0	0	19	20	51	22
60+	0	0	0	12	41	40
By education level						
0–8 years	0	0	11	26	33	24
9–12 years	0	0	0	13	45	16
High school	0	16	20	33	28	16
Some college	0	1	18	23	28	32
B.A.	0	5	12	27	45	43
Graduate degree	0	0	66	18	41	35
By gender						
Male	0	6	20	23	29	32
Female	0	6	21	27	39	29

Source: Current Population Survey, 1994.

usually take to prepare for their naturalization examinations expose them
to the most rudimentary facts about American government, but probably
have little or no impact on their preexisting political belief systems, their
general sense of political efficacy and trust toward government, or their
knowledge of the traditions, current policy debates, and political party
agendas of American politics. Learning about and, more important, becoming actively involved in politics "American style" through registering to
vote and voting in elections probably take place through a range of personal
and group experiences that go beyond citizenship classes and evolve over
time in conjunction with other aspects of becoming acculturated to American life and society.

The Asian Pacific American electorate is clearly undergoing a process of transformation and change. Its future characteristics and impact will be largely determined by the extent to which newly naturalized Asian immigrants and refugees are incorporated into the American political system and are encouraged to register to vote and to cast their ballots. An electorate that "looks like Asian America," especially one that is becoming predominantly foreign-born, may have far different partisan preferences and public policy priorities. For example, the changing electorate in the city of Monterey Park, California (Los Angeles County), where Asian Pacific Americans constituted 56 percent of all residents in 1990, is illustrative (Table 4.5). In 1984, among Chinese American registered voters, there was a plurality of Democrats (43 percent) over Republicans (31 percent), but also an extremely high proportion of persons (25 percent) who specified no party affiliations and considered themselves to be independents.[24] By 1997 Chinese American voters—most of whom were probably recently naturalized and who accounted for the vast majority of new registered voters in Monterey Park since 1984—were nearly evenly divided among Democrats (34 percent), Republicans (33 percent), and independents (30 percent).[25] By contrast, the Japanese Americans in Monterey Park, who experienced far less population growth, exhibited a different electoral profile than Chinese Americans; they showed a preference for the Democratic Party and a greater likelihood of declaring a party affiliation than registering as an independent. Moreover, the total Asian Pacific American electorate in Monterey Park changed its overall partisan orientation through the addition of these new, largely Chinese American registered voters. In 1984 Asian Pacific American voters as a whole in Monterey Park showed a slight majority preference for the Democrats. By 1997, with an increase of over four thousand new registered voters, the Asian Pacific American electorate in the city could no longer be characterized in this manner. Likewise, on a national scale the Asian Pacific American electorate at both the grassroots and leadership levels has undergone and will continue to undergo significant changes with the increased political participation of Asian immigrants and refugees.

BEYOND ELECTORAL POLITICS: SEARCHING FOR A PARADIGM OF ASIAN PACIFIC AMERICAN POLITICS

Asian Pacific American politics has received limited scholarly attention over the years. Early works such as Grodzins's *Americans Betrayed* (1949)[26]

Table 4.5

Asian Pacific American Registered Voters, Monterey Park,
1984 and 1997

	Number Registered	Democrats	Republicans	Other Parties	No Party
1984 (all voters)	22,021	13,657	5,564	368	2,290
	(100.0%)	(62.0%)	(25.0%)	(1.7%)	(10.4%)
1997 (all voters)	23,849	12,861	6,553	676	3,759
	(100.0%)	(53.9%)	(27.5%)	(2.8%)	(15.8%)
1984–1997 net gain/loss	+1,828	−796	+989	+308	+1,469
1984 (Asian Pacific voters)	6,441	3,265	1,944	54	1,178
	(100.0%)	(50.7%)	(30.2%)	(0.8%)	(18.3%)
1997 (Asian Pacific voters)	10,495	4,051	3,533	318	2,593
	(100.0%)	(38.6%)	(33.7%)	(3.0%)	(24.7%)
1984–1997 net loss/gain	+4,054	+786	+1,589	+264	+1,415
1984 (non–Asian Pacific voters)	15,438	10,392	3,620	314	1,112
	(100.0%)	(67.3%)	(23.4%)	(2.0%)	(7.2%)
1997 (non–Asian Pacific voters)	13,354	8,810	3,020	358	1,166
	(100.0%)	(65.9%)	(22.6%)	(2.7%)	(8.7%)
1984–1997 net loss/gain	−2,084	−1,582	−600	+44	+54
1984 (Chinese American voters)	3,152	1,360	972	23	797
	(100.0%)	(43.1%)	(30.8%)	(0.7%)	(25.3%)
1997 (Chinese American voters)	5,935	2,028	1,983	164	1,760
	(100.0%)	(34.0%)	(33.4%)	(2.7%)	(29.7%)
1984–1997 net gain/loss	+2,783	+668	+1,011	+141	+963
1984 (Japanese American voters)	2,586	1,429	838	21	298
	(100.0%)	(55.3%)	(32.4%)	(0.8%)	(11.5%)
1997 (Japanese American voters)	2,647	1,329	891	44	383
	(100.0%)	(50.2%)	(33.7%)	(1.6%)	(14.5%)
1984–1997 net gain/loss	+61	−100	+53	+23	+85

Source: Don Nakanishi, UCLA Asian Pacific American Voter Registration Project.

Note: In 1990 56 percent of the residents of Monterey Park were Asian Pacific American. In 1997 Asian Pacific Americans made up 44 percent of all voters in Monterey Park, 32 percent of all Democrats, 54 percent of all Republicans, and 69 percent of all individuals who registered as "No Party."

and Daniels's *The Politics of Prejudice* (1968)[27] focused on how American political institutions, especially the major political parties and West Coast state legislatures, had a decisive impact on creating and maintaining a system of exclusion and discrimination against Asian Pacific Americans. Few studies, however, were conducted on the flip side of that structural condition—namely, how Asian Pacific Americans responded to such treatment and, more generally, how they pursued a variety of political activities in both the domestic and nondomestic arenas during the course of their historical experiences.[28] Writing in the early 1980s, Massey concluded in his literature review of studies of different waves of immigrants to the United States, "There is no information on patterns of Asian political participation."[29]

Although almost no serious academic work was devoted to the political behavior and involvement of Asian Pacific Americans until recently, it has become apparent to most political commentators and practitioners that Asian Pacific Americans are becoming increasingly visible and influential political participants.[30] At no other period in the over 150-year historical experience of Asian Pacifics in U.S. society have so many individuals and organizations participated in such a wide array of political and civil rights activities, especially in relation to the American political system but also in relation to the tumultuous events in China, the Philippines, Korea, Indonesia, Vietnam, Pakistan, and other ancestral homelands in Asia. In U.S. electoral politics, what has become a routine occurrence in Hawaii since it achieved statehood in 1959—namely the election of Asian Pacific Americans to public office[31]—has become more commonplace in the continental United States with the election and appointment of Asian Pacific Americans to federal, state, and local positions from Texas to Delaware and from New Jersey to California. And, perhaps most significant, Asian Pacific Americans have demonstrated that they too have the organizational and leadership skills, financial resources, interethnic networks, and growing sense of political efficacy to assert their policy positions and to effectively confront the broad societal issues that are damaging their group's interests.[32]

Four widely reported grassroots campaigns of recent years illustrate this new collective determination, which is often characterized by significant interethnic and interracial coalition building and mobilization, as well as by electoral and nonelectoral political strategies. These campaigns were: (1) the successful drive by Japanese Americans to gain redress and reparations for their World War II incarceration; (2) the victorious mobilization of

Asian Pacific Americans in a coalition with other groups in defeating the nomination of Daniel Lundgren for California state treasurer; (3) the campaign to protest allegations of admissions quotas against Asian Pacific American applicants to colleges and universities; and (4) the national movement to appeal and overturn the light sentences given to two unemployed Detroit auto workers who, in 1982, used a baseball bat to kill a Chinese American named Vincent Chin (the two men mistook Chin for a Japanese and therefore someone they believed had taken away their jobs).[33]

This heightened interest in the electoral participation and potential of Asian Pacific Americans is all the more remarkable when it is considered in the context of the historical legacy of disenfranchisement of Asian Pacific Americans. Early Chinese and Japanese immigrants, for example, were disenfranchised and excluded from full participation in major aspects of American life because of a plethora of discriminatory laws and policies ranging from the Chinese Exclusion Act of 1882 to *Ozawa v. United States* (1922), which prohibited the naturalization of Asian immigrants.[34] These legal barriers prevented early Asian immigrants from participating in electoral politics of any kind—be it taking part in the type of ward politics practiced by European immigrants in the cities of the Atlantic or midwestern states or simply voting for their preferences in a local or presidential election. The barriers also effectively delayed the development of electoral participation and representation by Asian Pacific Americans in Hawaii, California, and elsewhere. Such development only began with the second and later generations during the post–World War II period—over a hundred years after their initial period of immigration. Moreover, even though the national news media have often since the mid-1960s touted Asian Pacific Americans as America's "model minority"—a label Asian Pacific leaders and scholars have disputed because of its simplistic implication that other minority groups can overcome racial and other discriminatory barriers by following the example of Asian Pacific Americans—this reputed success has disguised this group's historic lack of access and influence in the nation's most significant political and social decision-making arenas and institutions.[35] Meanwhile, Asian Pacific American civil rights groups have continued to remain vigilant in seeking elimination of the so-called "political structural barriers" such as unfair redistricting plans and lack of Asian language bilingual ballots, which many leaders believe have prevented Asian Pacific Americans from fully exercising their voting rights.[36]

Although electoral politics has increasingly gained the spotlight, it is only one of several major forms of political activity pursued by large and active sectors of the Asian Pacific American population. For one thing, Asian Pacific Americans have long been concerned about and affected by international events, issues, and relationships, particularly those affecting their ancestral homelands or other communities in their diasporic ethnic networks. The highly visible and determined responses in 1989 and the years that followed by Chinese foreign students and Chinese Americans alike to the repression of the pro-democracy movement in the People's Republic of China are testimony to that fact. Indeed, Asian Pacific Americans have been active transnational participants in the major revolutionary, nationalistic, and independence movements that have emerged in their respective homelands during the past century; they have protested against discriminatory and sometimes violent actions directed toward other diasporic communities; and they have sought to contribute to national economic and political development efforts in their countries of origin.[37] They also have been affected to a greater extent than other American immigrant groups by the dramatic shifts in bilateral relations between the United States and their homelands. For example, Japanese Americans were interned during World War II, and Asian Pacific American leftist activities were thwarted during the McCarthy era and other "cold war" periods in American diplomatic history.[38] During President Bill Clinton's second term in office, the controversial allegations that Chinese Americans and other Asian Americans were involved in espionage and inappropriate campaign finance activities for the Chinese and other Asian governments and corporate entities further underscored the continuing impact of bilateral and international politics on Asian Pacific Americans.[39]

For many Asian Pacific ethnic groups whose immigrant and refugee sectors have grown substantially and have remained in the majority since enactment of the Immigration and Nationality Act Amendments of 1965, homeland issues continue to dominate their political leadership agendas and the front pages of their media. These nondomestic issues often compete with, if not at times overwhelm, efforts to increase the electoral participation of the ever-growing numbers of naturalized citizens of these groups. As such, these immigrant-dominated groups are involved in the very familiar and yet normally conflict-filled process that earlier American immigrant populations underwent—that is, coming to grips with and seeking a balance between their domestic and nondomestic political orientations.[40] For example, in the early 1990s groups such as the Korean American Coalition and the Taiwanese American Citizens League, both of Los Angeles, were founded to enhance the participation of members of their largely immigrant communities in American electoral politics and to address the major domestic civil rights issues facing their ethnic groups. Both have gained footholds in their respective ethnic community power structures, which are dominated by elderly leaders whose attention is directed far more toward resolving highly volatile situations in their countries of origin. At times, major social conflicts and group tragedies, such as the 1992 civil unrest in Los Angeles in which over two thousand Korean and other Asian business establishments were apparently targeted and destroyed, can serve to accelerate the development of a domestic-oriented leadership agenda and organizations and meaningful accommodation between domestic issues and homeland concerns.[41]

At other times, however, the nondomestic-oriented issues, leaders, and groups within Asian Pacific American communities appear to be nearly autonomous from other political actors, especially those engaged in electoral politics. For example, in November 1997 major Asian Pacific American elected officials and civil rights organizations in Washington, D.C., and elsewhere were still complaining vigorously about the attempts by Tennessee senator Fred Thompson and syndicated columnist William Safire, among others, to portray a scandalous, disloyal relationship between agents of the People's Republic of China and certain partisan officials and business leaders of the Asian Pacific American population.[42] The same month, however, a major gala dinner was held in Los Angeles for Chinese president Jiang Zemin. Sponsored by over 140 local Chinese American groups and attended by two thousand largely Chinese American guests, the dinner attracted hundreds of protesters, most of whom were other Asian Pacific Americans voicing their concerns about Tibet, Taiwan, and human rights in China.[43]

Conventional wisdom suggests that interest in nondomestic issues declines with succeeding acculturated generations. Such a linear conceptualization, however, fails to consider the changing political economic conditions in states such as California, Washington, and Hawaii for Asian Pacific Americans and other groups. For example, large numbers of second- and third-generation Asian Pacific Americans, particularly those in business, law, journalism, high technology, and academics, are visibly involved in emerging Pacific Rim affairs and, more generally, in the structural transformations stemming from the internationalization of the political economies of many states. In the decades to come, some Asian Pacific American leaders may use their real and symbolic linkages with Pacific Rim issues to define a unique and highly significant niche in American domestic politics and business affairs. Yet the continued interest and involvement of groups as diverse as American Jews, Poles and other Eastern Europeans, Ukrainians, Cubans, Greeks, Armenians, Mexican Americans, and African Americans in their "homeland" issues demonstrate that acculturation does not automatically signal the end of involvement or interest.[44]

These nondomestic relationships and interests also may have provocative ramifications for interethnic and interracial conflicts and coalition-building situations, especially in local urban politics. In Los Angeles, for example, the leadership of the Japanese American community has become polarized in a bitter and prolonged multiethnic labor strike at a major Japanese-owned hotel in the Little Tokyo district of the city. Several small business and community-based organizations, leaders, and attorneys who have business and personal relationships with Japanese interests have lined up in support of the New Otani Hotel owners and management. The local union organizing campaign for the predominantly Latino and Japanese American hotel workers has attracted the support of, among others, several Asian Pacific American civil rights groups, including the National Coalition for Redress and Reparations (NCRR), which played a decisive role in the passage of the 1988 Civil Liberties Act that provided reparations and an apology to the Japanese Americans who were incarcerated during World War II. This controversy became transnational in scope when national and local labor leaders, members of the NCRR, and even African American activist Jesse Jackson traveled to Japan to enlist the support of Japan's largest labor unions. They managed to gain the unions' endorsement for a worldwide boycott of the New Otani hotel chain.[45]

In addition to their nondomestic political activities, Asian Pacific Americans, like other American racial minorities who historically have been disenfranchised, have engaged in an array of nonelectoral political activities such as social movements and legal challenges to advance or protect their group interests. As recent historical scholarship has documented, Asian Pacific Americans have been participants in labor organizing efforts in the Far West, Hawaii, New York, and the Rocky Mountain states, and indeed were at the forefront in creating labor unions for agricultural workers in California and Hawaii.[46] This legacy of organizing the working class and working poor sectors of the Asian Pacific American community continues with varying degrees of success, especially in urban areas.[47] In Los Angeles the Korean Immigrant Workers Advocates and the Thai Community Development Corporation are particularly active in the garment and service industries. In 1995 the latter, along with the Asian Pacific American Legal

Center and state and federal government officials, were instrumental in rescuing seventy-two Thai garment workers from slave-like working conditions in El Monte, California.[48] A growing network of local and national groups also has emerged, organized largely around various professions. They carry the banner of Asian Pacific American pan-ethnic unity.

Like other racial minorities, Asian Pacific Americans also have a long history of seeking social justice and equal treatment by engaging in legal challenges against discriminatory laws and practices in education, employment, housing, land ownership, immigration, and other significant public policy areas.[49] Many of their legal cases—such as *Korematsu v. United States* (1944), *Lau v. Nichols* (1974), and *Equal Employment Opportunity Commission v. University of Pennsylvania* (1989)—have become landmark civil rights decisions.[50] Moreover, since the 1980s the number of Asian Pacific Americans entering the legal profession has increased substantially, and the list of legal advocacy and civil rights organizations such as the National Asian Pacific American Legal Consortium has grown. The civil rights organizations are engaged in a range of interethnic and interracial collaborations. Among other activities, they educate the largely foreign-born Asian Pacific American population about the potentially adverse ramifications of major legislative acts dealing with immigration or welfare reform, as well as about ballot initiatives on issues such as affirmative action and bilingual education in states such as California.

And, finally, under the general rubric of nonelectoral politics are the leaders, activities, organizations, and issues of local, internal ethnic community politics. Past research usually focused on community power structures, with their elitist rather than pluralist power arrangements. Chinatowns, for example, were characterized as having a hierarchical set of relationships between the so-called Six Companies' elites (powerful traditional business and family leaders) and the masses of Chinatown residents.[51] More recent scholarship, however, such as Illsoo Kim's *New Urban Immigrants* (1981)[52] and Kyeyoung Park's *Korean American Dream* (1997),[53] captures a wider range of internal community institutions such as churches, the ethnic press, small business associations, social services agencies, and the political groups that better meet the needs of larger numbers of immigrants and refugees than their mainstream counterparts. By extension, the leaders and opinion makers whom the foreign-born sectors of the Asian Pacific American population are perhaps more likely to respect and follow are those who possess similar personal characteristics and experiences such as being immigrants, speaking the same Asian languages, and sharing the same transplanted values and dreams. This factor raises important questions not only about intergenerational cooperation and conflict among different groups of ethnic leaders, as mentioned earlier, but also about the types of leaders who come to represent the interests of specific ethnic communities in their relationships with a range of external groups. For example, no members of the Korean American community of Los Angeles who participated in the various Korean-black coalition activities or dialogues before and after the 1992 riots and civil unrest were elected officials because no Korean American has ever been elected to public office in Los Angeles. The same was not true for the African American community.

A conceptualization of Asian Pacific American politics in the multifaceted manner described here—domestic and nondomestic, electoral and nonelectoral—goes beyond what is customarily considered under the general rubric of minority politics.[54] Such an expanded conceptual framework is necessary, however, to highlight the fact that electoral politics is only one of several major competing forms of political activity that the diverse ethnic groups and sectors of the Asian Pacific American population have pursued and likely will continue to pursue in the years to come. A broader view that recognizes their extensive historical record, as well as their present wide-ranging participation in both nondomestic and nonelectoral political activities, should guard scholars against making unwarranted generalizations about the overall political participation of the Asian Pacific American population based solely on its seemingly low levels of electoral participation, especially voting. By taking these nonelectoral and nondomestic activities into account, scholars and others can focus their attention on the structural and legal barriers that led to the historical disenfranchisement of Asian Pacific Americans and that continues to have lasting consequences. At the same time, this inclusive perspective should steer researchers toward analyzing a number of points of intersection among these different forms of political activity in order to more fully and accurately capture the dynamic growth, dilemmas, and diversity of Asian Pacific American politics.

NOTES

1. Paul Ong and Don T. Nakanishi, "Becoming Citizens, Becoming Voters: The Naturalization and Political Participation of Asian Pacific Immigrants," in *The State of Asian Pacific America: Reframing the Immigration Debate*, ed. Bill Ong Hing

and Ronald Lee (Los Angeles: LEAP Asian Pacific American Public Policy Institute and UCLA Asian American Studies Center, 1966), 275–305.

2. Don T. Nakanishi, "When Numbers Do Not Add Up: Asian Pacific Americans and California Politics," in *Racial and Ethnic Politics in California,* Vol. 2, ed. Michael Preston, Bruce E. Cain, and Sandra Bass (Berkeley: Institute of Governmental Studies Press, 1998), 3–43.

3. Don T. Nakanishi and James Lai, *National Asian Pacific American Political Almanac* (Los Angeles: UCLA Asian American Studies Center, 1998).

4. Nakanishi, "When Numbers Do Not Add Up."

5. Don T. Nakanishi, "Japanese Americans in the City of Smog," in *Mutual Images: Essays in American-Japanese Relations,* ed. Akira Iriye (Cambridge: Harvard University Press, 1975), 223–257.

6. Daniel Akaka, "From the Senate Floor: Asian Americans and the Political Fundraising Investigation," in *National Asian Pacific American Political Almanac,* ed. Don Nakanishi and James Lai (Los Angeles: UCLA Asian American Studies Center, 1998), 22–28.

7. Leland T. Saito, "Asian Americans and Latinos in San Gabriel Valley, California: Interethnic Political Cooperation and Redistricting, 1990–1992," *Amerasia Journal* 19 (1993): 55–68; Pei-te Lien, "Ethnicity and Political Participation: A Comparison between Asian and Mexican Americans," *Political Behavior* 16 (1994): 237–264; Timothy P. Fong, *The First Suburban Chinatown: The Remaking of Monterey Park, California* (Philadelphia: Temple University Press, 1994); Larry Shinagawa, "Asian Pacific American Electoral Participation in the San Francisco Bay Area," Final Report, Asian Law Caucus, San Francisco, June 15, 1995; Wendy Tam, "Asians—A Monolithic Voting Bloc?" *Political Behavior* 17 (1995): 223–249; Joe Fong, "Los Angeles County Asian American Hidden Electorate," in *National Asian Pacific American Political Almanac,* ed. Don T. Nakanishi and James Lai (Los Angeles: UCLA Asian American Studies Center, 1998), 140–155; James Lai, "Racially Polarized Voting and Its Effects on the Formation of a Viable Latino-Asian Pacific Political Coalition," in *National Asian Pacific American Political Almanac,* ed. Don T. Nakanishi and James Lai (Los Angeles: UCLA Asian American Studies Center, 1998), 156–183; and Edward Park, "Competing Visions: Political Formation of Korean Americans in Los Angeles, 1992–1997," *Amerasia Journal* 24 (1998): 41–58.

8. Don T. Nakanishi, *In Search of a New Paradigm: Minorities in the Context of International Politics,* Studies in Race and Nations Series (Denver: Center for International Race Relations, University of Denver, 1975).

9. Don T. Nakanishi, "Surviving Democracy's 'Mistake': Japanese Americans and Executive Order 9066," *Amerasia Journal* 19 (1993): 7–35.

10. Matthew Ebnet, "A Divided Community Returns to Daily Life," *Los Angeles Times,* January 16, 2000, B1, 8.

11. Paul Ong and Suzanne Hee, "The Growth of the Asian Pacific American Population: Twenty Million in 2020," in LEAP Asian Pacific American Public Pol-

icy Institute, *The State of Asian Pacific America: Policy Issues to the Year 2000* (Los Angeles: LEAP Asian Pacific American Public Policy Institute and UCLA Asian American Studies Center, 1993), 11–24.

12. Judy Tachibana, "California's Asians: Power from a Growing Population," *California Journal* 17 (1986): 534–543; Bruce E. Cain, "Asian-American Electoral Power: Imminent or Illusory?" *Election Politics* 5 (1988): 27–30; Bruce Stokes, "Learning the Game," *National Journal,* October 22, 1998, 2649–2654; and John Miller, "Asian Americans Head for Politics," *American Enterprise* 6 (1995): 56–58.

13. Miller, "Asian Americans Head for Politics"; and Todd S. Purdum, "Asian-Americans Set to Flex Political Muscle Made Large," *New York Times,* November 15, 1997, A1, A9.

14. Don T. Nakanishi, ed. *National Asian Pacific American Political Directory* (Los Angeles: UCLA Asian American Studies Center, 1978).

15. Nakanishi and Lai, *National Asian Pacific American Political Almanac.*

16. Field Institute, "A Digest on California's Political Demography," November 1992, 6.

17. Don T. Nakanishi, "Asian American Politics: An Agenda for Research," *Amerasia Journal* 12 (1986): 1–27.

18. The 1990 CPS included 2,914 Asians out of a total sample of 105,875; the 1992 CPS, 3,443 Asians out of 102,901; and the 1994 CPS, 3,317 Asians out of 102,197. Both weighted and unweighted data were analyzed for this report.

19. Grant Din, "An Analysis of Asian/Pacific American Registration and Voting Patterns in San Francisco," M.A. thesis, Claremont Graduate School, 1984; John Horton, *The Politics of Diversity* (Philadelphia: Temple University Press, 1995); Shinagawa, "Asian Pacific American Electoral Participation in the San Francisco Bay Area"; and Tam, "Asians—A Monolithic Voting Bloc?"

20. Ong and Nakanishi, "Becoming Citizens, Becoming Voters."

21. Nakanishi, "Asian American Politics: An Agenda for Research"; Cain, "Asian-American Electoral Power"; Field Institute, "Digest on California's Political Demography"; Steven P. Erie and Harold Brackman, *Paths to Political Incorporation for Latinos and Asian Pacifics in California* (Berkeley: California Policy Seminar, 1993); and Lien, "Ethnicity and Political Participation," 237–264.

22. Ong and Nakanishi, "Becoming Citizens, Becoming Voters."

23. Zvi Gittleman, *Becoming Israelis* (New York: Praeger, 1982).

24. Other studies also have found that some groups of Asian American voters register in higher-than-expected proportions as "no party" or independents. See Din, "Analysis of Asian/Pacific American Registration and Voting Patterns in San Francisco," and Marion Chen, Woei-Ming New, and John Tsutsukawa, "Empowerment in New York's Chinatown: Our Work as Student Interns," *Amerasia Journal* 15 (1989): 199–206.

25. Nakanishi, "When Numbers Do Not Add Up."

26. Morton Grodzins, *Americans Betrayed* (Chicago: University of Chicago Press, 1949).

27. Roger Daniels, *The Politics of Prejudice* (New York: Atheneum, 1968).

28. Yung-Hwan Jo, ed., *Political Participation of Asian Americans: Problems and Strategies* (Chicago: Pacific/Asian American Mental Health Research Center, 1980); and Nakanishi, "Asian American Politics: An Agenda for Research."

29. Douglas S. Massey, "Dimensions of the New Immigration to the United States and the Prospects for Assimilation," *Annual Review of Sociology* 7 (1981): 57–85.

30. Nakanishi, "Asian American Politics: An Agenda for Research"; Cain, "Asian-American Electoral Power," 27–30; Su Sun Bai, "Affirmative Pursuit of Political Equality for Asian Pacific Americans: Reclaiming the Voting Rights Act," *University of Pennvania Law Review* 139 (1991): 731–767; Erie and Brackman, *Paths to Political Incorporation*; Lien, "Ethnicity and Political Participation"; Horton, *Politics of Diversity*; Shinagawa, "Asian Pacific American Electoral Participation in the San Francisco Bay Area"; Tam, "Asians—A Monolithic Voting Bloc?"; and Lai, "Racially Polarized Voting."

31. Tom Coffman, *Catch A Wave: A Case Study of Hawaii's New Politics* (Honolulu: University of Hawaii Press, 1973).

32. Nakanishi, "Asian American Politics: An Agenda for Research"; Tachibana, "California's Asians"; Stokes, "Learning the Game"; Rob Gurwitt, "Have Asian Americans Arrived Politically? Not Quite," *Governing* (November 1990): 32–38; Erie and Brackman, *Paths to Political Incorporation*; Horton, *Politics of Diversity*; Sam Chu Lin, "Candidates Keeping Tabs on Asian Pacific American Trends," *Asianweek*, November 2, 1995, 10; and Miller, "Asian Americans Head for Politics."

33. Rocky Chin, "The Long Road—Japanese Americans Move on Redress," *Bridge* 7 (1981): 11–29; Don T. Nakanishi, "A Quota on Excellence? The Debate on Asian American Admissions," *Change* (November/December 1989): 38–47; Nakanishi, "Surviving Democracy's 'Mistake' "; Leslie T. Hatamiya, *Righting a Wrong: Japanese Americans and the Passage of the Civil Liberties Act of 1988* (Stanford: Stanford University Press, 1993); and Mitchell Maki, Harry Kitano, and Megan Berthold, *Achieving the Impossible Dream: How Japanese Americans Obtained Redress* (Urbana: University of Illinois Press, 1999).

34. Frank Chuman, *The Bamboo People: Japanese Americans and the Law* (Del Mar, Calif.: Publisher's Inc., 1976); and Yuji Ichioka, "The Early Japanese Quest for Citizenship: The Background of the 1922 Ozawa Case," *Amerasia Journal* 4 (1977): 1–22.

35. Bob Suzuki, "Education and Socialization of Asian Americans," *Amerasia Journal* 4 (1977): 23–51; and Ki-Taek Chun, "The Myth of Asian American Success and Its Educational Ramifications," *IRCD Bulletin* 15 (1980): 1–12.

36. Bai, "Affirmative Pursuit of Political Equality for Asian Pacific Americans"; and Stewart Kwoh and Mindy Hui, "Empowering Our Communities: Political Policy," in

LEAP Asian Pacific American Public Policy Institute, *The State of Asian Pacific America: Policy Issues to the Year 2020* (Los Angeles: LEAP Asian Pacific American Public Policy Institute and UCLA Asian American Studies Center, 1993), 189–197.

37. Alexander Saxton, "The Army of Canton in the High Sierra," *Pacific Historical Review* 35 (1966): 141–152; Robert Keohane, "The Big Influence of Small Allies," *Foreign Policy* 2 (1971): 161–182; Kingsley Lyu, "Korean Nationalist Activities in Hawaii and the Continental United States, 1900–1945, Part I and II," *Amerasia Journal* 4 (1977): 23–90; Mark Juergensmeyer, "The Ghadar Syndrome: Nationalism in an Immigrant Community," *Center for South and Southeast Asian Studies Review* 1 (1978): 9–13; Shih-Shan Henry Tsai, "The Emergence of Early Chinese Nationalist Organizations in America," *Amerasia Journal* 8 (1981): 121–144; Renqiu Yu, "Chinese American Contributions to the Educational Development of Toisan, 1910–1940," *Amerasia Journal* 10 (1983): 47–72; Delber McKee, "The Chinese Boycott of 1905–1906 Reconsidered, The Role of Chinese Americans," *Pacific Historical Review* 55 (1986): 165–191; Madge Bello and Vince Reyes, "Filipino Americans and the Marcos Overthrow: The Transformation of Political Consciousness," *Amerasia Journal* 13 (1986–1987): 73–83; Edward Tea Chang, "Korean Community Politics in Los Angeles," *Amerasia Journal* 14 (1988): 51–68; Dick Clark, "The American-Vietnamese Dialogue," Aspen Institute, Queenstown, Maryland, 1993; L. Ling-Chi Wang, "The Structure of Dual Domination: Toward a Paradigm for Study of the Chinese Diaspora in the United States," *Amerasia Journal* 21 (1995): 149–169; Yuji Ichioka, "Beyond National Boundaries: The Complexities of Japanese-American History," *Amerasia Journal* 23 (1997): vii–xi; Matea Gold, "Arrest Unites Blacks, Korean Americans," *Los Angeles Times,* December 30, 1997, A1, A16; Jim Mann, "Korean Americans May See Old Home's Doors Opening," *Los Angeles Times,* December 24, 1997, A5; Sunita Sunder Mukhi and Sayu Bhojwani, eds., *Bridges with Asia: Asian Americans in the United States* (New York: Asia Society, 1997); "Pol Pot's Death Leaves Anger Unresolved," *Asianweek,* April 23, 1998, 8; and Darryl Fears, "Making Connections," *Los Angeles Times,* June 14, 1998, B1, B7.

38. H. Mark Lai, "China Politics and United States Chinese Communities," in *Counterpoint: Perspectives on Asian America,* ed. Emma Gee et al. (Los Angeles: UCLA Asian American Studies Center, 1976); Michi Weglyn, *Years of Infamy* (New York: Morrow, 1976); and Peter Irons, *Justice at War* (New York: Oxford University Press, 1983).

39. L. Ling-Chi Wang, "Race, Class, Citizenship, and Extraterritoriality: Asian Americans and the 1996 Campaign Finance Scandal," *Amerasia Journal* 24 (1998): 1–22.

40. Nakanishi, *In Search of a New Paradigm.*

41. Park, "Competing Visions"; and Kyeyoung Park, *The Korean American Dream: Immigrants and Small Business in New York City* (Ithaca: Cornell University Press, 1997).

42. Sam Chu Lin, "Commission on Civil Rights to Hear Asian-Bashing Complaints," *Rafu Shimpo*, December 4, 1997, 1, 4.

43. Dara Akiko, "Mission Accomplished," *Asianweek*, November 6, 1997, 13; and Henry Chu, "Jiang Talks Up Sino-L.A. Ties," *Los Angeles Times*, November 3, 1997, A1, A6.

44. Nakanishi, *In Search of a New Paradigm*; Stephen Ryan, "Explaining Ethnic Conflict: The Neglected International Dimension," *Review of International Studies* 14 (1988): 161–177; Yvonne D. Newsome, "International Issues and Domestic Ethnic Relations: African Americans, American Jews, and the Israel–South Africa Debate," *International Journal of Politics, Culture, and Society* 5 (1991): 19–48; Erie and Brackman, *Paths to Political Incorporation*; Norman Kempster, "U.S. Jews Back Push for Israel Peace, Poll Shows," *Los Angeles Times*, October 4, 1997, A11; Mark Fritz, "Pledging Multiple Allegiances," *Los Angeles Times*, April 6, 1998, A1, A14; Hugo Martin, "Group Hopes to Boost Armenian Americans' Political Role," *Los Angeles Times*, January 25, 1998, B3; Patrick J. McDonnell, "Cementing Ties to Mexico," *Los Angeles Times*, March 21, 1998, B1, B8; and Pacific Council on International Policy, "Advancing the International Interests of African-Americans, Asian-Americans, and Latinos," Pacific Council on International Policy, Los Angeles, 1998.

45. Martha Nakagawa, "Kajima Corp. in the Spotlight," *Rafu Shimpo*, December 19, 1995, 1.

46. Howard DeWitt, *Violence in the Fields: California Filipino Farm Labor Organizing during the Great Depression* (Saratoga, Calif.: Century Twenty-One Publishing, 1980); Peter Kwong, *Chinatown, New York: Labor and Politics, 1930–1950* (New York: Monthly Review Press, 1981); Cletus Daniel, *Bitter Harvest: A History of California Farm Workers, 1870–1941* (Ithaca: Cornell University Press, 1981); Karl Yoneda, *Ganbatte* (Los Angeles: UCLA Asian American Studies Center, 1983); Craig Scharlin and Lilia V. Villanueva, *Philip Vera Cruz: A Personal History of Filipino Immigrants and the Farmworkers Movement* (Los Angeles: UCLA Asian American Studies Center and UCLA Labor Center, 1992); and Arleen De Vera, "Without Parallel: The Local 7 Deportation Cases, 1949–1955," *Amerasia Journal* 20 (1994): 1–26.

47. Glenn Omatsu, "To Our Readers: Asian Pacific American Workers and the Expansion of Democracy," *Amerasia Journal* 18 (1992): v–xx; Edna Bonacich, "Editorial Forum: Reflections on Asian American Labor," *Amerasia Journal* 18 (1992): xxi–xxvi; Bert Elijera, "Union Gets Down to Business," *Asianweek*, August 15, 1997, 12; and Park, *Korean American Dream*.

48. Peter Liebhold and Harry R. Rubenstein, *Between a Rock and a Hard Place: A History of American Sweatshops, 1820–Present* (Los Angeles: UCLA Asian American Studies Center and Simon Wiesenthal Center Museum of Tolerance, 1999).

49. Chuman, *Bamboo People*; and Victor Low, *The Unimpressible Race: A Century of Educational Struggle by Chinese in San Francisco* (San Francisco: East-West Publishers, 1982).

50. L. Ling-Chi Wang, "Lau v. Nichols: History of a Struggle for Equal and Quality Education," in *Counterpoint,* ed. Emma Gee et al. (Los Angeles: UCLA Asian American Studies Center, 1976), 240–263; U.S. Commission on Civil Rights, *Civil Rights Issues of Asian and Pacific Americans: Myths and Realities* (Washington, D.C.: U.S. Commission on Civil Rights, 1979); Irons, *Justice at War;* and Deirdre Carmody, "Secrecy and Tenure: An Issue for High Court," *New York Times,* December 6, 1989, B8.

51. Stanford Lyman, *The Asian in the West* (Reno: Desert Research Institute, University of Nevada, 1970).

52. Illsoo Kim, *New Urban Immigrants* (Princeton: Princeton University Press, 1981).

53. Park, *Korean American Dream.*

54. Nakanishi, "Asian American Politics: An Agenda for Research."

PART TWO

VOTING BEHAVIOR

Asian Americans as the Median Voters: An Exploration of Attitudes and Voting Patterns on Ballot Initiatives

WENDY K. TAM CHO
BRUCE E. CAIN

If history is a reliable guide, immigration could have a substantial impact on the makeup of the United States and thus on U.S. electoral alignments in the near future. Immigration policies can preserve the dominant culture (the result of the pro-European bias in the pre-1965 U.S. immigration policies) or dramatically diversify the national mix (the unintended result of the post-1965 U.S. immigration policies).[1] Moreover, immigration policies can have an enduring effect on party loyalties, if allegiances are formed or solidified at the policy-making stage. A party that favors restrictionist immigration policies or nativist culture positions may be able to gain the immediate support of a dominant population group, but it may simultaneously risk losing the potential votes of immigrant groups for a generation or more. The same implications apply to policies that appear to primarily affect immigrant groups. Although these policies may not be immigration laws per se, they have the same potential impact on electoral alignments.

Once electoral alignments are created, they are strengthened by the inertial forces of party identification and collective memory. The predominantly Protestant Republican Party, for example, did not begin to make serious inroads into the Irish and Italian Catholic vote until the late 1960s and early 1970s, even though the processes of upward mobility were operating on these groups throughout the first half of the twentieth century.[2] Groups that are not predominantly affiliated with a given party are particularly vulnerable to important aligning events. Asian Americans are a case in point. At present, their loyalties, unlike those of blacks and Latinos, are not predetermined. Garnering Asian American support would benefit either party given its potential to swing an election.[3]

The loss of support from a generation of voters is heightened when policies have racial overtones. If the restrictionist, nativist party is predominantly white and the target groups are predominantly nonwhite, the restrictionist/nativist policy may have the appearance of being a racial policy even if the reality is more complex. The Republican Party has faced this situation at several recent junctures. The Clinton administration's appointment of Bill Lann Lee, for example, was embroiled in racial overtones. The Democrats claimed that the Republicans' unwillingness to confirm Lee's appointment as assistant attorney general for civil rights at the U.S. Department of Justice was evidence that they harbored anti-Asian sentiment. The Republicans countered that they opposed Lee based on his affirmative action stance, but the Democratic tactic clearly rattled them all the same. Similar types of arguments surrounded two initiatives on recent California ballots, Propositions 187 (1994) and 209 (1996). Proposition 187 dealt with the rights of undocumented immigrants to state services and Proposition 209 with affirmative action policies. Opponents of the initiatives dwelled on race and alleged prejudice; proponents talked about economics and the ideals of equal protection and equality. Both propositions passed, but there is a lingering suspicion that the rhetoric of the opponents "worked" insofar as most discussion of the propositions in the aftermath of their passage was couched in racial terms.

While it would be inaccurate to say that all restrictionists are Republicans and all opponents of such policies are Democrats, the more visible proponents of restrictionist policies (for example, presidential candidate Pat Buchanan and former California governor Pete Wilson) are Republicans and the more visible opponents (for example, the Latino congressional caucus) are Democrats. This situation has prompted at least one prominent Republican consultant to worry about the long-term consequences of recent Republican policies in the areas of immigration, language policy, and affirmative action.[4]

If immigration policies in the late twentieth century prove to have the political consequences they had in the early twentieth century, they may critically affect Asian Americans' political attitudes. Cultivating Asian American loyalties would be a highly coveted accomplishment. The overwhelming reason is that the Asian American population has recently experienced unparalleled growth. Like Latinos, Asian Americans constitute a major proportion of the recent immigration surge. Mexico provides the largest number of immigrants to the United States, but the next four countries are Asian: the Philippines, Korea, China, and Vietnam.[5] Latin America and Asia now account for over 80 percent of all immigration to the United States. Unlike Latinos, however, Asian American immigrants are less likely to be undocumented immigrants and the lag between their arrival and their naturalization is shorter. Thus, Asian Americans are uniquely poised to make a grand entrance onto the political scene. Although there is some question about whether they will make this grand entrance at all, there is even more uncertainty about what type of grand entrance they could make because their political attitudes remain largely unknown.

This chapter seeks to provide some insight into Asian American attitudes by exploring the roots of Asian American preferences on the two California initiatives. Because Asian Americans are predominantly foreign-born but legal immigrants, they have to contend with two potentially competing interests. The first interest opposes restrictionist and racially discriminatory policies toward immigrants. The other interest distinguishes between the restriction of legal versus illegal immigrants.

This chapter analyzes data from a 1996 California statewide survey that oversampled the minority populations. In particular, the chapter examines two specific questions. First, how do Asian Americans view other immigrants and minority groups? Second, to what extent do these perceptions and other factors, such as party and ideology, structure the Asian American vote?

PERCEPTION OF OTHER ETHNIC AND RACIAL GROUPS

Immigration has created an unusually multiracial mix in California. Outside of a few urban areas such as Miami, Chicago, New York, and Dallas, significant concentrations of more than one racial or ethnic minority are rarely found in the United States.[6] California, however, has a significant share of each of the major racial groups, Asian Americans (10 percent), blacks (9 percent), and Latinos (30 percent). Even though the distribution of these groups is far from uniform, all of the major urban areas (the San Francisco Bay Area, Los Angeles, and San Diego) have sizable numbers of all three minority groups. A consequence of this multiracial environment is that the Asian Americans in California experience not only the effects of their own group's rising immigrant numbers but also those of other groups—especially Latinos.

According to the survey described later in this chapter, in the uniquely multiracial environs of California, Asian Americans are the most residentially dispersed—that is, the least likely to live in a neighborhood in which their group is a majority (approximately 3 percent of California's Asian Americans live in such circumstances). Whites are the most concentrated; 85 percent of whites live in majority white areas. By contrast, 29 percent of blacks live in majority black areas, and 44 percent of Latinos live in majority Latino areas. Of the minority groups, Asian Americans are the most likely to live in majority white tracts—51 percent of Asian Americans live in these tracts compared with 31 percent of blacks and 35 percent of Latinos. In summary, the Asian American experience is unusually multiracial and almost evenly divided between those who live in predominantly white neighborhoods and those who live in more heavily Latino and/or black neighborhoods.

Through these multiracial circumstances, Asian Americans are exposed to the experiences of the other groups. The 1996 survey probed whether this environment produces positive or negative perceptions of other groups by asking respondents about their perceptions of other minority groups and types of immigrants. A special feature of this study was that it incorporated contextual information about the type of neighborhood and racial circumstances in which the respondent lived. This information allows a closer look at whether Asian Americans living in white neighborhoods have similar attitudes to those living in majority-minority neighborhoods.

Figure 5.1 reveals that, on the whole, Asian Americans have fairly positive perceptions of the other racial/ethnic groupings. When asked whether the effect of Latinos, blacks, and whites living in their neighborhood improved conditions, made them worse, or kept them about the same as before, the vast majority of Asian American respondents chose "better" or "about the same." They were somewhat more positive about the effects of whites than Latinos and blacks, and substantially more positive about Asian Americans than all the other groups. This preference for one's own group holds for blacks and Latinos as well.[7]

The most dramatic distinction made by Asian Americans was between legal and illegal/undocumented immigrants (Figure 5.2). Twenty-eight percent indicated that legal immigrants improved the neighborhood, but only 6 percent thought that illegal immigrants did. By comparison, 5 percent thought that legal immigrants made conditions in their neighborhood

Figure 5.1
Attitudes of Racial and Ethnic Groups toward Each Other

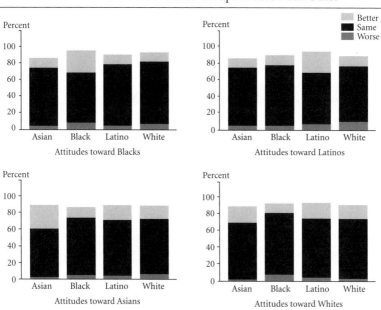

Respondents were asked: "Now I am going to ask you what effect different groups of people have had on the quality of life in the neighborhood where you live. After I give you the name of the group, please tell me whether that group has improved, made worse, or had no effect on the quality of life in your neighborhood."

worse versus 15 percent for illegal immigrants. Although all racial groups express similar attitudes, the Asian American preference for legal immigrants is distinctively stronger than those of Latinos and blacks. These numbers might suggest that even though most Asian Americans voted against Proposition 187, they were less opposed than Latinos or blacks.

The patterns just described hold for these ethnic groups when the groups are considered as a single bloc. However, as previously suggested, the neighborhood context may have a significant impact on these patterns and may serve as a dividing line for attitudes even within a single ethnic group.[8] Since daily interactions differ, it may be important to distinguish between Asian Americans who live in majority-minority neighborhoods and those who live in predominantly white neighborhoods. If in multiracial settings there is less tolerance for other groups, the future of race relations in Cali-

Figure 5.2
Attitudes of Racial and Ethnic Groups toward
Legal and Illegal Immigrants

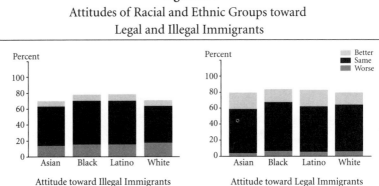

For question, see Figure 5.1.

fornia would not be promising. Fortunately, however, the data do not reveal such a pattern. Indeed, insofar as there is a difference, the data suggest a slightly more positive perception of other groups by those Asian Americans who live in majority-minority areas rather than elsewhere. Undocumented immigrants are the only case in which this pattern is reversed. The difference here, however, is not large.

PERCEPTIONS OF DIVERSITY AND RACE RELATIONS

In addition to questions about specific perceptions of other racial and ethnic groups, the 1996 survey included more general questions about race relations in California that are worth noting (Figure 5.3). Specifically, survey participants were asked to respond to the statement "People of different ethnic and racial groups are generally happier when they live and socialize with others of the same background." A majority (65 percent) of Asian American respondents, like all other racial groups, tended to prefer their own group; they replied with either "Agree somewhat" or "Agree strongly." The percentages for blacks (63 percent), Latinos (60 percent), and whites (64 percent) were about the same. This pattern holds for those who lived in majority-minority settings as well as those who did not. Combined with earlier observations, this finding suggests that while Asian Americans are more comfortable in purely Asian American settings, they

Figure 5.3

Perceptions of Diversity and Race Relations

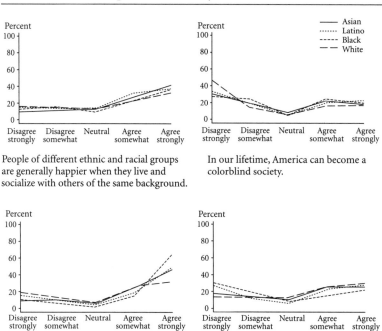

People of different ethnic and racial groups are generally happier when they live and socialize with others of the same background.

In our lifetime, America can become a colorblind society.

Members of certain ethnic or racial groups still have fewer opportunities to get ahead than other people.

Members of particular ethnic or racial groups use special programs to get more benefits than they deserve.

have overall positive or neutral views of other groups. The only exception lies in attitudes toward undocumented immigrants, and it would seem that Asian Americans distinguish between Latinos and undocumented immigrants.

Asian Americans' attitudes toward affirmative action are very similar to those of the other major racial/ethnic groups. Like Latinos and blacks, a majority of Asian American respondents tend to believe that minorities have fewer opportunities to succeed in America. In fact, Asian American and Latino responses are virtually identical (Figure 5.3). Blacks believe this statement most strongly, and whites trail behind all ethnic groups in supporting this claim. A significantly larger proportion of blacks also tended to disagree strongly with the claim that America could become a colorblind society in their lifetime; whites join Asian Americans and Latinos in yielding similar responses.

Finally, Figure 5.3 reveals that many Asian Americans believe that some groups receive more than they deserve from affirmative action programs, and a quarter claim to know an individual who received an undeserved position or promotion as a result of an affirmative action program. Asian American attitudes on this question mimic white attitudes. Despite their beliefs, a majority of Asian Americans still believe that Latinos, blacks, women, and Asian Americans need the affirmative action programs that Proposition 209 would eliminate. A vast majority of Asian Americans prefer a merit system over one that rewards sheer diversity. For them, affirmative action is a means of remedying unfairness in the merit system, not a rejection of that system per se.

None of the survey questions alone displays much evidence that the Asian American group differs much from other minority groups. The only notable difference is its weaker support for affirmative action. Given this finding, the next section describes a more sophisticated analysis of the two ballot propositions.

THE PROPOSITION 187 AND 209 VOTES

In California, Propositions 187 and 209 were two of the most controversial and hotly debated initiatives in recent memory. In 1994, Proposition 187 was passed overwhelmingly (59 percent to 41 percent) by California voters. The proposition made illegal aliens ineligible for public social services, nonemergency public health care services, and public school education at elementary, secondary, and postsecondary levels. It also required various state and local agencies to report persons who were suspected illegal aliens to the California attorney general and the U.S. Immigration and Naturalization Service. At a time when the California economy was slumping, support for the initiative ran high.

On November 5, 1996, the voters of California approved Proposition 209 by 55 percent to 45 percent. As a result, Section 31 was added to Article I of the California constitution. The first clause of the section succinctly describes the proposition: "The state shall not discriminate against, or grant preferential treatment to, any individual or group on the basis of race, sex, color, ethnicity, or national origin in the operation of public employment, public education, or public contracting." Some commentators believe that Proposition 209 was not a clear vote on affirmative action because of the way the initiative was worded and presented to the public. The concern began with the title of the proposition, which was "California Civil Rights Initiative." The implication was that Proposition 209 was building on civil rights laws that prohibit discrimination and that the new initiative would dispose of government-imposed quotas, preferences, and set-asides. Many felt that the true impact of the proposition, the abolition of affirmative action, was carefully veiled and that the civil rights wording was improper.

The data suggest that of all California's minorities, Asian Americans were the most divided by these two propositions, with about a third supporting them, 40–50 percent opposed, and the balance undecided. What distinguishes those Asian Americans who voted for the measures from those who opposed them? This question is explored further by means of two models that explain Asian American positions on these propositions as a function of various perceptions and background factors. Comparison of the Asian American model with similar models for blacks, whites, and Latinos allows an assessment of whether the factors that divide Asian American opinion are the same as the factors that explain the vote divisions of the other groups. Given the high level of opposition by blacks to Proposition 209 and Latinos to Proposition 187, these two specific models are not likely to account for a large degree of variation. With near consensus, there is little variance to explain. For this reason, the most interesting comparison is likely to be between the white and Asian American models.

The logic behind these models becomes clearer by examining three factors. The first is the partisan and ideological basis of the vote. Decades of public opinion research have revealed that opinions are often structured by a person's overall ideological orientation and party preference. Thus voters who are liberal or conservative may be predisposed to oppose or support a given measure. For Propositions 187 and 209, the expected mapping from ideology to issue would be from liberal to opposition and from conservative to support. This mapping seems initially plausible, but it is not without problems. Some liberals supported Proposition 187 because of environmental concerns (for example, the Sierra Club felt an influx of illegal immigrants would adversely affect the environment), or because they felt that immigrants should conform to the federal rules for entry and citizenship. Some economic conservatives may have voted against Proposition 187 because the loss of illegal immigrants would adversely affect the supply of labor to businesses such as agriculture and light manufacturing. Similarly, some liberals may have voted for Proposition 209 because they believed affirmative action programs were flawed and prone to abuse even though they believed that discrimination is an important residual problem. Some conservatives and moderates may have voted against it for fear that it would be too sweeping or might adversely affect women's rights. Generally, however, conservatives supported the measure, and liberals opposed it.

Party preferences also are likely to be important. Overall, Democrats were more likely to oppose both Propositions 187 and 209 and Republicans were more likely to support them. Because Asian Americans are more or less evenly divided between the parties, it is plausible to believe that this might be an important explanation for differences among Asian American voters. Yet, previous studies have suggested that partisanship is not as strong among Asian American voters as it is among other racial and ethnic groups.[9] If so, partisanship may be too weak to structure Asian American attitudes in any significant way.

The second factor is the circumstances and experiences in which Asian Americans finds themselves. These include their economic conditions, their perceptions of how other groups affect their neighborhood, the degree to which they see diversity as a positive, variable-sum experience (as opposed to a negative, zero-sum experience), and their perceptions about what government programs groups need in order to be successful. In contrast to ideology and party, these variables describe the direct experiences/effects of diversity rather than the symbolic element of these issues. If economic times are perceived to be poor, if respondents think that diversity leads to zero-sum competition, if the neighborhoods are thought to be adversely affected by demographic change, and if others seem to be benefiting from programs and preferences that they do not need, then Asian American voters will be inclined to support restrictionist measures.

The third factor is socioeconomic characteristics such as gender, age, education, and type of neighborhood. The relationship between these variables and voter preference is by now well established.[10] Among white voters, the better educated voters, younger people, and those living in a multiracial environment tend to be more liberal, more Democratic, and more tolerant. These predispositions may carry over to the issues prevalent in Propositions 187 and 209. The mapping here is likely to be fairly precise for nonminority voters and even for black and Latino voters. For Asian Americans, however, the direct translation from these predispositions to voter preference is less clear.

DATA ANALYSIS

The survey conducted among California voters in 1996 included a total of 1,500 respondents with an oversampling of minority groups. Of the total, 262 identified themselves as Asian American, 167 as black, 416 as Latino, and 427 as white. They were asked forty-two questions. The first step in analyzing the survey data was to create a manageable set of variables.[11] Although the survey encompassed forty-two questions, they fell into four distinct and logical categories: need for affirmative action, attitudes toward different groups, effect of diversity, and economic outlook.

The Proposition 187 Vote

Table 5.1 displays the results of a logistic regression analysis in which voting for Proposition 187 is the dependent variable. None of the variables appears to explain the black vote for Proposition 187, primarily because the heavy opposition of blacks to Proposition 187 produces little variation for the model to explain. For similar reasons, the model explaining the Latino vote also is not very illuminating. Two variables seem to matter for Latinos—whether they see a continued need for affirmative action and whether they think diversity is desirable. Figure 5.4 reveals, however, that Latino support for Proposition 187 runs from low to almost nonexistent based on these two variables. At no point is their support for Proposition 187 substantial.

For whites, Proposition 187 support is predominantly affected by partisanship, the state of the economy, and beliefs about diversity and affirmative action. Intuition says these are exactly the types of variables that would divide opinion on Proposition 187. They also are the variables that were stressed in the campaigns and by the politicians. It is curious, then, that these sets of variables explain the attitudes for whites but not for Asian Americans, blacks, or Latinos. The impact of these variables is dramatic for whites. Figure 5.4 shows that the change in support as the variables change is substantial, and that whites supported Proposition 187 at far higher rates than those of any of the minority groups.

Asian Americans display attitudes that are not as widely contrarian as those of blacks and Latinos but also are not as divided as those of whites. Some of the variables that divide whites do not divide Asian Americans. Most notably, party is not significant in predicting Asian American attitudes on Proposition 187, yet ideology plays a part. The more conservative

Table 5.1

Logistic Regression with Proposition 187 as Dependent Variable

	White	Asian	Black	Latino
Intercept	.7662	−.8908	−.7557	−.6893
	(.8619)	(1.2732)	(1.4996)	(.8051)
Factor 1: Need for	−1.0643[b]	−.6845[b]	−.1787	−.5059[b]
affirmative action	(.1651)	(.2175)	(.2792)	(.1590)
Factor 2: Attitude toward	−.2192	−.3884[a]	−.1209	−.1267
other groups	(.1443)	(.2133)	(.2560)	(.1580)
Factor 3: Effect of diversity	−.5329[b]	−.7090[b]	−.1616	−.8985[b]
	(.1669)	(.2415)	(.2342)	(.1812)
Factor 4: Economy	−.4324[b]	−.0330	−.3696	−.1218
	(.1551)	(.2032)	(.2379)	(.1605)
Age	.3080	−.1405	−.2071	.0741
	(.2033)	(.3214)	(.3486)	(.2231)
Democrat	−.5831[a]	.3562	.5725	−.5476
	(.3274)	(.4837)	(.7341)	(.3350)
Education	−.0124	−.1767	−.0505	.0235
	(.0994)	(.1481)	(.1653)	(.1071)
Ideology	.0055	.6556[b]	.0132	−.0698
	(.2298)	(.3291)	(.3292)	(.2120)
Nonminority neighborhood	−.2622	−.5768	−.5814	−.2487
	(.3140)	(.4566)	(.5120)	(.3308)
Gender	−.2375	.9447[b]	.2360	.1893
	(.3037)	(.4303)	(.5082)	(.3304)
n	290	135	98	233

a. $p < .10$

b. $p < .05$

the Asian American voter, the more likely he or she is to vote for Proposition 187. However, even the support of the most conservative Asian American hovers in the low 30 percent range. Finally, Asian American men are more likely to support Proposition 187 than Asian American women.

Like white opinions, Asian American opinions on Proposition 187 are affected by their attitudes toward diversity and the need for affirmative action. In addition, Asian American preferences on Proposition 187 are based on their experiences and attitude toward other racial groups. The signifi-

Figure 5.4
Change in Support for Proposition 187 Holding All
Other Variables at Their Mean

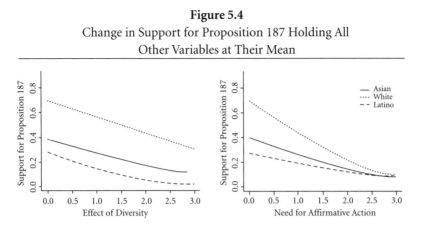

Note: Both the "Effect of diversity" and the "Need for affirmative action" variables are measured on a 3-point continuous scale. The higher the score, the greater is the level of support. Thus those scoring 3 on the "Effect of Diversity" value diversity the most; those with a score of 0 find the least value in diversity. The "Need for affirmative action" scale is similar, with 3 representing the attitude that affirmative action is very important.

cant factors thus tend to change from issue to issue. In summary, partisanship is not a defining variable for Asian Americans as it is for whites. Moreover, unlike for blacks and Latinos, Asian American opposition to Proposition 187 is not a foregone conclusion.

The Proposition 209 Vote

The results of a logistic regression model with the Proposition 209 vote as the dependent variable are displayed in Table 5.2. Again, the equation for blacks is strikingly unilluminating. Only a respondent's view about the effect of diversity provides any explanation; a respondent's education is marginally important. The level of black support for Proposition 209 declines insignificantly as beliefs about diversity change, suggesting that the model for blacks is interesting only insofar as it clearly indicates their strongly uniform opposition to Proposition 209.

The Latino model has many more significant variables than the black model, but the strength of these effects is not very substantial (Figure 5.5). For Latinos, support for Proposition 209 declines as the strength of one's belief in the need for affirmative action increases, but less dramatically than

Table 5.2

Logistic Regression with Proposition 209 as Dependent Variable

	White	Asian	Black	Latino
Intercept	.3537	−1.6469[a]	−2.0595	−1.2010[b]
	(.8343)	(.9368)	(1.3986)	(.5880)
Factor 1: Need for	−1.6215[b]	−1.0775[b]	−.2822	−.4578[b]
affirmative action	(.1824)	(.1767)	(.2093)	(.1202)
Factor 2: Attitude toward	−.0900	.0594	−.2314	−.1403
other groups	(.1481)	(.1588)	(.2753)	(.1241)
Factor 3: Effect of diversity	−.6123[b]	−.4871[b]	−.5537[b]	−.5211[b]
	(.1664)	(.1805)	(.2524)	(.1316)
Factor 4: Economy	−.5716[b]	−.3899[b]	.0524	.3506[b]
	(.1638)	(.1661)	(.2348)	(.1299)
Age	.3310	.3427	.4418	.1569
	(.2021)	(.2247)	(.3081)	(.1688)
Democrat	−.8600[b]	−.1418	.0194	−.7141[b]
	(.3337)	(.3531)	(.6839)	(.2550)
Education	−.0566	.1246	−.2762[a]	.0098
	(.1020)	(.1141)	(.1596)	(.0840)
Ideology	.2268	.0184	.3930	.1797
	(.2257)	(.2391)	(.3191)	(.1638)
Nonminority neighborhood	−.5650[a]	−.3316	−.3981	.2919
	(.3357)	(.3433)	(.5036)	(.2675)
Gender	.5995[a]	−.3654	.1976	−.0011
	(.3234)	(.3364)	(.4645)	(.2544)
n	354	220	142	362

a. $p < .10$
b. $p < .05$

for Asian Americans and whites. The same effect is evident for the economic variables: the stronger one thinks the economy is, the less likely one is to vote for Proposition 209. Likewise, the more one believes in the value of diversity, the less likely one is to support Proposition 209. Finally, Latinos demonstrate a party effect; Democratic Latinos are less likely to vote for the proposition. However, as shown in Figure 5.5, the support levels change but not dramatically. These effects are real, but the magnitude of their impact on the Latino vote is not substantial.

Figure 5.5

Change in Support for Proposition 209 Holding All
Other Variables at Their Mean

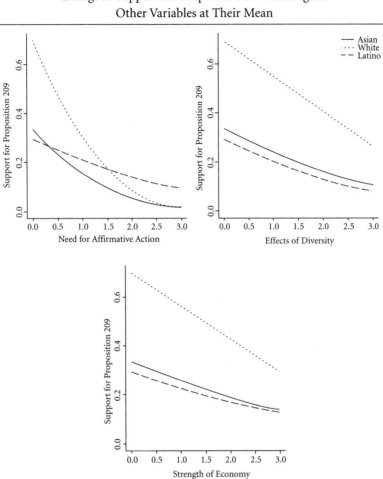

Thus the most interesting variations lie once again with the Asian American and white groups. The changes in the white response are dramatic (Figure 5.5). Levels of support for Proposition 209 decline precipitously as attitudes toward diversity and affirmative action change. These results are similar to those reported earlier for Proposition 187.

As with Proposition 187, Asian Americans hold the median position for Proposition 209—between the greater opposition of blacks and Latinos, on the one hand, and the greater support of whites, on the other. Although the impact of the various variables is less for the Asian American group than for the white group, in all significant respects, with the exception of partisanship, Asian American behavior weakly mimics white behavior. The strong effect of party on whites but not on Asian Americans is noteworthy. Party does not predict the Proposition 209 vote for blacks and Latinos because so few Republicans are in both groups. Because party positions were emphasized in the campaigns, one would expect that any variation in partisanship would serve as a source of division within a group. This expectation does not manifest itself in the Asian American attitudes, however.

CONCLUSION

Asian Americans, according to the data in this study, are the median voters. On immigration and race issues, their attitudes sit squarely between the attitudes of whites and those of other minorities. For the two measures examined here, Propositions 187 and 209, Asian Americans opposed both, but by smaller margins than blacks and Latinos. One reason may be the absence of strong party effects. Although race has increasingly defined party, and party has increasingly structured racial attitudes among whites particularly, neither is true for Asian Americans. Race does not define party for Asian Americans in the sense that Asian Americans, as a pan-ethnic category, do not have strong allegiances to one party, as is the case for blacks and Latinos. Disaggregating from the pan-ethnic category, this generalization does not hold completely for all the Asian American nationalities (for example, the Japanese are predominantly Democratic), but that caveat aside, it holds for most of the larger Asian American subgroups. Thus, uniquely among the major nonwhite minorities, Asian Americans are a genuine swing group. They are capable of voting predominantly for either party in a given election and are not bound by strong partisan identifications.

Indeed, unlike for white voters, party does not strongly influence attitudes among Asian American voters. For white voters, party is strongly correlated with views about immigration and race. In the 1994 gubernatorial race the Democratic candidate, Kathleen Brown, opposed Proposition 187, and the Republican incumbent, Pete Wilson, supported it as a centerpiece of his campaign. Exit polls and a county-based analysis of the returns revealed a similarly sharp partisan split among white voters.[12] The picture, however, is not quite so simple. White environmentalists may oppose immigration for quality of life reasons, and business-oriented groups on the right may support immigration for economic reasons. But all in all, party divisions often mirror attitudinal differences for whites. The statistical models described here, however, suggest that the pattern does not hold for Asian Americans. Asian American Republicans were no more likely to have supported Propositions 209 and 187 than Asian American Democrats. In other words, a party or candidate supporting these measures would have found a majority of the Asian Americans in his or her party in opposition to them. This finding is also consistent with the thesis that Asian American party identification seems to have less to do with race and immigration policy and more to do with other factors such as positions on economic and foreign policy matters.

As the models demonstrate, Asian American views on immigration and racial policies are derived from their perceptions of and experiences with other racial groups. Socioeconomic status and partisanship are not as prominent.[13] As noted earlier, Asian Americans have an unusually multiracial experience; only a small percentage live in majority Asian American neighborhoods. California's Asian American community has relatively positive perceptions of other racial and ethnic groups as neighbors. It also believes that the problems of discrimination are real and that the needs for programs such as affirmative action still exist. The one exception—and even here Asian Americans are relatively neutral—is undocumented aliens. This finding relates to the point made at the beginning of this chapter: Asian Americans differ from Latinos in the ratio of documented immigrants to undocumented noncitizens in their respective communities. Anyone concerned about an Asian-Latino rift might do well to focus on this aspect of immigration policy and the similarly pessimistic views both groups share about the future of race relations and the job opportunities. But on the whole, despite the Los Angeles riots in 1992 sparked by the Rodney King case and the party differences that separate Asian Americans from Latinos and blacks, Asian Americans and Latinos appear to have more in common than not on issues of race and immigration.

NOTES

The authors of this chapter would like to thank Gordon Chang, Brian Gaines, and participants at the Asian Americans and Politics Conference in Washington, D.C., March 1998, for their helpful comments.

1. On the influx of the Irish, see George E. Reedy, *From the Ward to the White House: The Irish in American Politics* (New York: Scribner's, 1991). On immigration in New York, see Nathan Glazer and Daniel P. Moynihan, *Beyond the Melting Pot* (Cambridge: MIT Press, 1963). For a polemical, contemporary argument, see Peter Brimelow, *Alien Nation: Common Sense about America's Immigration Disaster* (New York: Harper-Perennial Library, 1996).

2. See Raymond E. Wolfinger, "The Development and Persistence of Ethnic Voting," *American Political Science Review* 59 (1965): 896–908.

3. Other discussion of the swing vote potential includes Don T. Nakanishi, "The Next Swing Vote? Asian Americans and California Politics," in *Racial and Ethnic Politics*, ed. Byran O. Jackson and Michael B. Preston (Berkeley: IGS Press, 1991).

4. Personal correspondence with Stuart Spencer, former top Reagan adviser and current GOP consultant.

5. Bill Ong Hing, *Making and Remaking Asian America through Immigration Policy, 1850–1990* (Stanford: Stanford University Press, 1993).

6. Bruce E. Cain, "Racial and Ethnic Politics," in *Developments in American Politics*, Vol. 2, ed. Gillian Peele, Christopher Bailey, Bruce Cain, and B. Peters (Chatham, N.J.: Chatham House, 1995).

7. For an analysis of American attitudes to neighborhood integration in general, see, for example, William G. Mayer, *The Changing American Mind: How and Why American Public Opinion Changed between 1960 and 1988* (Ann Arbor: University of Michigan Press, 1993).

8. William L. Miller, *Electoral Dynamics in Britain since 1918* (New York: St. Martin's Press, 1977).

9. See, for example, Wendy K. Tam, "Asians—A Monolithic Voting Bloc?" *Political Behavior* 17 (1995): 223–249.

10. See, for example, Angus Campbell, Philip E. Converse, Warren E. Miller, and Donald E. Stokes, *The American Voter* (Chicago: University of Chicago Press, 1964); Norman H. Nie, Sidney Verba, and John R. Petrocik, *The Changing American Voter* (Cambridge and London: Harvard University Press, 1976); Raymond E. Wolfinger and Steven J. Rosenstone, *Who Votes?* (New Haven: Yale University Press, 1980); Warren E. Miller and J. Merrill Shanks, *The New American Voter* (Cambridge: Harvard University Press, 1996).

11. Including forty-two independent variables in a model depletes a significant number of the degrees of freedom. Even more troublesome, however, is the fact that many of the survey items attempt to tap the same attitudes. This portends a high degree of multicollinearity in the potential regressors. Thus, even if the degrees of freedom could be afforded, the high variance of the estimated coefficients is likely to produce an unnecessary and unworkable degree of insignificance.

12. Bruce E. Cain, Karin MacDonald, and Kenneth McCue, "Nativism, Partisanship, and Immigration: An Analysis of Proposition 187," paper presented at the an-

nual meeting of the American Political Science Association, San Francisco, August 29–September 1, 1996.

13. Although socioeconomic status (SES) factors are well known to have a strong relationship with political acts such as voting turnout and voter preferences, Tam shows that these general theories need to be adapted to the immigrant communities with caution. In short, SES variables have their expected impact only when immigrant communities are socialized in a fashion similar to the native community. The findings in this paper further back this claim. See Wendy K. Tam Cho, "Naturalization, Socialization, Participation: Immigrants and (Non-) Voting," *Journal of Politics* 61 (November 1999).

APPENDIX: FACTOR ANALYSIS

Each of the four factors resulting from the factor analysis was labeled, and the questions encompassed by each factor are listed below. In the actual factor analysis, a varimax rotation was used.

Factor 1. Need for affirmative action
Q6. As you know, Proposition 209 will eliminate all state and local governmental actions which in the past have provided special programs intended to benefit certain groups of people. Which of the following groups do you think still need the programs eliminated by Proposition 209?

Q6a. Blacks
Q6b. Latinos
Q6c. Asians
Q6d. Women

Factor 2. Attitude toward other groups
Q4. Now I am going to ask you what effect different groups of people have had on the quality of life in the neighborhood where you live. After I give you the name of a group, please tell me whether that group has improved, made worse, or had no effect on the quality of life in your neighborhood.

Q4a. Blacks
Q4b. Latinos
Q4c. Asians
Q4d. Illegal Immigrants
Q4e. Legal Immigrants
Q4f. Whites

Factor 3. Effect of diversity

Q10. I am going to read you some statements which some people agree with, while others do not. Please tell me if you agree strongly, agree somewhat, are neutral, disagree somewhat, or disagree strongly.

Q10a. The more good jobs and places in college provided to minorities, the fewer there are for people who are not members of those groups.

Q10d. Members of particular ethnic or racial groups use special programs to get more benefits than they deserve.

Q10e. People of different ethnic and racial groups are generally happier when they live and socialize with others of the same background.

Q11. Which of these statements comes closer to the way you feel?

1. Diversity benefits our country economically and socially, so race, ethnicity and gender should be a factor in determining the type of person who is hired, promoted or admitted to college.
2. Hiring, promotion and college admissions should be based solely on merit and qualifications and not on characteristics of race, ethnicity or gender.

Factor 4. Economic outlook

Q18. Would you say over the past year your personal finance situation has gotten better, worse or stayed the same?

Q19. What about the economy of California? Would you say over the past year it has gotten better, worse or stayed the same?

CHAPTER SIX

CHANGING OF THE GUARD? THE EMERGING IMMIGRANT MAJORITY IN ASIAN AMERICAN POLITICS

PAUL M. ONG
DAVID E. LEE

This study examines a remarkable transformation that is reshaping the nature of politics within Asian American communities, the emergence of an immigrant majority. The last quarter-century has seen three demographic transitions among Asian Americans as the population has moved from majority U.S.-born to majority immigrant: first in the adult population, then in the subgroup with citizenship, and, most recently, in the pool of voters. These changes could potentially restructure Asian American politics and the voices representing this population. While there are many other forms of politics, this study focuses on participation within the electoral arena because it is central to understanding the political life of this population. Elections are particularly important to immigrants; participation is tied to acculturation and assimilation—and to gaining political rights.

Several sources of information are used in this study, including the Current Population Survey, *Los Angeles Times* surveys of Asian Americans in southern California, voter registration rolls, a 1998 CAVEC (Chinese American Voters Education Committee) survey of Chinese American voters in San Francisco, and experiential knowledge. Each source alone has its limitations, yielding insights to only part of the emerging picture. Taken together, they provide an intriguing and consistent story, albeit an incomplete and unfinished one.

This chapter begins by examining the population dynamics and acculturation process that have produced the immigrant voting majority. The analysis indicates that the growing number of adult immigrants and the rising voter registration rate are behind this phenomenon. The chapter then examines the political orientation of naturalized Asians and, when possible, compares it with that of U.S.-born Asians. This examination yields a systematic difference in party registration, with immigrants less likely to be Democrats and more likely to have no preference. Party affiliation, however, is not a reliable measure of political orientation because identification with a party is shallow or not deeply held. Finally, the chapter takes a closer look at one potential implication of the emerging immigrant majority: the threat it poses to progressive activism, which has been an important force within Asian American communities. Although the discussion is speculative, based in part on a case study of recent events in San Francisco, what it reveals is intriguing—a possible changing of the guard in Asian American politics.

DEMOGRAPHIC TRANSITIONS

Adult Population

The three demographic transitions among Asian Americans have been driven by a renewal of large-scale immigration after the federal government eliminated racial quotas in 1965. The influx of a new wave of immigrants rapidly transformed the composition of the adult Asian American population (Table 6.1). U.S.-born Asians were still in the majority in 1970, but they became the minority a decade later. While the number of U.S.-born increased by about 250,000 from 1970 to 1980, the number of foreign-born increased by over 250,000 for the same period. The difference in growth rates continued in the 1980s as the U.S.-born grew by over 250,000 and the foreign-born by over 2 million, increasing the immigrant share of the adult population by an additional 9 percentage points. The U.S.-born regained some ground during the 1990s, but today naturalized immigrants still outnumber the U.S.-born. This trend will probably continue in the twenty-first century.[1]

Citizenship

Among those with citizenship, the U.S.-born lost ground after 1965, and in the mid-1980s they went from being a majority to a minority among those eligible to vote. The emergence of an immigrant majority among citizens was driven by an increase in the 1980s in the overall naturalization rate (the

Table 6.1
Asian American Adult Population, United States, 1970–1996

	Total Asian Americans (thousands)	Percent U.S.-born	Percent Naturalized	Percent Noncitizen Foreign-Born
1970	969	52	20	28
1980	2,498	30	25	45
1990	4,938	21	34	45
1996	6,775	24	33	43

Sources: Paul Ong and Don T. Nakanishi, "Becoming Citizens, Becoming Voters: The Naturalization and Political Participation of Asian Pacific Immigrants," in *The State of Asian Pacific America: Reframing the Immigration Debate* (Los Angeles: LEAP Asian Pacific American Public Policy Institute and UCLA Asian American Studies Center, 1996); and Current Population Survey, November 1996.

Note: Adults are persons eighteen years and older. Numbers for most recent years include a small number of Pacific Islanders.

naturalized population as a percentage of the immigrant population) and the continued growth in the absolute number of immigrants during the 1990s. The temporal change in the naturalization rate is evident in the bottom row of Table 6.2. The rate increased from 36 percent in 1980 to 43 percent in 1990 and remained at roughly 43–44 percent in the early 1990s. The rate increase in the 1980s, however, is misleading, or at least an incomplete picture. The most important factor determining naturalization is length of residency in the United States. As the statistics in Table 6.2 reveal, there is considerable consistency in the naturalization rates within cohorts by length of residency. A comparison by cohorts shows that Asian immigrants are naturalizing at a pace equal to or greater than that for non-Hispanic whites and Latinos. In other words, Asian immigrants are no more resistant to becoming citizens than their counterparts from other parts of the world.

The one group of Asians exhibiting a noticeable temporal variation is made up of longtime residents (twenty or more years). The lower rate in 1970 among longtime residents stemmed from the dominance of pre–World War II immigrants, many of whom had been prohibited from becoming citizens for much of their lives. This historic exclusion left a legacy by dampening the desire to naturalize even after the government abolished the racist restriction on the right to citizenship. The influence of this history waned, however, with the passage of time and the passing of this generation. For

Table 6.2

Naturalization Rates of Adult Immigrants, United States, 1970–1996
(percent)

	Asians				Non-Hispanic Whites	Latinos
	1970	1980	1990	1996	1996	1996
Number of years in United States						
0–10	17	19	19	16	14	8
11–20	67	67	66	64	59	27
Over 20	68	79	81	88	83	64
All	41	36	43	44	54	23

Sources: Public Use Micro Samples, 1970, 1980, 1990; Current Population Survey, November 1996.

post-1965 immigrants, the data indicate that about nine in ten will eventually become citizens, with some attaining this status later in life than others.

As noted, the increase in the overall naturalization rate in the 1980s (from 36 percent to 43 percent), combined with dramatic growth in the absolute number of immigrant adults (from 1.2 million to 3.9 million), was sufficient to create an immigrant majority among Asian American citizens. The pattern changed in the 1990s, but not enough to eliminate the immigrant majority. The relative number of U.S.-born increased during that period, in part because of the maturing of the American-born children of immigrants. At the same time, the overall naturalization rate stopped increasing; it had reached a plateau of around 43–44 percent. This leveling off in the rate was offset by the continued growth in the number of adult Asian immigrants, from 3.9 million in 1990 to 5.2 million in 1996. This expanding population base and the constant naturalization rate were sufficient to maintain the immigrant majority among Asian American citizens.

What Table 6.2 does not show are the variations by ethnicity and the interest in becoming citizens among those not yet naturalized. Table 6.3 partially fills that gap by providing data on four Asian groups in southern California. The table indicates that most Vietnamese, Chinese, and Filipino immigrants want to become U.S. citizens. About two-thirds of the Chinese and Filipinos achieved that status, a high rate that reflects in part the fact

Table 6.3

Asian Naturalization Rates in Southern California, by Ethnic Group
(percent)

Group	Naturalized (A)	Intend to Naturalize (B)	(A) + (B)
Korean	34	25	59
Vietnamese	48	42	90
Chinese	66	25	91
Filipino	67	22	89

Source: *Los Angeles Times* surveys, No. 276, February–March 1992; No. 331, March–April 1994; No. 350, November 1994; No. 370, December 1995; No. 396, May 1997.

that these groups are more established in the United States. Slightly less than half of the Vietnamese were citizens, a lower rate that can be attributed to the relatively recent arrival of this population, most of whom came to this country in 1975 or later. Although information is not available on Asian Indian immigrants, the national data reported by Aneesh Chopra et al. indicate that a majority (56 percent) of this population is naturalized.[2] Of those not yet citizens in southern California, a large majority of Vietnamese, Chinese, and Filipinos intend to become citizens. Interestingly, when the percentage of those already citizens is combined with the percentage of those planning to become citizens, the results indicate that nine out of ten will be citizens, a finding consistent with the long-run statistics in Table 6.1. Koreans are the exception to the pattern of high rates of actual and desired naturalization. Only a quarter were citizens at the time of the 1992 *Los Angeles Times* survey, and their low propensity to naturalize holds even after accounting for number of years in the United States. Moreover, only a minority of the noncitizens intend to become naturalized. There is no good explanation for this pattern.[3]

Voter Registration Rates

Although the naturalization rate of Asians did not increase during the 1990s, the voter registration rate among naturalized Asians did increase enough to produce a third demographic transition, the emergence of an immigrant majority among registered Asian American voters. By the late 1980s, immigrants already constituted a majority of Asian American citi-

Table 6.4

Asian American Registration and Voting Rates, 1996

	Percent Who Registered to Vote	Percent Who Actually Voted
Naturalized		
Pre-1965	64	52
1965–1974	61	48
1975–1985	54	42
1986–1996	57	46
Overall	57	44
U.S.-born	57	45

Source: Current Population Survey, November 1996.

zens, but they were still a minority among Asian American registered voters because of a low registration rate.[4] Even in the early 1990s, slightly less than half of naturalized immigrants had signed up to vote, whereas a majority of U.S.-born had done so. This difference soon changed. By 1996 the registration rates were identical (Table 6.4). The increase in voter registration was particularly pronounced among more recent immigrants. Prior to 1996, registration rates were highly correlated with length of residency in the United States; the rate for long-timers was twice as high as that for newcomers. By 1996 the rates were fairly uniform across the cohorts reported in Table 6.4. Combined with a larger population base, the increase in overall registration among naturalized Asians was sufficient to create an immigrant majority (58 percent) among registered Asian Americans. Moreover, because the voter turnout rates were nearly identical for both groups, immigrants were a majority of the voting Asians (58 percent) as well.

Although the national data indicate that the emergence of an immigrant majority is a recent phenomenon, the transition probably occurred earlier for some regions than for others. In states such as Hawaii, U.S.-born Asian Americans still constitute a clear majority of the adult population and the voting population. In California the transition occurred in the 1990s. In the *Los Angeles Times* exit poll for the 1992 elections in California, 58 percent of the Asian Americans interviewed were immigrants. This percentage may be biased downward because those with limited English language skills may have been less willing to be interviewed. The use of absentee ballots also may affect the estimate. An analysis of the San Francisco voting rolls indicates that immigrants are more likely to vote through the mail. Despite the limitations of exit polls, the results of those conducted in 1992 suggest that by then immigrants were a majority, albeit a small majority, of registered Asian Americans and of Asian American voters. By the mid-1990s immigrants were well established as a majority. In fact, 62 percent of the Asian Americans on the 1996 registration rolls for San Francisco and Alameda County were foreign-born. One might reasonably hypothesize, then, that an immigrant majority emerged in California in the early 1990s, if not earlier.

This analysis sheds some light on the much-publicized increase in Asian American naturalization and voter registration in response to anti-immigrant sentiments. A September 16, 1996, article in the *San Jose Mercury News* is representative of the naturalization argument. The headline read "Citizenship classes inundated—fear of impending welfare cuts spurs signups by legal immigrants," and it went on to report that demand for enrollment in English-as-a-second-language classes had gone up by as much as 1,000 percent in less than three months. Furthermore, the article cited an astounding statistic from the U.S. Immigration and Naturalization Service (INS). Some 1.1 million U.S. immigrants had become citizens that year, 1996, breaking the previous record set in 1944 when 441,979 foreign-born residents became citizens. Reporter Carolyn Jung declared that the region was in the midst of an unprecedented immigrant citizenship boom.

If increased naturalization has had a measurable impact, it appears to be concentrated. As noted earlier, citizenship rates have increased secularly for those in the country the longest (more than twenty years), but this growth occurred over the last quarter of the twentieth century. Certainly, the higher rates during the 1970s, and perhaps also the 1980s, stemmed from the replacement of pre–World War II immigrants, who had suffered from blatant racism, by post–World War II immigrants who were subjected to less-overt discrimination. The increase during the 1990s, however, may well have been driven by the growing fear of not being a citizen. Unfortunately, the increase in the naturalization rate of those resident in the United States at least twenty years was offset by a decrease in rates for more recent immigrants (those in the country no more than ten years and those in the country eleven to twenty years). Consequently, the naturalization rate for all Asian immigrants did not change significantly between 1990 and 1996. If there was an acceleration in the overall naturalization process, it would have occurred after 1996. Moreover, the data indicate that the achievement of significant future gains will depend on increasing the ability and willingness of the more recent immigrants to become citizens.

Registering to vote as a response to growing anti-immigrant sentiments appears to be more pronounced than the naturalization response. Efforts to register immigrants with citizenship are not new. Organizations such as CAVEC (Chinese American Voters Education Committee) in the San Francisco Bay Area were established to promote voting (and naturalization).[5] Today, organizations such as APPPCON (Asian Pacific Policy and Planning Council), a consortium of community-based organizations in Los Angeles, are launching new campaigns promoting political participation. These recent efforts are reactions to proposed changes in the law that could have profound implications for Asian immigrants, such as the Personal Responsibility and Work Opportunity Reconciliation Act of 1996 (welfare reform) and California's Proposition 227, which severely restricts the use of bilingual education in public schools.

It is difficult to gauge the effectiveness of the registration drives. Some argue that the outcomes are significant. For example, Jack Vaitayanonta asserts that "efforts on the part of activist interest groups led to increased APA [Asian Pacific American] voter registration and turnout and naturalization in 1996."[6] Because the registration drives coincided with the jump in registration, particularly among recent immigrants, it is clear that whatever stimulates immigrants to participate in electoral politics has had its most profound impact on newer citizens. This finding is not surprising because this group probably feels that it has much to lose from anti-immigrant sentiments. One must not, however, mistake the temporal correlation between the registration drives and increased registration for causality. Undoubtedly, Asian American groups have made a concerted and sincere effort to promote political participation, but it was a common historical event (the rise of anti-immigrant sentiments) that motivated the activists to action and also prompted immigrants to become involved. The result was a landmark event during the mid-1990s—the emergence of an immigrant political base.

POLITICAL ORIENTATION

The emergence of an immigrant majority is reshaping the political orientation of Asian American voters. One indicator of this development is party affiliation.[7] The changes in Monterey Park—a California city that had a majority Asian American population in 1990—illustrate this phenomenon.[8] In 1984 Chinese American Democrats outnumbered their Republican counterparts 43 percent to 31 percent. Five years later, after a significant increase in registration by immigrants, Chinese American Republicans slightly out-numbered their Democratic counterparts 37 percent to 35 percent. The shifting of partisanship has differentiated Asian Americans from other ethnic/racial groups. For California, the 1992 *Los Angeles Times* exit poll indicated that Asian Americans were closer to non-Hispanic whites in party affiliation than the other minority groups. Forty-two percent of Asian Americans were Democrats—compared with 40 percent of whites, 70 percent of Latinos, and 80 percent of blacks—and 40 percent of Asian Americans were Republicans—compared with 46 percent of whites, 16 percent of Latinos, and 8 percent of blacks. In the much more liberal Bay Area, Asian Americans in 1996 were less likely to be Democrats than non-Asians (43 percent to 62 percent), and they were more likely to be Republicans than non-Asians, but not by much (23 percent to 19 percent). The biggest difference between the two groups was the percentage not affiliated with the two major parties—34 percent of Asian Americans compared with only 19 percent of non-Asians. For Asians, then, the choice is not just which party but also whether to identify with a party at all. An astonishing one-third has chosen to be unattached.

Asian American voters demonstrate considerable heterogeneity across subgroups (Table 6.5). As a general rule, in both northern and southern California foreign-born Asian Americans are less likely to be Democrats and more likely to be Republicans. Among immigrants, there are sizable differences in party affiliation. For example, although a majority of the Vietnamese in southern California are Republican (which is probably related to the strong anticommunist sentiment in this predominantly political refugee population), Koreans, Chinese, and Filipinos are more evenly divided between the two major parties, with neither party claiming a majority. A noticeable difference between immigrants and U.S.-born Asian Americans is the extent of nonaffiliation. Immigrants are less likely to affiliate with either of the two major parties (Table 6.5).

The immigrant–U.S.-born difference in party affiliation holds across class lines (see Table 6.6, an analysis based on the median income of neighborhoods). Although there is a danger of an ecological fallacy (that is, incorrectly ascribing the characteristics of the geographic unit to individuals), the patterns reported in Table 6.6 are consistent with the literature, which finds a correlation between income and the likelihood of being a Republican. For both foreign-born and U.S.-born Asian Americans, the percentage of Democrats drops only for the highest income category. By contrast, the percentage of Republicans increases across most of the income range. A com-

Table 6.5

Party Affiliation of Asian Americans, San Francisco/
Alameda County and Southern California
(percent)

	Democrat	Republican	Other
San Francisco and Alameda County			
All Asians	43	23	34
U.S.-born	52	20	28
Foreign-born	41	23	36
Southern California			
U.S.-born	44	38	18
Foreign-born			
Vietnamese	24	62	14
Korean	42	48	10
Chinese	27	28	45
Filipino	35	41	25

Source: CAVEC and *Los Angeles Times* surveys, various years.

parison of the two groups within income categories reveals that foreign-
born Asian Americans are more likely to be Republicans or unaffiliated.

Party affiliation, however, may not be a highly reliable measure of political orientation for Asian Americans. When they state a party preference,
most are not strongly attached to that party,[9] and support for candidates
based on party is not consistent over time.[10] The data collected for this
study suggest that party affiliation is partly emulating the predominant
choice within the larger environment. For example, Asian immigrants are
much more likely to be Democrats in liberal northern California than in the
relatively more conservative southern California. Even the Vietnamese,
known for their conservative leanings, appear subject to a strong regional
influence: Republicans outnumber Democrats by more than two to one in
southern California, but the opposite is true in San Francisco. Zip code–
level data for Alameda County (Oakland) show an extremely strong correlation between the political party composition of Asian immigrants and that
of their non-Asian neighbors. This may stem from voting with one's feet
(that is, selecting a local government and neighborhood through residential
choice), which produces neighborhoods in which residents share similar
tastes. Most people, however, do not choose a neighborhood based on party

Table 6.6

Party Affiliation of Asian Americans by Median Income
of Neighborhood, Alameda County
(percent)

Neighborhood Median Income	Party Affiliation		
	Democratic	Republican	Other
Foreign-born			
<$34K	42	27	38
$34K–$41K	42	27	31
$42K–$47K	42	29	29
$48K+	36	33	31
U.S.-born			
<$34K	60	17	24
$34K–$41K	61	20	19
$42K–$47K	59	23	19
$48K+	53	28	19

Note: Sum may be greater than 100 percent because of rounding. The income categories are based on the median incomes for zip code areas as reported in the 1990 census. The categories contain roughly equal numbers of registered foreign-born Asians.

Source: 1996 voter registration rolls, Alameda County, California.

composition. They consider instead the quality of education, housing, and other nonpolitical factors. Thus, although there is no concrete evidence to verify or reject the hypothesis, the available evidence is consistent with the assertion that many Asian Americans, and immigrants in particular, do not hold a party affiliation based on a deeply held political philosophy.

For alternative measures of political orientation, the results are mixed (Table 6.7). When asked to choose an ideological label, U.S.-born and foreign-born Asian Americans produce very similar responses. The plurality falls in the middle, and there are more conservatives than liberals. The similarity disappears, however, in actual voting records on the candidates; the U.S.-born are less likely to vote for Republicans. For voting records on state initiatives, the outcomes are mixed and only slightly different. An overwhelming majority of both groups supported the three-strike initiative (Proposition 184), which prescribed a mandatory sentence for persons convicted of a third serious crime. Both groups were equally divided on Propo-

Table 6.7

Alternative Measures of Political Orientation among
Asian Americans, 1992 Election
(percent)

	Foreign-Born Voters	U.S.-Born Voters
Political ideology		
Liberal	19	21
Middle	49	49
Conservative	32	30
U.S. Senate race		
Feinstein (D)	48	54
Huffington (R)	45	30
Gubernatorial race		
Brown (D)	42	61
Wilson (R)	57	30
State initiatives (percent yes)		
Proposition 184 (three strikes)	81	77
Proposition 187		
(illegal immigrants)	46	46

Source: 1992 *Los Angeles Times* exit poll.

sition 187, which prohibited illegal immigrants from receiving publicly supported services. Asian Americans may hesitate to support initiatives approved by non-Asian voters out of fear that the proposition is not just about
undocumented aliens but is a part of the growing anti-immigrant sentiments. Exit polls conducted by the Asian Law Caucus in the San Francisco
Bay Area and the Asian Pacific Legal Center in Los Angeles revealed that opposition to Proposition 187 was greater in neighborhoods with high concentrations of Asian Americans, which also tend to have a higher percentage of immigrants. This pattern implies that Asian immigrants felt they had
the most to lose and thus were more likely to vote against the initiative.

The vote on Proposition 187 indicates the potential for ethnic-based or
race-based voting. This group behavior is certainly not new in American
politics, and other examples of this behavior among Asian immigrants are
available. For example, in Monterey Park, the vast majority of Chinese
voted in 1988 and again in 1990 along ethnic lines (for a Chinese American candidate), with the most recent immigrants exhibiting the strongest
ethnic affinity.[11] Another example comes from a 1998 pre-election survey

of Chinese voters in San Francisco sponsored by CAVEC. Among the immigrants who expressed an opinion (51 percent), those supporting Matt Fong, the Republican U.S. Senate candidate, outnumbered those supporting Democrat Barbara Boxer by four to one. Even among Chinese immigrants registered as Democrats, the ratio was three to one in favor of Fong, indicating that ethnic affinity is stronger than party affiliation. Ethnic-oriented voting, however, may be even stronger than indicated by the preference for U.S. senator. For example, in the 1998 CAVEC survey, 88 percent of the Chinese American respondents offered an opinion on Proposition 227, which would have severely restricted bilingual education in the state's public schools, whereas only 51 percent offered an opinion on the Senate race. Moreover, the responses on the initiative were very one-sided—73 percent expressed their support and 15 percent their opposition. The high response rate probably stemmed from the fact that Chinese Americans found bilingual education to be important to their community and their children.

Little is known about whether ethnic-oriented voting among Asian immigrants extends to pan-Asian-oriented voting. Other studies have revealed that some Asian American groups are willing to support Asian American candidates not of their own ethnicity. For example, Japanese American voters in Monterey Park (including immigrants) crossed ethnic lines to support a Chinese American candidate, exhibiting some degree of racial unity.[12] It is unclear, however, whether significant numbers of Asian immigrants would cross ethnic lines to support an Asian candidate. Pan-Asian solidarity at this time is more a possibility than a reality for Asian immigrant voters.

Finally, although Asian immigrants are a part of a minority group that has been subjected to past acts of overt racism, they are not strongly aligned with the civil rights agenda. For many immigrants, Asian American history is not their history, so they have no sense of membership in a historically victimized population. Although Asian immigrants do experience discrimination, many attribute that discrimination to cultural and linguistic differences rather than race. Moreover, discrimination against Asian Americans is far less extensive and severe than that faced by African Americans and Latinos. As a consequence of this contemporary status and a lack of history, most Asian immigrants do not readily support minority-oriented efforts and programs. For example, only 32 percent of the immigrants in the CAVEC survey opposed Proposition 209, the initiative to end the use of affirmative action programs in the public sector (it was on a ballot prior to the survey). While 32 percent of Chinese voters polled in the June 1998 survey opposed Proposition 209 compared with 21 percent who supported it, 48 percent did not even know about the issue. In other words, a plurality was ambivalent about this heated wedge issue, and even though the majority of those with an opinion opposed it, a sizable minority also supported it. The lack of support for affirmative action may be rooted in the perception that affirmative action hurts Asian Americans. When asked about their opinions on admission quotas for San Francisco's elite public Lowell High School, 45 percent of the immigrant respondents thought it was a "bad idea," 32 percent thought it was a "good idea," and 23 percent expressed no opinion. The opposition is not surprising because quotas have restricted the number of academically qualified Chinese admitted while increasing the number of other minorities. A third, however, supported the plan despite this differential impact, indicating potential for support for the broad civil rights agenda. The most accurate observation may be that most Asian immigrants are likely to vote against measures they view as discriminatory toward their own ethnic group, but they have not yet formed strong opinions about many of the issues that matter to most other minorities.

CHANGING OF THE GUARD?

The emergence of an immigrant majority can have profound implications for Asian American politics. One impact of such a majority is the threat it might pose to progressive activists, who constitute one of the most visible forces representing this population.[13] At the core of this group are those activists who cut their teeth on the social movements of the late 1960s and early 1970s, particularly those aligned with the civil rights movement, the War on Poverty, and the ethnic studies movement. In fact, they were the leaders of the "Asian American Movement," which had its heyday between 1965 and 1980.[14] The more recent generation of progressive activists has tended to be a loose collection of social service providers, civil rights advocates, and their supporters, who share a liberal or progressive agenda centered on social justice, economic equality, and ethnic/racial pride. Another prominent characteristic of both the first and subsequent generations of progressives is the dominance of U.S.-born Asian Americans, particularly in leadership roles. In major urban areas, they have emerged as the primary spokespersons for the "Asian American community" by displacing the leaders of older and more politically conservative ethnic institutions rooted in earlier waves of Asian immigrants.

While many of the progressive activists have been self-described radicals, at least some were involved in mainstream politics at the early stages of the Asian American Movement, and, over time, more have moved from alternative politics to electoral politics. They have worked within and through traditional institutions with the goal of establishing a visible Asian American presence. Despite some flirtation with third-party alternatives, most have accepted the established parties as a realistic channel for political empowerment and for airing Asian American concerns. Not surprising, they have mainly aligned themselves with the Democratic Party; they find Democrats more sympathetic to minority and Asian American causes. This sympathy was evident in the campaign for Japanese American redress carried out during the 1970s and 1980s; Democrats spearheaded the required legislation.[15] Moreover, many of the Asian Americans elected to public office are Democrats who occasionally worked with the activists on Asian American issues.[16] Thus through electoral politics and the Democratic Party, the activists have been able to assume the role of visible and vocal spokespersons for Asian Americans.

Ironically, it was the very small numbers of naturalized and voting Asian immigrants that created an opportunity for the progressives to gain prominence. This situation produced an interesting juxtaposition of the two groups, with U.S.-born Asian Americans dominating organizations whose legitimacy depended in large part on representing foreign-born Asians. This dominance is a component of a larger phenomenon within the social service and advocacy communities, whose leaders are primarily U.S.-born Asian Americans and whose clients and constituents are immigrants.[17]

An intriguing question is whether progressive activists can continue to represent the new immigrant majority, which is less liberal, less aligned with the civil rights agenda, and less affiliated with the Democratic Party. Differences in political priorities between the progressive leadership and the voting base can create a sense of alienation on the part of the immigrants; however, this sense alone is probably not sufficient to displace the progressives. What is required is the emergence of alternative political forces. Some challengers are Republican loyalists, a few of whom have won elections in non-Asian districts. The interest here, however, is not with this group, whose members are often only marginally tied to politics within Asian American communities. They are challenging the prominence of progressives by becoming prominent through nonethnic channels. This discussion will focus on the challengers who are actively seeking to become the new voice for the immigrant majority, and in doing so are coming into direct conflict with the progressives over who will be able to organize and represent Asian Americans.

Recent events in San Francisco indicate that such a process is starting. The changes have centered on the San Francisco Neighborhood Association (SFNA), an organization established in 1995 to represent immigrant Chinese American homeowners. The organization is largely an immigrant Chinese American citizens group led by two Chinese American immigrants new to such ventures. Many of the active members are even newer to electoral politics. Of the sample of 128 Chinese Americans who received voter registration forms during an SFNA forum, an overwhelming majority were foreign-born and first-time voters, and less than a quarter were registered as Democrats (71 percent were registered as "Decline to State"). Unlike the social service activists of the 1970s and 1980s, the new Chinese activists are organizing around "quality of life" issues and around property rights rather than social justice.

Since its establishment, SFNA has compiled a remarkable record of victories. It began by quashing the Residential Code Amendment (RCA), a proposal to limit the expansion and destruction of older homes in San Francisco, thereby preserving "neighborhood character." For many Chinese homeowners, who constituted about a fifth of all homeowners in the city, the RCA was a threat to their property rights. Using a weekly SFNA-sponsored Cantonese radio talk show (Voice of the Neighborhood), the nascent leaders tapped into what one observer described as a "wellspring of pent-up frustration stemming from a century of political isolationism" in San Francisco's ethnic Chinese community. Employing confrontational tactics reminiscent of those used earlier by progressive activists, SFNA and its supporters beat back the RCA. The organizing effort was described as a "stunning victory for the San Francisco Neighborhood Association, a month-old, largely Chinese American, homeowners' coalition."[18]

Six months later, in March 1996, SFNA was in the headlines again, this time over its opposition to a city-proposed ban on the sale of live animals for food—a proposal that would have had a disproportionate impact on Chinatown. Unlike issues such as Proposition 209, live-animal sales were something new Chinese immigrants were familiar with. In the 1998 CAVEC survey, 83 percent of Chinese American registered voters supported the right of merchants to sell live animals for food; only 8 percent felt such sales were cruel to animals. The social service agencies and social justice advocacy organizations were slow to act on this issue, because the right to sell live animals as food did not readily fit within the progressive agenda. Moreover, many of the leaders of these agencies and organizations were unaware of the depth of concern over this issue because of the language and cultural gap with the immigrants. SFNA, however, was more than willing to fill the political void created by a lack of attention from progressives. It mobilized Chinese merchants and their supporters by characterizing the prohibition as a racist affront to the Chinese community. In response to this pressure politics, the Board of Supervisors eventually decided not to adopt the recommendation. As for the SFNA, in pursuing and winning this fight, it was able to expand beyond its initial base of homeowners and gain credibility within the broader immigrant community.

In 1997 the San Francisco Neighborhood Association plunged into the cutthroat world of San Francisco electoral politics. Using what was by then a form of populist politics in California, SFNA became involved through an initiative drive that centered on the Central Freeway, a major transportation artery damaged by the 1988 Loma Prieta earthquake. Claiming that this infrastructure was vital to Chinese Americans who had used it to commute to and from work, SFNA launched a drive to put the rebuilding of the freeway on the ballot. By then, the organization had developed a repertoire of effective public relations techniques. It conducted its early organizing through the SFNA Cantonese radio talk show, a primary vehicle for mobilizing supporters for press events. The press events generated additional coverage from the Chinese news media, which reached thousands more voters. As the campaign progressed, volunteers spent weekends gathering signatures to qualify the initiative, known as Proposition H. In three weeks SFNA gathered some thirty thousand signatures, enough to place the proposition on the November 4, 1997, ballot. To the surprise of many, SFNA won. A front-page article in the *San Francisco Chronicle* reported on the astonishing success of the citizen-sponsored ballot initiative, using phrases like "political earthquake" and "triumphant emergence of a new force" to recount how a largely immigrant Chinese American citizens group led by two Chinese American immigrants had taken on every major political force in San Francisco—including Mayor Willie Brown, a majority of the Board of Supervisors, the San Francisco Democratic Central Committee, San Francisco Tomorrow (a citizens group and urban environmental organization), and both the city's major daily newspapers and its alternative news media—and won.[19]

A movement that is able to shake up San Francisco's political establishment certainly has the power to restructure Asian American politics. This development, then, presents a major challenge to progressive activists, who had dreamed of the day when Asian Americans would emerge as a major political force. They got their wish in the form of a larger voter base, but it is highly questionable that they are finding many supporters among immigrants. The progressive leadership has not been able or willing to address many of the daily concerns of the new majority. Thus San Francisco and other areas such as Monterey Park have witnessed the emergence of new ethnic-specific forces to fill the political vacuum. It is unclear whether SFNA will mature into a viable and sustainable organization, but even if it does not, the underlying conditions will continue to offer opportunities to others to form alternatives to the progressives. In a worst-case scenario, the new forces will supplant the progressives as the voices representing Asian Americans, an ironic repeat of the dethroning of the prior political establishment two decades ago, now only with a different victim.

CONCLUSION

The analysis presented in this chapter demonstrates the remarkable transformation under way in Asian American politics with the growth of the immigrant voting population. Some elements are not in dispute. On average, in its ideological orientation and political concerns this group is distinctly different from the old Asian American activist group. The leaders of the progressive old guard have been promoting naturalization and voter participation, but they have not formulated an effective strategy to incorporate a meaningful segment of the newly emerging majority into their camp. Activists' inability to find a common ground has created a crisis of legitimacy for the progressive activists, undermining their ability to continue as spokespersons for Asian Americans. But the resulting political vacuum did not remain empty for long, as demonstrated by the events in San Francisco. There and elsewhere are formidable political entrepreneurs who share and understand the daily concerns of the new majority and are able to assume the mantle of leadership.

Yet the dislocation of the old progressive guard is not inevitable. As we have seen, the emerging immigrant majority is a heterogeneous and evolving group in composition and political orientation. Continued acculturation will refine the concerns and values of these immigrants, creating perhaps a stronger sense of a minority identity. The old guard, then, will have opportunities to influence this political development, but that will require a revolutionary change in the way it operates. Even within the best scenario, however, the old guard will have to share the podium with others. The world of Asian American politics has changed and will continue to change.

NOTES

1. Based on projections by Paul Ong and Suzanne Hee, "The Growth of the Asian Pacific American Population: Twenty Million in 2020," in *The State of Asian Pacific America: Policy Issues to the Year 2020* (Los Angeles: LEAP Asian Pacific American Public Policy Institute and UCLA Asian American Studies Center, 1993), 11–23.

2. Aneesh Chopra, Ajay Kuntamukkala, and Keith Reeves, "Survey of the Public Policy Concerns of Indian Americans," *Asian American Policy Review* 7 (1997): 115–131.

3. One could argue that the 1992 L.A. civil unrest (riots), which disproportionately affected Koreans, made this group disenchanted with life in the United States; however, the survey was conducted just prior to the civil unrest. It is likely that even before the 1992 riots many Koreans felt alienated because they were economically marginalized when they assumed the role as merchants in black and Latino areas. That alienation translated into a low naturalization rate. See Paul Ong and Suzanne Hee, "Lists of the Damaged Properties and Korean Merchants and the L.A. Riot/ Rebellion," in *Losses in the Los Angeles Civil Unrest: April 29–May 1, 1992* (Los Angeles: UCLA Center for Pacific Rim Studies, 1993).

4. Paul Ong and Don T. Nakanishi, "Becoming Citizens, Becoming Voters: The Naturalization and Political Participation of Asian Pacific Immigrants," in *The State of Asian Pacific America: Reframing the Immigration Debate* (Los Angeles: LEAP Asian Pacific American Public Policy Institute and UCLA Asian American Studies Center, 1996), 275–303.

5. William Chin, "Cultivating the Asian Pacific American Vote: A Survey of Voter Registration Strategies in the San Francisco Bay Area," in *National Asian Pacific American Political Almanac,* ed. Don T. Nakanishi (Los Angeles: UCLA Asian American Studies Center, 1996).

6. Jack Vaitayanonta, "Asian American Political Participation, Voting Patterns and the Reshaping of American Politics, 1984–1996," *Asian American Policy Review* 7 (1997): 183–199.

7. Grant Din, "An Analysis of Asian/Pacific American Registration and Voting Patterns in San Francisco," M.A. thesis, Claremont Graduate School, 1984; and Don T. Nakanishi, *The UCLA Asian Pacific American Voter Registration Study* (Los Angeles: Asian Pacific American Legal Center, 1986).

8. Don T. Nakanishi, "The Next Swing Vote: Asian Pacific Americans and California Politics," in *Racial and Ethnic Politics in California,* ed. Bryan O. Jackson and Michael B. Preston (Berkeley: IGS Press, 1991), 25–54.

9. Chopra et al., "Survey of the Public Policy Concerns of Indian Americans."

10. Vaitayanonta, "Asian American Political Participation."

11. John Horton, "The Politics of Ethnic Change: Grass-Roots Responses to Economic and Demographic Restructuring in Monterey Park, California," *Urban Geography* 10 (1989): 578–592; and Leland T. Saito and John Horton, "The New Chinese Immigration and the Rise of Asian American Politics in Monterey Park, California," in *The New Asian Immigration in Los Angeles and Global Restructuring,* ed. Paul Ong, Edna Bonacich, and Lucie Cheng (Philadelphia: Temple University Press, 1994).

12. Saito and Horton, "New Chinese Immigration."

13. Our definition of progressive politics and activists within Asian American politics is a useful conceptual construction for the purpose of this chapter, but we recognize that this group is very heterogeneous and that many activists would find our definition too broad and even objectionable. Its analytical usefulness, however, is that it allows a comparison of this group with the newly emerging immigrant majority.

14. See the insightful discussions about this political phenomenon in: Yen Le Espiritu and Paul Ong, "Class Constraints on Racial Solidarity among Asian Americans," in *The New Asian Immigration in Los Angeles and Global Restructuring,* ed. Paul Ong, Edna Bonacich, and Lucie Cheng (Philadelphia: Temple University Press, 1994), 295–321; and William Wei, *The Asian American Movement* (Philadelphia: Temple University Press, 1993).

15. Harry H. L. Kitano and Mitchell Maki, "Japanese American Redress: The Proper Alignment Model," *Asian American Policy Review* 7 (1997): 55–72.

16. Nakanishi, "Next Swing Vote"; and Don T. Nakanishi, ed., *National Asian Pacific American Political Almanac* (Los Angeles: UCLA Asian American Studies Center, 1996).

17. Espiritu and Ong, "Class Constraints on Racial Solidarity."

18. Kandace Bender, "Home Expansion: A Hot Issue," *San Francisco Examiner,* July 23, 1995.

19. Edward Epstein and Ramon G. McLeod, "New S.F. Voter Bloc Shows Clout, Chinese Americans Were Key to Freeway Retrofit Ballot Victory," *San Francisco Chronicle,* November 5, 1997, A1.

CHAPTER SEVEN

VOTING PARTICIPATION: RACE, GENDER, AND THE COMPARATIVE STATUS OF ASIAN AMERICAN WOMEN

PEI-TE LIEN

The dual identities of *Asian* and *female* emit contrary signals about the likelihood of Asian American women participating in U.S. elections.[1] On the one hand, Asian women belong to a racialized group that, despite its remarkable level of socioeconomic achievement, has voting registration and turnout rates that do not compare well with those of other groups of Americans.[2] On the other hand, Asian women also belong to a gender group whose members have been able to overcome generations of underparticipation. In recent elections they registered and voted at rates at least on a par with those of Asian males.[3] Which of these two identities—race or gender—may prevail in determining the likelihood that Asian women will participate in electoral politics? And how does their experience differ from that of other groups of men and women?

Unfortunately, the literature on mass political behavior provides few clues about the answers to these questions. Past research on the gender gap in mass political behavior has tended to base its findings almost exclusively on observations of the white-dominated electorate. When the opinions of African and Hispanic Americans were the focus in a small number of empirical studies, the evidence of a gap appeared to be somewhat mixed and its contours different.[4] When the role of gender among Asian Americans has been examined at all, the research has been limited in geographic region, sample size, or both.[5] Moreover, almost all of these studies have been driven by empirical concerns. There has been very little attempt to theorize gender roles and

173

their possible intersections with race and class. Particularly lacking in this type of research is an account of women of color whose experiences "formed through the intersecting processes of racial formation, labor exploitation, and gender subordination" may manifest political differences that set them apart from white males and females with similar characteristics.[6]

According to recent Current Population Surveys (CPS) collected each March by the U.S. Bureau of the Census, Asian American women have attained an overall level of educational achievement and income status comparable to or even surpassing that of non-Hispanic white women. Their seemingly privileged socioeconomic position presents an interesting opportunity to study the interactive effect of race and gender on a group of nonwhite women whose economic class is not predominantly a lower one. The case of Asian American women is an intriguing one, for, as explained later, their apparent prosperity in the present day may not shield them from sexual and racial discrimination in the economic sphere. The intersectionality of race, class, and gender studied here suggests that race may matter more than gender in structuring the political behavior of Asian American women. This thesis is developed in the rest of this chapter by examining the comparative status of Asian Americans in the national setting, statistically tested with census data for the 1992 and 1996 elections.

CONSIDERING ASIAN AMERICAN WOMEN AND MEN

Historically, Asian women were prevented from participating in U.S. mainstream politics. At first, very few Asian women were even permitted to enter the United States; later they were denied their legal rights to become naturalized upon petition; and still later they were subjected to social segregation and subordination.[7] Not until 1952 were all groups of Asian-born men and women able to overcome the barriers to U.S. citizenship created by the 1790 Naturalization Act which limited naturalization petitions to "free, white persons." Even U.S.-born women of Asian ancestry who married Asian immigrants were at risk of losing their citizenship because a clause in the Cable Act, enforced between 1922 and 1931, stipulated that women who married "aliens ineligible for citizenship" would be stripped of their citizenship. In addition, Asian women were discouraged from political participation by the patriarchal cultural forms and values found in many of their homelands as well as in U.S. society.

The status of Asian women in America did not begin to change until World War II. Other milestones followed, such as the lifting of anti-Asian immigration quotas in 1965 and the passage of the civil rights acts. Today, Asian women have come a long way toward attaining an overall level of educational achievement and income status comparable to or even surpassing that of white women. According to the March 1994 Current Population Survey, almost two-fifths of Asian and Pacific Islander American women twenty-five years and older hold at least a bachelor's degree.[8] Only one-fifth of white women attain this level of education. The median household income of families maintained by women with no spouse present is $28,920 among Asians and $21,650 among whites. The median income and median earnings of persons fifteen years and older also are higher among Asian women than white women.

Although Asian women appear to hold a socioeconomic position superior to that of white women, it would be a mistake to conclude that Asian women are a "model minority" without taking into account the factors contributing to greater economic success, such as education and length of work. Whereas in 1993 the median earned income of college-educated, year-round, full-time workers was similar for white and Asian women—but about three-fourths of that earned by their white male counterparts—the earnings of workers with a high school education were lower among Asian than white women. Furthermore, compared with Asian men, a smaller percentage of Asian women continued their education beyond high school (55 percent versus 66 percent) or earned an income equal to or greater than $30,000 (19 percent versus 26 percent). The result is that Asian women receive only a portion of what Asian or white men earn, and the less-educated Asian women receive less income than their white male or female counterparts.

These observations of the discriminatory effects of race and gender on the socioeconomic status of Asian American women are consistent with the findings of previous studies.[9] Like white women, highly educated Asian women still suffer from gender discrimination. But unlike white women, less-educated Asian women have to confront an additional form of oppression related to race. The same census survey also indicated that Asian men receive only a portion of what white men earn, except that this racial gap affects both high school and college graduates. Thus, in spite of a gender gap in earnings, many Asian men and women share the experience of receiving fewer dollars in return for their education and work time than white men and women. Perhaps because of this dual oppression in race and class, the gender gaps in earned income and median income among Asians are rendered smaller than those separating white women and men. In this sense, race, gender, and class are indeed interconnected axes of social structure.[10]

The American experience of Asian women and men may overlap—at least in part—with that of other nonwhite groups. In fact, a cursory reading of America's multiracial history suggests that through genocide, removal, slavery, and conquest, American Indians, blacks, and Latinos share many aspects of the Asian experience of exploitation, exclusion, subordination, and disenfranchisement in America. Women in these groups may be particularly vulnerable to the triple oppression of race, class, and gender.[11] Not even ascendance to middle-class status can help these women and men escape discriminatory treatment in the workplace and other public sites.[12] Undeniably, regardless of class status, race continues to have a significant influence on the lives of nonwhite Americans. However, is it more important than gender in structuring political behavior?

Scholars interested in the intersection of race and gender have unfortunately failed to reach agreement on the answer to this question. Although some emphasize the equal significance of these forms of oppression,[13] some insist that racism and sexism are not analogous forms of oppression and that the experience of nonwhite women is different from that of white women.[14] The answer seems clear in the case of Asian Americans.

If overall level of socioeconomic achievement can be used to predict political involvement, Asian women as a group would be expected to participate at least on a par with their white counterparts or women of equal background. Yet Asian women are not monolithic in class, and the gender differences in earnings among Asians may be suppressed by the presence of racial oppression. Indeed, the literature shows that being Asian may hinder the translation of socioeconomic resources into participation in mainstream politics.[15] This hindrance affects both women and men and may have something to do with racist U.S. immigration and naturalization policies, limited resocialization processes among adult Asian immigrants, Asians' nonassertive cultural norms, mainstream political mobilization bias, and other psychological and structural barriers. Moreover, Asians are far from a monolithic voting bloc.[16] The community is fragmented not only in class but also in ethnicity, national origin, gender relation, religion, language, and immigration history. This tremendous internal diversity may prevent the spontaneous formation of any sense of a pan-Asian identity except under special conditions.[17] The situational and volatile nature of pan-ethnicity implies that a gender-based solidarity among Asians may not be as easy to form or as established and fixed as that observed among white and black women.[18] As a result, race appears to matter much more than gender in influencing the political behavior of Asian Americans.

Based on the Asian American experience, for other nonwhite groups race as a determinant of political differences may matter more than gender. Barring dramatic social and institutional changes, race may continue to suppress the political mobility of nonwhite men and women and undermine the significance of gender in structuring political behavior and attitudes. Thus the racial gap between white and nonwhite men or women in rates of electoral participation (registration and voting) may continue. Furthermore, racial differences in registration and voting between whites and each of the nonwhite groups may be greater than gender differences within each race. Nevertheless, because of the prevailing significance of race and the distinct history and development of each group, the role of gender may vary across racial groups. Political differences by gender among Asians, Latinos, or American Indians may be small relative to the gender gaps existing within groups with a more salient history of participation in the development of feminist consciousness such as whites and blacks. An examination of the empirical data presented in the next section suggests support for these hypotheses.

DATA AND METHODS

In the study described here, the comparative status of Asian American women in voting participation is assessed by analyzing two national surveys conducted by the U.S. Bureau of the Census within a week of the 1992 and 1996 general elections. Although only voting participation and sociodemographic data are available for analysis, a distinct advantage of these data sets is the huge number of nonwhite respondents and the opportunity they present to generalize to the nation's population by race.

In 1992, 105,815 adults were interviewed in person for the base sample: 84,196 non-Hispanic whites, 10,020 blacks, 7,093 Latinos, 3,542 Asian or Pacific Islanders, and 964 American Indians. In 1996, 90,054 adults were interviewed either in person or by phone for the base sample: 70,374 non-Hispanic whites, 8,440 blacks, 6,995 Latinos, 3,213 Asian or Pacific Islanders, and 1,032 American Indians. Interviews were conducted only in English or Spanish. The language restriction may mitigate the effects of race for Asians because only those proficient in one of the two languages could be included in the pool of respondents. Findings about the roles of race and gender in this study also may be influenced by the race and sex of interviewers, as in the face-to-face interviews with one-third of the respondents in 1996. Much more information is needed, however, before the extent and impact of these factors can be estimated.

To distinguish the roles of race and gender and the interaction of the two in voting participation, the study described here uses a multivariate regression procedure that controls for possible confounding factors such as socioeconomic status and indicators of social involvement or connectedness.[19] The dependent variables are registration and voting in presidential elections. Because of the dichotomous nature of the dependent variables, logistic regression analysis is performed using the maximum likelihood method. The interpretation of the beta coefficient is similar to that in a linear regression model, except that the change in the dependent variable is the logarithm of the odds of two probabilities. For each dependent variable, column I tests the independent effect of gender, column II tests the independent effect of race, and column III tests the interactive effect of race and gender. Interactive terms are introduced here to capture the unique contributions found in the dual identities of being female and nonwhite, beyond what race and gender each can explain independently.

Socioeconomic factors (such as education and family income), which the literature has identified as important for predicting political attitudes and behavior, are controlled in the analyses. In addition, indicators of social connectedness such as age, length of residence, marital status, residence in the southern United States, and nativity (for 1996 models) are controlled. When minority racial group identities are controlled (column II), whites are the reference group. When interactive terms are introduced (column III), white males are the reference group and the coefficient for gender stands for white females.

Broad racial categories are used here for theoretical reasons and because of the lack of ethnic data in both surveys. It is important to keep in mind that Asian, black, Latino, and American Indian are pan-ethnic/racial labels that may mask great variations along generation, class, language, gender, and ethnicity lines within each group. Their separate impacts on political participation will need to be addressed in future studies.

EMPIRICAL EVIDENCE FROM THE CURRENT POPULATION SURVEY

Registration and voting rates by race and gender in the general elections of 1992 and 1996 are reported in Table 7.1. The percentage distribution re-

Table 7.1

Registration and Voting, 1992 and 1996 Elections, by Race and Gender

1992 Election N (× 1,000)	Asian 5,070	Latino 14,688	Black 20,777	White 143,963	American Indian 944
Citizenship (percent)	53[a]	58	95	98	99
Registration	31 (62)[b,c]	35 (63)	64 (70)	74 (77)	61 (63)
College graduate	39 (75)	60 (86)	81 (89)	89 (93)	89 (90)
Age 45+	40 (70)	47 (73)	73 (78)	80 (84)	73 (74)
Male	32 (63)	32 (60)	61 (67)	73 (76)	58 (60)
Female	31 (61)	38 (64)	67 (72)	74 (78)	64 (66)
Voting	27[c] (56)[c]	29 (54)[c]	55 (63)	67 (72)	51[c] (55)[c]
College graduate	35 (70)	56 (82)	77 (87)	85 (90)	81 (86)
Age 45+	37 (65)	40 (65)	65 (72)	74 (79)	62 (65)
Male	28 (57)	27 (53)	51 (61)	66 (71)	49 (52)
Female	27 (55)	31 (55)	57 (64)	68 (72)	54 (57)
Registered	88[c]	83[c]	85[c]	91[c]	84[c]

1996 Election N (× 1,000)	Asian 6,580	Latino 18,426	Black 21,918	White 145,343	American Indian 1,385
Citizenship (percent)	57[a]	61	96	98	99
Registration	33[c] (58)[b,c]	36 (59)	64 (67)	72 (73)	61[c] (62)[c]
College graduate	42 (69)	60 (78)	80 (83)	84 (86)	82 (85)
Age 45+	40 (64)	48 (70)	73 (75)	78 (80)	70 (71)
Male	33 (57)	33 (56)	60 (63)	71 (72)	59 (59)
Female	33 (58)	39 (61)	67 (69)	73 (74)	64 (65)
Voting	26[c] (46)[c]	27 (44)	51 (53)	60 (61)	45[c] (46)[c]
College graduate	34 (57)	55 (71)	77 (87)	85 (90)	81 (86)
Age 45+	33 (53)	41 (60)	65 (72)	74 (79)	62 (65)
Male	26 (46)	24 (41)	47 (49)	59 (60)	43 (44)
Female	26 (45)	29 (47)	54 (56)	60 (62)	47 (47)

(continues on next page)

Table 7.1 *(continued)*

Registration and Voting, 1992 and 1996 Elections, by Race and Gender

1996 Election N (× 1,000)	Asian	Latino	Black	White	American Indian
	6,580	18,426	21,918	145,343	1,385
Registered	79[c]	75[c]	80	83[c]	73[c]
Male	81	74	77	83	74
Female	78	76	81	83	73

Source: U.S. Bureau of the Census, *Current Population Survey: Voter Supplement File, 1992, 1996,* ICPSR version (Washington, D.C.: U.S. Department of Commerce, Bureau of the Census [producer], 1997; Ann Arbor, Mich.: Inter-university Consortium for Political and Social Research [distributor], 1997).

Note: All populations are age eighteen or over. Unlike figures previously released by the Census Bureau, those reported here fall into mutually exclusive racial categories. Thus "white" refers to "non-Hispanic white," "black" refers to "non-Hispanic black," and "Asian" refers to "non-Hispanic Asian or Pacific Islanders." All tests of significance are conducted with reweighted data calculated from the original weights to adjust for the sizes of standard errors.

a. Entries are in percentages. Those reported for citizenship are among the valid responses.

b. Entries in parentheses are those among citizens.

c. Chi-square test fails to reject the hypothesis of no gender difference at $\alpha = .05$. All other differences by race, gender, or both are statistically significant at the .05 level or better.

veals clear racial differences in registration and voting between whites and nonwhites—nonwhites are much less likely to register and vote than whites (this participation disparity applies to both males and females). However, the size of the racial gap is much smaller for African and Native Americans than for Asians and Latinos. Although the racial gap in participation rates between whites and Asians or Latinos shrinks significantly with adjustment for citizenship status, the same is less true with adjustments for education and age differences. In fact, among all citizens the racial gap in registration and voting for college-educated Asians is consistently larger than that for Asians of all educational backgrounds. Thus, even though the participation rates for Asians with citizenship status are at least 20 percentage points higher than those for voting-age Asians as a whole, the voting registration and turnout rates of college-educated citizens of Asian ancestry still trail those of equally educated whites by 17–33 percentage points in both elections. The racial divide between whites and Asians begins to diminish, however, after the level of voting registration is controlled. When turnout rates are calculated only for citizens who registered to vote, 88 percent of Asian Americans went to the polls in 1992 and 79 percent in 1996. Although these figures are only 3–4 percentage points short of the rates for whites, the Asian turnout deficit in the 1996 presidential election is still statistically significant among registered voters, a finding that differs from that of Paul Ong and Don T. Nakanishi for the 1994 midterm election.[20]

Compared with racial gaps, differences in registration and voting rates by gender are far less distinct, and they too vary across racial groups (Table 7.1). Asian women acquired citizenship, registered, and voted in both 1992 and 1996 at virtually the same rates as Asian men. The same can be said of American Indians except that American Indian women registered at a significantly higher rate than American Indian men in 1992. Other groups of women tended to register and vote at higher rates than their male counterparts in both elections. Results of chi-square tests indicate, however, that the female edge in turnout may hold up only for black registered voters in 1996. In that election, black female registered voters surpassed black male registered voters in turnout by 4 percentage points, even though this rate was still 2 percentage points behind that for white women.

Can the observed racial and gender gaps in the aggregate be explained away by controlling for individual differences in socioeconomic class and social connectedness? Table 7.2 shows that among the registered voters in 1992, females in general had a slight (0.09 percent) but significant edge in voting turnout. Blacks, Latinos, and Asians all tended to vote less than whites by 0.8–5.4 percent. But neither Asian nor Latino nor Native American women were significantly more likely to vote than males in the same groups. The female edge in voting applied only to blacks and whites, and the size of the gap was greater among blacks (1.7 percent) than among whites (0.07 percent). Among voting-age citizens in 1992, women in general were more likely to register to vote than men by 3 percentage points. When race enters the equation, being female remains a booster factor for both whites and blacks, but not for Asians, Latinos, or American Indians. In 1992 white women were more likely to register to vote than white men, by 2.4 percent; the female edge for black women was greater, at 3.4 percent. The multivariate results also indicate that, other conditions being equal, Asians may be much less likely to register than whites, by 19.8 percent; blacks may be more likely to register than whites, by 5 percent; and Latinos and American Indians may not register at a rate different from that of whites of equal status.

Table 7.2
Logistic Regression Estimation of Voting, 1992 Election

	Voting			Registration		
	(I)	(II)	(III)	(I)	(II)	(III)
Female	.10		.08	.16		.13
	(.03)		(.03)	(.02)		(.02)
Asian		−.60	−.69		−1.06	−1.07
		(.12)	(.18)		(.07)	(.10)
Black		−.09	.19		.27	.17
		(.04)	(.06)		(.03)	(.05)
Latino		−.29	−.26		.03[a]	−.03[a]
		(.05)	(.09)		(.04)	(.06)
American Indian		−.32[a]	−.25[a]		−.13[a]	.01[a]
		(.18)	(.28)		(.12)	(.14)
Asian women			.18[a]			.01[a]
			(.25)			(.14)
Black women			.19			.18
			(.08)			(.06)
Latino women			−.05[a]			.14[a]
			(.12)			(.08)
American Indian women			−.11[a]			.16[a]
			(.36)			(.24)
Education	.18	.18	.18	.26	.27	.26
	(.01)	(.01)	(.01)	(.00)	(.00)	(.00)
Income	.06	.06	.06	.06	.06	.07
	(.00)	(.00)	(.00)	(.00)	(.00)	(.00)
Married	.40	.39	.40	.21	.22	.23
	(.03)	(.03)	(.03)	(.02)	(.02)	(.02)
Age (raw score)	.03	.03	.03	.03	.03	.03
	(.00)	(.00)	(.00)	(.00)	(.00)	(.00)
Length of residency	.15	.15	.15	.17	.16	.16
	(.01)	(.01)	(.01)	(.01)	(.01)	(.01)
South	−.28	−.28	−.25	−.12	−.16	−.16
	(.03)	(.03)	(.03)	(.02)	(.02)	(.02)
Constant	−1.57	−1.40	−1.44	−3.99	−3.99	−4.06

Table 7.2 *(continued)*
Logistic Regression Estimation of Voting, 1992 Election

	Voting			Registration		
	(I)	(II)	(III)	(I)	(II)	(III)
−2 Log likelihood	34,091			76,891		
At convergence	31,517	31,485	31,467	66,399	66,171	66,086
% Predicted correct	89.87	89.88	89.88	77.04	77.19	77.17
Reweighted N	68,180			89,341		

Source: U.S. Bureau of the Census, *Current Population Survey: Voter Supplement File, 1992, 1996* (computer files), ICPSR version (Washington, D.C.: U.S. Department of Commerce, Bureau of the Census [producer], 1997; Ann Arbor, Mich.: Inter-university Consortium for Political and Social Research [distributor], 1997).

Note: Numerical entries are logistic coefficients or log odds except where noted. Standard errors are in parentheses. All coefficients are statistically significant at the .05 level or better except those denoted with a superscript *a* (p > .05). The dependent variable for voting is scored 1 if R voted in the general election of November 1992. The dependent variable for registration is scored 1 if R was registered to vote in the 1992 election. Only registered voters are included in the voting models, and only voting-age citizens are included in the registration models. The average voting rate is 90.0. The average registration rate is 75.2.

Note that the variable "Education" was coded in sixteen categories with Ph.D. having the highest score; the variable "Income" was coded in thirteen categories with those having an annual income of $75,000 or more being assigned the highest score; and the variable "Length" has six categories with those respondents having lived in the same residence for five years or more being assigned the highest score.

South is a dummy variable. The census definition of South does not include Delaware, Maryland, and the District of Columbia.

Similar roles for race and gender and the interaction of the two are observed for the 1996 election (Table 7.3), except that the size of the gender gap is larger than in 1992 and there are changes in the meaning of the racial gap. For example, among registered voters the female edge in turnout increases to 1.7 percent, with white and black women more likely to turn out and vote than white and black men by 1.2 percent and 4.5 percent, respectively. Compared with the 1992 election, being Asian in 1996 suggests a larger turnout deficit among registered voters (6.8 percent). Conversely, being black signi-

Table 7.3

Logistic Regression Estimation of Voting, 1996 Election

	Voting			Registration		
	(I)	(II)	(III)	(I)	(II)	(III)
Female	.12		.08	.18		.15
	(.03)		(.03)	(.02)		(.02)
Asian		−.47	−.34		−.67	−.60
		(.10)	(.15)		(.07)	(.10)
Black		.34	.17		.33	.21
		(.04)	(.06)		(.03)	(.05)
Latino		−.06[a]	−.12[a]		.03[a]	−.03[a]
		(.05)	(.09)		(.04)	(.06)
American Indian		−.22[a]	−.16[a]		.05[a]	−.03[a]
		(.14)	(.19)		(.11)	(.16)
Asian women			.25[a]			−.13[a]
			(.19)			(.14)
Black women			.31			.21
			(.08)			(.06)
Latino women			.11[a]			.12[a]
			(.10)			(.08)
American Indian women			−.09[a]			.03[a]
			(.28)			(.22)
Education	.18	.18	.18	.25	.25	.25
	(.01)	(.01)	(.01)	(.00)	(.00)	(.00)
Income	.05	.05	.05	.05	.05	.05
	(.00)	(.00)	(.00)	(.00)	(.00)	(.00)
Married	.26	.28	.29	.25	.27	.28
	(.03)	(.03)	(.03)	(.02)	(.02)	(.02)
Age (raw score)	.03	.03	.03	.03	.03	.03
	(.00)	(.00)	(.00)	(.00)	(.00)	(.00)
Length of residency	.11	.11	.11	.20	.20	.20
	(.01)	(.01)	(.01)	(.01)	(.01)	(.01)
South	−.23	−.26	−.26	.02[a]	−.02[a]	−.02[a]
	(.03)	(.03)	(.03)	(.02)	(.02)	(.02)
Foreign-born	.06[a]	.20	.20	−.50	−.33	−.33
	(.06)	(.07)	(.07)	(.04)	(.05)	(.05)
Constant	−2.50	−2.55	−2.60	−4.10	−4.15	−4.22

Table 7.3   *(continued)*
Logistic Regression Estimation of Voting, 1996 Election

	Voting			Registration		
	(I)	(II)	(III)	(I)	(II)	(III)
−2 Log likelihood	40,894			65,446		
At convergence	37,631	37,557	37,519	56,668	56,558	56,472
% Predicted correct	82.17	82.21	82.22	76.37	76.49	76.49
Reweighted N	54,731			72,386		

Source: U.S. Bureau of the Census, *Current Population Survey: Voter Supplement File, 1992, 1996* (computer files), ICPSR version (Washington, D.C.: U.S. Department of Commerce, Bureau of the Census [producer], 1997; Ann Arbor, Mich.: Inter-university Consortium for Political and Social Research [distributor], 1997).

Note: Numerical entries are logistic coefficients or log odds except where noted. Standard errors are in parentheses. All coefficients are statistically significant at the .05 level or better except those denoted with a superscript *a* (p > .05). The dependent variable for voting is scored 1 if R voted in the general election of November 1996. The dependent variable for registration is scored 1 if R was registered to vote in the 1996 election. Only registered voters are included in the voting models, and only voting-age citizens are included in the registration models. The average voting rate is 82.3. The average registration rate is 70.9.

Note that the variable "Education" was coded in sixteen categories with Ph.D. having the highest score; the variable "Income" was coded in thirteen categories with those having an annual income of $75,000 or more being assigned the highest score; and the variable "Length" has six categories with those respondents having lived in the same residence for five years or more being assigned the highest score.

South is a dummy variable. The census definition of South does not include Delaware, Maryland, and the District of Columbia.

fies a greater propensity to turn out (5 percent), while being Latino can no longer be associated with a significant turnout deficit. Among voting-age citizens, the female edge in registration grows to 3.7 percent, and this edge stems more from the higher registration rate of black women (4.3 percent) than from the higher registration rate of white women (3.1 percent). Although being Asian in 1996 may still be associated with a registration deficit, the size of the deficit drops by 6 percentage points to 13.8 percent. Blacks, on the other hand, expand the registration edge to 6.8 percent over whites of similar status. For both Latinos and American Indians, neither race nor gender appears to play a significant role in determining their likelihood to register and vote, compared with whites, in the two elections studied.

Although the roles of the control variables are consistent with the literature—that one is more likely to register and vote if one is better-educated, better-off, married, older, lives a longer time in the same residence, or resides outside the American South—there also are some differences in results between the two elections. For example, residence in the South was no longer a significant factor hindering voter registration in 1996. Instead, being foreign-born could decrease one's likelihood to register. And yet once registered, being foreign-born could increase one's likelihood to vote.

DISCUSSION

These survey results on voting participation display a general pattern of support for the research hypotheses. In the two elections examined, the average voting registration and turnout rates of Asians, blacks, Latinos, and American Indians are all lower than those for whites, even though there is significant variation in the distance between whites and each nonwhite group. Comparatively, the scope of gender differences in participation within each nonwhite race is much smaller than political differences by race, particularly for Asians and Latinos. However, the significance of the gender factor also varies across racial groups, with Asian and American Indian women most likely to register and vote at rates similar to those of Asian and American Indian men with the same background.

When individual differences in socioeconomic status and social connectedness are taken into account, the racial gap in turnout among registered voters remains significant for all nonwhite groups except American Indians in 1992. For 1996, however, only Asians are found to suffer from a continuous turnout deficit. In fact, among individuals of equal status, blacks would be more likely to vote in 1966, and both Latinos and American Indians would not be any less likely to vote than whites in 1996. This latter pattern of racial differences in turnout can be used to predict voter registration in both elections. Compared with whites, Asians were much less likely to register in 1992 and 1996; for blacks the opposite was true.

This finding of the persistent and unique Asian deficit in voter registration and turnout places this study on a very short list of studies adopting inferential statistics that found that sociodemographic factors may be able to account for most or all of the participation differences between whites and blacks or Latinos but not between whites and Asians.[21] A comparison of the bivariate and multivariate results for Asians further reveals that, unlike findings about other nonwhite groups, statistical controls not only cannot explain away participation disparity, but also add to the depth of frustration encountered in trying to solve the puzzle of Asian underparticipation. It is hoped that the slightly reduced registration gap among citizens in 1996 after the controls (from 15 percent to 13.8 percent) is not only an exception but the beginning of a new trend in political behavior among Asians.

When the gender factor is added to the logistic regression equations of race, only black and white women may be predicted to participate at significantly different rates than black and white men of equal background. The insignificant interactive terms associated with Asian as well as Latino and American Indian women suggest that, for these races, being female may not contribute much to what race itself can predict about the level of participation. This shows that for these nonwhite groups participation behavior may be structured more by race than by gender—even though Asians are the only group that shows consistent racial gaps at both the bivariate and multivariate levels. The hyperactive image of black and white women in voting and registration, after accounting for differences in socioeconomics and social connectedness, also reveals that the role of gender in political participation does vary across racial groups. Relative to other races, gender differences are greater among blacks and whites. Compared with women in other racial groups, black and white women may benefit from the greater sense of gender consciousness developed in these more established racial communities.

In all, the aggregated results of significant racial gaps in rates of voting participation and the near absence of a significant gender gap within certain races demonstrate support for the main thesis of this research. The racial disparity in voting participation between white and nonwhite men or women persisted into the mid-1990s, even though the color and culture of nonwhites were much more diversified and the contours of gender were different. When differences in possible correlates of voting turnout among the registered as well as voting registration among adult citizens are controlled, race remains important as a factor suppressing the participation of Asians in both 1992 and 1996, whereas being female is not useful in increasing the level of participation of Asian women. For Latinos and American Indian women, their racial disparity may be overcome if given equal opportunities to access social resources and establish connections; being female does not appear to interfere with the process. For black women, both their racial and gender identities may help overcompensate the deficit in participation suppressed by resource deprivation and social segregation. Finally, although the confluence of race and gender cannot provide much explanation beyond what race can explain about the variation in political behavior for women of Asian, Latino, and indigenous origin, it can provide an explanation in the case of black and white women. More research is needed, however, to further investigate the interracial group differences and coalitional opportunities for groups of men and women.

CONCLUSION

In response to criticism that feminist theory neglects the influence of race and class, scholars in that field are now tending to emphasize the importance of race, class, and gender as interlocking systems of oppression and power. However, they have not clearly specified exactly how this concept of intersectionality operates in structuring political behavior. This study is a preliminary attempt to examine the confluence of race and gender while controlling for class. By comparing the experience of Asian American women with that of other groups of men and women, this chapter has explored the dynamics of race, gender, and class in structuring political participation in multiracial America.

The findings reported here underline the centrality of race when considering the political experience of Asian men and women. They echo the calls made by many feminists of color to recenter race in the study of gender. And yet findings on the marginalization of gender because of the dual oppression of race and class among Asians also highlight the importance of studying and presenting these categories of difference as relationally constructed. Therefore, to conclude that race is more significant than gender in structuring political attitudes and behavior is not to be interpreted as denying the persistence of gender oppression or, by the same token, capitalist exploitation. In fact, findings on the political behavior of other groups affirm the importance of gender and class in understanding the political experience of American women. Nevertheless, findings on the various gender gaps between whites and nonwhites and among different nonwhite groups do present a challenge to the prevailing conceptualization of presenting race, class, and gender as black/white, under-class/upper-class, and men/women dichotomies. In this sense, this study supports Yen L. Espiritu's call for moving beyond dualism in studying the dynamics of race, class, and gender.[22]

Finally, concerns over the contradictions in feminist methodology are addressed here by calling attention to the methodological limitations of this study and soliciting more inquiries. The findings reported in this chapter represent the opinions of survey respondents only at a given time and cover a very narrow scope of political behavior and opinions. Although the CPS survey has the advantage of its huge sample size, it collects information only on two forms of electoral participation and also is limited in terms of providing alternative explanations for the continuing underparticipation of Asians. Furthermore, it may suffer from problems such as over-reporting of turnout and undercounting of racial minorities. Potential biases associated with issues of interview language and interviewers' race and sex also may need to be addressed. More important, this empirical approach may not be sufficient to discover the "hidden determinants of oppression."[23] It is therefore imperative to conduct more research looking at a wider range of political behavior and using various research designs, theories, methodologies, and political contexts.

NOTES

1. In this chapter umbrella racial terms are used to represent Americans of European, African, Hispanic, Asian or Pacific Islander, and indigenous descent. For convenience, *black* and *African American* are used interchangeably as are *Latino* and *Hispanic American,* (*non-Hispanic*) *white* and *European American, Asian* and *Asian American, American Indian* and *Native American.* Unless noted otherwise, these terms refer to both males and females in each group, and these categories are mutually exclusive.

2. Don T. Nakanishi, "Asian American Politics: An Agenda for Research," *Amerasia Journal* 12 (1986): 1–27; Don T. Nakanishi, "The Next Swing Vote? Asian Pacific Americans and California Politics," in *Racial and Ethnic Politics in California,* ed. Bryan O. Jackson and Michael B. Preston (Berkeley: IGS Press, 1991), 25–54; Don T. Nakanishi, "When Numbers Do Not Add Up: Asian Pacific Americans and California Politics," in *Racial and Ethnic Politics in California,* 2d ed., ed. Michael Preston, Bruce Cain, and Sandra Bass (Berkeley: IGS Press, 1998), 3–43; Carole J. Uhlaner, Bruce E. Cain, and D. Roderick Kiewiet, "Political Participation of Ethnic Minorities in the 1980s," *Political Behavior* 11 (1989): 195–232; Jane Junn, "Assimilating or Coloring Participation? Gender, Race, and Democratic Political Participation," in *Women Transforming Politics,* ed. Cathy Cohen, Kathleen Jones, and Joan Tronto (New York: New York University Press, 1997), 387–397; Pei-te Lien, "Ethnicity and Political Participation: A Comparison between Asian and Mexican Americans," *Political Behavior* 16 (1994): 237–264; and Pei-te Lien, *The Political Partici-*

pation of Asian Americans: Voting Behavior in Southern California (New York: Garland Publishing, 1997).

3. Sandra Baxter and Marjorie Lansing, *Women and Politics: The Visible Minority* (Ann Arbor: University of Michigan Press, 1993); M. Margaret Conway, *Political Participation in the United States*, 2d ed. (Washington, D.C.: CQ Press, 1991); Ruy A. Teixeira, *The Disappearing American Voter* (Washington, D.C.: Brookings, 1992); Steven J. Rosenstone and John M. Hansen, *Mobilization, Participation, and Democracy in America* (New York: Macmillan, 1993); Kay Schlozman, Nancy Burns, Sidney Verba, and Jesse Donahue, "Gender and Citizen Participation: Is There a Different Voice?" *American Journal of Political Science* 39 (1995): 267–293; Kay Schlozman, Nancy Burns, and Sidney Verba, "Gender and the Pathways to Participation: The Role of Resources," *Journal of Politics* 56 (1994): 963–987; M. Margaret Conway, Gertrude Seuernagel, and David Ahern, *Women and Political Participation* (Washington, D.C.: CQ Press, 1997); and Richard A. Seltzer, Jody Newman, and Melissa Leighton, *Sex as a Political Variable: Women as Candidates and Voters in U.S. Elections* (Boulder: Lynne Rienner, 1997).

4. Richard D. Shingles, "Black Consciousness and Political Participation: The Missing Link," *American Political Science Review* 75 (1981): 76–91; Baxter and Lansing, *Women and Politics*; Robert Brischetto, "The 1984 Election Exit Polls," in *Ignored Voices: Public Opinion Polls and the Latino Community*, ed. Rodolfo de la Garza (Austin: Center for Mexican American Studies, University of Texas, 1987), 76–94; Katherine Tate, *From Protest to Politics: The New Black Voters in American Elections* (Cambridge: Harvard University Press, 1993); Susan Welch and Lee Sigelman, "A Gender Gap among Hispanics? A Comparison with Blacks and Anglos," *Western Political Quarterly* 45 (1992): 181–199; F. Chris Garcia, John Garcia, Rodolfo de la Garza, and Angelo Falcon, "The Effects of Ethnic Partisanship on Electoral Behavior," paper delivered at the annual meeting of the American Political Science Association, Chicago, 1992; and Lisa Montoya, "Latino Gender Differences in Public Opinion: Results from the Latino National Political Survey," *Hispanic Journal of Behavioral Sciences* 18 (1996): 255–276.

5. Junn, "Assimilating or Coloring Participation?"; Lien, "Ethnicity and Political Participation"; Pei-te Lien, "Ethnicity and Political Adaptation: Comparing Filipinos, Koreans, and Vietnamese in Southern California," paper presented at the annual meeting of the Association for Asian American Studies, Seattle, 1997; and Lien, *Political Participation of Asian Americans*.

6. Lisa Lowe, "Work, Immigration, and Gender: Asian 'American' Women," in *Making More Waves: New Writing by Asian American Women*, ed. Elaine Kim, Lilia Villanueva, and Asian Women United of California (Boston: Beacon Press, 1997), 272.

7. Lucie Cheng and Edna Bonacich, eds., *Labor Immigration under Capitalism: Asian Workers in the United States before World War II* (Berkeley: University of California Press, 1984); Sucheta Mazumdar, "General Introduction: A Woman-Centered Perspective on Asian American History," in *Making Waves: An Anthology*

of Writings by and about Asian American Women, ed. Asian Women United of California (Boston: Beacon Press, 1989), 1–22; Ronald Takaki, *Strangers from a Different Shore* (Boston: Little, Brown, 1989); Sucheng Chan, *Asian Americans: An Interpretive History* (Boston: Twayne, 1991); Bill Ong Hing, *Making and Remaking Asian America through Immigration Policy, 1850–1990* (Stanford: Stanford University Press, 1993); and Yen L. Espiritu, *Asian American Women and Men: Labor, Laws, and Love* (Thousand Oaks, Calif.: Sage Publications, 1997).

8. U.S. Bureau of the Census, *The Nation's Asian and Pacific Islander Population—1994,* Statistical Brief (Washington, D.C., 1995).

9. See, for example, Deborah Woo, "The Socioeconomic Status of Asian American Women in the Labor Force: An Alternative View," *Sociological Perspectives* 28 (1985): 307–338; Deborah Woo, "The Gap between Striving and Achieving: The Case of Asian American Women," in *Making Waves: An Anthology of Writings by and about Asian American Women,* ed. Asian Women United of California (Boston: Beacon Press, 1989), 185–194; Wu Xu and Ann Leffler, "Gender and Race Effects on Occupational Prestige, Segregation, and Earnings," *Gender and Society* 6 (1992): 376–392; Paul Ong and Suzanne Hee, "Economic Diversity," in *The State of Asian Pacific America: Economic Diversity, Issues and Policies* (Los Angeles: LEAP Asian Pacific American Public Policy Institute and UCLA Asian American Studies Center, 1994); and Vilma Ortiz, "Women of Color: A Demographic Overview," in *Women of Color in U.S. Society,* ed. Maxine Baca Zinn and Bonnie Thornton Dill (Philadelphia: Temple University Press, 1994), 13–40.

10. Margaret Andersen and Patricia Hill Collins, *Race, Class, and Gender: An Anthology,* 2d ed. (Belmont, Calif.: Wadsworth Publishing, 1995); and Espiritu, *Asian American Women and Men.*

11. Bell Hooks, *Ain't I a Woman? Black Women and Feminism* (Boston: South End Press, 1981); Bell Hooks, *Feminist Theory from Margin to Center* (Boston: South End Press, 1984); Evelyn Nakano Glenn, "Racial Ethnic Women's Labor: The Intersection of Race, Gender and Class Oppression," *Review of Radical Political Economics* 17 (1985): 86–108; Patricia Zavella, *Women's Work and Chicano Families: Cannery Workers of the Santa Clara Valley* (Ithaca: Cornell University Press, 1987); Aida Hurtado, "Reflections on White Feminism: A Perspective from a Woman of Color," in *Social and Gender Boundaries in the United States,* ed. Sucheng Chan (Lewiston, N.Y.: Edwin Mellen Press, 1989), 155–186; Patricia Hill Collins, *Black Feminist Thought: Knowledge, Consciousness, and the Politics of Entitlement* (New York: Routledge, 1990); M. A. Jaimes and Theresa Halsey, "American Indian Women: At the Center of Indigenous Resistance in Contemporary North America," in *The State of Native America,* ed. M. A. Jaimes (Boston: South End Press, 1992), 311–344; Teresa Amott and Julie Matthaei, *Race, Gender, and Work: A Multicultural Economic History of Women in the United States,* 2d ed. (Boston: South End Press, 1996); Beatriz Pesquera and Denise Segura, "With Quill and Torch: A Chicana Perspective on the American Women's Movement and Feminist Theories," in *Chicanas/Chicanos at*

Crossroads: Social, Economic, and Political Change, ed. David Maciel and Isidro Ortiz (Tucson: University of Arizona Press, 1996); and Lowe, "Work, Immigration, and Gender."

12. Joe R. Feagin, "The Continuing Significance of Race: Antiblack Discrimination in Public Places," *American Sociological Review* 58 (1991): 101–116; Denise Segura, "Chicanas in White Collar Jobs: 'You Have to Prove Yourself More,' " *Sociological Perspectives* 35 (1992): 163–182; and Elizabeth Higginbotham, "Black Professional Women: Job Ceilings and Employment Sectors," in *Women of Color in U.S. Society,* ed. Maxine Baca Zinn and Bonnie Thornton Dill (Philadelphia: Temple University Press, 1994), 113–131.

13. Maxine Baca Zinn and BonnieThornton Dill, "Difference and Domination," in *Women of Color in U.S. Society,* ed. Maxine Baca Zinn and Bonnie Thornton Dill (Philadelphia: Temple University Press, 1994); and Esther Ngan-Ling Chow, "Introduction: Transforming Knowledgment: Race, Class, and Gender," in *Race, Class, and Gender: Common Bonds, Different Voices,* ed. Esther Chow, Doris Wilkinson, and Maxine Baca Zinn (Thousand Oaks, Calif.: Sage Publications, 1996), xix–xxvi.

14. Collins, *Black Feminist Thought;* Cynthia Deitch, "Gender, Race, and Class Politics and the Inclusion of Women in Title VII of the 1964 Civil Rights Act," in *Race, Class, and Gender: Common Bonds, Different Voices,* ed. Esther Chow, Doris Wilkinson, and Maxine Baca Zinn (Thousand Oaks, Calif.: Sage Publications, 1996), 288–307; Audre Lorde, "Age, Race, Class, and Sex: Women Redefining Difference," in *Race, Class, and Gender in the United States: An Integrated Study,* 3d ed., ed. Paula Rothenberg (New York: St. Martin's Press, 1995); Doris Wilkinson, "Gender and Social Inequality: The Prevailing Significance of Race," *Daedalus* 124 (1995): 167–178; Aida Hurtado, *The Color of Privilege: Three Blasphemies on Race and Feminism* (Ann Arbor: University of Michigan Press, 1996); and Pesquera and Segura, "With Quill and Torch."

15. Nakanishi, "Asian American Politics"; Nakanishi, "Next Swing Vote?"; Uhlaner et al., "Political Participation of Ethnic Minorities in the 1980s"; Steven P. Erie and Harold Brackman, "Paths to Political Incorporation for Latinos and Asian Pacifics in California," California Policy Seminar, University of California, 1993; Lien, "Ethnicity and Political Participation"; and Lien, *Political Participation of Asian Americans.*

16. Grant Din, "An Analysis of Asian/Pacific Registration and Voting Patterns in San Francisco," master's thesis, Claremont Graduate School, 1984; Wendy Tam, "Asians—A Monolithic Voting Bloc?" *Political Behavior* 17 (1995): 223–249; and Lien, "Ethnicity and Political Adaptation."

17. Yen L. Espiritu, *Asian American Panethnicity* (Philadelphia: Temple University Press, 1992).

18. Esther Ngan-ling Chow, "The Development of Feminist Consciousness among Asian American Women," *Gender and Society* 1 (1987): 284–299; and Sonia Shah, "Presenting the Blue Goddess: Toward a National Pan-Asian Feminist Agenda," in

Women Transforming Politics, ed. Cathy Cohen, Kathleen Jones, and Joan Tronto (New York: New York University Press, 1997), 541–548.

19. For literature on these and other determinants of voting participation, see Teixeira, *Disappearing American Voter;* Conway, *Political Participation in the United States;* Rosenstone and Hansen, *Mobilization, Participation, and Democracy in America;* and Sidney Verba, Kay Schlozman, and Henry Brady, *Voice and Equality: Civic Voluntarism in American Politics* (Cambridge: Harvard University Press, 1995).

20. Paul Ong and Don T. Nakanishi, "Becoming Citizens, Becoming Voters: The Naturalization and Political Participation of Asian Pacific Immigrants," in *Reframing the Immigration Debate,* ed. Bill Ong Hing and Ronald Lee (Los Angeles: LEAP Asian Pacific American Public Policy Institute and UCLA Asian American Studies Center, 1996), 275–305.

21. Uhlaner et al., "Political Participation of Ethnic Minorities in the 1980s"; and Lien, *Political Participation of Asian Americans.*

22. Espiritu, *Asian American Women and Men.*

23. Sherry Gorelick, "Contradictions of Feminist Methodology," in *Race, Class, and Gender: Common Bonds, Different Voices,* ed. Esther Chow, Doris Wilkinson, and Maxine Baca Zinn (Thousand Oaks, Calif.: Sage Publications, 1996), 385–401.

PART THREE

EMERGING
POLITICAL IDENTITIES

U.S.-Born, Immigrant, Refugee, or Indigenous Status: Public Policy Implications for Asian Pacific American Families

KENYON S. CHAN

The role of the family has been a central theme in the discourse on Asian Pacific American (APA) communities since the first APA immigrants landed on U.S. soil.[1] Whether it is the story of nineteenth-century immigrants separated from their families to pursue economic rewards or the story of the refugee families escaping war-torn Asia in the 1970s and 1980s, one observation is heard often: families and family values are the strength and core of Asian Pacific communities. The concept of family crosses ethnic, cultural, linguistic, and socioeconomic boundaries, yet like most social constructions, it is complex and multilayered. This chapter investigates the concept of family within the Asian Pacific American context and examines its implications for social policy and politics in the United States.

Any analysis of the APA community is a difficult task, however. Its rapidly changing nature over the past three decades has perplexed social scientists trying to find order in these growing communities and frustrated public policy analysts attempting to determine the nature and priorities of these moving targets. Meanwhile, it has become quite clear that even though the application of the overarching Asian American or Asian Pacific American nomenclature to so many distinct ethnic groups has social and political advantages, such a designation is a thin tie for such diversity.[2] An examination of the aggregate APA profile reveals significant differences *between* the APA community and other racial and ethnic groups in the United States.

More important, however, disaggregation of the APA profile uncovers important differences *within* the APA population. Thus the concept of APA *communities* is more appropriate than that of APAs as a single community.

It is common practice now among social scientists and public policy analysts to disaggregate any analysis and discussions of APA communities as much as possible, particularly across ethnic lines (see Figure 8.1). The current ethnic configuration is a dramatic change from 1960 when Japanese Americans constituted the largest APA ethnic group; Filipinos, Asian Indians, and Koreans were small in number; and the presence of Southeast Asians was negligible. With the addition of new APA ethnic groups over the last quarter-century, the APA population is one of the most diverse racially and ethnically in the United States.[3] APA groups vary in language spoken, religion, cultural beliefs, social class, and historical location in the United States.

Compounding this diversity, there are as many differences within APA ethnic groups as there are among APA ethnic groups. Within specific ethnic groups behavior and culture vary widely by region of origin and by social

Figure 8.1
APA Population by Selected Ethnic Groups, 1990

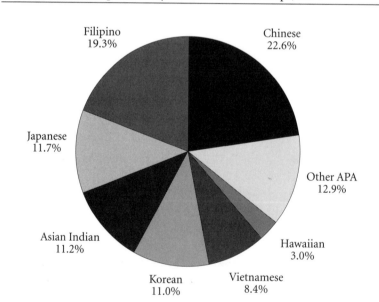

Source: U.S. Bureau of the Census, *1990 Census of Population, Social and Economic Characteristics, CP-2-1* (Washington, D.C., 1993).

class. For example, the Chinese American community is really made up of multiple communities. Some Chinese Americans are third- or fourth-generation U.S.-born; many others are recent arrivals. Recent arrivals are from different regions of Asia, including Hong Kong, China, Southeast Asia, and Taiwan, and from places outside of Asia, such as Canada, the Caribbean, and New Zealand. These communities differ in language spoken at home and in many cultural traditions. Class differences also are quite evident when comparing Chinese Americans from Taiwan, China, or Vietnam.

Within the Vietnamese American community, segments are from the former ruling elite in Vietnam; others have distinctly working-class and peasant backgrounds. Some families are headed by former Vietnam government and military officials; others are families of foot soldiers and service personnel. Some adults within this community are highly educated with college educations obtained in Europe or the United States; others have had little formal education at all. These complexities within the Chinese and Vietnamese American communities mirror the complexities within most APA ethnic groups and confirm the notion of "communities."

Even with these complexities, an examination of Asian Pacific Americans by ethnic group remains useful in conceptualizing the characteristics and needs of APAs in the United States. Yet any attempt to disaggregate APA communities by APA ethnic group may itself conceal important distinctions. Thus it is necessary to go beyond such disaggregation and seek alternative configurations of these complex communities. In this chapter I examine the complexities of APA families within the context of APA ethnic groups, but I also configure the data by adding four proxy categories that represent U.S.-born APA communities, immigrant-impacted communities, refugee-impacted communities, and indigenous communities. This additional configuration will offer new insights into the complications of policy making and political participation among APAs. Furthermore, it will illuminate social class issues that are an important divide within the context of the larger APA nomenclature.

A NEW CONFIGURATION FOR ANALYSIS

Since 1965 APA communities have experienced a tidal wave of new immigrants and refugees. As a result, the APA population has shifted from a largely U.S.-born one to a predominantly foreign-born one of first-generation Americans. The predominance of recent immigrants and war refugees

Figure 8.2
APA Foreign-Born by Ethnic Group, 1990

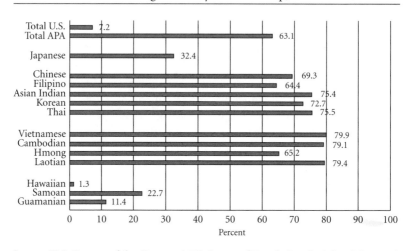

Source: U.S. Bureau of the Census, *1990 Census of Population, Social and Economic Characteristics, CP-2-1* (Washington, D.C., 1993).

among APAs was evident in the 1990 U.S. Census. Only 7.2 percent of the U.S. population reported being foreign-born in 1990, but 63.1 percent of APAs were born in a country other than the United States. By contrast, 36 percent of Hispanics and 3.3 percent of whites were foreign-born.[4] Of all foreign-born persons in the United States in 1990, 51 percent were white, 40 percent Hispanic, 23 percent APA, and 7 percent black.[5]

APA communities did not experience this tidal wave of new immigration evenly, however. For example, 65.6 percent of those of Asian descent are foreign-born compared with only 12.9 percent of Pacific Islanders. The total percentage of foreign-born persons for each APA ethnic group also varies widely (Figure 8.2). Although the rate of foreign-born Japanese Americans is four and a half times the rate of the nation as a whole, it is half the rates of other Asian American communities. Nearly 70 percent of the Japanese American community is U.S.-born, often third-, fourth-, or fifth-generation. Its cultural, economic, and social experiences are largely modulated by the American context and represent an almost completely American experience. Japanese Americans thus serve as an imperfect, yet revealing, proxy for the *U.S.-born* Asian American population in the United States.

The high percentage of foreign-born Americans of Chinese, Filipino, Asian Indian, Korean, and Thai descent reflects the rapid immigration experienced by these communities since 1965 (Figure 8.2). Although these ethnic communities are different in many ways, as immigrants they share certain common experiences. Immigrants usually plan their departure, have opportunities to prepare for their arrival, and, at the very least, anticipate their immigrant status and economic conditions. They may immigrate as families or plan for temporary family separation and eventual reunification. They can retain strong ties with relatives and friends in their country of origin and may join family and friends in the United States. They also are often able to integrate into well-established social networks in the United States developed by earlier immigrants from similar backgrounds. Immigration is generally a positive, deliberate action. APA ethnic groups that have experienced a large influx of new immigrants serve here as a proxy for *immigrant-impacted communities.*

The generally high percentage of foreign-born among Vietnamese, Cambodian, Hmong, and Laotian Americans reflects their post–Vietnam War refugee status (Figure 8.2).[6] These communities are far from homogeneous. They differ widely in their cultural practices, religion, language, educational experiences, social class, and historical experiences with the U.S. military. Yet, unlike immigrants, these Americans from Southeast Asia share the refugee experience—they were not voluntary immigrants to the United States. Refugees flee their home countries unwillingly in the face of traumatic situations; they often do not have the opportunity to plan an orderly exit; and they arrive with few resources and no plans for the future. They also are often separated from their families temporarily or permanently and lose contact with families and friends in their countries of origin. Furthermore, Southeast Asian refugees, who were among the first to arrive in the United States, have had to establish new social networks and organizations to support community and economic development rather than benefit from networks established by previous immigrants. Broadly conceived, the Vietnamese, Cambodian, Hmong, and Laotian communities in the United States will serve here as a proxy for *refugee-impacted communities.*

Finally, Americans with Hawaiian, Samoan, and Guamanian backgrounds share similar experiences because their Pacific Island homelands were absorbed into the U.S. sphere of influence. They are indigenous cultural groups in territories acquired by the United States by force of colonization, military intrusion, or political and economic conquest. They are neither voluntary immigrants nor refugees. And, as expected, they report relatively low rates of foreign-born individuals (Figure 8.2) because Hawaii is one of the fifty U.S. states and American Samoa and Guam are U.S. territories. Some members of these groups reside on the U.S. mainland, but most reside in Hawaii or in the territories of Samoa or Guam. While included in the APA social construction, Americans of Hawaiian, Samoan, and Guamanian backgrounds share few historical, cultural, or religious bonds with Americans who trace their origins to Asia. Any bonds between indigenous communities and other APAs tend to take the form of pragmatic politics and shared social influence and power rather than natural cultural or behavioral affinities. Therefore, treating *indigenous communities* as a separate proxy category is warranted.

REVEALING COMPLEXITIES: A DEMOGRAPHIC POLICY ANALYSIS

In this chapter selected demographic characteristics of Asian Pacific American families are compared with the characteristics of all persons in the United States and those of the other major ethnic and racial groups, including Hispanics. The characteristics of APA communities are disaggregated by specific APA ethnic groups. And, as noted, the data on specific ethnic groups are intentionally presented according to the four proxy categories: (1) U.S.-born communities—those of Japanese descent; (2) immigrant-impacted communities—those of Chinese, Filipino, Asian Indian, Korean, and Thai descent; (3) refugee-impacted communities—those of Vietnamese, Cambodian, Hmong, and Laotian descent; and (4) indigenous communities—those of Hawaiian, Samoan, and Guamanian descent. While ethnic affiliation remains important, dividing APA communities into these four categories may be ultimately more useful in public policy analysis than ethnic configurations.

One caveat is in order, however. Use of these categories as proxies does not imply that the categories are homogeneous. Rather, these four categories hint at the underlying construct they represent and offer intriguing ideas for further research and policy studies related to APA families. These proxies, along with dimensions such as ethnic group, gender, and social class, demonstrate the complexities of examining communities, families, and individuals with multiple identities.

Growth Rates

The increased diversity in Asian Pacific American communities has been accompanied by the rapid growth of most APA ethnic groups (Table 8.1).

Table 8.1

APA Population and Growth Rates, by Selected Proxy Categories
and Ethnic Group, 1970–1990

		Population			Percent Change	
		1970	1980	1990	1970–1980	1980–1990
Total APA		1,356,638	3,726,440	7,273,662	174.7	95.2
U.S.-born	Japanese	588,324	716,331	847,562	21.8	18.3
Immigrant-	Chinese	431,583	812,178	1,645,472	88.2	102.6
impacted	Filipino	336,731	781,894	1,406,770	132.2	79.9
	Asian Indian	NA	387,223	815,447	NA	110.6
	Korean	69,510	357,393	798,849	414.2	123.5
Refugee- impacted	Vietnamese	NA	245,025	614,547	NA	150.8
Indigenous	Hawaiian	NA	172,346	211,014	NA	22.4
communities	Samoan	NA	39,520	62,964	NA	59.3
	Guamanian	NA	30,695	49,345	NA	60.8
	Other APA	NA	254,054	934,001	NA	267.6

Source: U.S. Bureau of the Census, "The Nation's Asian and Pacific Islander Population—1994," Statistical Brief, SB/95-24, November 1995.

Note: NA = data not available.

The Japanese American and native Hawaiian communities may have experienced relatively modest growth, but Chinese, Filipino, Asian Indian, and Korean Americans have seen rapid gains in population since 1965, resulting in new communities that now constitute major segments of the APA population. The Vietnamese American community grew fourfold from 1970 to 1980 and more than doubled from 1980 to 1990. These rates reflect those experienced by other refugee-impacted APA communities.[7]

The task of examining growth rates configured by proxy categories is difficult because the historical data for Thais and most refugee groups, for example, are only available for 1990 and later. Yet, even with these limitations, the available data on growth rates confirm the causal observations of low growth rates among U.S.-born APAs, very high growth rates among immigrant- and refugee-impacted communities, and moderate growth rates among indigenous communities. There is little doubt that ethnic composition and growth rates among APAs are related to immigration and refugee policies in the United States and economic and political conditions in the sending regions. Whether these rapid growth rates will continue into the next decades is open to speculation. Some demographers have projected astounding gains in the APA population over the next thirty years,[8] but recent changes in U.S. immigration policies, particularly related to family reunification, economic opportunities in Asia and the Pacific Rim, and the general lack of major military conflicts around the Pacific Rim may significantly moderate Asian emigration to the United States. Furthermore, the rise of "transnational" immigrants who spend time in both the United States and Asia may complicate notions of immigration.[9]

Residential Patterns

Although Asian Pacific Americans can be found in every region of the country, nearly 58 percent of all APAs live in the western United States compared with 21 percent of the U.S. population and 19.5 percent of whites. Seventy percent of the APA population is concentrated in just six states—Hawaii, California, Washington, Texas, Illinois, and New York—and there are significant populations in the Boston and Washington, D.C., areas.[10]

Within the regions in which they reside, APA families are concentrated in urban areas. In 1990, 90 percent of all APAs lived "inside urbanized areas," as defined by the U.S. Bureau of the Census—that is, approximately 47 percent of APAs lived in central cities and 42 percent lived in urban fringe areas.[11] By contrast, only 64 percent of the total U.S. population, 58 percent of whites, 78 percent of blacks, 82 percent of Hispanics, and 39 percent of American Indians lived inside urbanized areas. Los Angeles–Long Beach, California, had the largest number of APA households (276,886), followed by New York City (167,261), Honolulu (155,189), San Francisco (96,493), and Oakland, California (77,154). The highest percentage of APA households in an urban area was in Honolulu; nearly 60 percent of its households were listed as APA.[12]

Place of residence for APA families has several policy implications. First, comparisons of APAs to others living in the west or inside urbanized areas are more instructive than national comparisons because the demographic and economic characteristics of the west and urban areas, where APAs are concentrated, are significantly different from those of other regions of the United States and suburban or rural areas.[13] Second, the geographic concentration of APAs in the west and in urbanized areas is important for policy making and political influence. "National" policy making, undifferentiated by region, places APA families at a disadvantage; policy makers from regions with few APA families may misinterpret or ignore the needs of APA communities, thereby perpetuating the dualistic black/white paradigm in public policy discussions. Yet the concentration of Asian Pacific Americans in certain areas has allowed them some regional influence, especially, for example, in Honolulu and the San Francisco Bay Area.

Family Composition and Characteristics

Table 8.2 compares the characteristics of Asian Pacific American families with those of all U.S. families and families in other racial and ethnic groups. In 1990, 78.1 percent of the 7.2 million persons of Asian or Pacific Islander descent residing in the United States lived in family households, which is higher than the comparable percentage (70.7) for the nation as a whole.[14] Nearly 2 million or 28 percent of those living in family households were under eighteen years of age. Of the APAs living in households, 63.8 percent resided in married couple families, 10.4 percent in households headed by women, 3.6 percent in households headed by men, and 22.2 percent in non-family households.[15]

The average size of APA families was 3.74 persons in 1990, well over the average size of all U.S. families and families of other racial and ethnic groups except Hispanics (Table 8.2). Furthermore, when compared with the nation as a whole, APAs had nearly double the percentage of households made up of five persons (11 percent), six persons (4.2 percent), and seven or more persons (3.1 percent).[16]

A closer look at the 1990 data by proxy categories suggests that U.S.-born APAs are less likely than other APAs and the nation as a whole to reside in family households (Table 8.3). Immigrant-impacted and indigenous communities generally reside in family households at rates higher than those for the total U.S. population, and, of all groups, refugee-impacted communities have the highest rate of residing in family households. On this demographic dimension, within the refugee-impacted communities the Vietnamese community most closely resembles the immigrant-impacted communities.

Although the average APA family was larger than the average American family in 1990, family size differed among APA ethnic groups (see Table 8.3). It ranged from an average of 3.07 persons per family for Japanese Americans to 6.38 persons per family for Hmong Americans. Once again, differences among proxy categories can be observed. The U.S.-born proxy

Table 8.2

Comparative Family Characteristics, by U.S. Population, Race, and Ethnic Group, 1990

Family Characteristic	APA	U.S. Population	Non-Hispanic white	Black	Hispanic	American Indian
In family household (percent)	78.1	70.7	69.6	71.0	81.3	74.2
Persons per family	3.74	3.16	3.1	3.46	3.84	3.57
Median family income	$41,251	$35,225	$37,628	$22,429	$25,064	$21,750
Median family income—inside urban only	$41,285	$38,233	$42,246	$24,302	$25,993	$27,008
Per capita income	$13,638	$14,420	$16,074	$8,859	$8,400	$8,328
Per capita income—inside urban only	$13,772	$15,707	$18,274	$9,501	$8,718	$10,702
Below poverty line—families (percent)	11.6	10.0	7.0	26.3	22.3	27.0
Below poverty line—inside urban only families (percent)	11.6	9.5	5.5	24.6	21.4	19.8
Families with three or more wage earners (percent)	19.8	13.4	13.0	13.4	17.4	12.0

Source: U.S. Bureau of the Census, *1990 Census of Population, Social and Economic Characteristics, CP-2-1* (Washington, D.C., 1993).

Table 8.3

Selected Structural Characteristics of U.S. Population and APA Families,
by Proxy Category and Ethnic Group, 1990

	APA Ethnic Group	In Family Household (percent)	Persons per Family	Median Age	Fertility Rate
U.S. population		70.7	3.16	33.0	1.6
All APAs		78.1	3.74	30.1	1.5
U.S.-born	Japanese	66.0	3.07	36.5	1.1
Immigrant-	Chinese	76.5	3.58	32.3	1.2
impacted	Filipino	82.3	3.97	31.3	1.5
	Asian Indian	82.5	3.73	29.4	1.6
	Korean	80.8	3.55	29.1	1.4
	Thai	70.6	3.4	32.3	1.4
Refugee-	Vietnamese	84.0	4.26	25.6	2.0
impacted	Cambodian	93.8	4.90	19.7	2.3
	Hmong	97.0	6.38	12.7	5.2
	Laotian	92.8	4.90	20.5	2.8
Indigenous	Hawaiian	77.4	3.82	26.2	2.0
communities	Samoan	89.4	4.76	21.3	2.4
	Guamanian	81.6	3.82	25.9	2.1

Source: U.S. Bureau of the Census, *1990 Census of Population, Social and Economic Characteristics*, CP-2-1 (Washington, D.C., 1993).

Note: Fertility rates were calculated by dividing the number of women ages twenty-five to forty-four by the number of children born to them.

had the smallest family size; in fact, it is even slightly smaller than the average American family size. Immigrant-impacted and indigenous communities have moderately larger families than U.S.-born communities, and the average size of refugee-impacted families is significantly larger than those of almost all other groups.

Striking differences in median age across APA proxy categories and ethnic families can be observed (Table 8.3). The U.S.-born proxy category has the highest median age; immigrant-impacted families have lower median ages compared with the national average; and refugee-impacted and indigenous families are significantly younger than other groups. The large differences in median age among the four proxy categories suggest differences in the structure of proxy families. U.S.-born families are older with fewer young children; refugee-impacted families are younger with more young children within the family unit.

In summary, as aggregated, APA families are composed of married couple families, larger in size than most other American families. Disaggregation of APA family composition by proxy categories and ethnic groups reveals complexities within APA communities. U.S.-born APAs are older, are less likely to live in family households, and have few persons per family. Immigrant-impacted families are moderately younger than the national average, are likely to live in a family household, and live in larger families than most other Americans. Refugee-impacted families are much younger than the Americans as a whole and other APAs and are very likely to live in a family household that is significantly larger than other households. Finally, indigenous families are much younger than the national average age and generally live in family households that are larger than the national average size. These differences in the structural characteristics of APA families by proxy categories suggests that generic social policies or social research on APAs would not be as effective as targeting policies, resources, and research at a specific configuration. It then follows that family-related services should be tailored to specific proxy categories. For example, housing policy or job training aimed at U.S.-born APAs should differ from that for refugee-impacted families because of differences in family size, median age, and fertility rates. Refugee and indigenous families require assistance in parenting and economic development designed specifically for their status and experience as refugees or indigenous communities as compared with immigrant families.

Characterized by an extremely low median age, large size, high fertility rate, and relatively low percentage of foreign-born persons, Hmong families appear to be headed by refugee parents with many U.S.-born children. This interpretation supports the need for more field research on the Hmong in the United States and for culturally sensitive social policies designed specifically for this unique segment of the APA community.[17]

Income

Median family income, per capita income, and poverty data are presented in Table 8.2 for groups living anywhere in the United States and those living "inside urbanized areas." A comparison of groups living anywhere in the United States reveals that APAs have the highest median family income. Deconstruction of these oft-quoted statistics, however, reveals a more complex picture. The median family income for APAs living "inside urban areas" is approximately the same as the nationwide median for APAs, but for every other comparison group the median incomes of those residing inside urban areas is higher than its national median. This finding confirms the intense concentration of APAs in urban areas and provides evidence that for all Americans incomes are generally higher in urban areas than outside urban areas. When compared with all American families living inside urban areas, APAs continue to have significant median family incomes, but they fall below the median incomes for white families.

The relatively high median family income reported by APA families also reflects in part the larger number of wage earners per family (Table 8.2). In 1990 nearly 20 percent of APA families had three or more wage earners, many more than any other comparison group. This high number may stem from the lower per capita income of APA families when compared with those for the nation as a whole and for whites. A substantially higher percentage of APAs live below the poverty line than Americans generally or whites. Thus, although the APA median family income is quite robust, it reflects the larger number of wage earners per family who make less per capita and live inside urbanized areas. Median family income, then, masks a significant number of families living below the poverty line and the higher percentage of multiple wage earners per family.

Disaggregation of income data by proxy categories and by APA ethnic groups is even more revealing (Table 8.4). In 1990 median family incomes ranged from a high of $51,550 for Japanese Americans to a low of $14,227 for Hmong Americans. Lower median family incomes are concentrated among refugee-impacted and indigenous families. Per capita income data also show differences among APA ethnic groups, with Japanese Americans having the highest per capita incomes and Hmong Americans the lowest. Once again, APA refugee-impacted families have significantly lower average per capita incomes than other APA groups.

Family poverty rates also demonstrate significant differences among APA groups. The family poverty rate for the U.S.-born proxy category is remarkably low, whereas the poverty rate for immigrant-impacted groups suggests complexities in this proxy group. The significantly lower poverty rates for Filipino and Asian Indian Americans probably reflect the higher levels of educational attainment and greater proportion of professional workers among these immigrants compared with other immigrant-impacted families.[18] The family poverty rates for the refugee-impacted families—and for Samoan Americans—are alarmingly high.

Table 8.4

Selected Income Characteristics of the U.S. Population and APA Families, by Proxy Category and Ethnic Group, 1990

	APA Ethnic Group	Median Family Income	Per Capita Household Income	Percent of Families Below Poverty Line	Percent of Families with Three or More Wage Earners	Percent of Families with No Wage Earners
U.S. Population		$35,225	$14,420	10.0	13.4	13.0
All APAs		$41,251	$13,638	11.6	19.8	8.3
U.S.-born	Japanese	$51,550	$19,373	3.4	15.3	8.7
Immigrant-impacted	Chinese	$41,316	$14,877	11.1	19.0	7.9
	Filipino	$46,698	$13,616	5.2	29.6	4.1
	Asian Indian	$49,309	$17,777	7.2	17.8	2.3
	Korean	$33,909	$11,178	14.7	15.8	7.6
	Thai	$37,257	$12,140	10.8	15.5	5.0
Refugee-impacted	Vietnamese	$30,550	$9,057	23.8	21.3	13.6
	Cambodian	$18,126	$5,098	42.1	13.5	38.1
	Hmong	$14,227	$2,694	61.8	6.7	49.9
	Laotian	$23,101	$5,606	32.2	18.8	26.7
Indigenous communities	Hawaiian	$37,269	$11,576	12.7	20.0	9.5
	Samoan	$27,228	$7,101	24.5	19.5	11.1
	Guamanian	$33,020	$10,804	12.3	19.1	5.9

Source: U.S. Bureau of the Census, *1990 Census of Population, Social and Economic Characteristics, CP-2-1* (Washington, D.C., 1993).

In all proxy categories the percentages of families with three or more wage earners exceed the national average of multiple wage earners. This is particularly remarkable for the immigrant-impacted, refugee-impacted, and indigenous families. The high percentage of multiple wage earners suggests that in APA families both parents and often older children are working. Because for many APA families per capita income is quite low and poverty rates are quite high, parents and older children are working in low-wage jobs. Focused on economic survival, they have little time or energy for alternative activities, including parenting, leisure, and self-development.

The very low percentage of three or more wage earners found for Hmong American families not only is much lower than those of the APAs, but also is associated with a very high rate of families with no wage earners, 49.9 percent. Cambodians and Laotians have high rates of no wage earners as well, indicating worrisome high levels of total disengagement from wage earning for all these groups. Furthermore, the median family income for Hmong Americans is less than half the average income for Americans as a whole, and that of Hmong and Cambodian Americans is less than half the median income for APAs as a whole. These observations suggest that refugee-impacted families are in economic crisis—a conclusion supported by the high rates of Cambodian, Hmong, and Laotian Americans in the social welfare system.[19] Recent changes in the social welfare system have had a disproportionately negative impact on refugee families. Many of them regard government assistance as partial payment for their participation in the Vietnam War in behalf of the United States.[20] Whatever the case, their lack of preparation for economic survival in the United States places them at greater economic risk than other APAs. Moreover, the poverty rates and low per capita incomes of APA refugee families and Samoan Americans suggest some needs are masked in any examination of the aggregate APA data. Culturally sensitive, targeted public policy and interventions are required for APA families living at the margins of the U.S. economy.

Based on median family income, per capita income, poverty rates, and numbers of wage earners within families, the four proxy categories used here roughly coincide with four socioeconomic levels. The U.S.-born proxy with high median incomes, high per capita incomes, low poverty rates, and moderate numbers of wage earners approximates an upper-middle-class economic environment. Immigrant-impacted families with moderate median incomes and moderate per capita incomes but with mixed rates of poverty and more families with multiple wage earners can be characterized as a struggling working class but engaged in the economic environment.

Refugee-impacted families, by contrast, have significantly lower median and per capita incomes than other proxy categories, accompanied by very high rates of poverty, multiple wage earners per family, and very high levels of families with no wage earners reported. They represent a working community steeped in poverty. Even with the relatively higher median income of Vietnamese Americans, refugee-impacted families are significantly different from the U.S.-born proxy and immigrant-impacted families.

For indigenous families, the picture is more complicated. The category is characterized by mixed levels of median income but generally lower levels of per capita income, higher levels of poverty, and more multiple wage earners than other American families. In its entirety, the economic picture of indigenous families falls somewhere between that of immigrant-impacted families and refugee-impacted families. These divisions by social class require further investigation and may be another critical configuration of APAs worthy of careful examination.

The economic picture of APA families is, then, complex. Although APA median family income is comparatively high, this phenomenon is a product of several intervening variables, including the fact that APAs cluster in higher-cost, higher-income urban areas, have more wage earners per family, and have lower per capita incomes than the U.S. population and whites. Furthermore, the higher median family income of APA families is moderated by their larger family size. Thus APA family incomes must be considered within the context of APA families who are deeply engaged in a struggle for economic stability and mobility rather than families resting well with the comforts and leisure of the average middle-class American.

Housing

The housing characteristics of Asian Pacific American families are another indicator of their economic condition. APA families are more likely than whites to live in crowded conditions as defined by the U.S. Bureau of the Census. Within metropolitan areas, APAs are eight times more likely to live in crowded households than whites (24 percent versus 3 percent). In central city areas, 28 percent of APAs live in crowded conditions as compared with 4 percent of whites.[21]

The median value of homes owned by APAs in 1990 was $184,000, double that for whites ($91,700). The high value of homes owned by APAs can be explained by the concentration of APA homeowners in California and Honolulu where median home costs are well above the U.S. norm. By contrast, white homeowners are not as highly concentrated in high-cost urban areas; rather, they may be found in lower-cost suburban and rural areas. APA home values in metropolitan areas in California were generally comparable to those of whites, but in Honolulu the median home value for white owners was $324,900 compared with $274,000 for APA owners.[22]

As for renters, within the top twenty-five metropolitan areas APAs paid a median rent of $447 a month, or 15 percent more than whites ($390). In suburban areas, APAs paid $579 a month versus $443 for whites, or a difference of 31 percent.[23] Clearly, because APAs tend to live in more costly areas of the country, they require more income to meet their housing expenses than they would need if they settled in less costly areas.[24] Disaggregated data on housing costs among APAs are not available and remain a subject for further research.

Language

APAs are over five times more likely than the total U.S. population to speak a language other than English (Table 8.5). In 1990, 38.4 percent reported not speaking English "very well" and 24.2 percent said they live in "linguistically isolated" households.[25] Of particular interest is the linguistic environment of school-age children (ages 5–17). Over 60 percent of APA children speak a language other than English and 25 percent do not speak English "very well" and live in "linguistically isolated" households. In the United States as a whole, relatively few persons live in non-English-speaking environments.

Among APA ethnic groups, 44 percent of Japanese Americans, the proxy category for U.S.-born APAs, speak a language other than English and only one-fourth report not speaking English "very well." Thus U.S.-born APAs still experience some level of a non-English language environment, perhaps through older members of the community and recent immigrants.

Immigrant-impacted families report significant language diversity at home. Particularly those families with immigrants from non-English-speaking countries report high levels of individuals who speak a language other than English, who do not speak English "very well," and who live in "linguistically isolated" households. As expected, Filipino and Asian Indian Americans, whose language use and training in their country of origin often included English, report lower rates of individuals who do not speak English "very well" or who live in linguistic isolation. Individuals from these families, however, are very likely to be bilingual, speaking a language other than English as well.

Table 8.5

Language Spoken at Home by U.S. Population and APA Families,
by Proxy Category and Ethnic Group, 1990
(percent)

	APA Ethnic Group	Speak Language Other than English	Do Not Speak English "Very Well"	Linguistically Isolated Household
U.S. population		13.8	6.0	3.5
Total APA population		73.3	38.4	24.2
APA ages 5–17		60.6	25.7	24.8
U.S.-born	Japanese	44.0	25.2	14.8
Immigrant-impacted	Chinese	84.0	50.5	34.8
	Filipino	68.4	24.2	9.7
	Asian Indian	77.7	23.5	11.2
	Korean	82.2	51.6	35.1
	Thai	80.0	46.2	26.6
Refugee-impacted	Vietnamese	93.8	60.8	42.1
	Cambodian	96.0	70.0	54.6
	Hmong	97.4	67.0	59.8
	Laotian	96.8	67.8	51.5
Indigenous communities	Hawaiian	10.0	2.7	1.0
	Samoan	66.4	21.8	7.2
	Guamanian	46.1	16.3	8.1

Source: U.S. Bureau of the Census, *1990 Census of Population, Social and Economic Characteristics, CP-2-1* (Washington, D.C., 1993), tables 40 and 106.

Note: Statistics apply to age group five years and older. Linguistic isolation refers to persons in households in which no one fourteen years or older speaks only English and no one who speaks a language other than English speaks English "very well."

Nearly all members of refugee-impacted families speak a language other than English, with the majority reporting not speaking English "very well" and living in "linguistically isolated" households. Because these families are largely new to the United States and do not have a historical population base prior to 1975, the high levels of limited English and linguistic isolation are to be expected. Nevertheless, these language data suggest the need for targeted public policy that would help refugee families acquire the English language skills necessary for full involvement in the economic and civic life of the United States.

Data on indigenous families present a mixed and misleading picture. For example, few Hawaiians report speaking a language other than English and few also claim to live in a linguistically isolated household. Yet mastery of "standard" English is often regarded as an educational challenge for native Hawaiian children. The reason: Hawaiian Creole English (pidgin English) is spoken by many Hawaiians and is classified as "English" in surveys of home language environments. The implications of Hawaiian Creole for the development of the Hawaiian community require special study. Hawaiian Creole is tied to a long linguistic history and political issues of "home rule" among Hawaiians. It has political significance for many native Hawaiians, yet its implications for the education and economic, social, and political success of native Hawaiians remain controversial.[26] For Samoan and Guamanian Americans, the reported language factors suggest that their families include a significant number of bilingual persons.

Educational Attainment

The comparative data on educational attainment by persons twenty-five years and older in 1994 reveal that the percentage of APAs with a high school education or more exceeds the rate for the total U.S. population and is nearly identical to that for whites (Table 8.6).[27] In education, the APA community shows a bimodal distribution. APAs are nearly twice as likely as the total population or whites to have achieved bachelor's degrees or more, and yet APAs also are one and a half times more likely than the total population or whites to have only an eighth-grade education or less.

A different picture emerges when comparing only those residing in the western United States where the majority of APAs reside. In general, those residing in the west have obtained more education than the nation as a whole. Whites in the west have the highest rate of high school graduation or beyond (90.3 percent), exceeding both the total population and APAs in the west. By contrast, over 10 percent of APAs have an eighth-grade education or less, which is over three times the rate for the white population in the west. While APAs still lead whites in those with bachelor's degrees or more, the gap between APAs and whites closes in the west, and the bimodality found in APA communities is enhanced.

An examination of educational attainment by proxy category and APA ethnic groups reveals that some groups are educationally at risk (Table 8.7).

Table 8.6

Comparison of Educational Attainment in the United States,
by Race and Residence in West, 1994
(percent)

United States	Total Population	Asian Pacific Americans	Whites
Eighth grade or less	8.8	9.8	6.2
Ninth grade to high school graduate	44.6	30.0	44.3
Some college or associate degree	24.3	19.1	25.2
Bachelor's degree or more	22.2	41.2	24.3
High school graduate or more	80.9	84.8	84.9
West Only			
Eighth grade or less	9.1	10.8	3.1
Ninth grade to high school graduate	37.3	32.6	36.5
Some college or associate degree	29.4	21.9	32.3
Bachelor's degree or more	24.2	34.7	28.1
High school graduate or more	82.6	83.9	90.3

Source: U.S. Bureau of the Census, *The Asian and Pacific Islander Population in the United States,* 1994 Current Population Survey (Washington, D.C., March 1994).

Note: Statistics apply to age group twenty-five years and older.

The U.S.-born proxy exceeds the educational attainment of the average American population. The immigrant-impacted communities have higher rates of persons with bachelor's degrees than the national average, but they also exceed the rate of those with less than a fifth-grade education. In part, these data reflect preferences in U.S. immigration policy since 1965 that favor well-educated, highly skilled immigrants and family reunification. The high rates of persons with bachelor's degrees or more, particularly among immigrant communities, stem from the large numbers of foreign educated. Thus educational attainment for immigrant-impacted communities may not reflect an American educational experience but rather a foreign education often not recognized in the United States. This lack of certification of foreign education is social policy that inhibits the full economic potential of foreign-educated immigrants. At the same time, immigration policy also has favored family reunification, in which family members of U.S. citizens may apply for admission to the United States. Some of these immigrants may be the elderly parents of U.S. naturalized citizens, and they may have little formal education.

Table 8.7
Educational Attainment, by Proxy Category and Ethnic Group, 1990

		Less than Fifth Grade	High School or More	Some College	Bachelor's or More
U.S. population		2.7	75.0	45.2	20.3
All APAs		6.9	77.5	59.0	36.6
U.S.-born	Japanese	1.4	87.5	61.5	34.5
Immigrant-	Chinese	9.4	73.6	59.1	40.7
impacted	Filipino	4.2	82.6	66.3	39.3
	Asian Indian	3.8	84.7	73.2	58.1
	Korean	4.6	80.2	55.4	34.5
	Thai	8.6	74.0	57.3	32.8
Refugee-	Vietnamese	11.4	61.2	43.7	17.4
impacted	Cambodian	40.7	34.9	23.1	5.7
	Hmong	54.9	31.1	20.6	4.9
	Laotian	33.9	40.0	20.9	5.4
Indigenous	Hawaiian	1.3	79.5	40.9	11.9
communities	Samoan	4.3	70.6	34.8	8.0
	Guamanian	4.7	72.3	41.0	10.0

Source: U.S. Bureau of the Census, *1990 Census of Population, Social and Economic Characteristics, CP-2-1* (Washington, D.C., 1993).

Educational risk is clearly revealed in the data for refugee-impacted communities. Their rates of higher education (some college or a bachelor's degree) are well under the rates for all APAs and for the nation, and their rates of those with less than fifth-grade education are quite high. The high rates of limited education for the Cambodian, Hmong, and Laotian communities require special attention because in the United States level of education is related to economic potential and preparation for citizenship through naturalization. Without a substantial formal educational experience in either the United States or their country of origin, some refugees and their children are at risk of failure. Adult education can provide refugee adults with opportunities to increase their English language skills, obtain the training needed for high-skill jobs and steady employment, and prepare for citizenship examinations. It also can help them help their children succeed in school. Clearly, social and educational policies must be carefully targeted to the specific needs of the refugee-impacted communities.

The educational attainment of indigenous communities, who are largely U.S.-born and have had their full educational experience in the American educational system, is also problematic. They negotiate high school in reasonable numbers, although in slightly fewer numbers than other groups. The proportions of those who attend or graduate from college, however, are very low in comparison with those of all APAs and the total U.S. population. Given the relatively small population of indigenous communities, culturally sensitive and targeted intervention to raise their college completion rate would have a good probability for success. The educational needs of indigenous communities in the United States have gone largely unattended, however.

DEMOGRAPHIC SUMMARY

The demographic profile of APA families is complex and multilayered, but U.S. Census data do provide a general but limited outline of APA families. In broad strokes APA families can be described as:

- ethnically diverse;
- rapidly growing;
- married family households;
- larger-than-average households;
- composed of more wage earners per family than average households;
- possessing significant income diversity—from relatively high incomes to alarmingly low incomes;
- living in greater poverty than average households;
- concentrated inside urban areas and largely in the western United States;
- living in crowded and high-cost housing areas;
- largely foreign-born;
- linguistically diverse, with many living in non-English environments; and
- educationally diverse, with some groups at educational risk.

PUBLIC POLICY IMPLICATIONS

Even with the limitations of the broad survey data, the demographic picture of APA families illuminates several important public policy issues for both advocates of APA communities and policy makers.

Culturally Sensitive and Targeted Public Policy

Advocates and public policy makers must continue to be sensitive to the complex diversity within Asian Pacific American communities. Any attempts to base public policy on the aggregate conception of APA communities will be extremely problematic, will mask significant issues, and may not be effective or reach families in greatest need. For example, public policy based on aggregate family income data would overlook significant issues affecting APA refugee-impacted and indigenous families. By disaggregating and deconstructing the APA concept, policy makers will be better able to develop targeted and specific interventions and policies.

Interventions and remediations that are more precisely designed and culturally sensitive should be a goal as well. For example, the refugee-impacted communities in the United States are a direct result of the U.S. military intervention in Southeast Asia in the 1960s and early 1970s and the withdrawal of the U.S. military in 1975. It is unlikely that many Vietnamese, Cambodians, Hmong, and Laotians would have chosen to leave their homelands in Southeast Asia had not their service to the Central Intelligence Agency and U.S. military forced their military evacuation.

The economic crisis in which these relatively small ethnic groups find themselves deserves special attention. Yet rather than meeting the special needs and concerns of these groups, new national "welfare reform" policies have thrust many of these refugees further into economic chaos. For example, an estimated 20,000 Hmong in California have lost their food stamp support and will lose other public assistance as well.[28] Without other means of support and with very little education or job skills relevant to the U.S. environment, Hmong Americans face a grave economic situation. Culturally sensitive and targeted social policy—for example, specifically designed "welfare reform" for Hmong Americans and other APA refugee families—is urgently needed and is independent of the needs or concern of other APAs.

Influence over Local and National Policy

As noted earlier, Asian Pacific Americans are largely concentrated in the urban areas of six states. This concentration of the APA population has public policy advantages and disadvantages. In California the increase in the APA population has contributed to a moderate increase in political power and social influence; proof is offered by the election of local APA politicians and a greater awareness of the cultural and economic contributions of this segment of the U.S. population. Yet the heavy concentration of Asian Pacific Americans in particular areas and their relatively small numbers in other regions lead to various levels of ignorance or lack of concern by policy makers who have little or no contact with APAs. Because the overall APA population in the United States is less than 3 percent, APA communities are often disregarded by national policy makers as inconsequential segments of the American mosaic. While some policy makers believe that most politics is local, public policy made at the national level has a profound effect on the allocation of resources and the definition of social concerns, both of which too often disregard the needs of APAs because of the lack of APA constituencies throughout the country.

Naturalization and Voting Rights

For immigrants and refugees, exercising the right to vote begins by obtaining citizenship through the naturalization process. Although APAs have high rates of naturalization, they also have very low rates of voter registration when compared with other groups.[29]

The influx of foreign-born APAs over the past three decades now faces the naturalization process and incorporation into the political process. The naturalization process, however, discriminates against non-English speakers and those who did not attend Western-style educational systems. As a result, APA immigrants and refugees are at a distinct disadvantage. For example, the naturalization process includes minimum competencies in both English literacy and basic civics (U.S. history and government). While the minimum standards in both areas do not appear to be overly onerous for well-educated people, they do discriminate against segments of APA communities.

The English literacy requirements and basic civics requirements are particularly difficult for older immigrants and refugees who have little formal education and who may be illiterate even in their home language.[30] For example, a typical citizenship course may require that students spend over one hundred hours of class time memorizing the answers to trivial multiple-choice questions about U.S. history and government. Because the instructions and tests are in English, non-English-speaking immigrants often memorize the questions and associated answers without comprehending the concepts under study.

The relevancy of the English literacy or civics requirements to competent or appropriate citizenship behavior has never been demonstrated. Instead, they represent sturdy barriers to many who would welcome naturalization and full participation in the United States. A more efficient naturalization process might allow non-English-speaking immigrants to learn about U.S. political processes and traditions in their own language. Indeed, they could be required to acquire a higher level of civics competence in their home language than is currently required. They also could devote more and separate attention to learning English (which would improve their civic and economic participation) rather than memorizing answers to specific test items and to learning the values and behavior of good citizenship (which might include parenting and work skills).

Permanent resident aliens not only are excluded from selecting national and statewide officeholders, but also are powerless to influence their local governments and, in particular, their local school boards. Moreover, although they pay their fair share of taxes, they are unable to influence the election of their local, state, and federal representatives. Their inability to vote silences their concerns and diminishes their ability to influence local policies that affect them intimately. Some Asian Pacific immigrant and refugee parents have complained that they are voiceless within their schools because they have no right to vote for local school boards. In this case, the traditional relationship of citizenship to voting produces public policy that works against local control and political influence for many Asian Pacific families.

Language Policy

Significant numbers of Asian Pacific Americans live in non-English-speaking environments. Currently, bilingual education policies are designed to be "subtractive" processes aimed at preparing students to make a smooth, rapid transition from their home language to English proficiency. Subtractive approaches to bilingualism, however, devalue the home language and diminish a student's language proficiency in that language. This process contributes to the alienation between parents and children. New initiatives to completely eliminate even subtractive bilingual education and encourage English-only policies will further exacerbate family divisions within many APA families.

Language barriers and cultural conflicts between parents and youth are found in many APA families, but especially those in the immigrant-impacted and refugee-impacted communities. Although many APA children and youth are thought to be completely bilingual, their skills in their home language are often marginal. They may be able to communicate with their parents on simple matters, but many APA "bilingual" youth are unable to discuss complex or emotional issues with their parents in either their home language or in English. Miscommunication, lack of communication, and cultural conflicts between APA youth and parents are quite common. For many APAs, language barriers are significant obstructions to full participation in the U.S. economic system as well. Lacking English, many APA immigrants and refugees are restricted to low-paying jobs and limited upward mobility. Even some highly educated APAs who may speak English fluently but with an accent often encounter job discrimination and glass ceilings.[31] Contrary to popular belief, APA immigrants and refugees, like most immigrants and refugees in the United States, are eager to learn English, yet the opportunities for adults to learn English are quite limited. Not only does economic survival take precedence over English language training, but even if immigrants and refugees can find the time to enroll in English-as-second-language (ESL) courses, they will find that such courses at adult education schools are filled to capacity.

Language barriers also prevent many APAs from full participation in the political system. While bilingual ballots and government documents have been important advances, bilingual documents are limited to the largest APA ethnic groups and ignore many APAs illiterate in their home language. Breaking down the language barriers in a multicultural and multilingual society requires a stronger commitment to multilingual environments. Language policies that preserve and develop home languages other than English would enhance family life for many APA families. Development of home language competence by APA youth would not only improve family communications but may provide a rich language resource for participation in a global economy. Support for adult education and English language training in the workplace and other settings is an important public policy goal that would enhance the potential for economic and political participation by many APA adults currently unable to fully participate in American society.

Policies that Support Families

Policy makers and educators often assume that the strong concern for families and education expressed by many Asian Pacific Americans goes hand in hand with equally strong parental supervision. Although the generally strong educational ethos among APA families is often interpreted as some underlying dimension of the Asian culture, more recent analysis suggests that many immigrants see education as a highly valued tool for improving economic status and combating discrimination.[32]

But strong parental support for education and the general well-being of their children is not a proxy for strong parental involvement or supervision. Many APA children report being in unsupervised homes where both parents spend more hours outside the home working than they do at home. Although APA parents vocalize their concerns for their children and may even establish harsh "family rules" and environments to ensure educational progress, many APA parents may not be physically available for the positive parenting necessary for positive child development. The alienation between parents and youth, a growing problem in many APA families, is in part a product of absentee parenting and conflicts between parental values and culture and peer values and culture. The sixteen-hour workdays in sewing factories, restaurants, or mini-markets have a negative impact on parenting and participation in community and civic affairs.

When asked to propose solutions to this strain between APA youth and parents, some APA youth suggest programs that would pay their parents to acquire the basic English skills and job skills needed to escape low-paying, long-hours jobs. In short, language barriers and long working days for parents create a culture of alienation within high-risk APA families. Dual "careers" for APA immigrant and refugee couples are often low-prestige, low-paying hourly jobs, frequently with no benefits. Because APA immigrant and refugee women often are initially more "employable" than their husbands, the traditional power relationships between husbands and wives and between parents and daughters may be disrupted. Although the disruption of traditional patriarchal dominance may ultimately be a worthy goal, family disruption caused by gender differences in employability has resulted in family stress and even increases in domestic violence directed at APA women. Efforts to balance economic necessities and opportunities in APA families may enhance the roles and opportunities of mothers and daughters, but the social costs incurred require the attention of advocates and policy makers.[33]

Policies Related to Children of Newcomers

The children of newcomers present special problems. All immigrant and refugee children are "involuntary" immigrants who are rarely consulted about being uprooted from their home environment to move to the United States. Numerous life histories suggest that immigration for children can be quite traumatic. Often they are not consulted or notified about the impending move until shortly before departure, they are not able to say goodbye to their friends and relatives, and they do not understand parental motivations for moving. Even in the harsh conditions of war, life histories suggest that children often live protected lives and find moving to a safer but strange location quite puzzling.

Compounding their dislocation, immigrant and refugee children generally acquire English faster than their parents and often face greater responsibilities than other children and youth. They help their parents and other adults learn to negotiate the American environment, often serving as the interface between their families, particularly their non-English-speaking parents, and the greater society. It is not unusual to see newcomer children serving as translators for their parents in grocery stores, doctors' offices, social service agencies, or schools. Children of newcomers also often face a loss of childhood and have greater responsibilities within the home for housekeeping, babysitting, and essential home care compared with other children and youth. Many APA youth are important economic contributors to the family income as well, either working outside the family or as unpaid workers in small family-operated businesses. Advocates on behalf of APAs and public policy makers should develop interventions and policies that especially target newcomers and their children.

Policy Issues Related to Indigenous Families

The political history of Asian Pacific American indigenous groups gives rise to a different interpretation of the complexities of their communities and families than those of other APAs. Indigenous Pacific Islanders are neither immigrants nor refugees to the United States. Rather, their homelands were absorbed into the U.S. sphere of influence either as a state or as "protected" territories. Simply put, indigenous Pacific Island communities did not choose to be Americans.

Located on both the U.S. mainland and in the Pacific Islands, Pacific Island indigenous groups may share more political identity with mainland American Indians than with their Asian American counterparts. Their desires and motivations to integrate into the American economic and social mainstream are moderated by their desires for self-determination and identities as independent peoples.[34]

The desire of indigenous communities for self-determination influences the effectiveness of educational and economic interventions designed for them. Policies intended to further absorb indigenous communities into the mainstream of American life may be met with skepticism at best and open hostility at worst. Educational attainment and economic participation are important concerns facing these communities. Yet advocates and public policy makers need to consider the perspectives of Pacific Islanders on issues of sovereignty and indigenous rights as they work with indigenous groups to design social and political policy. Finally, scholars, advocates, and policy makers must separate indigenous Pacific Islander voices from Asian American voices. Under current practices, the perspectives, concerns, and needs of indigenous Pacific Islanders are overwhelmed by the larger, more dominant Asian American communities in the pan-ethnic alliance among Asian and Pacific Islander Americans.

CONCLUSION

Asian Pacific American families are multilayered and complex. Significant differences are found not only between APA families and other Americans, but also among APA ethnic groups and APA proxies for U.S.-born, immigrant-impacted, refugee-impacted, and indigenous groups. Indeed, this analysis suggests that the proxy configuration of APAs provides a relevant method for assessing the qualities and needs of APA families. By understanding the characteristics of the four proxy categories, advocates and policy makers can formulate more appropriate public policy and interventions than by using ethnic configurations alone. Use of both the proxy and ethnic configurations in combination would yield analysis more sensitive to the cultural and social complexities of these communities.

APA families and communities also have dimensions beyond those examined in this chapter. For example, women and men within APA families and communities have somewhat different perspectives and needs. The growing rate of intermarriage among APAs and between APAs and others further compounds notions of APA families and communities. No single configuration or disaggregation of APAs is satisfactory. Multiple dimensions require multiple analyses and multiple strategies.

Analysis of the proxy categories also leads to speculation about the commonalities and differences existing between APA proxy categories and similar proxy categories in other racial and ethnic groups. For example, what are the similarities and differences among APA immigrant families and Hispanic immigrant families? What are the commonalities and differences shared by APA refugee families and refugees from Central America and elsewhere? What role do race and culture play in modulating proxy features and needs? It could easily be suggested, for example, that U.S.-born APAs are more like other U.S.-born populations in the United States, particularly whites. Yet U.S.-born APAs are not white in the racialized U.S. society. Although many U.S.-born APAs have reached certain levels of economic and educational parity, the experiences of U.S.-born APAs are still tempered by racial barriers, discrimination, and glass ceilings not experienced by U.S.-born whites.[35] One need only look at the relationship between educational level and income to note that while some APAs may attain reasonable levels of education, their incomes are not commensurate with their educational attainment.[36] Thus, although the new proxy categories can provide another important perspective on APA communities, race and ethnic background still matter.

NOTES

1. The author wishes to thank Gordon H. Chang for his leadership on this project, Warren I. Cohen and the staff of the Woodrow Wilson Center for their support, and Shirley Hune and Purnima Mankekar for their critical reading of the manuscript.

In this study the term *Asian Pacific American (APA)* is used to refer to both Asian Americans and Pacific Islanders. It includes persons of Chinese, Filipino, Japanese, Asian Indian, Korean, Vietnamese, Cambodian, Hmong, Laotian, Thai, Hawaiian, Samoan, and Guamanian descent. It also includes important but relatively small communities such as Burmese, Sri Lankan, Malayan, Indonesian, Pakistani, Bangladeshi, Tongan, Fijian, Palauian, Tahitian, and other distinct cultural, linguistic, and national groups with roots throughout the Pacific Rim. The term *Asian American* remains common usage, but *Asian Pacific American* is a more inclusive term. Where pertinent and possible, Asian Americans and Pacific Islanders are discussed separately and a distinction is made between the two groups.

2. Yen Le Espiritu, *Asian American Panethnicity* (Philadelphia: Temple University Press, 1992).

3. For a more complete discussion of the demographic shift within the APA community since 1970, see Kenyon Chan and Shirley Hune, "Racialization and Panethnicity: From Asians in America to Asian Americans," in *Toward a Common Destiny: Educational Perspectives on Improving Race and Ethnic Relations,* ed. Willis Hawley and Anthony Jackson (San Francisco: Jossey-Bass, 1995), 393–404; and Shirley Hune and Kenyon Chan, "Special Focus: Asian Pacific American Demographic and Educational Trends," in *Fifteenth Annual Status Report on Minorities in Higher Education,* ed. Deborah Carter and Reginald Wilson (Washington, D.C.: American Council on Education, 1997), 39–67, 103–107.

4. U.S. Bureau of the Census, *1990 Census of the Population* (Washington, D.C., 1993), tables 1, 9, 11.

5. U.S. Bureau of the Census, *We the Americans: Foreign Born* (Washington, D.C., September 1993). In this study the term *white* refers to non-Hispanic whites; *Hispanic* refers to Hispanics of any race; *American Indian* includes American Indians, Eskimos, and Aleuts; and *black* is used interchangeably with *African American.*

6. The relatively lower rate of foreign-born among the Hmong (65.2 percent) stems in part from the very high birthrate and very low median age (12.7 years) found for the Hmong in the United States.

7. U.S. Bureau of the Census, *The Nation's Asian and Pacific Islander Population—1994,* Statistical Brief SB/95-24 (Washington, D.C., November 1995).

8. Paul Ong and Suzanne Hee, "Twenty Million in 2020," in LEAP Asian Pacific American Public Policy Institute, *The State of Asian Pacific Americans: Policy Issues to the Year 2020* (Los Angeles: LEAP Asian Pacific American Public Policy Institute and UCLA Asian American Studies Center, 1993).

9. See, for example, Linda Basch, Nina Glick Schiller, and Christina Slanton, *Nations Unbound* (Luxembourg: Gordon and Breach Publishers, 1994); and Aihwa Ong, "On the Edge of Empire: Flexible Citizenship among Chinese in the Diaspora," *Positions* 1 (winter 1993): 3, 745–778.

10. U.S. Bureau of the Census, *1990 Census of Population, Social and Economic Characteristics,* CP-2-1 (Washington, D.C., 1993).

11. U.S. Bureau of the Census, *1990 Census of Population,* table 9. "Inside urbanized areas" is defined by the Census Bureau as central places and urban fringe areas inhabited by fifty thousand or more persons.

12. U.S. Bureau of the Census, *Housing in Metropolitan Areas: Asian or Pacific Islander Households,* Statistical Brief SB/95-6 (Washington, D.C., April 1995).

13. U.S. Bureau of the Census, *1990 Census of Population.* A comparison of the demographic data, particularly on economic matters, for either "inside urbanized areas" or the west with the aggregate U.S. data reveals striking differences. According to the Census Bureau, the west comprises the following states: Alaska, Hawaii, Washington, Oregon, California, Montana, Idaho, Wyoming, Colorado, Utah, Nevada, Arizona, and New Mexico.

14. U.S. Bureau of the Census, *1990 Census of Population, Social and Economic Characteristics,* CP-2-2 (Washington, D.C., 1993), table 40.

15. U.S. Bureau of the Census, *The Asian and Pacific Islander Population in the United States,* (Washington, D.C., March 1994), table 7.

16. Ibid.

17. See Nancy Donnelly, *Changing Lives of Refugee Hmong Women* (Seattle: University of Washington Press, 1994); and Wendy Walker-Moffat, *The Other Side of the Asian American Story* (San Francisco: Jossey-Bass, 1995).

18. Fifty-eight percent of Asian Indians and 39.3 percent of Filipinos twenty-five years and over in the United States had bachelor's degrees or higher compared with

36.6 percent of all APAs and 20.3 percent of all Americans. Although 40.7 percent of Chinese Americans had bachelor's degrees or higher, their rate of persons with less than a fifth-grade education was over double those of Asian Indians and Filipino Americans (U.S. Bureau of the Census, *1990 Census of Population,* table 106). The percentages of professionals admitted as immigrants from India and the Philippines were higher than the corresponding figures for other parts of Asia. See Hune and Chan, "Special Focus," for a more detailed discussion.

19. See Ngoan Le, "The Case of the Southeast Asian Refugees: Policy for a Community 'At-Risk,' " in LEAP Asian Pacific American Public Policy Institute, *The State of Asian Pacific Americans: Policy Issues to the Year 2020* (Los Angeles: LEAP Asian Pacific American Public Policy Institute and UCLA Asian American Studies Center, 1993).

20. Virginia Ellis, "Hmong Seek Exemption from Food Stamp Cuts," *Los Angeles Times,* November 2, 1997, A3.

21. U.S. Bureau of the Census, *Housing in Metropolitan Areas.* A metropolitan area as defined by the Census Bureau is a large geographical area with a large population nucleus. It is usually larger than an urbanized area. Ninety-four percent of APAs live in metropolitan areas. The Census Bureau defines "crowded" households as more than one person per room.

22. Ibid.

23. Ibid.

24. Disaggregated data on housing by APA ethnic groups are not available.

25. "Linguistically isolated" is defined by the U.S. Bureau of the Census as a household in which no one fourteen years and older speaks only English and no one who speaks a language other than English speaks English "very well."

26. Charlene Sato, "Sociolinguistic Variation and Language Attitudes in Hawaii," in *English around the World: Sociolinguistic Perspectives,* ed. Jenny Cheshire (Cambridge: Cambridge University Press, 1991).

27. U.S. Bureau of the Census, *1994 Current Population Survey, The Asian and Pacific Islander Population in the United States* (Washington, D.C., March 1994). See Hune and Chan, "Special Focus," for a thorough discussion of the educational attainment of APAs.

28. Ellis, "Hmong Seek Exemption from Food Stamp Cuts."

29. Paul Ong and Don T. Nakanishi, "Becoming Citizens, Becoming Voters: The Naturalization and Political Participation of Asian Pacific Immigrants," in *The State of Asian Pacific America: Reframing the Immigration Debate,* ed. Bill Ong Hing and Ronald Lee (Los Angeles: LEAP Asian Pacific Public Policy Institute and UCLA Asian American Studies Center, 1996.)

30. The author is familiar with a citizenship training course designed for Vietnamese refugees in which they spend over one hundred hours attempting to master or memorize the questions on the history and government knowledge test. One wonders what benefit might be derived if an equal number of hours were spent developing English competencies and job skills.

31. Deborah Woo, *The Glass Ceiling and Asian Americans* (Washington, D.C.: U.S. Department of Labor, Glass Ceiling Commission, 1994).

32. For a discussion of the model minority myth, see Stacey J. Lee, *Unraveling the "Model Minority" Stereotype* (New York: Teachers College Press, 1996); and Hune and Chan, "Special Focus."

33. See Donnelly, *Changing Lives of Refugee Hmong Women*; Carl Bankston, "Gender Roles and Scholastic Performance among Adolescent Vietnamese Women: The Paradox of Ethnic Patriarchy," *Sociological Focus* (1995): 161–176; and Nazil Kabria, *Family Tightrope: The Changing Lives of Vietnamese Americans* (Princeton: Princeton University Press, 1993).

34. See Haunani-Kay Trask, "Politics in the Pacific Islands: Imperialism and Native Self-Determination," *Amerasia* (1990): 1–19.

35. See Woo, *Glass Ceiling and Asian Americans*.

36. See Hune and Chan, "Special Focus."

CHAPTER NINE

ASIAN PACIFIC AMERICAN YOUTH:
PATHWAYS FOR
POLITICAL PARTICIPATION

PETER NIEN-CHU KIANG

We can make phone calls but I don't think we should be going door-to-door.
Some people might not like it because of the way we look.

Although we were sitting on opposite sides of the meeting room, Kiko, my
Japan-born ninth-grade classmate, came over specifically to caution me as
we each prepared to join the volunteer ranks of Democratic senator George
McGovern's 1972 U.S. presidential campaign. We were the only two Asian
American youth in the room, but I confess I had not thought about the
racial implications and cultural dimensions of my own intent to work for
McGovern's election, until Kiko's warning.

Four years earlier I had delivered bundles of campaign brochures around
town by bicycle to support Sen. Eugene McCarthy's bid for the Democratic
presidential nomination. He, like McGovern, advocated an end to the war
in Vietnam. As a nine-year-old during that summer of McCarthy's campaign, I had watched the gloved fists of Tommie Smith and John Carlos rise
proudly from the Mexico City Olympics victory stand. Their demonstration of Black Power, as the fastest humans in the world, touched me deeply,
though I was unable to articulate how or why at that time. Then, in junior
high school, after the 1970 slaying of four students at Kent State University,
I found myself unable to stand any longer for the daily Pledge of Allegiance
to the American flag. Politics was personal, and it mattered.

Despite Kiko-chan's admonition not to participate in McGovern's 1972 campaign because of the way we looked, I naively refused to restrict my activities and proceeded to canvass voters door to door with great optimism every day after school until the November election. Even though McGovern carried my home state of Massachusetts, his crushing defeat—losing forty-nine of fifty states to the Republican incumbent, President Richard Nixon, in one of the biggest landslides in U.S. history—left me cynical and bitter about politics and my own participation. I did not reengage in political activities again until the movement of Asian American and Third World students at my college campus several years later enabled me to connect my core sensibilities of peace and justice with the realities of my racial and cultural identity—a fact of life Kiko-chan had recognized at a much earlier age.

I never discussed with my parents or friends any of these early experiences of political involvement, even though they had profound meaning for me personally. As I consider how today's generation of Asian Pacific American youth finds relevant ways to participate politically, images from these experiences of roughly thirty years ago still persist vividly in my own memory and lead me to suggest that we—as researchers, teachers, community leaders, and parents—may know very little about what really matters in politics to young people, until we watch and listen closely.

Much of the literature on Asian Pacific American political participation, including the chapters in this volume, focuses either on broad theoretical and historical perspectives or on quantitative, empirical analyses of demographic profiles and voting patterns. I want to argue alternatively for the value of considering how Asian Pacific Americans—and youth specifically—make meaningful, concrete choices at a micro level about their political participation as individuals with group identities across multiple domains.

This chapter presents examples of Asian Pacific American youth who have chosen to participate in mainstream political activities, including student government and advocacy within their high schools, political campaigns of family members, and citizenship education activities in their communities. The cases reveal some of the diverse backgrounds within Asian Pacific American populations among ethnicities, generations, and urban/suburban status, and illustrate how young people, primarily from immigrant backgrounds, view themselves in relation to the opportunities and obstacles associated with mainstream political participation. The examples are based on in-depth individual and focus group interviews, participant observation, and an analysis of reflective writings by Asian Pacific American young people.[1]

By locating Asian Pacific American youth political participation in relation to the social domains and influences of family, school, and community,
I wish to challenge the glaring absence of research and representation of
young people's perspectives in much of the social science literature on
Asian Pacific American politics[2] and the parallel dearth of Asian Pacific
American perspectives in the education literature on youth development,
identity, and empowerment.[3]

MAKING COMMITMENTS TO
ASIAN PACIFIC AMERICAN YOUTH

With the doubling of the school-age population of Asian Pacific Americans
during the 1990s, the unmet needs of these youth have escalated dramatically in schools and communities throughout the country. In most settings,
adults with professional responsibilities for supporting Asian Pacific American youth, including teachers, counselors, and administrators, do not share
their ethnic, linguistic, and racial backgrounds. Constrained by limited resources, an increasingly hostile, anti-immigrant climate, and their own
stereotypical assumptions based often on popular media images that portray
Asian Pacific American young people as either hardworking overachievers
or violent gangbangers, many educators and adult professionals have been
unable to respond effectively to the full range of academic, social, and personal challenges that face the growing numbers of these young people.[4]

At the same time, faced with linguistic barriers, cultural differences, and
economic pressures, Asian Pacific American parents, most of whom are immigrants, typically do not participate or intervene consistently in their children's schooling, even if they express high expectations at home for their
children's educational success. Thus Asian Pacific American students are
often left on their own to manage and mediate their experiences in school
and society.[5]

Two significant reports document these needs nationally across the
decade of the 1990s. The first, a 1992 landmark study produced by the U.S.
Commission on Civil Rights and dealing with a range of civil rights issues
facing Asian Pacific Americans, includes a chapter on the conditions facing
Asian Pacific American young people. The commission concluded:

> Asian American immigrant students all too often find schools that are unpre-
> pared to deal with diversity, teachers who do not know their languages and

culture and are insensitive to their needs, and an atmosphere that is un-
friendly and charged with racial hostility. . . . Quickly, Asian American immigrant children are made to feel like outsiders in our schools, which detracts
from their ability to concentrate on school work and often has devastating
consequences for their self-esteem.[6]

The commission's findings have since been validated in several other studies.[7]

In 1998 the national advocacy organization, Asian Americans/Pacific Islanders in Philanthropy (AAPIP), implored grant makers to recognize that
"an urgent educational crisis threatens the futures of a growing number of
Asian Pacific American students, both immigrant and American-born."
Foremost among its recommendations, AAPIP urged funders to support
"activities that offer parents, community members, and youth opportunities
for leadership development . . . and that promote a sense of well-being, community ownership, and civic pride for young people and their families."[8]

MODELS AND AGENDAS FOR YOUTH, COMMUNITY, AND CIVIC DEVELOPMENT

Within the social domains of school, family, and community, a wide range
of Asian Pacific American youth organizations, programs, and projects
have emerged in recent years. Many Asian Pacific American social and cultural student clubs, for example, operate as extracurricular activities within
schools.[9] Youth service initiatives also have been established as programs
within larger community-based or mainstream institutions such as
churches, neighborhood centers, and multiservice agencies. Some, like the
Filipino Youth Organization (FYO) of Seattle, are the legacies of more than
four decades of community-based commitments to youth empowerment;
others, like the school-based Vietnamese Student Association described in
this chapter, come and go within a few months. A few, like the East Bay
Asian Youth Center in Berkeley, have elaborate funding streams and
staffing patterns, while others, such as the youth education and empowerment program of the Filipino American National Historical Society in
Hampton Roads, Virginia, survive strictly through the commitments of
volunteers. Only a handful of Asian Pacific American youth organizations,
however, such as South Asian Youth Action! (SAYA!) in Queens, New York,
have explicit missions to develop leadership and ethnic pride, together with
practices of empowerment. Even fewer, such as the Coalition for Asian Pa-

cific American Youth (CAPAY) in Massachusetts, are consciously youth-run in governance and pan-Asian in representation.

Analyzing the status, history, and impact of these various Asian Pacific American youth organizations is an important task for researchers in the areas of youth development and Asian American Studies, but it is beyond the scope of this chapter. My intent here is to suggest that Asian Pacific American youth acquire sensibilities for and competence in mainstream politics by developing skills, resources, and visions through their experiences with the dynamics of power, representation, and identity. Asian Pacific American youth organizations offer important settings in which these processes can occur.

Furthermore, although no one yet seems prepared to take on this challenge, it is time to consider how participants in these various Asian Pacific American youth organizations throughout the country might gather together to share lessons, strategies, and resources, while striving to articulate a collective, national Asian Pacific American youth agenda. Such an agenda, whether national or local in scope, must inform the commitments of researchers and community advocates who are working more broadly to strengthen Asian Pacific American political participation through various means, including those presented in this volume.

In light of the persistent inequities and urgent needs facing Asian Pacific American youth, which are highlighted in the AAPIP and U.S. Commission on Civil Rights reports and other studies, it is important to consider how larger dimensions of Asian Pacific American political participation and community development intersect with the specific domains of activity and meaning that matter to Asian Pacific American youth. For example, participants in the 1995 Wingspread national conference, "Emerging Best Practices: Weaving the Work of Youth and Civic Development," concluded that "young people's efforts connect with the large civic challenges and questions of meaning in our time." They also asked: "How are the primary networks of relationships in which young people live and work strengthened and renewed? How does youth work become less focused on 'fixing' youth through service delivery, and more focused on building youth capacities for productive contributions?"[10]

These perspectives are helpful in explicitly linking the goals and processes of civic development with those of youth development—an important challenge that faces Asian Pacific American politics. It is unfortunate that Asian Pacific American voices or examples are typically missing at gatherings like the Wingspread conference, which document innovative practice and theory in youth development work. Nevertheless, Asian Pacific American young people have much to share and show.

SCHOOL AS A DOMAIN OF POLITICAL PARTICIPATION

What are the domains that matter to Asian Pacific American young people, particularly in relation to their socialization toward political participation? Given the sheer amount of time that most young people spend in school each day and the formal role school plays in acculturating "citizens," particularly through the social studies curriculum,[11] school is an essential domain in which Asian Pacific American youth develop sensibilities toward political participation based on their own direct experiences.

Within schools, young people participate politically in two principal ways. They run for elected office in student government, or at the very least, vote in elections for student government representatives. Outside of formal student government structures, they become involved in school politics as members and leaders of student organizations. This section offers examples of each possibility through the voices of individual Asian Pacific American young people.[12] The sections that follow examine the related domains of family and community.

Student Government as a Site of Opportunity, Resistance, and Accommodation

Serena,[13] a charismatic young woman of mixed Lao-Thai heritage, came to the United States with her family from Laos and Thai refugee camps and grew up in a predominantly white, working-class city where many Asian immigrants and refugees had settled. The strains of changing demographics were evident throughout the city during that period. A fifteen-year-old at the time of these reflections, Serena was playing a leadership role in both the Asian club of her high school and in a regional Asian Pacific American youth network. One of the formative experiences that motivated her activism had occurred when she tried to participate politically in the student government of her junior high school. She recalled:

> Growing up, I was taught to be an obedient child who listened to the words of your parents and believed that I always had to carry on a straight A's report card to make my parents proud. I was always instructed to be the proper

daughter, by doing house chores at a young age and to convey large responsibilities such as babysitting my baby sister at the age of nine.... As soon as I got into junior high, I felt I was older and thought they can trust me more and allow me to take part in school activities. So I began to be more active in the school activities such as sports, joining clubs, and actually becoming an important part of the first Student Council in junior high. All in that one school year, I've changed from an obedient daughter to a stubborn and independent youth who had a thirst to go out and discover what's outside in the world and what every thing is about. That, of course, started conflict within my family.... Every day my mom would cry about how she missed her little daughter who was so obedient and how she hated this new daughter of hers....

While I was running for Student Council, I actually ran for President. I won the election by 73 votes, but it turns out that I did not become President of the Student Council. President of the Student Council was given to a Jewish girl who was also running for the position. The student body objected towards the decision. The excuse that the teachers gave the student body for the decision was that the representative of the school should be chosen because of work and effort, not because of popularity, when my work and hers was equivalent. I did not sit down to take that. I got all the student body together to petition and was able to negotiate only the Vice President position. Still, I am proud of my work and I think I left that year with something for all the Asians after me to remember. We never really talked into detail about why I did not get the position because we tried to keep the gossip about the teachers to a certain limit. But there was a teacher in that board that did not think that it was suitable for an Asian girl to hold the position of President in their first Student Council.

Within the constraints of her setting, Serena found ways to accommodate and resist the limitations she faced from both home and school. She also consciously set an example of leadership, both in running for the position of class president and in not backing down when her majority vote was rejected by adults who exercised ultimate authority to decide the election's outcome. In this example, Serena internalized valuable lessons about her own political persistence as well as the ways in which seemingly democratic structures and processes often reveal themselves to be exclusive and arbitrary.

In contrast to Serena's setting, Silvertown was a very wealthy suburban community, though it too was predominantly white. There, Asian Pacific American students achieved substantial success within their high school's electoral process. For example, Sri, of Indian heritage born in Japan, and Nicole, born in the United States of Korean immigrant parents, each served as student government council members of Silvertown High's senior class. Sri, in fact, had been elected a member of the student government council every year since ninth grade; Nicole had run and lost in ninth grade, but eventually won as a junior. Reflecting on her motivations to persist with her own political participation, Nicole explained:

> I originally wanted to run so that I could feel closer and more connected and more a part of the whole student body. I know everyone, but I don't feel like I am really involved in their lives even though we go to school together, and I think being part of the government and representing them and doing what people want is a great way of getting to know everyone better. Like you're an important person, you're a part of other people's lives.

A third student, Amanda, was elected as a representative of Silvertown High's ninth-grade class. Born in the United States of parents from Taiwan, Amanda analyzed her own electoral success and that of two other Chinese American ninth-graders:

> I was kinda surprised that three out of the eight officers happened to be Chinese this year. Two of us were born here and the third one moved here in fifth grade or something like that. Two are pretty well known in sports, and I was born here and living here my whole life and I know basically everyone pretty well. I think a lot of people don't really even like consider them Asians, like a different race almost. But like people [more recent immigrants] who come later, they are kinda separated. It's more difficult.

Expanding on Amanda's observation, Sri added:

> Many Asians move here late in high school. They don't start in elementary school, or grow up in the States, so moving here they don't know what's required of them. . . . I don't think there is enough of an effort by the school to reach out. I think everyone is accepted but there is no action taken to say what people feel. It's because people say, "Oh, I'm accepting," but what actions are taken by students on a personal level? So, I think it's difficult for people who move here and for the Asian community to really get involved.

Sri explained some of the difficulties facing Asian newcomer students in gaining popularity or acceptance within Silvertown High: "Because they speak Korean or Chinese or whatever and they don't speak much English, they seclude themselves maybe to people of their own race or ethnicity."

Upon further critical reflection about the school's social dynamics and his own status within them, Sri observed:

> People I hang out with don't perceive me as being different or Asian, but sometimes they will make comments about other people. They're not racists, but they think of different Asians like they just don't think of me in the same way, because to them I'm just another one of them. I know they're not racists per se, but they have certain stereotypes about Asians in school and I guess they feel I don't fit those.

Nicole also distinguished herself from the more recently arrived Asian American students in the school, albeit with ambivalent senses of both pride and loss related to her identity: "My parents are American citizens and they chose to become citizens. It's all a reflection of how they decided to live their lives. In a sense, I live the same way. I can speak Korean very well for someone who is born here, but besides being able to speak the language, there isn't too much that I know."

Thinking out loud, Nicole then found words to articulate the strategy and price of her own social and political success. Her insight also resonated deeply for Sri and Amanda: "I feel like if you really want to immerse yourself in Silvertown and take advantage of everything, I think that most people that do who are Asian Americans almost, in a sense, have to detach themselves from their own culture."

Unlike municipal, county, state, and federal elections in which only U.S. citizens have the right to register to vote—making electoral participation by massive numbers of immigrants impossible—there are no formal barriers like citizenship or length of residency requirements to student participation as either candidates or voters in a school's student government process. Yet, as Amanda, Sri, and Nicole concluded from their own "successful" experiences as elected student council members at Silvertown High, there are social and cultural requirements in school which, though unstated, are fully operational with real meaning and consequence. In this sense, their realizations echo Serena's and raise important questions about whether school student governments provide effective, open structures for genuine democratic participation and leadership by all Asian Pacific American youth.

Claiming Space and Representation through Student Clubs

Beyond student government, an alternative vehicle for political participation is the web of student organizations that have missions and mandates, both real and perceived, to represent specific constituencies in school. The blossoming of Asian student clubs in schools throughout the country reflects both the objective realities of rapid Asian Pacific American demographic growth and the resulting ethnicization/racialization of student bodies, as well as the subjective desires of individuals and groups to claim space and voice through their organized assertion of identity.[14]

City South High School is a nonselective urban high school. Its student body is 12 percent Asian, 24 percent Latino, 27 percent white, and 37 percent black. The school has no Asian administrators, counselors, or regular education teachers; Khmer and Vietnamese bilingual teachers and paraprofessionals are the school's only Asian Pacific American staff members.

In interviews conducted for a larger study with fifteen Vietnamese American tenth- through twelfth-graders at City South, every student recounted examples of witnessing or experiencing racial harassment, including name-calling and physical assault, as part of their daily lives.[15] A senior sighed, "I feel like I get stepped on every day in that school." One student noted, "The white kid is always messing with the Asian"; another stated, "I experience problems with blacks more than any other group"; and still others described conflicts with Latino and Haitian students.

In just three years, the number of Vietnamese students at City South had tripled from thirty to more than a hundred. Most were newly arrived immigrants. School officials never publicly discussed the implications of this dramatic demographic change within the school community. Many non-Asian students, therefore, disregarded the Vietnamese students' ethnic, linguistic, and cultural identities as Vietnamese and instead assigned them a racialized identity as "Chinese" and "Chinks." The confusion surrounding the Vietnamese students' presence was evident in the experiences of almost every student interviewed. Thuy, a Vietnamese junior, recalled: "When we pass by them [other students] they give you some kind of like a dirty look. . . . They say, 'Look at that Chinese girl,' and then they call like, 'Chinks, go back to where you belong.' "

Whether because of personal experience, observation, or advice from friends and siblings, Vietnamese students at City South crafted individual survival strategies to get through school—typically by choosing to be quiet in class, rushing through the hallways in groups, confining themselves to particular tables in the cafeteria, and avoiding certain areas like the bathrooms where they expected and frequently experienced racial conflict. Ky, a twelfth-grader, explained: "I try to keep myself very, very careful, you know. I think about where I'm going before I'm going there.... My eye open ... so I can get out some situation quickly as I can."

A few students, however—those who had lived in the United States longer than five years and who were more proficient in English—asserted themselves as equal members of the school community. This challenged the school's social dynamics, according to Kieu, another senior:

> I see other Asian students.... After the class change they just go straight to the class or they walk in a whole group.... [But] Ky and I or even Thuy, it seems like we speak more English, and we walk like [we're] a part of the school.... That's why the problems started.... They want to be power in the school.... When I walk in school I feel like I'm equal to anybody else. And I guess that what they not wanted.

With the escalating needs of Vietnamese students going unrecognized and no other forms of collective political participation or representation available, Thuy, Ky, and Kieu decided to launch a Vietnamese club for the school. Thuy's idea for the club grew out of her middle school experience in another state:

> They have all kind of ESL, bilingual programs for Asian kids [at the middle school] ... and they have this club called the ESL club ... and all Asian kids can join the club and the teachers, the ESL teacher, she do a lot of activity with us.... Then I went to City South. I saw a lot of Vietnamese kids, right, they don't speak English at all, but the school didn't do anything for them. It's like either they learn or they don't.... So I felt kind of bad, and I start talk to my teacher.... I complain to her. And I say that they should have an ESL program or something you know. Or at least a Vietnamese club that we could help those students.

Assisted by a Vietnamese tutor from a local university, a Cambodian bilingual teacher, and another teacher of English, the group attracted roughly thirty students to its first meeting. Ky and Kieu delivered the welcome speech:

> None of us wants, ten to twenty years later when we travel half our lives, to not have any nice memory about our first steps into life at our student age. The Vietnamese Student Association is going to be the first means to help us to build those memories.... Of course, the Vietnamese Student Association is not going to be a place only for fun. But it is also the place for studying....

We will have occasions to improve and exchange our experiences as students and the initial difficulties when trying to adapt into new schools and a new society. We can share the good poems, the good novels and songs in order to help keep the national [Vietnamese] culture in our hearts. This is also a good way that we can prove to the foreigners that even though we have to take their culture daily, we are not going to forget to improve our national culture.

Participants in the first meeting discussed their hopes that the club would provide academic and ESL tutoring, advice about cultural expectations in U.S. society, and ways to share Vietnamese language and culture. After three well-attended meetings, however, the club had still not gained any backing from the school administration and found itself without an approved time and place to meet. Although some teachers were willing to help when asked, others criticized the new club for encouraging segregation. Thuy observed, "They [school personnel] are not so happy about [the club] . . . it's so hard up here to do those things."

The club also faced internal conflicts, reflecting gender dynamics and differences in acculturation. Thuy recalled: "At every meeting when I open my mouth, he [Ky] always jump in and say let him handle it. . . . The guy try to be the head, you know. They don't want any young lady or woman to take their place. So every thing I say, he always jump in and cut me off. So that's a problem." These gender conflicts represented important issues for the students to work through. Ky asserted, "Most of the girls I know who've been here more than two years, they always act that way. They're bolder, aggressive." Thuy countered: "A lot of Vietnamese kids go to school, whatever the people say, they just sit there. They sit there and be quiet. . . . I say no! I'm not gonna sit there and be quiet. I won't. I won't be quiet."

Because no one helped the students analyze their attitudes or guided their actions, they were unable, individually or collectively, to sustain their organizing initiative and overcome the school administration's lack of formal, institutional support. Not surprisingly, then, the Vietnamese Student Association dissolved after two months and was not reactivated the next year. Ironically, instead of embracing the Vietnamese students' leadership and resourcefulness in responding to a growing need within the school, some adults at City South labeled students' efforts to organize themselves and support their newcomer peers as separatist and divisive. Although examples of highly effective and generously supported Asian Pacific American student organizations in schools across the country do exist and should be documented, the City South case is useful in capturing some of the complex motivations and frustrations experienced by many Asian Pacific American youth who seek voice and space, identity and representation, within the political possibilities and asymmetrical power relations that define their domain of school.

LEARNING WITHIN THE DOMAIN OF FAMILY

Students in the City South case also found little support or understanding for their concerns at home. This section explores how the domain of family limits and contributes to the political socialization and participation of Asian Pacific American youth.

The Rhetoric and Realities of Parents' Roles

None of the students interviewed at City South had told their parents about either their interests in establishing a Vietnamese Student Association or their problems with racial harassment at school. A junior noted, "They don't know what happened, and they feel okay because they don't know everything. My mother and father don't speak English." Ky described the relationships between Vietnamese students and their parents in these terms: "Our parents not involved enough in our schools. One of the things is English barrier. They try and protect themselves inside their house . . . and sometime they too busy with their work, trying to earn a living, trying to survive in this society. So they try so hard they just forget about us. . . . I don't blame at all. They try so, make a living so hard."

Though very conscious of the sacrifices and hardships their parents endured in order to provide a better life for their families, most students did not describe close relationships with their parents. While challenging Vietnamese students' silence in school, Thuy sighed that her parents viewed her as "too Americanized." Kieu also felt discouraged that her parents did not understand the difficulties she faced at school. She revealed to them some of the more dramatic incidents of racism she had experienced only after they criticized her for receiving mediocre grades. Kieu explained, "I go home and struggle. When I go outside, outside I struggle."

At Westlake High, a suburban high school, Asian Pacific American students organized as members of the school's Multicultural Club to protest offensive "Chinamen" stereotypes in the school's spring musical, *Anything Goes,* by Cole Porter. Interviews with these students revealed another situation in which parents did not understand or share their children's desire to give priority to that issue over other commitments in the school.[16] Unlike at City South High where students' working-class, immigrant/refugee parents knew little about and did not participate directly in their children's school experiences, the Westlake High Asian Pacific American parents were able to intervene more directly in their children's school lives, in large part because of their own bicultural, professional backgrounds. Yet parental intervention did *not* mean support for students' political participation. If anything, the Westlake High parents consciously limited students' involvement with the *Anything Goes* issue. Cara, chair of the school's Multicultural Club which served as the principal vehicle for asserting Asian Pacific American students' concerns, revealed at the height of the controversy, one month before the play was scheduled to open: "Just about everyone is upset, frustrated and fed up. Anita had a big fight with her parents last night because they want her to concentrate on school. My parents are concerned with the scholarship issue. It's a bummer but my Dad is the one who's gonna pay my college tuition. . . . We really do not have support from other parents/kids."

Indeed, Cara's Taiwan-born parents were counting on her winning a major scholarship to a local university, but this depended on receiving outstanding recommendations from her teachers and the principal. Not wanting to risk those relationships, Cara's father halted her activism. He stated in a phone conversation at the time, "I don't think Cara should be involved in this any longer. Living in this country, I've learned you have to look out for number one."

Even within the Coalition for Asian Pacific American Youth—a nationally recognized model for Asian Pacific American youth organizing and leadership development[17]—most of its activist youth leaders have not received direct support or understanding from their parents for their participation. For example, in a focus group interview with former steering committee members and officers, a young Chinese immigrant woman stated, "I have never fully explained to my parents what CAPAY is. It's just something I have always done. I don't know if any of our parents know exactly what CAPAY is." A young Chinese immigrant man agreed, "I don't bother to explain to them. They don't understand a younger group that is action-oriented." A young Indian American male with immigrant parents further clarified that the lack of initiative to discuss one's political participation is two-way. He noted, "My parents actually have politics, but never talk about it. You have to ask them what party did you vote for in that election."

In the singular case of Silvertown High where Asian Pacific American students ran successfully for elected office within the governing councils of their grade levels, students reported nothing like the active discouragement of Cara's parents or the distance described by the City South students. Nicole, for example, did not experience parental pressure or discouragement related to her own political participation. Nevertheless, even in her case, she did not inform her parents about running for a student government position until after the election. She recalled: "My parents never pushed me to do anything I don't want to do, but I didn't even tell them I was going to run senior year. I came home and my mom was like really surprised. She was happy. But she didn't like have a hand in it or anything."

Despite the rhetoric and rationalizations articulated by so many immigrant adults that their decisions to come to the United States reflect their commitments to do what they think is best for their children's futures, it seems clear from these cases that many Asian Pacific American parents understand little about their children's daily lives, struggles, and dreams. In turn, many Asian Pacific American young people seem unwilling or unable to share their questions, interests, and agendas for political participation within the domain of family.

Ironically, though, when asked which Asian Pacific Americans in their own lives and in society inspire them to be active, the Asian Pacific American young people in my research typically identify family members—usually mothers or an older sibling. Clearly, then, the depictions of parents and family members as discouraging or unengaged in the day-to-day realities of their children's lives need to be balanced with appreciation for the genuine caring and sacrifice that characterize so many relationships within the domain of family for Asian Pacific Americans.

Furthermore, many alternative scenarios are possible for families, particularly when older siblings—typically with 1.5-generation backgrounds—provide models and bridges of understanding between generations. Although this chapter centers on Asian Pacific American youth, some of my previous research directly challenges the view that immigrant parents, due to language barriers and cultural differences, are helpless or passive in relation to mainstream political participation. The multilingual coalition of Southeast Asian and Latino parents who successfully sued the city of Lowell, Massachusetts, for discriminatory segregation of immigrant children in the public schools, and who subsequently mobilized to support their Latino and Cambodian organizers in the Lowell school board election, represents a compelling case in point.[18]

Similarly, although many mainstream and Asian Pacific American analysts attribute Asian Pacific Americans' perceived low levels of political participation to immigrants' negative homeland experiences with politics, particularly in countries governed by communist parties, such explanations seem overly simplistic, ideological, and removed from the diverse backgrounds and stances of real people at the micro level. Cases such as a parent-organizing effort in a bilingual preschool in Boston's Chinatown and lessons from a statewide immigrant leadership training program in Massachusetts clearly demonstrate that many newcomers—including both former cadres and members of resistance movements from China, Vietnam, and the Philippines (or Haiti, El Salvador, and Lebanon, for that matter)—bring sophisticated theories and grounded practices of political analysis, mass organizing, popular education, and coalition building from training and political participation in their home countries.[19]

Far from being cynical or fearful about politics, these sectors of immigrants represent vital, albeit largely untapped, capacities and aspirations for expanded political participation within their communities. The next section describes the case of an Asian immigrant who successfully won election to a citywide office. It also examines the effects of his political campaign on his children within their shared domain of family.

Political Participation and the Meaning of Home

In 1997 a Chinese Cambodian immigrant became the first Asian Pacific American ever elected to the board of selectmen (comparable to a city council) of a mixed-income, suburban town where many working-class Asian immigrant families had settled in recent years. He had run and lost in the previous selectmen's race and also had lost a race for state representative from the district several years earlier. His success as the top vote-getter in the 1997 election signified the impact of incremental social and demographic change within the town as well as his own persistence. He explained:

> The racial makeup of the [five-member] Board [of Selectmen] is white white white white. I'm the only non-white in the town's 204-year history to serve on the board. They did not expect an Asian American would win, let alone top the ticket. They did not expect that change in the town is such that more people now realize that maybe having a non-white serving is okay after all. So when I first began there was obvious hostility, but now I think the level of hostility is kind of softened.

Although his electoral platform spoke to broad cross-cutting issues for the town as a whole, his professional training and career history linked him closely to Asian Pacific American concerns, particularly in the areas of mental health, refugee resettlement, and education. In explaining what motivated him to run, he asserted: "I feel that running for office is a very strong and concrete statement to indicate that I belong. This is my home. I am not coming here as a visitor. . . . We cannot sit at home and wait for the mainstream community to come to the realization that all these Asian Americans are also part of our community. No, we need to let them know that we are part of this place."

This view of political participation as a way to claim a sense of home or belonging in the town contrasted sharply with his own socialization to politics, growing up as an ethnic Chinese in Cambodia. He recalled: "We were taught to despise politics, not realizing that politics is something that affects our daily lives. The idea is that politics is dirty. People will use whatever means at their disposal to get wherever they are. Politicians are self-serving: they cheat; they're hypocrites. I think we saw the dark side of politics more often than the positive side."

His political socialization in Cambodia also included a cultural dimension that complicated his own campaign process:

> Culturally we were taught to be humble, to be moderate. We were taught that if you are good, people will recognize you, just as they would recognize a flower. A flower doesn't have to yell out and say, "Look, how beautiful I am, look how good I smell." If you're so good, people recognize it. This directly contradicts the kind of self promotion you often find in American life. But how can someone run for political office without remembering to say, "Look, this is what I can do; this is what I want to do; these are my credentials." So the whole system is not really compatible with our upbringing.

In most analyses of Asian Pacific American political participation, the story might stop here—highlighting this inspiring example of immigrant empowerment based on vision, persistence, and effective organizing. A closer look at this case with those themes in mind offers many lessons about seeking election and sustaining political leadership at the local level in settings without a large base of Asian Pacific American voters.[20] But this case also reveals insights about the meaning of political participation within the domain of family itself, from the perspectives of the candidate's children—points of view rarely considered when analyzing or promoting Asian Pacific American political campaigns.

The candidate's two daughters, who were active in his campaign, each had vivid images and very frank opinions about the significance and impact of their father's political participation. The older daughter recalled her father's first campaign for state representative:

> I was in the middle of fourth grade. I recall the excitement and how important I felt at the fact that my father was doing what I had only seen people do on TV. I delighted in seeing my dad's name plastered around town, and I especially loved putting as many of his campaign buttons on my bookbag as possible. The functions and the fundraisers became a sort of entrance into the fast lane and gave me a glimpse of what it felt like to live in what I thought was the real world. Above all, being involved and present to stand by my father made me feel grown up. In the beginning, I didn't mind going up to his campaign office on the third floor of a stuffy old building in the center of town. I could fold, address, stamp, and stuff envelopes for hours.

Her enthusiasm, however, soon gave way to stress and resentment as the campaign demanded more and more from the family:

> My father's campaign really affected the family in a negative way. My father quit a job that was quite prestigious and sought after. Everything was put on the line so that what he wanted came first. . . . I knew that we were having financial difficulties, using up the savings for my father's campaigns while trying to pay for our private school tuition. Getting by became a big question in my mind, as I am the eldest, and my mother often shares her feelings and worries with me. I hated seeing my mother put on a brave front and lock all her feelings inside of her while she rooted for my dad on the outside. Most of all, I hated the fact that I had to be the one to hear the long list of problems that the campaign was causing when I felt that my father should be the one to deal with it. I wanted so much for him to know that the family had to sacrifice so much for him to reach toward his dream.

The younger daughter's reflections on the campaign experience were similarly ambivalent:

> I remember holding signs on election day as the bitter wind pounded against my face and resenting the fact that I said I would help my father. After learning that my father had topped the ticket, I was not only overwhelmed with happiness, but I also was a bit afraid of the idea that there would be many changes that would have to take place from that point on now that my father

was a selectman. . . . At first, I thought that my family was wasting their time, money, and effort for something that was for and that would only affect my father, but as time went on I saw how much my father wanted to win the election and those feelings I had before went away.

Because of commitments by both parents to Asian Pacific American issues and organizations, the two daughters had grown up with strong senses of their cultural and racial identities. Although she did not name any instances of discrimination or exclusion in her own life, the older daughter clearly felt the impact of racism on her father's status in the electoral process:

Sadly, and I am ashamed to admit it, I did not think that he was going to win. In some ways, his previous losses were embarrassing and I had begun to feel that nobody would ever vote for an Asian. . . . Politics in my town are pretty tricky and most of the town's leaders try to keep their own in the top positions. My father represented a threat, and the retaliation came in the form of questioning how well a Chinese man could hold up in the public spotlight. I also feel that because of my father's race, a lot of people didn't take him seriously and believe in his abilities and the gifts and talents that he could bring to the Board.

Though not yet in high school, the younger daughter also recognized the dynamic of racism that her father confronted in running for selectman: "I think that being Chinese or Asian American was a barrier that made it more difficult for my father to be elected because many people viewed my father as an outsider and a person who was not tightly woven into the community [in which] he was about to be entrusted with the [responsibility for] representation and protection of its interests." Balancing these various dimensions in her own assessment of the more recent campaign's meaning, the older daughter added:

I am glad that my father has achieved one of his dreams. I still feel that he doesn't realize how things have changed so much ever since the first campaign. I still don't like the fact that our financial situation is not as stable as it could be due to the campaign. In terms of time and effort, I constantly remind myself that what I did for my father came out of love despite my initial unhappiness. I am proud of him, and I take pride in knowing that my father has done what a lot of people—much less Asians—would never have the courage to do. Yet, I do know for sure that in my mind, enough is enough.

U.S. teenagers often criticize their parents' choices, of course. But it seems unlikely that anyone encouraging Asian Pacific Americans to run for political office would expect or intend for the children of those candidates to conclude that the campaign process represents a tremendous burden for those who are closest and care most for the person running—even in exemplary campaigns with inspiring messages, committed community support, and winning margins. Yet it is hard to deny the clarity and realism that underlie the daughters' sentiments. For example, in her advice to other families involved in political campaigns the older daughter counseled:

> A political campaign is very emotionally, physically, spiritually, and financially taxing. A lot of time and energy is involved in selling oneself or an image, as well as just taking care of all the logistics. The family must be prepared to sacrifice things such as money, time spent together, and personal time to work on the campaign or to be supportive of the candidate. . . . The family will often be stressed out, tired, discouraged, or frustrated, and patience is a must in order to get through the campaign without severely destroying the relationships within the family.

The older daughter further declared, "I don't think that I will be running for political office," and went on to list six specific reasons why she would not follow her father's example. She later admitted, however, "at some point in the future, I will participate in some form of politics in terms of working on a committee. I think that I would be a very good campaign organizer."

Regardless of their future personal choices, the daughters' observations reveal how the domain of family serves as a site of powerful learning for young people about the meaning of political participation. Researchers and analysts, not to mention candidates and campaign organizers, have much to gain from paying greater attention to this domain and its importance in the lives and perspectives of Asian Pacific American young people.

YOUTH DEVELOPMENT AND THE
DOMAIN OF COMMUNITY

Both researchers and organizers typically conceptualize Asian Pacific American political participation in terms of interests, issues, and voting patterns defined by ethnic and geographic communities.[21] Youth-defined interests and issues are seldom included in those political analyses, however, and youth are rarely viewed as a significant voting bloc. Nevertheless, linkages between the theory and practice of youth development and community development can strengthen the capacities and visions of both. In turn, the domain of community can represent a significant site of learning for Asian Pacific American young people as they struggle to understand broader contexts of power, democracy, and inequality.

Citizenship Education and Meaning across Generations

The case described in this section draws on extensive observations by Phi, a former CAPAY leader who served as a volunteer instructor in a community-based citizenship education class for Vietnamese elders. Her descriptions of the learning process she shared with her "students" illustrate how the domain of community offers profound meaning for Asian Pacific American young people in relation to the goal and process of political participation. Phi's reflections also reveal the substantial obstacles and bitter realities that face many Asian Pacific American immigrants who are desperately struggling to become citizens.

Phi came to the United States as a child, having escaped from Vietnam by boat with her family. Within the domain of the community, her status as a young person in the role of "teacher" with "students" the age of her grandparents symbolized some of the cultural struggles and shifts that immigrant youth and elders are forced to confront in the United States. Furthermore, although her conversational Vietnamese was quite good, Phi had far less native language fluency than her elders who were much more recently arrived, having spent their entire lives in Vietnam. Again, the contradictions built into this role reversal for Phi as the "teacher" emerged in deeply troubling ways. She confessed:

> As I was teaching the chapter on the American Constitution, I was unable to translate many of the English words into the Vietnamese language. I depended on my students to translate the phrases into Vietnamese. While I think it is great how the students are willing to help each other, I can't help but feel that I have lost a sense of who I am as a Vietnamese. I couldn't even communicate with my people. . . . In some ways I don't feel qualified to be standing in front of my students. One of my reasons for teaching this class is to stay in touch with the Vietnamese culture and language. Is it selfish of me to be teaching this class? I wonder if they respect me? I wonder if they think that I could care less for my Vietnamese culture? What has happened to the

Vietnamese part of my Vietnamese American identity? I am very afraid that my Vietnamese identity will disappear the longer I stay in the U.S. What will become of my identity? Will I then just be American? But what is American? I don't think there is a term in which I could truly convey my identity, my confusion. Once again, I am stuck in a binary opposition. I am not totally Vietnamese, nor am I a complete American. I label myself as a Vietnamese American but this identity is slowly shifting to the American side, I think. But I am not American. Others do not see me as an American either. What culture do I belong to? I feel outcasted in both. Where do I go from here?

The explicit purpose of the community-based citizenship class was to prepare immigrant elders to pass the official examination required for naturalization. Much of Phi's reflections focused on the elders' experience of "anguish as a second language" [22] during the preparation and test-taking process.

We practiced dictation because it is the first part of their exam. If the students do not get one out of two correct of the dictation, then the exam corrector would not even look at the other part of their exam. The elders definitely have problems listening to spoken English. Some complained that it sounded too fast. Another person said she could read the statement and answer it on paper, but when it came to listening, she was clueless. I could not imagine how hard this is on these elders. They have to go home and study this book until they know it by heart because passing the exam means life or death to them, especially because of the changes in the welfare reform and immigrant laws. . . . Finally the exams were passed out. We helped the test-giver person by helping the students filling in their answer sheet. Some students did not understand to fill in the oval corresponding to the letter. Finally the test-giver said that I along with my group were no longer allowed to speak. I felt a little tingle inside because I wanted to speak Vietnamese the whole time during the test to help explain it to them. During the practice section, one woman filled in the wrong ovals which would have made her test completely wrong. I quickly told the test giver. She was lucky it wasn't during the test.

Phi's documentation of this process is rich and significant, not only in relation to her own political socialization as a young person, but also in contrast to the distorted yet dominant images of wealthy, transnational Asians trying to buy political influence in Washington, D.C., and corrupt rings of smugglers and service providers using extortion and forgery to pass thousands of illegal and ineligible aliens as naturalized citizens. Phi's reflections provide crucial grounding in the reality faced by many honest and vulnerable working-class immigrants within the community domain:

The test-giver took ten minutes to correct the exams. Everyone passed except one woman who did not know how to read and write. She had been in the class before. On her last test she got only two correct. This time she got ten correct. She was very ashamed [at the class celebration the next day]: "Teacher, I'm so embarrassed. I sit in the back of the room because I'm afraid to look at you and the other students. I feel like I'm letting you down because you spent so much time to teach me. I'm so stupid. Why do I have to have this despair. I stayed up all night last night and cried because I failed the test again. I'm so embarrassed. Teacher, if I don't pass the next test, I don't know what I will do." I felt so much empathy for her. I, as well as the group, are determined to help her in every way to get her to pass next time. Her comment gives me further reasons why I am particularly working in the Vietnamese community. There is so much to do. . . .

Throughout the process, Phi also engaged in her own research as a participant observer to explore how the elders actually viewed the meaning of "citizenship." Were they motivated to take the citizenship class simply to protect themselves and their families against the drastic elimination of benefits and rights for noncitizens—as many agency workers pragmatically advised and many advocates for immigration and welfare reform cynically portrayed? Did they feel or act on any sense of civic responsibility to the ethnic community or geographic neighborhood that defined much of their day-to-day social interactions outside the domain of family? How did they "translate" their indigenous concepts of "citizenship" to the context of their lives and futures in the United States, given that in Vietnam the reference points and implications of the term *citizenship* differed dramatically from those in U.S. society?

Perhaps because these were Phi's own questions rather than ones generated simply to fulfill an assignment from school, she pursued them with passionate dedication—getting up at six o'clock in the morning each week for the hour-long bus trip to the Sunday morning citizenship class. Her initiative suggests the value of the domain of community as a source or setting for inspired learning and integrated social/academic development for Asian Pacific American youth.

People thought that I was like insane for driving back and forth for maybe once or twice a week to do this. I don't know, it was something that I really wanted to do. I wanted to help teach the class, but at the same time, it was for myself to learn more about the environment and also what that environment could help me learn about myself. I have never grown up particularly in a

Vietnamese community so that is why I taught citizenship there. It was to just make me more aware of Vietnamese issues, because I know that this is where my life is going to be at—just getting myself more acquainted and associated with the community like in the long run. Because I know I have a commitment to improving all the injustices I think I see or will see. This year I have seen a lot.

Finally, in answer to her own questions, Phi concluded: "By listening to these elders I realize that achieving citizenship is not only to get benefits but to also get a sense of belongingness, 'home.' "

In linking the elders' efforts to gain citizenship with their desires to establish a sense of "home," Phi's analysis echoes the way in which the Chinese Cambodian immigrant father described why he struggled to become his town's first Asian Pacific American selectman. He explained that "running for office is a very strong and concrete statement to indicate that I belong. This is my home." Such was also the case for Nicole at Silvertown High who wanted to run so she could feel "closer and more connected and more a part of the whole student body." Indeed, perhaps this suggests that the shared desires for "home" and "belonging" that emerge thematically across domains, ethnicities, and even generations in these micro-level cases should be analyzed more specifically as meaningful motivating forces, distinct from the rational choice dynamics of power and representation that are more typically highlighted as the factors instrumental in the participation of Asian Pacific Americans and other "minorities" in mainstream political activities.

CONCLUSIONS

Beyond the electoral commitments described in this chapter, a wide range of Asian Pacific American youth programs, projects, and actions deserve attention. Throughout the United States Asian Pacific American young people are actively engaged in what Bill Flores, Rina Benmayor, Renato Rosato, and other Chicano/Latino studies practitioners have termed "cultural citizenship." Flores and Benmayor explain:

Cultural citizenship can be thought of as a broad range of activities of everyday life through which Latinos and other groups claim space in society, define their communities, and claim rights. It involves the right to retain difference, while also attaining membership in society. . . . It includes how excluded groups interpret their histories, define themselves, forge their own symbols and political rhetoric, and claim rights. It includes how groups retain past cultural forms while creating completely new ones.[23]

The daily assertions of voice, identity, space, and rights by Asian Pacific American young people are important to affirm, in part because their gains and prospects in mainstream political life seem quite bleak. Indeed, the day-to-day structures and supports for Asian Pacific American young people wishing to develop as effective participants in the democratic practice are limited and arbitrary, but young people are not at fault for this limitation. Rather, the adults who have important roles to play within and across the domains of school, family, and community are themselves frequently out of touch with the motivations and meanings that matter most to the youth. With or without assistance, though, young people do create their own pathways for political participation—often with desires to find "home." Their strivings demand and deserve far greater recognition and support.

NOTES

1. This chapter builds on an invited presentation to a conference on Asian Americans and politics hosted by the Woodrow Wilson Center's Asia Program and held in Washington, D.C., March 13–14, 1998. I limit my discussion in this chapter primarily to "mainstream" or electoral political participation to accommodate the stated focus of the Wilson Center's conference. A much broader range of Asian American and youth political activities also deserves analysis and reflection. My work on this chapter is part of a larger study on Asian American youth leadership supported by a Spencer Foundation Post-Doctoral Fellowship Award administered by the National Academy of Education. I also acknowledge the assistance and contributions of Nguyen Huu Luyen, Leland Honda, Vivian Wai-fun Lee, Dan Lam, ThaiDuong Phan, the Coalition for Asian Pacific American Youth (CAPAY), and all the young people whose voices and experiences have informed this work.

2. See, for example, Yung-Hwan Jo, ed., *Political Participation of Asian Americans: Problems and Strategies* (Chicago: Pacific/Asian American Mental Health Research Center, 1980); Paul Ong and Don T. Nakanishi, "Becoming Citizens, Becoming Voters: The Naturalization and Political Participation of Asian Pacific Immigrants," in *The State of Asian Pacific America: Reframing the Immigration Debate*, ed. Bill Ong Hing and Ronald Lee (Los Angeles: LEAP Asian Pacific American Public Policy Institute and UCLA Asian American Studies Center, 1996), 275–305; Stewart Kwoh and Mindy Hui, "Empowering Our Communities: Political Policy," in LEAP Asian Pacific American Public Policy Institute, *The State of Asian Pacific*

America: Policy Issues to the Year 2020 (Los Angeles: LEAP Asian Pacific American Public Policy Institute and UCLA Asian American Studies Center, 1993), 189–197.

3. See Josephine A. van Linden and Carl I. Fertman, *Youth Leadership: A Guide to Understanding Leadership Development in Adolescents* (San Francisco: Jossey-Bass, 1998); Richard D. Lakes, *Youth Development and Critical Education: The Promise of Democratic Action* (Albany: State University of New York Press, 1996); and Shirley Brice Heath and Milbrey W. McLaughlin, eds., *Identity and Inner-City Youth: Beyond Ethnicity and Gender* (New York: Teachers College Press, 1993).

4. Henry T. Trueba, Li-Rong Lilly Cheng, and Kenji Ima, *Myth or Reality: Adaptive Strategies of Asian Americans in California* (London: Falmer Press, 1993); and Peter N. Kiang and Vivian W. Lee, "Exclusion or Contribution: Education K–12 Policy," *State of Asian Pacific America* (Los Angeles: LEAP Asian Pacific American Public Policy Institute and UCLA Asian American Studies Center, 1992), 25–48. For examples of critiques of popular media stereotypes of Asian Pacific American youth during the past twenty years, see Thomas K. Nakayama, "Stereotyping by the Media: Framing Asian Americans," in *Images of Color—Images of Crime,* ed. Coramae Richey Mann and Marjorie S. Zatz (Los Angeles: Roxbury Publishing, 1998); Stacey J. Lee, *Unraveling the "Model Minority" Stereotype* (New York: Teachers College Press, 1996); Bob H. Suzuki, "Asian Americans as the 'Model Minority,' " *Change* (November/ December 1989): 13–19; Ki-Taek Chun, "The Myth of Asian American Success and Its Educational Ramifications," *IRCD Bulletin, Teachers College* 15 (1980): 1–12; and Bob H. Suzuki, "Education and Socialization of Asian Americans: A Revisionist Analysis of the 'Model Minority' Thesis," *Amerasia Journal* 4 (1977): 23–51.

5. M. Tran, "Maximizing Vietnamese Parent Involvement in Schools," *NASSP Bulletin* (National Association of Secondary School Principals) (1992): 76–79; R. D. Morrow, "Southeast Asian Parent Involvement: Can It Be a Reality?" *Elementary School Guidance and Counseling* 23 (1989): 289–297; and Margie Kitano and Philip C. Chinn, eds., *Exceptional Asian Children and Youth* (Reston, Va.: Council for Exceptional Children, 1986).

6. U.S. Commission on Civil Rights, *Civil Rights Issues Facing Asian Americans in the 1990s* (Washington, D.C., February 1992), 69–70.

7. Peter N. Kiang, "When Know-Nothings Speak English Only: Analyzing Irish and Cambodian Struggles for Community Development and Educational Equity," in *The State of Asian America: Activism and Resistance in the 1990s,* ed. Karin Aguilar-San Juan (Boston: South End Press, 1994), 125–145; Peter N. Kiang, Nguyen Ngoc-Lan, and Richard L. Sheehan, "Don't Ignore It: Documenting Racial Harassment in a Fourth Grade Vietnamese Bilingual Classroom," *Equity and Excellence in Education* 28 (1995): 31–35; Delia Pompa, *Looking for America: Promising School-Based Practices for Intergroup Relations* (Boston: National Coalition of Advocates for Students, 1994); M. Semons, "Ethnicity in the Urban High School: A Naturalistic Study of Student Experiences," *Urban Review* 23 (1991): 137–158; Mary Poplin and Joseph Weeres, *Voices from the Inside: A Report on Schooling from Inside*

the Classroom (Claremont, Calif.: Institute for Education in Transformation, Claremont Graduate School, 1993); and Rachel Sing and Vivian W. Lee, *Delivering on the Promise: Positive Practices for Immigrant Students* (Boston: National Coalition of Advocates for Students, 1994).

8. Laurie Olsen, *An Invisible Crisis: The Educational Needs of Asian Pacific American Youth* (New York: Asian Americans/Pacific Islanders in Philanthropy, 1998), 7, 33–34.

9. Although students clubs are typically organized as after-school extracurricular activities, educators also should determine how to integrate lessons and learning from these student-initiated activities within the traditional curriculum of the regular school day.

10. Johnson Foundation, "Principles of Vital Practice for Youth and Civic Development," in *Emerging Best Practices: Weaving the Work of Youth and Civic Development,* Wingspread Conference Summary (Racine, Wis.: Johnson Foundation, 1995), 1.

11. See, for example, Kathleen Bennet deMarrais and Margaret D. LeCompte, *The Way Schools Work: A Sociological Analysis of Education* (New York: Longman, 1995); Alan R. Sadovnik, Peter W. Cookson Jr., and Susan F. Semel, *Exploring Education: An Introduction to the Foundations of Education* (Boston: Allyn and Bacon, 1994); James W. Loewen, *Lies My Teacher Told Me* (New York: New Press, 1995); and James A. Banks, *Teaching Strategies for the Social Studies* (New York: Longman, 1990).

12. For other examples of research presented through the voices of Asian Pacific American youth, see: Patricia Phelan, Ann Locke-Davidson, and Hanh Thanh Cao, "Speaking Up: Students' Perspectives on School," *Phi Delta Kappan* 73 (1992): 695–704; and Sonia Nieto, "Lessons from Students on Creating a Chance to Dream," *Harvard Educational Review* 64 (1994): 393–426.

13. The names of individuals and schools featured in this chapter have been changed.

14. See Kiang and Lee, "Exclusion or Contribution"; and Stacey J. Lee, *Unraveling the "Model Minority" Stereotype* (New York: Teachers College Press, 1996).

15. This section draws on a larger case study focusing on racial conflict in an urban high school. See Peter N. Kiang and Jenny Kaplan, "Where Do We Stand? Views of Racial Conflict by Vietnamese American High-School Students in a Black-and-White Context," *Urban Review* 26 (1994): 95–119; and Peter N. Kiang and Jenny Kaplan, "Race/Space Relations in School," *NABE News* (National Association for Bilingual Education) 17 (1994): 5–6, 30.

16. For a full description of this case study, see Peter N. Kiang, "We Could Shape It: Organizing for Asian Pacific American Student Empowerment," Occasional Paper No. 1, Institute for Asian American Studies, University of Massachusetts Boston, 1996.

17. For further description of CAPAY as a model for organizing Asian Pacific American youth, see ibid and http://omega.cc.umb.edu/~capay/.

18. For a full discussion of this case, see Peter N. Kiang, "Southeast Asian and Latino Parent Empowerment: Lessons from Lowell, Massachusetts," in *Education Reform and Social Change: Multicultural Voices, Struggles, and Visions*, ed. Catherine E. Walsh (Mahwah, N.J.: Lawrence Erlbaum Associates, 1996), 59–69. In a more recent development, Chanrithy Uong, a progressive Cambodian community leader and bilingual guidance counselor at Lowell High School, was successfully elected to the Lowell City Council in November 1999. In so doing, he became the first person of color ever to be elected in Lowell and the first ethnic Cambodian American to be elected to office in any major city in the United States. His campaign success and the evolving story of community politics and empowerment in Lowell are the subject of continuing research. See Brian Mooney, "Immigrant's Story Wins with Lowell Electorate," *Boston Globe*, November 4, 1999, B1, B6.

19. See, for example, Joan Arches, Marion Darlington-Hope, Jeffrey Gerson, Joyce Gibson, Sally Habana-Hafner, and Peter Kiang, "New Voices in University-Community Transformation," *Change* 29 (1996): 36–41.

20. See Chapter 13 in this volume for an example of those kinds of lessons from the successful gubernatorial campaign of Gary Locke in Washington State.

21. But as Kenyon S. Chan notes in Chapter 8 of this volume, other background factors related to generation and immigrant/refugee or indigenous status also are productive ways to sort Asian Pacific American demographic data and analyze policy needs/impacts.

22. Thanks to Vivian Zamel, director of the ESL program at the University of Massachusetts Boston, for this phrase.

23. William V. Flores and Rina Benmayor, *Latino Cultural Citizenship: Claiming Identity, Space, and Rights* (Boston: Beacon Press, 1997), 262–263.

CHAPTER TEN

SEEN, RICH, BUT UNHEARD?
THE POLITICS OF ASIAN INDIANS
IN THE UNITED STATES

SANJEEV KHAGRAM
MANISH DESAI
JASON VARUGHESE

More than one million Asian Indians currently live in the United States, and this number is growing rapidly as a result of their larger-than-norm family sizes and high rates of immigration (355,000 between 1985 and 1995).[1] In 1993 Asian Indians (once again) became the third largest Asian American group in the United States behind the Chinese and Filipinos and ahead of the Japanese, Koreans, and Vietnamese. Today, they are one of the wealthiest, if not the wealthiest, ethnic groups in the United States. Asian Indians manage small retail shops, own hotels, and drive taxicabs, and they are often engineers, computer specialists, medical doctors, and scientists. As this population grows and younger generations mature, Asian Indians are increasingly entering corporate business, law, academics, journalism, even the arts.

But what about the politics of Asian Indians? What is the political role of this "seen, rich, but unheard" group in the United States? What are the issues that mobilize and politicize Asian Indians? What are their modes of political participation and representation? How do they vote and how successful have they been in securing positions of political authority? How does the politics of Asian Indians compare with that of other Asian American and non–Asian American groups in the United States? How have the answers to these questions changed historically, and what can be expected in the future?

The politics of Asian Indians in the United States is basically uncharted territory. This chapter will begin to fill in some of the unknowns in this area by integrating existing secondary sources with the initial results of ongoing primary research. It begins by describing the historical experience of Asian Indians in the United States and then examines the current socioeconomic and demographic profile of this population. These sections are followed by an analysis of current themes and trends in Asian Indian politics in the United States, a discussion of the practical implications of the findings, and future directions for research.

Transnational dynamics, shaped by the global political economy and the domestic political economies of India and the United States, have profoundly shaped the historical experience and politics of Asian Indians in America.[2] The Asian Indian experience in the United States can be divided into two broad historical periods, before and after the 1965 immigration reform act, which is roughly similar to that of other major Asian American groups such as the Japanese, Chinese, Filipinos, and Koreans.[3] During both of these periods, albeit in fits and starts, Asian Indians have contributed to the formation of the field of racial meanings and practices in the United States, and especially to the construction of the categories Asian American and white American.[4]

As we shall see, Asian Indians have had a much longer history in the United States than is conventionally known. Between 1900 and 1920, for example, Asian Indians constituted the third largest Asian community in the country. But several factors—British colonial rule in South Asia, an overwhelming male-to-female ratio among immigrants, racism from white Americans, and progressively severer immigration restrictions—prevented Asian Indians from becoming a more substantial minority group in the United States during their historical period. Before 1947 Asian Indian immigrants had virtually no support from their homeland government (compared with Chinese and Japanese immigrants, for example) because India remained a British colony. In fact, many did what they could to support the independence movement back in India. During this first historical period, Asian Indians also were politically active in fighting against the pervasive legal and societal discrimination they encountered in the United States. But, even though Asian Indians did organize and mobilize politically to promote their interests, coalitions among the various Asian American immigrant groups were virtually nonexistent.

The historical experience and politics of Asian Indians in the United States over the last three decades have similarly been conditioned by transnational dynamics, driven by the changing relations between global and domestic political economies. Japan's defeat in World War II, India's independence from Great Britain in 1947, the communist revolution in China, and the effects of the Korean War globally, as well as the strides made by the civil rights movement and the increasing demand for skilled labor in the United States all contributed to the passage of the 1965 Immigration and Nationality Act Amendments (also known as the Hart-Cellar Act).[5] This act produced a dramatic growth in Asian Indian immigration to the United States from the mid-1960s on. Although most of the immigrants during this second phase have been well educated, and many have been economically prosperous, greater use of the family reunification clauses in U.S. immigration law (among other factors) has resulted in a growing percentage of less-educated, working-class, and even poor Asian Indians in the United States since the 1980s.

In the twenty-first century in the United States, both the structure and the politics of the Asian Indian community are far more complicated than the "model minority" myth could ever capture. During this more recent historical period, Asian Indians continue to be concerned about immigration and discrimination, as well as U.S.-India relations, but they also have strong political interest in issues such as crime and education. They have established political organizations, have accepted appointments to high-level public policy positions, and are beginning to run for elected office in greater numbers, often facing barriers similar to those hampering other minorities in the United States. Coalition building with other Asian American and non–Asian American groups is becoming more noticeable as well. Thus, despite the popular perception of this group as apathetic, Asian Indians have been politically active in the United States for nearly a century, and their degree of political empowerment continues to grow.

ASIAN INDIANS IN THE UNITED STATES: A HISTORICAL PERSPECTIVE

The first significant wave of Asian Indian immigration to the United States arrived at the turn of the twentieth century.[6] The most likely route these early pioneers took to the "New World" was from Calcutta in eastern India to Hong Kong and then on to North America via the Philippines. Indian immigrants often went first to Canada, which was a British Dominion at the time, and then traveled down the west coast of the United States to settle in California. As immigration restrictions in Canada increased, however, more and more Indians came directly to the United States.[7]

A substantial proportion of these early Asian Indian pioneers had learned about the possibilities of immigrating to North America, particularly Canada, while serving in the British military. Asian Indians served overseas from East Africa to the Middle East to Hong Kong and participated in China's Boxer Rebellion in 1900. By World War I, more than 65 percent of Indian combat troops in the British military came from the northern region (and later state) of India known as Punjab. Of the six to seven thousand Indians who came to the United States between 1899 and 1914, approximately 85 percent came from Punjab and practiced the Sikh religion—a faith that emerged from Hinduism and Islam in India during the fifteenth century.[8]

Asian Indians faced not only societal ignorance but also intense racism upon arrival in the United States. Although most Asian Indian immigrants were Sikhs, they were all called Hindus and were generally discriminated against by officials and nonofficials alike. As one U.S. immigration official stated at the time, "The Hindus are regarded as the least desirable, or, better, the most undesirable, of all the eastern Asiatic races which have come to our soil."[9] In 1907 openly hostile white American workers chased seven hundred Indians out of Bellingham, Washington, because the Indians were willing to work longer hours for lower wages in the town's lumber mills. A similar incidence of violence against Asian Indians occurred two months later in the nearby town of Everett. U.S. authorities, including President Theodore Roosevelt, turned a blind eye to the incidents.

A 1908 comment by Samuel Gompers, president of the American Federation of Labor, vividly captured the animosity of white workers toward Asians, the ethnic category into which immigrants from India were placed: "Sixty years' contact with the Chinese, and twenty five years' experience with the Japanese and two or three years' acquaintance with Hindus should be sufficient to convince any ordinarily intelligent person that they have no standards . . . by which a Caucasian may judge them."[10] A year earlier, in 1907, the Japanese and Korean Exclusion League of San Francisco had renamed itself the Asian Exclusion League (AEL) to ensure that people from India would be targeted by its campaign to halt Asian immigration to the United States. The AEL also fought to exclude Asian immigrants already in the country, including Asian Indians, from naturalization and other citizenship rights. But despite this common foe, Asian immigrants from many different countries did not forge coalitions to further their political interests.

Immigration policy, however, was a central focus of the politics of Asian Indians during this early historical period.[11] It quickly became clear that British colonial officials would not object to the exclusion of Asian Indians from immigration and citizenship; those officials were worried that Asian Indians in the United States would support the independence movement in India. Thus in 1908 "the chief of the bureau of naturalization asked all United States attorneys to oppose actively the granting of naturalization to 'Hindoes or East Indians.' "[12] U.S. officials, in turn, also began to limit the number of Indians allowed to stay after arriving. In 1907 less than 10 percent of the Indians who applied for entry to the United States were rejected, but by 1913 that figure had risen to more than 50 percent.[13]

In response, Asian Indians began to empower themselves individually, often pursuing legal strategies via the U.S. judicial system to fight for their rights. An early victory was won in 1910 when a federal court determined in the case of *United States v. Balsara* that Asian Indians, as descendants of Aryans, were Caucasian and thus, unlike Chinese and Japanese immigrants, could not be discriminated against because of their race. As a direct result of the *Balsara* ruling, more than 70 percent of Asian Indian immigrants who arrived around 1910 were naturalized.[14] Between 1909 and 1923, however, the courts ruled that Asian Indians were "white persons" eligible for citizenship rights in only four out of eight cases, and in no cases after 1923 when the U.S. Supreme Court handed down its infamous *Thind* decision (discussed later in this chapter).[15]

Asian Indians also began to establish themselves collectively, both culturally and politically. For example, the first Sikh *gurdwara* was built in Stockton, California, in 1912. This and other temples became not only places of worship, but also meeting places to organize political activities in the promotion of Asian Indian interests. In 1913 Indian nationalists in northern California founded the Ghadar Party to support India's independence from Great Britain.[16] During this period, Tarak Nath Das, a political activist and Asian Indian immigrant, played a central role in many of the battles against anti–Asian Indian laws and in the movement to support Indian Independence. He eventually won his own long battle for U.S. citizenship in 1914 but later was arrested and almost deported for his political activities during World War I.[17] In 1917 one hundred Asian Indians involved in the Ghadar movement were convicted of violating U.S. neutrality laws in an ambitious but ill-conceived plot to overthrow the British colonial government in India.

During this same period, an array of public officials and several domestic interest groups aggressively campaigned against Asians residing in the United States. In response to the mounting political pressure, California enacted in 1913 the Alien Land Act, which restricted land ownership to citizens or those eligible for citizenship. The Asian Exclusion League fought for a halt to Asian Indian immigration by citing "the undesirability of Hindus, their lack of cleanliness, disregard for sanitary laws, petty pilfering, especially of chickens, and insolence to women."[18]

After several years of intense lobbying, domestic anti-Asian groups began to have an impact on federal policy. The 1917 federal Immigration Act delineated an "Asian barred zone" that excluded the Philippines and Japan but included India. The Philippines was a U.S. colony and the Japanese government strongly supported its population in the United States, but the British colonial government in India agreed with the restrictive policy, and Indians were no longer allowed to migrate to or petition for citizenship in the United States.[19]

Even after the 1917 immigration reform Asian exclusionists continued to lobby against the rights of Asian Indians. They were eventually successful when, in 1923, the Supreme Court overturned the *Balsara* ruling in the case of *United States v. Thind*. The Court determined that the Asian Indian immigrant Bhagat Singh Thind could not be granted citizenship because he was not white in culture or color. Thind was a U.S. Army veteran who, like many other aliens, had been drafted during World War I.[20] The *Thind* decision followed closely on the heels of the *Ozawa v. United States* Supreme Court case in which Japanese American Takao Ozawa's petition for U.S. citizenship was denied because he was not Caucasian. As historian Mai Ngai notes, "By ruling that Japanese and Asian Indians were racially ineligible for citizenship, the two decisions cast Japanese and Asian Indians with Chinese as unassimilable aliens and helped constitute the racial category Asian.' "[21]

The scientific term *Caucasian,* according to the justices in the *Thind* case, did not reflect popular understanding in the United States and thus could not be the basis for legal decision making with respect to Asian Indians. The Court stated unequivocally: "In the popular conception he is an alien to the white race and part of the 'white man's burden.' . . . Whatever may be the white man's burden, the Hindu does not share it, rather he imposes it." The Court went on to say, "We venture to think that the average well-informed white American would learn with some degree of astonishment that the race to which he belongs is made up of such heterogeneous elements."[22] As a result of the *Thind* decision, the U.S. Immigration and Naturalization Service began a denaturalization program to retroactively cancel citizenships that had been granted to Asian Indian immigrants between 1923 and 1926.[23]

Anti-immigration and naturalization laws were not the only forms of institutional racism facing Indian immigrants. From the 1880s on, California law prohibited any marriage between a Negro, mulatto, or Mongolian and a white.[24] Very few Asian Indian women migrated to the United States during this historical period. Of the approximately seven thousand Asian Indians who entered the United States from 1904 to 1911 only three or four were women.[25] By 1930 there were more than 1,572 Asian Indian men per 100 Asian Indian women in the United States.[26] Thus, even though categorized by scientists as Caucasian and legally considered white before the 1923 *Thind* ruling, Asian Indian men found it difficult to marry white citizens. Most married Mexican women.[27]

Further complicating the situation, in 1922, prior to the *Thind* decision, Congress enacted a federal bill that revoked the citizenship of American women who married immigrants ineligible for citizenship. Political activist Tarak Nath Das, for example, had married a white American, Mary K. Das, who was later refused a U.S. passport under the law. Tarak Das fought against the decision and the broader denaturalization program that targeted Asian Indians. He even met with the chief justice of the United States, former president William Howard Taft, and convinced Taft to send a letter to the U.S. secretary of labor in which Taft called the condition of Asian Indians "a real injustice" and recommended that special legislation be enacted.[28]

Within weeks of the 1923 *Thind* decision, California attorney general Ulysses Sigel Webb began nullifying, under the state's 1913 Alien Land Act, land titles held legally by Asian Indians. Appeals by Asian Indians to the British ambassador in Washington, D.C., for assistance proved fruitless.[29] To evade California's Alien Land Act, Asian Indians often registered their lands in the names of their Mexican American wives or their mixed children (these young "Punjabi Mexicans" were automatically citizens by virtue of their birth in the United States). They also "sold property to trusted friends, other times friends held leases, and frequently there were simply verbal leasing agreements." But these arrangements sometimes led to real conflicts. In 1925 rancher Pahkar Singh murdered his two white "partners" after they claimed his entire harvest. Earlier he had leased his ranch to them in a verbal contract to prevent his land from being taken back by California authorities, but he had remained the sole investor and primary tiller of the land. Singh was later brought up on criminal charges and spent fifteen years in jail.[30]

Asian Indians persisted in the struggle against legal discrimination after the 1923 *Thind* decision and passage of the 1924 Immigration and Naturalization Act, which solidified the exclusion of Asian Indians from the United States. S. G. Pandit, an Asian Indian immigrant who had been naturalized in 1914 and admitted to the California bar as a practicing attorney, argued against the Immigration and Naturalization Service's denaturalization program in a series of court cases, including his own.[31] Organizations such as the Indian Welfare League and the Friends for the Freedom of India, which was founded by Tarak Das, were active in supporting both the Indian independence movement as well as citizenship rights for Asian Indians living and working in the United States. In 1927 and again in 1939, these organizations successfully lobbied for the introduction of bills in Congress that would halt legal discrimination against Asian Indians. These acts never made it out of Congress, however, because of the strong opposition of anti-Asian groups such as the American Federation of Labor and Asian Exclusion League. Nevertheless, Asian Indians did not give up. In 1940, for example, an Asian Indian named Khairata Ram Samras filed yet another petition to overturn the Supreme Court's *Thind* decision of 1923, although he was ultimately unsuccessful.[32]

In the end, however, it was the global geopolitics of the 1940s that turned the tide toward the relegalization of naturalization rights for Asian Indians in the United States. In 1941 the Atlantic Charter, which upheld the right of peoples to self-determination, was signed by President Franklin D. Roosevelt and British prime minister Winston Churchill. In turn, groups such as the India League of America increased their lobbying efforts with the U.S. government to reinstitute naturalization rights for Asian Indian immigrants and to pressure the British to grant Indian independence based on the norms in the charter. America's promotion of democracy abroad was being contrasted with its discriminatory and undemocratic policies at home and British colonialism in India. Perhaps more important, the United States needed to strengthen relationships with India to prevent Japan from taking South Asia or the formation of a Japanese-Indian alliance during World War II. U.S. alliances with India, as well as with China and the Philippines, contributed to changes in its anti-Asian laws and regulations. The combination of extensive lobbying by domestic Asian Indian political organizations and the increasing likelihood that India would soon become independent proved critical in finally pushing the reforms through. Congress passed the Luce-Cellar Act in 1946 (also called the Filipino Naturalization Act), which ended the 1917 "Asian barred zone" and the quotas established in the 1924 Immigration and Naturalization Act, allowed 105 Asian Indians to immigrate per year, and permitted members of this group to apply for citizenship for the first time since the 1923 *Thind* decision. After the final withdrawal of Great Britain from South Asia in 1948, the four new nations of South Asia—India, Pakistan, Sri Lanka, and Burma—were each granted an annual immigration quota of 105. The immigration quota for European countries was much higher. Poland's, for example, was 6,524 per year. But had Congress not passed the Luce-Cellar Act in 1946, or the McCarran-Walter Act of 1952 (also known as the Immigration and Naturalization Act) which ended all further exclusion regulations against Asian immigrants, the Asian Indian community in the United States would likely have died out. Rather, about 1,770 Asian Indians were naturalized as citizens between 1947 and 1962.[33]

Asian Indians quickly attempted to parlay the victory of the Luce-Cellar Act of 1946 into further political empowerment. For one things, in 1956 they helped elect Dalip Singh Saund from California's Imperial Valley to the House of Representatives, where he became the first Asian American member of Congress in U.S. history and the only Asian Indian elected to national political office to date. Saund had been granted citizenship in 1949 based on the recently passed immigration reforms. As he later wrote in his autobiography, "I saw the bars of citizenship were shut tight against me. I knew that if these bars were lifted I would see much wider gates of opportunity open to me, opportunity as existed for everybody else in the United States of America."[34] Saund was reelected for a second term in 1958 but had to resign before completing it because of ill health.

Until 1965 and passage of the Hart-Cellar Act, the total number of Asian Indians in the United States remained quite low. The act was the result of a combination of factors, including the changing global political context, the increasing immigration of Korean and Japanese brides of U.S. servicemen from the Korean War, the growth and success of the civil rights movement which highlighted domestic racial injustice internationally, as well as the greater demands for skilled labor to support the booming U.S. economy. The provisions of the new law thus gave priority to family reunification and certain occupational categories as preferred bases for immigration to the United States.[35]

In the years just after passage of the 1965 immigration reform act, the Asian Indian immigrants admitted were primarily those selected on the basis of occupational and investor characteristics (approximately 60 percent), followed by spouses, children under twenty-one, and the parents of pre-1965 and early post-1965 immigrants. In addition, from the 1950s, and even more so from the 1960s, Asian Indian students seeking a higher education constituted a steady stream of immigrants.[36]

And where did these immigrants settle? During the 1940s, the geographical distribution of Asian Indian settlement in the United States began shifting away from California to other states (see Table 10.1). This trend turned around again during the 1980s, although this reversal was not a return to the settlement pattern of rural-based Asian Indian concentration in California that had characterized the late 1800s and early 1900s.

ASIAN INDIANS IN THE UNITED STATES: A DEMOGRAPHIC AND SOCIOECONOMIC PROFILE

The demographic and socioeconomic dynamics—and thus political potential—of the post-1965 Asian Indian population in the United States are markedly different from those of the pioneers who arrived during the late nineteenth and early twentieth centuries. Certainly the increasing size of the population bodes well for a greater presence of Asian Indians in U.S. politics over time. By 1990 Asian Indians constituted the fourth largest Asian American community in the United States (Table 10.2). Less than three years later, this group had moved into the third position, not far behind

Table 10.1

Asian Indian Population Distribution by Decade, 1910–1990

Decade	United States	California	Percent in California
1910	2,544	1,948	77
1920	2,544	1,723	69
1930	3,130	1,873	59
1940	2,405	1,476	60
1950	2,398	815	34
1960	8,746	1,586	17
1970	13,149	1,585	16
1980	387,223	57,901	15
1990	815,447	236,078	29

Source: Karen Isaksen Leonard, *The South Asian Americans* (Westport, Conn.: Greenwood Press, 1997), 70.

Table 10.2

U.S. Population, 1980–1990

	1980	1990	Percent Increase
Total United States	226,545,805	248,709,873	9.8
Non-Hispanic white	180,602,838	188,128,296	4.2
African American	26,482,349	29,986,060	13.2
Native American Indian, Eskimo, Aleut	1,534,336	1,959,234	27.7
Asian/Pacific Islander	3,726,440	7,273,662	95.2
Asian Indian	387,223	815,447	110.6
Chinese	812,178	1,645,472	102.6
Filipino	781,894	1,406,770	79.9
Japanese	716,331	847,562	18.3
Korean	357,393	798,849	123.5

Source: Timothy P. Fong, *The Contemporary Asian American Experience: Beyond the Model Minority* (Upper Saddle River, N.J.: Prentice Hall, 1998), 3.

Note: The percentage change between 1980 and 1990 for Asian/Pacific Islander in this table is lower than the 107.8 percent found in some other published reports. Other reports based their calculations on the count of all Asian Pacific Americans in 1990 but only nine specific Asian American groups in 1980. The 95.2 percent figure cited in this table is more accurate and comparable and is the percentage change of only the nine specific Asian American groups between 1980 and 1990.

Chinese and Filipino Americans.[37] Not surprisingly, then, and like other Asian American groups, this population has grown most dramatically since the 1970s.[38] Of the 605,090 Asian Indians that immigrated to the United States between 1820 and 1994, 564,294 (or 93.3 percent) came between 1971 and 1994 (Table 10.3).

The figures on birthplace, rates of naturalization, and age structure suggest possible reasons why Asian Indians have had lower rates of political participation in the United States in the recent past.[39] According to the 1990 census, of the major Asian American groups the Asian Indian population is composed of the largest percentage of foreign-born individuals, 75.4 percent. This figure is nearly as high as that of the smaller Southeast Asian communities (see Table 10.4). Moreover, the Asian Indian immigrants of the 1970s had a naturalization rate of 53.6 percent. If Asian Indians had fol-

Table 10.3

Immigration to the United States, 1820–1994

Region	Total 1820–1994	Between 1971 and 1994	Percent of Immigrants since 1971
All countries	61,503,866	16,341,228	26.6
Europe	37,732,981	2,193,839	5.8
Asia	7,334,013	5,641,167	76.9
India	605,090	564,294	93.3
China[a]	1,084,567	641,264	59.1
Japan	494,226	128,842	26.1
Korea	719,149	678,285	94.3
Philippines	1,275,119	1,152,217	90.4
North America	4,407,840	414,490	9.4
Mexico	5,969,623	3,584,830	60.1
Caribbean	3,139,648	1,049,648	65.3
Central America	1,087,219	830,062	80.0
South America	1,487,918	995,203	66.9
Africa	442,790	336,317	82.7
Oceania	229,468	111,293	48.5

Source: Timothy P. Fong, *The Contemporary Asian American Experience: Beyond the Model Minority* (Upper Saddle River, N.J.: Prentice Hall, 1998), 21.

a. Beginning in 1957, China includes Taiwan.

lowed the trend for Asian Americans as a whole, their naturalization rate should have risen during the 1980s and 1990s to approximately 80 percent.[40] Recent research suggests, however, that Asian Indians have continued to have one of the lowest naturalization rates of any immigrant group in the United States.[41] As for age structure, close to three-quarters of this population is less than forty-five years of age.

Asian Indian political activity is more likely to be found in the cities and states with high concentrations of this population. About 70 percent of Asian Indians are located in eight major states: California, New York, New Jersey, Texas, Illinois, Pennsylvania, Michigan, and Ohio. The first five states in this list have Asian Indian populations in excess of fifty thousand. Significant Asian Indian communities are found in the cities of New York, Chicago, San Jose (California), Los Angeles/Long Beach, and Houston.[42] Yet Asian Indians are the most geographically dispersed of all the major Asian

Table 10.4

Percentage of Foreign-Born Asian Americans
by Ethnic Group, 1990

Group	Percent
Total United States	7.9
Asian/Pacific Islander	65.6
Asian Indian	75.4
Chinese	69.3
Filipino	64.4
Japanese	32.3
Korean	72.7

Source: Timothy P. Fong, *The Contemporary Asian American Experience: Beyond the Model Minority* (Upper Saddle River, N.J.: Prentice Hall, 1998), 40.

American groups. The statistics suggest that more than one-third of Asian Indians can be found in the Northeast and about one-quarter in the western and southern United States. By contrast, more than 50 percent of Chinese, nearly 70 percent of Filipinos, and more than 75 percent of Japanese reside in the west (see Table 10.5).

The internal diversity within the Asian Indian community (as for Asian Americans as a whole) probably has had a dampening effect on their col-

Table 10.5

Regional Distribution of Ethnic and Racial Groups, United States, 1990
(percent)

Group	West	Midwest	Northeast	South
Total United States	21.2	24.0	20.4	34.8
White	20.0	26.0	21.1	32.4
Black	9.4	19.1	18.7	52.8
Asian/Pacific Islander	55.7	10.6	18.4	15.4
Asian Indian	23.1	17.9	35.0	24.0
Chinese	52.4	8.1	27.0	12.4
Filipino	70.5	8.1	10.2	11.3
Japanese	75.9	7.5	8.8	7.9
Korean	44.4	13.7	22.8	19.2

Source: Timothy P. Fong, *The Contemporary Asian American Experience: Beyond the Model Minority* (Upper Saddle River, N.J.: Prentice Hall, 1998), 43.

lective political activism. Newer Asian Indian immigrants are not overwhelmingly Punjabi like those in the earlier historical period; they also include Gujarati, Hindi-speaking, and many South Indian groups, such as those from the states of Kerala and Karnataka. The Asian Indian immigrants who have arrived over the last three decades also are not overwhelmingly Sikh; they are mostly Hindu, followed by Muslim and smaller numbers of Christians, Parsis, Ismalis, and Sikhs.[43]

Yet compared with other Asian American groups, Asian Indians do not generally find language and education to be considerable barriers to political empowerment. Many Asian Indians do speak English quite well (see Table 10.6), and they are one of the most educated of all groups in the United States. The 1990 census revealed that 87.5 percent of Asian Indians in America have completed high school, and 62 percent have had some college education. More than 58 percent hold bachelor's degrees or higher, which is the highest percentage among all Asian American groups (see Table 10.7). However, Asian Indian men (65.9 percent) are much more likely to have four or more years of college than Asian Indian women (48.7 percent), and older women are likely to constitute a larger percentage of the population that has difficulty speaking English.

Public policy linked to sectors of the U.S. economy such as medicine, technology, small business, and higher education should be of particular interest to large numbers of Asian Indians. A recent survey of 375 Asian Indians found that 20 percent were business owners, 17 percent were engineers,

Table 10.6

Asian Americans Who Do Not Speak English "Very Well,"
Five Years Old and Over
(percent)

Group	All	Native	Foreign-born
Total United States	6.1	2.3	47.0
Asian	39.8	12.2	51.4
Asian Indian	23.5	10.0	26.6
Chinese	50.4	15.0	63.1
Filipino	24.2	6.3	32.2
Japanese	25.2	8.5	58.7
Korean	51.6	12.0	62.3

Source: Timothy P. Fong, *The Contemporary Asian American Experience: Beyond the Model Minority* (Upper Saddle River, N.J.: Prentice Hall, 1998), 41.

Table 10.7

Educational Attainment by Ethnic and Racial
Group, Twenty-five Years and Older, 1990

Group	Percent Attending College 4+ Years
United States	20.3
White	21.5
Black	11.4
Hispanic	9.2
Asian/Pacific Islander	36.6
Asian Indian	58.0
Chinese	40.7
Filipino	39.3
Japanese	34.5
Korean	34.5

Source: Timothy P. Fong, *The Contemporary Asian American Experience: Beyond the Model Minority* (Upper Saddle River, N.J.: Prentice Hall, 1998), 58-59.

13 percent were business managers or executives, and 8 percent were either computer programmers or physicians. An estimated five thousand Asian Indians are currently faculty members at U.S. universities. It is also estimated that Asian Indians "own more than half of the nation's 24,000 economy hotels and more than a quarter of all hotels," and that over 40 percent of the taxicabs in New York City are driven by Asian Indians.[44] These figures are likely to be much higher for men than for women.

The general wealth of this population could be translated into considerable political power, if other factors were held equal. Growing economically at a pace matched only by one other Asian group, Japanese Americans, Asian Indians now earn more than any other ethnic community in the United States. As of 1990 the median family income of Asian Indians was $49,309, only slightly behind the $51,550 for Japanese Americans and much higher than the $30,056 for the United States as a whole (see Table 10.8). By 1994 Asian Indians had surpassed Japanese Americans, earning a mean family income of $59,777. A more recent survey of Asian Indian families found a median family income of close to $64,000.[45]

Part of the reason for the high family incomes of Asian Indians is the number of workers per household. Nearly 70 percent of Asian Indian fam-

Table 10.8

Median Family Income and Poverty Status by Ethnic or
Racial Group, 1990

Group	Median Family Income (U.S. dollars)	Percent below Poverty Line
Total United States	30,056	10.0
White	37,152	7.0
Black	22,429	26.3
Asian	41,583	11.4
Asian Indian	49,309	7.2
Chinese	41,316	11.1
Filipino	46,698	5.2
Japanese	51,550	3.4
Korean	33,909	14.7

Source: Timothy P. Fong, *The Contemporary Asian American Experience: Beyond the Model Minority* (Upper Saddle River, N.J.: Prentice Hall, 1998), 64.

ilies have two or more workers (Table 10.9). In fact, nearly 60 percent of Asian Indian women over age sixteen in the United States work.[46] Yet in 1990 a significant percentage of Asian Indians (7.2 percent) lived below the poverty line (Table 10.8). More recent research found that over 10 percent of the Asian Indian population in the western states of California, Oregon, and Washington lives below the poverty line. Another study discovered that 14 percent of Asian Indian children in California live in poverty, much higher than the national average of 9 percent.[47]

Unemployment and poverty, particularly among female-headed households, are real public policy issues facing Asian Indians in the United States. The statistics on income distribution partially reflect the fact that Asian Indian immigrants who have entered the country since 1965 are more likely to have come under the Family Reunification Act and are less educated and skilled than their predecessors. There is also some evidence that second-generation Asian Indians have much higher levels of unemployment and lower levels of educational attainment than first-generation immigrants, Asian Americans, or non-Hispanic whites. Moreover, while there are far fewer female-headed Asian Indian households than is the case for other Asian American groups, the percentage of female-headed Asian Indian

Table 10.9

Workers in Family by Ethnic Group, 1990

(percent)

Group	One Worker	Two Workers	Three + Workers
Total United States	28	45.6	13.4
Asian	26.2	45.7	19.8
Asian Indian	27.7	51.8	17.8
Chinese	25.5	47.6	19.0
Filipino	18.1	48.2	29.6
Japanese	33.2	42.9	15.3
Korean	31.8	44.8	15.9

Source: Timothy P. Fong, *The Contemporary Asian American Experience: Beyond the Model Minority* (Upper Saddle River, N.J.: Prentice Hall, 1998), 67.

households below the poverty line was quite high in 1990, 35.1 percent (see Table 10.10).

In summary, the factors that favor political participation by Asian Indians are their rapidly increasing numbers, high levels of education and wealth, and general fluency in the English language. In the recent past, these positive attributes may have been dampened by Asian Indians' low rates of naturalization, the internal diversity within the Asian Indian community,

Table 10.10

Female-Headed Households and Poverty Rates of Asian Americans, 1990

Group	Percent of Female-Headed Households	Percent of Female-Headed Households below Poverty Line
Asian Americans	10.7	34.7
Asian Indian	3.9	35.1
Chinese	7.8	28.3
Filipino	13.8	19.9
Japanese	11.0	17.9
Korean	10.5	30.4

Source: Timothy P. Fong, *The Contemporary Asian American Experience: Beyond the Model Minority* (Upper Saddle River, N.J.: Prentice Hall, 1998), 210.

and the relatively youthful age structure of this group. The latter factors will probably become less important with the passage of historical and generation time. It is likely that Asian Indians will be the most politically active in the cities (such as New York, San Jose, and Houston) and states (such as New York, California, and Texas) where their numbers are greatest. They also should be politically important in the sectors of the economy in which they are highly represented: engineering, science, medicine, and small business. In terms of public policy, however, the various demographic and socioeconomic differentials between men and women warrant attention, as well as the growing rates of poverty and unemployment among women, newer immigrants, and second-generation Asian Indian Americans.

THE POLITICS OF ASIAN INDIANS IN THE UNITED STATES: RECENT THEMES AND TRENDS

Immigration, discrimination, and U.S. relations with India have remained the political issues that most galvanize the Asian Indian population. The rising tide against immigration and immigrants has clearly provoked action from many Asian Indian organizations, ranging from the long-established national associations to the newly formed groups at the local and state levels. Moreover, since the murder of two Asian Indian Americans in New Jersey in 1987 by "dotbusters," violence and discrimination have become more prominent concerns among this population. "Dotbusters" are racist white youth gangs that have formed to harass and intimidate Asian Indians. The term itself alludes to the *bindhi* decorative dot that Asian Indian women wear on their foreheads (red *bindhis* are traditionally worn by married women).[48]

A 1996 survey of the public policy concerns of the Asian Indian American community revealed that immigration, discrimination, and U.S.-India relations are not the only political issues of concern for Asian Indians.[49] This survey of a national cross section of 402 Asian Indian Americans was conducted by telephone between September 23 and 28, 1996, and its results are (in theory) statistically significant with 95 percent confidence, with a margin of plus or minus 6 percent. Sixty-two percent of the respondents were male; 76 percent had completed some college or more; 82 percent were either doctors, engineers, other professionals, small business persons, or full-time students; nearly 60 percent had household incomes of $30,000 or greater; 61 percent were citizens but only 12 percent were born in the United States; and approximately 80 percent or more had come to this country after 1970.

The survey revealed that the political issues that Asian Indians give priority to are in fact not just group-specific. Some 80 percent of the respondents did state that a political candidate's position on immigration, affirmative action in higher education, and U.S. relations with India was important to them, but in a question asking respondents to choose the most important issue facing the United States, 32 percent selected crime and 26 percent education. The next most important issue chosen was the economy (13 percent). These three issues—crime, education, and the economy—have repeatedly been found to be three of the top concerns of Americans generally.

Responses to questions on political participation were mixed. Only one-third of the respondents were registered to vote, but of those registered more than 90 percent actually voted in the 1992 presidential election. In the preceding two years a paltry 4 percent had worked for a political party or candidate, 10 percent had contributed money to a political party or candidate, 11 percent had contacted a public official, and 12 percent had been contacted by a public official. Yet, by contrast, 64 percent said they followed events at the local government or community level some or most of the time, and 76 percent said they followed the federal government or national affairs some or most of the time. Although television was reported to be the most important source of political information by far (67 percent), 72 percent responded that ethnic newspapers were somewhat or very important sources of news.

Indeed, an important vehicle for political discussion and organizing among Asian Indians in the United States has been the development of a sophisticated and wide range of print media published by and for this population. Some of the major newspapers include *India Abroad, India West, Indian Post, India Tribune,* and *India Currents.* Leading journals include *South Asia Bulletin, South Asia Forum/Quarterly, South Asian Magazine for Action and Reflection,* and *Committee on South Asian Women.* The circulations of these journals vary from the hundreds to the thousands and continue to grow annually. The major political issues facing the Asian Indian community, from immigration and discrimination to crime and education, are regularly featured and hotly debated in the Asian Indian press.[50]

Survey responses to questions on political ideology and political party preference also were quite diverse. Although the survey revealed overwhelming support for Democrat Bill Clinton over Republican Bob Dole and independent candidate Ross Perot in the 1992 presidential election, 36 percent also supported the initiatives of the Republican Congress elected in 1994. More generally, 42 percent thought of themselves as Democrats, 24 percent as independents, and 13 percent as Republicans. But about 20 percent did not select any of the political parties, and only 44 percent of the self-identified Republicans and Democrats considered themselves to be strong party supporters. Finally, in terms of overall political ideology, 50 percent considered themselves moderate, 25 percent liberal or very liberal, and 19 percent conservative or very conservative.

Contrary to conventional wisdom and most scholarship,[51] however, Asian Indians have clearly become more involved in U.S. politics over the last three decades. Five national Asian Indian organizations dedicated partly or wholly to political activities have been established during this historical period. One of the largest is the Association of Indians in America (AIA). AIA is also probably the oldest such group; it was founded in the mid-1960s. Both AIA and the National Federation of Indian Associations (NFIA), which was formed under a different name in the Northeast in 1971, promote political, social, and cultural activities within the Asian Indian community. Since its founding, NFIA has grown dramatically and currently consists of more than eighty smaller associations throughout the United States.[52]

The three other major national Asian Indian organizations are exclusively political in scope. They are the National Association of Americans of Asian Indian Descent (NAAAID), the Indian American Forum for Political Education (the Forum) and, most recently, the India Abroad Center for Political Awareness (IACPA) which was founded in 1993. NAAAID, which represents only naturalized Asian Indian citizens and concentrates on funding candidates for political office, joined with AIA during the 1970s in the campaign to make "Asian Indian" a subcategory under the broader Asian American heading in the 1980 U.S. Census. A primary motive for this effort was to make Asian Indians eligible for affirmative action programs.[53] In 1982 NAAAID successfully obtained the right to have the Asian Indian population recognized as a socially disadvantaged minority by the U.S. Small Business Administration.[54] A few years later, the Forum and NFIA collaborated to fight against a 1985 proposal to substantially cut Medicare funding to hospitals employing foreign medical graduates and against the 1986 Simpson-Mazzoli bill, which called for severely cutting back use of the fifth preference in the 1965 Hart-Cellar Act which enabled siblings of citizens and their spouses and children to migrate to the United States.[55]

The mission of IACPA, the youngest of the five organizations, is to pursue political activities that will dispel the notion that Asian Indians in the United States are foreigners. This nonprofit, nonpartisan organization based in Washington, D.C., has focused its activities on politicizing Asian Indian youth through a congressional internship program, as well as analyzing, lobbying, and building coalitions around public policy issues that affect the Asian Indian and Asian American communities. Most recently, IACPA spearheaded a broad-based campaign against two provisions of the 1998 Campaign Reform and Election Integrity Act because they banned legal permanent residents (which most Asian Indians in the United States are) from contributing to political campaigns.[56]

Asian Indian business and professional associations have proliferated and become increasingly active politically during the 1980s and 1990s as well. The American Association of Physicians of Indian Origin (AAPI), for example, was founded in 1984 and now has one hundred chapters across the country. The largest ethnic association of doctors in the United States, AAPI has successfully lobbied against restrictive policies that set quotas for foreign-born medical graduates, promoted equal access to managed care, and advocated for the patients' bill of rights. AAPI also has built coalitions with other groups working to pass anti-tobacco laws, because minorities and immigrants are the prime targets of tobacco companies (67 percent of Indian men smoke). On March 26, 1998, AAPI organized its first congressional briefing in Washington, D.C. More than thirty members of Congress, including four senators, attended the meeting.[57]

The Asian American Hotel Owners Association (AAHOA) links Asian hotel and motel owners nationally to promote their interests. Since consolidation with the Indo-American Hospitality Association, which was formed in 1985, AAHOA has grown to represent four thousand members, who in turn represent more than eighteen thousand hotels and motels (it is estimated that 25 percent of all small hotels and motels in the United States are owned by Asian Indians). In view of its powerful business presence, AAHOA recently formed a Governmental Affairs and Political Action Committee. Charged with influencing legislators and policy that affects the lodging industry, this committee is fighting to lower state income and property taxes, increase deductions on business taxes, and lower the minimum wage. Although AAHOA mainly focuses on issues directly facing the hospitality industry, the organization also plans to tackle issues of immigration reform as well as U.S. security and economic policies toward India.[58]

In addition to these and other business and professional organizations, literally hundreds of nonprofit organizations established by Asian Indians have been critical to the politics of this community in the United States. Cultural groups based on different religions, castes, and communities, such as the Federation of Kerala Associations in North America, have engaged in political activities from time to time. Nonprofit service and advocacy organizations, such as SAHARA and Sakhi (dedicated to empowering women of South Asian descent) and Trikone and SALGA (dedicated to serving the needs and promoting the interests of gays and lesbians of South Asian descent), also have proliferated, especially in those cities and states with large Asian Indian populations.[59]

Student groups, like the South Asian Association at Harvard University and the South Asian Students Association at Brown University, have become increasingly popular on college campuses throughout the country. Although these student associations are mostly social and cultural in orientation, they too have become progressively more involved in political activities both on campus and off.[60] They also have provided a vehicle for Asian Indian American students who want to develop their political ideas and skills.[61] In 1997 a South Asian American student group at Stanford University, Sanskriti, successfully co-led a nationwide campaign to overturn the denial of tenure to Akhil Gupta, a prominent Asian Indian professor of anthropology at Stanford.

Asian Indians have begun to identify and form coalitions with other Asian American groups, albeit with mixed success.[62] Many of the student associations and nonprofit organizations, such as those just described, are examples of such coalitions,[63] as was the 1994 merger of the Indo-American Hospitality Association and the Asian American Hotel Owners Association. Prior to that, in 1988, the Forum and NFIA had successfully coordinated with other Asian American organizations to keep the smaller country-of-origin categories under the "Asian American" census heading. Periodic attempts to enact discriminatory immigration or campaign finance laws in the United States often result in more broad-based collective action among Asian American groups, including the India Abroad Center for Political Awareness, Japanese American Citizen League, Organization of Chinese Americans, and National Asian Pacific American Legal Consortium.

Despite this growing political activity, Asian Indian Americans have not been able to make significant inroads into positions of political authority similar to those made by other Asian American groups. Although many candidates have run campaigns, Dalip Singh Saund remains the only Asian Indian to have won a congressional seat.[64] After front-runner Ramakrishnan Nagarajan lost a 1998 Indiana Democratic primary to a once-convicted felon, the Democratic leader for the Sixth Congressional District, Allan Radless, reckoned that "Nag is a fine candidate but his name conjures up some Middle East Monster for voters, I guess."[65] And the executive director of the Indiana State Democratic Party, Mark Harmless, intimated the underlying racism that Asian Indians like Nagarajan face when he said, "I guess Nagarajan is not a Hoosier-sounding name."[66] Asian Indians have gained some voice, however. In 1994 U.S. Representative Frank Pallone of New Jersey, along with seven other members of Congress, established the Congressional Caucus on India and Indian-Americans, which now includes more than one hundred members of Congress.

At the state level, at least three Asian Indian Americans have been elected to state legislatures—in Wyoming, Minnesota, and Maryland. At the local level, Asian Indians were recently elected a council member in New Jersey, a mayor in California, and an alderman in Chicago.[67] And several Asian Indians have been appointed to high-level public policy positions, including Dharmendra K. Sharma as an administrator in the U.S. Department of Transportation, Arati Prabhakar as director of the National Institute of Standards and Technology (U.S. Department of Commerce), Preeta Bansal as a counselor in the Office of the White House Counsel, and Bobby Jindhal as executive director of the President's Bipartisan Commission on Medicare Reform.

The politics of Asian Indians in this country continue to be shaped by, as well as shape, transnational dynamics driven by the global political economy and the domestic political economies of the United States and India. But the impact of Asian Indians on the relations between the United States and India has been largely negligible since 1965. They have tended to generally be sympathetic to the foreign and domestic policies of India, except for Sikh Americans who have regularly lobbied Congress to criticize the civil rights abuses perpetrated by the Indian government against its Sikh population.[68] In addition, for some years Asian Indians in the United States have hoped that India would change its policy and allow dual citizenship, although this is unlikely to occur.

The Indian government, acting on the neoliberal economic reforms inaugurated in India in 1991, has urged Asian Indians in the United States to increase trade with India, as well as invest money and establish businesses there. At the same time, the U.S. government has begun to build linkages with Asian Indian businesspeople in the United States in the hope of generating greater and more beneficial economic ties with India. The two countries continue to have significant foreign policy differences, however; evidence of these differences is the U.S. response to India's nuclear tests in May 1998.[69]

Underlying the confrontation between the United States and India on the nuclear issue, as anthropologist Hugh Gusterson so convincingly demonstrated in a recent essay, lies a racist "Orientalism" that constructs Asians as impulsive, emotional, effeminate, traditional, and even treacherous.[70] This "Orientalism," as we saw earlier in this chapter, has deep historical roots. Asian Indians' contributions to improving U.S.-India relations in the twenty-first century will depend on whether or not they will be able to deconstruct this dominant set of "Orientalist" understandings through increased political activity, broadly construed.

CONCLUSION

Asian Indians will not be "seen, rich, but unheard" in the United States for much longer, if they ever really have been. They will continue to be active in community, cultural, and college campus politics, and, as they continue to grow in numbers, educational attainment, and wealth, they could become a broader political force to be reckoned with in the twenty-first century. Political parties that have not "discovered" Asian Indian Americans, particularly in those geographical areas in which they are concentrated, are likely to lose out over the medium to long term. Asian Indians also are likely to contribute more substantially to a wide array of public policy issues ranging from immigration and discrimination to health care, to small business, high technology, and U.S.-India relations. And they are likely to be increasingly concerned with and vocal about unemployment, poverty, and gender justice.

For this to happen, however, Asian Indians will have to increase their political involvement by becoming citizens, registering, and voting in greater numbers; forming new and strengthening existing political organizations; building coalitions with other groups; and vigorously contesting the pervasive ignorance and racism that continue to exist in the United States. Coalition building with other Asian American groups is paramount because of their shared historical experiences and interests and the practical exigencies of U.S. politics. This is undoubtedly a critical period in the political life of Asian Indians in the United States given the rapidly changing profile of this population and the dynamic global and domestic interactions in which it is embedded.

NOTES

1. We would like to thank Gordon Chang, Akhil Gupta, Rajini Srikanth, Debasish Mishra, and the participants in the conference on "Asian Americans and Politics," held at the Woodrow Wilson International Center for Scholars, March 13–14, 1998, for their insightful comments. The authors, however, are entirely responsible for the content of this essay.

2. Arjun Appadurai and Carol Breckenridge, "Asian Indians in the United States: A Transnational Culture in the Making," paper presented at the Asia Society symposium, New York, 1986.

3. Bill Ong Hing, *Making and Remaking Asian America through Immigration Policy, 1850–1990* (Stanford: Stanford University Press, 1993).

4. Mae M. Ngai, "Illegal Aliens and Alien Citizens: U.S. Immigration Policy and Racial Formation, 1924–1945," Ph.D. dissertation, Columbia University, 1997; and see Chapter 2 in this volume.

5. Timothy P. Fong, *The Contemporary Asian American Experience: Beyond the Model Minority* (Upper Saddle River, N.J.: Prentice Hall, 1998), 16–20.

6. There is some evidence that a small number of Asian Indians, usually young Christian men, were brought to the United States as early as the 1790s as slaves and indentured servants with their British colonial masters. Between 1820 and 1898, 523 Asian Indians immigrated to the United States; most were agricultural workers and unskilled laborers. Reportedly they married and soon disappeared into the black slave population. Joan M. Jensen, *Passage from India: Asian Indian Immigrants in North America* (New Haven: Yale University Press, 1988).

7. Ibid.

8. Ibid.

9. H. A. Millis, "East Indian Immigration to the Pacific Coast," *Survey* 29 (1912): 381.

10. Lan Cao and Himilce Novas, *Everything You Need to Know about Asian American History* (New York: Penguin, 1996), 289.

11. Ngai, "Illegal Aliens and Alien Citizens."

12. Jensen, *Passage from India,* 249.

13. Harold S. Jacoby, "More Thind against than Sinning," *Pacific Historian* 11 (1967): 37.

14. Fong, *Contemporary Asian American Experience,* 16.

15. Ian F. Haney López, *White by Law: The Legal Construction of Race* (New York: New York University Press, 1996).

16. Karen Isaksen Leonard, *The South Asian Americans* (Westport, Conn.: Greenwood Press, 1997), 54.

17. Cao and Novas, *Everything You Need to Know,* 291; and Jensen, *Passage from India.*

18. Cao and Novas, *Everything You Need to Know,* 289.

19. Hing, *Making and Remaking Asian America,* 32–39.

20. Haney López, *White by Law.*

21. Ngai, "Illegal Aliens and Alien Citizens," chaps. 2 and 4.

22. Ibid., 19–20.

23. Fong, *Contemporary Asian American Experience,* 16.

24. Ronald Takaki, *Strangers from a Different Shore: A History of Asian Americans* (New York: Penguin Books, 1989), 330–331.

25. Rajanki K. Das, *Hindustani Workers on the Pacific Coast* (Berlin: Walter De Bruyter, 1923), 77.

26. Leonard, *South Asian Americans,* 23.

27. Ibid., 51.

28. Jensen, *Passage from India,* 262–263.

29. Ibid., 266.

30. Min Song, "Pakhar Singh's Argument with Asian America: Color and the Structure of Race Formation," in *A Part, Yet Apart: South Asians in Asian America,* ed. Lavina Dhingra Shankar and Rajini Srikanth (Philadelphia: Temple University Press, 1998), 79–102.

31. Jensen, *Passage from India,* 255–262.

32. Cao and Novas, *Everything You Need to Know,* 292–293.

33. Ibid., 292.

34. Ibid., 296.

35. Hing, *Making and Remaking Asian America.*

36. Fong, *Contemporary Asian American Experience,* 22–27.

37. LEAP Asian Pacific American Public Policy Institute, *The State of Asian Pacific America: Policy Issues to the Year 2020* (Los Angeles: LEAP Asian Pacific American Public Policy Institute and UCLA Asian American Studies Center, 1993).

38. See Chapter 6 in this volume.

39. Ibid.

40. Leonard, *South Asian Americans,* 74.

41. Aditi Kinkhabwala, "Asian Indians Have Yet to Succeed in Political Arena," *Home News Tribune,* August 17, 1997, 1.

42. See Maxine P. Fisher, *The Indians of New York City: A Study of Immigrants from India* (New Delhi: Heritage Publishers, 1980).

43. Leonard, *South Asian Americans,* 69–70.

44. David M. Levitt, "Entrepreneurs Share Hard Work, Risk and Big Dreams," *Home News Tribune,* August 15, 1997, 2–4; and Cao and Novas, *Everything You Need to Know,* 293.

45. Levitt, "Entrepreneurs Share Hard Work," 6.

46. Fong, *Contemporary Asian American Experience,* 212.

47. Leonard, *South Asian Americans,* 82.

48. Cao and Novas, *Everything You Need to Know,* 295–296.

49. Aneesh P. Chopra and Ajay Kuntamukkula, "The 1996 Survey of Public Policy Concerns of the Indian American Community," draft manuscript, John F. Kennedy School of Government, Harvard University, 1996.

50. Leonard, *South Asian Americans,* 71, 90, 96.

51. Amrita Basu, "The Last Wave: Political Involvement of the Indian Community in the United States," paper presented at the Asia Society symposium, New York, 1986; and Myron Weiner, "The Indian Presence in America: What Difference Will It Make?" in *Conflicting Images: India and the United States,* ed. Sulochna Raghavan and Nathan Glazer (New York: Riverdale, 1990), 252–253.

52. Inder Singh, "NFIA: Mobilizing the Indian Community since 1980," *India-West,* September 13, 1996, A5, A31.

53. Cao and Novas, *Everything You Need to Know,* 295.

54. Robert J. Fornaro, "Asian Indians in America: Acculturation and Minority Status," *Migration Today* 12 (1984): 30–31.

55. Leonard, *South Asian Americans,* 90; and Weiner, " Indian Presence in America."

56. Personal interview with Debasish Mishra, executive director, IACPA, Washington, D.C., May 1998.

57. Personal interview with Neil Parekh, legislative director, AAPI, Washington, D.C., May 1998.

58. Telephone interview with Fred Schwartz, executive director, AAHOA, May 1998.

59. Sandip Roy, "The Call of Rice: (South) Asian American Queer Communities," in *A Part, Yet Apart: South Asians in Asian America,* ed. Lavina Dhingra Shankar and Rajini Srikanth (Philadelphia: Temple University Press, 1998), 168–185.

60. Anu Gupta, "At the Crossroads: College Activism and Its Impact on Asian American Identity Formation," in *A Part, Yet Apart: South Asians in Asian America,* ed. Lavina Dhingra Shankar and Rajini Srikanth (Philadelphia: Temple University Press, 1998), 127–145.

61. Sumantra Tito Sinha, "From Campus to Community Politics in Asian America," in *A Part, Yet Apart: South Asians in Asian America,* ed. Lavina Dhingra Shankar and Rajini Srikanth (Philadelphia: Temple University Press, 1998), 146–167.

62. Nazli Kibria, "The Racial Gap: South Asian American Racial Identity and the Asian American Movement," in *A Part, Yet Apart: South Asians in Asian America,* ed. Lavina Dhingra Shankar and Rajini Srikanth (Philadelphia: Temple University Press, 1998), 69–78.

63. Gupta, "At the Crossroads"; and Roy, "Call of Rice."

64. For a fascinating account of the Uppuluri primary campaign—by an author whose mother is Japanese and father is Asian Indian—see Rajini Srikanth, "Ram Yoshino Uppuluri's Campaign: The Implications for Panethnicity in Asian America," in *A Part, Yet Apart: South Asians in Asian America,* ed. Lavina Dhingra Shankar and Rajini Srikanth (Philadelphia: Temple University Press, 1998), 186–214.

65. Francis X. Clines, "An Unlikely Candidate Rattles the Establishment," *New York Times* (national section), May 24, 1998.

66. Ibid.

67. Personal interview with Debasish Mishra.

68. Weiner, "Indian Presence in America," 252–253.

69. James Benet, "Clinton Calls Test a 'Terrible Mistake' and Announces Sanctions against India," *New York Times,* May 14, 1998, A14.

70. Hugh Gusterson, "Iraqnophobia: America's Racist Discourse on Nuclear Proliferation," unpublished manuscript, Center for International Security and Arms Control, Stanford, Calif., June 11, 1998. The original work on this subject is by Edward Said, *Orientalism* (New York: Vintage Books, 1978).

CHAPTER ELEVEN

THE IMPACT OF MAINSTREAM POLITICAL MOBILIZATION ON ASIAN AMERICAN COMMUNITIES: THE CASE OF KOREAN AMERICANS IN LOS ANGELES, 1992–1998

EDWARD J. W. PARK

From April 29 to May 2, 1992, the nation witnessed one of the most devastating civil unrests in its modern history. Sparked by the "not guilty" verdict of four white officers of the Los Angeles Police Department in the beating case of black motorist Rodney King, street corner disturbances in South Central Los Angeles quickly spread to engulf a sixty-square-mile area. The three days of largely unmitigated violence, arson, and looting resulted in the loss of fifty-two lives, 16,291 arrests, and almost $1 billion in damage. While the precipitating event could be framed through the familiar black and white lens, the broader social significance of the civil unrest could not.

Reflecting the multiracial realities of Los Angeles, Latinos represented the plurality of those arrested, and Korean Americans alone sustained nearly half of the almost $1 billion in property damage. In the nation's first "multiracial riot," Korean Americans found themselves at the center of American race relations—not just as passive victims of the violence but also as one of its root causes. Even before the verdict was handed down, the media speculated whether the tension between Korean American merchants and African American customers would result in violence. During the civil unrest itself, broadcasters showed the raw footage of a Korean American merchant, Soon Ja Du, shooting an African American girl, Latasha Harlins, in a dispute over a bottle of orange juice—alternately explaining and seemingly justifying the pattern of looting that appeared to fall disproportionately on Korean Americans.

The Los Angeles civil unrest also became the major source of political fodder in that presidential election year. Conservatives used the event to rally support for cracking down on undocumented immigrants and getting tough on crime, and liberals called for a national dialogue on race relations and creating empowerment zones to bring more private capital into the inner cities. The major political initiatives of the 1990s—ranging from California's successful Proposition 187 (1994), which sought to withhold public education and services to undocumented immigrants, to President Bill Clinton's Presidential Commission on Race Relations—have their origins in the Los Angeles civil unrest.[1]

On May 28, 1992, the Korean Federation of Los Angeles (KFLA) called an emergency meeting of Korean American community leaders. Held less than a month after the nation's largest civil unrest, the meeting grew increasingly heated over competing visions and strategies of how to organize the community's political response to the event that left the community in an unprecedented crisis. Frustrated with the increasingly divisive discussion, a representative of the Korean consulate pleaded with the activists: "I beg you to put aside your political differences. In this time of crisis, we cannot afford to be a Republican or a Democrat, or a conservative or a liberal. We must all be Koreans first and pursue a singular Korean interest."[2] Two days later, his call for political unity was echoed in an editorial in the *Korea Times,* the largest Korean language daily in the United States: "Although there has been a lot of political differences in the community, we should establish or choose a single Korean American political organization to represent all interests of Korean Americans. In engaging the mainstream society, we must speak with a singular, united voice."[3] Korean Americans in Los Angeles, however, disregarded the pleas of the consulate and the *Korea Times.* Within six months of the civil unrest, they established two political organizations in response to the event—the Korean American Republican Association (KARA) and the Korean American Democratic Committee (KADC).

Despite this division, the first two explicitly partisan political organizations in the Korean American community won major victories. In November 1992 KARA celebrated the election of the first Korean American to Congress, archconservative Republican Jay Kim. A few years later KADC celebrated the appointment of Angela Oh—a criminal defense attorney and one of the most progressive political activists in Los Angeles—to President Bill Clinton's Commission on Race Relations.[4] Reflecting on the changing fortunes of Korean American politics, a longtime observer of the community commented in 1998, when asked to recall the KFLA meeting on May 28, 1992:

> I guess a lot of us were wrong when we thought that political division would be a barrier to political empowerment. While Korean Americans have become more politically divided than ever before, they have also achieved a level of political representation that many of us could not have dreamed possible. But I wonder what the cost is. I mean, how has all this politicking changed our community?

After a pause he answered his own question: "In the last six years, our community has been fundamentally changed."[5]

Much of the discussion of Asian American politics has focused on the impact of Asian American participation on the mainstream political process. In this literature some scholars have examined Asian Americans' voting patterns and candidacies, partisanship and ideology, policy preferences and fund-raising; others have examined the many barriers to their incorporation in the political process, ranging from their transnational ties to racial discrimination by mainstream political institutions and the media.[6] Scholars have paid little attention, however, to how this political mobilization is reshaping the internal political dynamics of Asian American communities themselves. Yet it is clear that mainstream political mobilization reconfigures community politics by bringing new political actors, institutions, and issues into Asian American communities. This chapter examines the impact of mainstream political mobilization on Asian American communities by means of a case study of Korean Americans in Los Angeles. Their effort to find political integration in the mainstream political system has indeed left the community "fundamentally changed."

WHAT GOOD IS LEADERSHIP?

The civil unrest of 1992 had a tremendous impact on Korean Americans. Representing less than 2 percent of the population of Los Angeles, they lost 2,300 businesses and sustained $350 million of the total $785 million in property damage.[7] Confronted with their first major political crisis, the political leaders of the Korean American community in Los Angeles found themselves woefully unprepared to exercise leadership. Indeed, nineteen days before the civil unrest, the *Korea Times* had run a strongly worded editorial criticizing the entrenched leadership in the Korean American community. In his editorial entitled "Problems of Korean American Community: No Leadership," Sang Ho Ahn, an editorial writer, took direct aim at the KFLA, calling it an immigrant generation–dominated organization that derived its political legitimacy from its ties to the South Korean government and the Korean consulate in Los Angeles. After pointing to the "moral crisis" of some key leaders who were accused of financial improprieties and to the "lack of qualifications" of some of KFLA's officers, he lamented the insularity of the Korean American political leadership. Korean American political leaders do no good for the Korean American community, he asserted, unless they have an impact on mainstream political organizations in behalf of that community. Otherwise, he questioned, "what good is leadership other than for self-aggrandizement?"[8]

Bound by language barriers and lack of institutional ties to the mainstream political organizations, the KFLA vented its frustration during the civil unrest within the confines of the Korean American media. Members of the KFLA also charged local African American and Latino politicians with turning their backs on Korean Americans in spite of having received financial support for their political campaigns through various Korean American organizations, including the KFLA. Their charges, however, simply underscored their political ineffectiveness in the eyes of the broader Korean American community. In fact, in his *Korea Times* editorial Sang Ho Ahn had raised a prophetic warning about the political ineffectiveness of the existing leadership:

> Korean Americans have confused money with politics. You don't participate in American politics just with money. You participate by developing ties with the mainstream political parties first and then deliver money and votes. Then the politicians feel some accountability. But, Korean Americans just gave money without building political relationships. The politicians saw us as just donors, not a political force. This is the major problem.[9]

Unable to move the mainstream political and media institutions, the KFLA saw its influence slip away to a new group of political leaders.

Hindsight reveals that the civil unrest generated two different, but ultimately interrelated, changes in the leadership of the Korean American community. The first change, in political legitimacy, has taken place at the community leadership level, brought on by the political discourse surrounding the civil unrest and, more concretely, the politics of rebuilding. The second change has been the widening political divisions among the emerging political leadership, and, for the first time within the Korean American community, the prominent injection of openly partisan politics. These changes have transformed Korean American politics and have set the stage for the future political development of the community.

ASSIGNING BLAME AND REBUILDING

Even as Los Angeles erupted in flames on April 29, 1992, the political discourse on the causes of the civil unrest implied that Korean Americans' strained relationship with African Americans was largely to blame.[10] And the Soon Ja Du incident of 1991, cited by many observers as the central metaphor for a decade of black-Korean tensions in the inner city,[11] was cited as one of the major contributing factors. Moreover, the incident was used to explain and, in some cases, justify the inordinate economic loss suffered by Korean Americans.[12] Particularly within the mass media, the Soon Ja Du incident was invoked in a casual and reckless way, with some outlets interspersing a replay of the 1991 video footage with live footage of burning Korean American stores. KPFK, the Los Angeles radio affiliate of the Public Broadcasting System, celebrated the looting of Korean American stores as "payback."[13]

From the Korean American perspective, the invocation of the Soon Ja Du incident and the black-Korean tension to explain both the cause of civil unrest and the ethnic pattern of looting was an attempt to scapegoat Korean Americans for the civil unrest and politically minimize the economic loss that the community suffered.[14] Many Korean Americans felt "revictimized" by this discourse that blamed them for the civil unrest and seemed to offer a justification for the ethnic pattern in looting.[15] A Korean American student at the University of California Los Angeles (UCLA) recalls being told repeatedly by some non–Korean American students who linked the Soon Ja Du incident with the civil unrest and that "Korean Americans got what they deserved."[16] K. W. Lee, a longtime journalist and observer of the Korean American community, argued that "this scape-goating was the real victimization that Korean Americans were made to suffer. We were told in a back-handed way that we were to blame for the riots and that we should rightly bear the burden."[17]

As frustration and anger within the community grew, the existing Korean American political establishment—represented most powerfully by the immigrant generation–led KFLA—was unable to defend the community. A Korean American volunteer at a senior citizen center complained: "I lost all respect I had for the KFLA. They have always claimed that they were the leaders of the community, even calling the President the 'Mayor of Koreatown.' But during the riot, our mayor could not even come on the television and tell the rest of America that Korean Americans should not be blamed for the riots and that our suffering is as real as anyone else's."[18]

While Korean Americans were frustrated and angered by what they perceived to be an effort to place the blame for the civil unrest on their community, the politics of rebuilding further demonstrated the ineffectiveness of the existing Korean American political power structure. In the aftermath of the civil unrest, Korean Americans had little or no representation in the official rebuilding efforts. For example, they were notably absent from the leadership of "Rebuild Los Angeles" (RLA), the sole official response to the civil unrest from City Hall. Even after RLA's leadership was diversified with the creation of four co-chairs, the "Asian co-chair" went to Linda Wong, a Chinese American.[19] In addition, as both of the 1992 presidential candidates—George Bush and Bill Clinton—toured Los Angeles in the midst of election year politicking, Korean Americans were conspicuously absent from their entourage as locally elected officials took the spotlight and articulated the rebuilding agenda.[20] In response, the Korean American community, still reeling from the unprecedented crisis, keenly felt its marginality in the politics of rebuilding and was reminded of the real cost of such marginality. Frustrated at the inability on the part of Korean Americans to participate in the political process, Edward Chang, a professor of ethnic studies at the University of California Riverside, declared to the *Los Angeles Times,* "We have no allies . . . politically, Korean Americans found they are on the bottom of the society."[21]

In the discourse surrounding the causes of the civil unrest, the Korean American community found a new leader in Angela Oh literally overnight—in the May 6, 1992, broadcast of ABC's *Nightline.*[22] A second-generation Korean American criminal defense lawyer who had been active in liberal circles in Los Angeles politics but who was an unknown in the Korean American community, Oh finally articulated a Korean American perspective on the civil unrest. With enormous poise and passion, she protested the media's coverage of Korean Americans as dehumanized, gun-toting vigilantes and faulted the media's failure to discuss the decades of neglect of the inner cities that created the conditions for the civil unrest. Her appearance on *Nightline* may have done little to reshape the discourse on the civil unrest, but her entry into the debate marked an important turning point in Korean American politics: for the first time in the community's short history, a spokesperson emerged whose political ties lay outside of the entrenched Korean American community power structure. Moreover, by winning the support of Korean Americans who saw in her an articulate spokesperson who could advocate on behalf of the community in the main-stream media, Oh created a space in which others could fill the political vac-uum within the community.[23] She was quickly joined by other Korean Americans—such as Marcia Choo, executive director of the Asia-Pacific American Dispute Resolution Center, and Ryan Song, a 1.5-generation[24] attorney, who spoke for the first time as representatives of the Korean Americans in Los Angeles.

The politics of rebuilding thus began to fuel the rise of a new generation of Korean American leaders. It unfolded through new institutions that placed a premium on interracial and interethnic collaboration.[25] "Rebuild Los Angeles," with its Anglo, Latino, African American, and Asian Ameri-can co-chairs, signaled that racial consolidation would be a key strategy in facilitating the rebuilding effort. The major rebuilding efforts outside of City Hall also placed a premium on interracial and interethnic coalitions in an effort to exercise greater leverage on mainstream political institutions. In fact, the new organizations that provided much of the "unofficial" political leadership in the rebuilding effort—such as the Multicultural Collaborative (MCC, which brought together social service agencies from all major racial groups), Asian Pacific Americans for a New Los Angeles (APANLA), and the Asian Pacific Planning Council (APPCON)—demanded interracial and interethnic coalition building in return for their participation in the re-building process.[26] These organizational efforts collectively had the effect of bringing into the Korean American community a new group of political leaders who had the requisite language skills and political familiarity to par-ticipate effectively in multiracial and multiethnic settings. For example, Bong Hwan Kim, executive director of the Korean Youth and Community Center (KYCC), and Roy Hong, executive director of Korean Immigrant Workers Advocates (KIWA), a progressive labor organization, became key Korean American figures in the rebuilding effort and new political figures within the Korean American community.[27]

The shift in the Korean American political leadership occurred along two dimensions. Most visibly, it represented a generational change in which many of the immigrant-generation leaders stepped aside as the second generation and the 1.5 generation emerged as key political leaders. The political ascendancy of Angela Oh, Bong Hwan Kim, Roy Hong, Cindy Choi (cochair of MCC), and Michelle Park-Steel (a Republican activist and a key figure in the Korean American Coalition's Youth Leadership Conference) was evidence of this generational shift within the Korean American political leadership. A less-visible transition was the decline of those whose political base was rooted in "homeland" politics and the rise of others (first generation included) who had political ties with mainstream political institutions.[28] On this front, Congressman Jay Kim and Tong Soo Chung (a Democrat activist and a Clinton appointee to the U.S. Department of Commerce) represented first-generation Korean Americans whose political ties to the mainstream political system leveraged their political careers to unprecedented levels for Korean Americans. In an unequivocal sign of concession to the changing political realities within the Korean American community, the KFLA changed its main organizational mission from "representing the collective interest of Koreans living in the United States" to "supporting the effort of Korean Americans for political representation."

DIVIDED WE STAND

While Korean Americans in Los Angeles have agreed on the need to participate in mainstream politics, they have been profoundly divided over how best to channel their political resources and community support in the complex political landscape of contemporary American society.

The Partisan Divide

At the center of this division lies the explicit partisan politics that has emerged within the Korean American community. This partisan division reflects both the changes in the community's political leadership just described and the political developments facing the Korean American community since the civil unrest. The changes in political leadership brought in new political leaders who had clear party loyalties. Liberals such as Angela Oh and Bong Hwan Kim were clearly identified with the Democratic Party; conservatives such as Jay Kim and Michelle Park-Steel brought with them clear institutional ties to the Republican Party.

As Korean Americans have embarked on their road to political empowerment, Korean American liberals have argued that the community ought to align itself with the traditional civil rights coalition within the Democratic Party.[29] In particular, they argue that Korean Americans are victims of racial oppression in America; they have been excluded in turn from immigration, the mainstream economy, and equal protection under the law. They also argue that whatever rights and equality Korean Americans currently enjoy stem largely from the civil rights struggles of African Americans and Latinos, including passage of the Hart-Cellar Act (Immigration and Nationality Act Amendments of 1965) which finally removed the racial barriers to immigration. From this vantage point of racial oppression and historical linkages with other racial minority groups, Korean American liberals maintain, then, that the civil unrest of 1992 was the culmination of racial injustice in America, in which decades of inner-city neglect and racial oppression resulted in the explosion that victimized communities of color. Thus in their opinion the best hope for Korean Americans in their effort to find lasting political empowerment is to join other communities of color and white liberals who are committed to issues of racial equality and justice. Linking the Korean American experience with the civil unrest to the broader history of racial inequality in America, the Reverend Jae Hwang, a pastor at the Oriental Mission Church in Koreatown, reflected: "Without this crisis, we would not have realized that America is not the dreamland that we all thought it was. Now we know firsthand about racial injustice in America."[30] In practical terms, this vision of Korean American political incorporation urged the community to join the Democratic Party and its established structure of racial minority incorporation.

This vision gained prominence in the Korean American community immediately after the civil unrest, and Angela Oh became one of the first openly liberal political leaders within the community by linking the civil unrest with Republican neglect of the inner cities and the racial inequality perpetuated by mainstream political institutions, including the criminal justice system.[31] In the massive "Peace Rally" organized by Korean Americans and attended by thirty thousand participants on May 11, 1992, placards such as "Justice for All People of Color" and "More Jobs for the Inner City" implicated institutional racism and economic inequality as the primary causes of the civil unrest. Moreover, these messages reflected a sense of common victimization and destiny that Korean Americans felt with the African American and Latino communities.

A Korean American labor activist who participated observed that

there was a definite racial tone to the march. Korean Americans were angry at the white power structure, even more than at those who took part in the looting. The Koreans felt that they paid the cost of a racist justice system and years of inner-city neglect. More than that, they felt that the white power structure sacrificed Koreatown to take the full brunt of people's anger. Only when the looting spread to places like Hollywood or the West Side did [Los Angeles police chief] Daryl Gates and [California governor] Pete Wilson send in the troops to quell the looting. Many Koreans marching through the heart of the heavily Latino and African American Koreatown were yelling "Join us! We want racial justice just like you." And, many Latinos and African Americans did just that.[32]

A Korean American secondary school teacher had a similar experience: "I thought Korean Americans would use the march to show our anger at the looters and the march would be a display of our narrow nationalism. However, I was completely wrong. The march was really about Koreans reaching out to other groups, especially to African American and Latino communities."[33]

The political protest in the peace march took on a partisan tone. Among the marchers, a woman held up a large red sign that read "Is This a Kinder, Gentler Nation?" in reference to President Bush's 1988 campaign; another woman carried a sign that read "Wilson—You Were Three Days Too Late" in reference to Governor Wilson's decision to send in the National Guard on May 2, three days after much of south central Los Angeles and Koreatown lay in ruins. For many Korean Americans, the timing of the civil unrest, coming after over a decade of Republican control of both the White House and the governor's mansion, indicated that the blame should be placed squarely on Republican leadership and their policies of fiscal austerity and political hostility toward the inner cities. A middle-aged member of the board of directors of Korean Immigrant Workers Advocate commented on the situation:

I was surprised by the political insights of so many Korean Americans. They felt that the American government systematically ignored the plight of poor in the inner city and abused racial minorities. Especially in the peace march, there was no difference between what Koreans were saying and what the African Americans and Latinos were saying. "We want justice for Rodney King [a black motorist beaten by Los Angeles police], we want jobs in the inner cities, we want racial equality, and we want you to stop abusing our communities." Old-time liberals like us who felt we were a small minority in the community was really quite stunned with what we saw.[34]

Within the Korean American community, the Korean American Democratic Committee has become a platform from which liberals and progressives can organize their political activities. Founded in 1992, KADC had difficulties for much of its early existence because most visible liberals and progressives channeled their political activities toward coalition efforts. Leaders such as Angela Oh and Bong Hwan Kim played key roles in the formation of the Multicultural Collaborative and Asian Americans for a New Los Angeles and did not actively provide leadership in Korean American partisan politics.[35] In addition, KIWA, perhaps the most progressive organization in the community, engaged in a bitter fight with the Korean American Relief Fund to win Korean American and Latino workers a share of the relief money that flowed into the community after the civil unrest.[36] Things changed, however, in the summer of 1996. The presidential campaign was in full swing, and bitter partisan fights were beginning to erupt over issues of affirmative action in state programs (California's Proposition 209) and immigration and welfare reform in national politics. Against this backdrop, KADC was revitalized that summer, and Angela Oh, Bong Hwan Kim, and K. S. Park (an organizer at KIWA) joined KADC as officers. The revitalized KADC launched an ambitious program to politically organize Korean Americans for the 1996 election that included a voter registration drive, compilation of a voter's guide (a first for the community in a nonprimary election), and a coordinated voter education drive through the Korean American ethnic media.

Although they only recently entered mainstream Los Angeles politics, Korean American liberals already have had some major impacts, especially in the formation of new liberal coalitions. Both Angela Oh and Bong Hwan Kim have played an instrumental role in the formation of the MCC and APANLA, and Cindy Choi has become one of the founding co-directors of the MCC.[37] The MCC is now one of the most important and powerful progressive voices within Los Angeles politics, and APANLA has made Asian Americans more politically visible than ever.[38] As for other political victories, Korean American journalist K. Connie Kang was hired by the *Los Angeles Times* and President Clinton appointed T. S. Chung to the Department of Commerce. In addition, KIWA has engaged in a number of highly visible labor conflicts in which it has worked with predominantly Latino rank-and-file labor unions. With KIWA's help, unions such as Justice for Janitors and Local 11 were able to resolve labor conflicts that involved Latino workers and Korean or Korean American employers without having these conflicts grow into racial conflicts and thereby pointing a way to multiracial organizing and cooperation.[39] Similarly, the Korean Youth and Community Center worked with the Community Coalition for Substance Abuse Prevention and Training (a predominantly African American anti–substance abuse organization headed by Karen Bass) to convert Korean American liquor stores damaged during the civil unrest to other types of businesses. This cooperative effort received a great deal of media coverage for representing a new possibility in black-Korean relations.[40] In a short period of time, then, Korean American liberals have become important figures in Los Angeles politics and have brought a new set of issues to the city's political agenda.

On the other side of the partisan divide, conservative Korean American activists have urged the Korean American community to align itself with the conservative politics of the Republican Party. Whereas liberals cite racial injustice and inner-city neglect as the cause of the civil unrest, Korean American conservatives assert that at the root of the civil unrest was the failure of the liberal welfare state and the civil rights coalition. Moreover, they argue that the Korean American community, with its large segment of small entrepreneurs and accelerating residential suburbanization, can best pursue its political interest through the Republican Party, which has championed fiscal conservatism and law and order.[41] While appealing to the material interests of Korean Americans, they also point out the recent evidence that the Republican Party is now inclusive of racial minorities and "legal" immigrants. For example, they cite the rise in the party of racial minorities such as Gen. Colin Powell, Ward Connelly (an African American member of the University of California Regents and a key architect of the effort to undermine the state's affirmative action programs), Jay Kim, and Wendy Gramm (a Korean American appointee to the Department of Commerce under Bush and the wife of Texas senator Phil Gramm). Kim himself has stressed this theme of new inclusiveness within the GOP, especially for "Asian Americans . . . who hold conservative values."[42] While Korean American liberals credit the civil rights coalition and the Democratic Party for removing past discriminatory policies, Korean American conservatives hail the symmetry of the Republican political agenda and the material interests of the Korean American community and the new politics of inclusion within the Republican Party.

In Los Angeles the strain between the locally elected politicians (nearly all liberal Democratic African Americans and Latinos) and some segments of the Korean American community (most notably the Korean American Grocers Association, or KAGRO) erupted under the strain of the civil unrest. Because the disturbance raged for nearly a week and Korean Americans sustained nearly half of all economic damage, they looked to the local politicians to come to their aid. A Republican activist recalls:

> I went to a meeting called by Councilman Nate Holden with members of KAGRO to urge him to pass a measure to provide financial relief to Korean Americans who lost their businesses. When we showed up, he made it clear that we were not a priority. Instead, his only concern was to free people who were jailed during the riots. Can you imagine? We walked out in sheer disgust. Holden's response was typical of most Democrats—siding with the perpetrators and turning their backs on the real victim. From a political point of view, this was a crucial mistake. KAGRO's leadership decided that it was impossible to work with these people, and we began explicitly supporting the Republican Party.[43]

The shift of KAGRO, one of the largest and the most influential organizations in the community, from a nonpartisan to a Republican supporter became consolidated in the politics surrounding the rebuilding of the liquor stores. If the peace march represented a high point in the Korean American community's public display of liberal sentiments, the politics surrounding the rebuilding of the liquor stores represented a low point when the profound barriers between the Korean American community and the civil rights coalition emerged and created an opportunity for conservatives to make their appeal to the Korean American community.

Well before the civil unrest, liquor stores in the inner cities were a major source of tension between the African American and Korean American communities.[44] African Americans charged that the stores saturated inner-city communities and served as magnets for criminal activities ranging from drug dealing to prostitution. Korean Americans countered by citing their basic right to engage in a legal commercial activity.[45] The civil unrest provided an unexpected opportunity to settle this impasse between the two communities when 200 liquor stores were destroyed. The racial dimension of rebuilding the liquor stores became apparent when it was learned that 175 of the 200 liquor stores destroyed were owned by Korean Americans and that local African American politicians were seizing this opportunity to severely curtail the number of stores.[46] Indeed, local African American politicians saw the situation as an opportunity to show their accountability to their largely African American and Latino constituencies. Korean American conservatives, however, saw it as an opportunity to rally the community toward the Republican Party and reframe the civil unrest and its aftermath from a conservative perspective.

Working with white and Latino liberals on the Los Angeles City Council, local African American political leaders, headed by City Council members Mark Ridley-Thomas and Rita Walters and state assembly member Marguerite Archie-Hudson, launched the "Campaign to Rebuild South Central without Liquor Stores." In doing so, they successfully imposed a conditional use variance process that would allow City Hall, in consultation with local residents, to impose conditions for rebuilding the liquor stores such as restricting hours of operation and requiring uniformed security guards.[47] KAGRO, representing the Korean American liquor store owners, sought to bypass City Hall altogether by going directly to the California legislature where it worked with Paul Horcher, then a conservative Republican from East San Gabriel Valley. In consultation with KAGRO and KARA, Horcher sponsored AB 1974 in the state legislature that would have removed the conditional variance process in Los Angeles. Ultimately, AB 1974 was defeated in committee by a coalition of Democrats over the strong objections of Republicans. Two years later, only 10 of the 175 Korean American–owned liquor stores were back in business.[48]

Although Korean American conservatives clearly lost the policy battle, the politics surrounding the liquor stores became a major victory for the newly emerging Korean American conservative activists. First, the liquor store controversy allowed many Korean American conservatives to gain political visibility within the Korean American community for the first time. New conservative activists such as Michelle Park-Steel, whose political ties with the Republican Party ran deep (her husband, Shawn Steel, also was a Republican Party activist), and Jerry Yu, who placed his mainstream legal career on hold to advocate full time for KAGRO, became highly visible in the Korean American community through the liquor store controversy. Much like their liberal counterparts, they gained their political legitimacy by demonstrating to the community that they could have an impact on mainstream politics and move mainstream political institutions on its behalf.

Second, Korean American conservatives were able to use the liquor store controversy to sharpen the political differences between the Korean American and African American communities and undermine the liberals' vision of rallying Korean Americans quickly and easily into the civil rights coalition. In their defeat over the liquor store controversy, Korean American conservatives pulled no punches as they blamed the African American community for depriving Korean Americans of their economic rights. In an editorial published in the *Korea Times,* Michelle Park-Steel and Shawn Steel urged Korean Americans in Los Angeles to use the liquor store controversy to "carefully assess who are their friends and who are their enemies" as they charged African American politicians for "unleashing a legislative terror."[49] Jerry Yu linked the liquor store controversy to the more fundamental failing of the civil rights coalition and the Democratic Party. He claimed that "these African American politicians" are blaming the Korean Americans for "decades of their own failed policies in the inner-cities that caused the riots in the first place." [50] Others agreed with this assessment. One Korean American student whose family store was burned down during the civil unrest and remained closed after four years states:

My family's American Dream died when the city prevented us from rebuilding our store. We were victimized by the racism of the black community who want us out of South Central. Never mind that we have the right to conduct business and make a living. We are the wrong skin color from their point of view, and we don't belong in their community. However, last time I checked, there were no signs that read "You Are Now Entering the Black Community" at the borders of South Central. If whites did this to Blacks, then this would be a huge incident. But, I guess Black racism against Koreans is okay.[51]

A member of KARA pointed out that "the liquor store issue really stopped the rise of liberals like Angela Oh and Bong Hwan Kim. [It] made [Oh's and Kim's] claim that Korean Americans must join Blacks and Latinos to fight white racism seem simple and idealistic." He also pointed out that "it was clear to all Korean Americans that it was the white Republicans who fought for our community and it was the blacks [who] wanted nothing less than to drive us out." Another KARA member observed that "the liquor store controversy showed to Korean Americans that African American and Democratic politicians would rather go after some bogeyman such as white racism or evil Koreans rather than telling people they have to work hard, get off welfare, and rebuild the economy."[52]

Meanwhile, KARA has become one of the most visible political forces in the Korean American community since the civil unrest. Its major political victory came only months after the disturbance with the election of Jay Kim to the

House of Representatives in November 1992. As the very first Korean American elected to a federal office, Kim brought immediate legitimacy to KARA and energized Korean American conservatives. Until his conviction for improper fund-raising undermined his 1998 campaign, Kim aggressively pursued his ultraconservative agenda, refusing to join the Democratic-dominated Asian American Caucus in the House and becoming a cosponsor of California's politically charged Proposition 187 that sought to deny government benefits to undocumented immigrants.[53] In 1995 KARA stepped up its activities to the presidential level when it successfully hosted a fund-raising dinner for Phil Gramm's presidential campaign and, in 1996, co-hosted Bob Dole's victory speech in California primaries. Finally, Mark Kim, a Korean American assistant deputy in the Los Angeles District Attorney's Office and president of KARA, took a leadership role within the Korean American community in advocating California's Proposition 209 which was intended to preempt affirmative action policies in state government agencies, including public employment and government contracting. Overall, then, Korean American conservatives have joined other conservative racial minorities to bring new legitimacy to the Republican Party's claim for racial inclusion—a central theme in the Republican Party's 1996 and 2000 national conventions—and new complexities to the racial politics surrounding affirmative action and immigration reform.[54]

The Generational Divide

In addition to the partisan divide, the Korean American community has undergone a very public and painful conflict between the generations. Immediately after the civil unrest, the participation of the 1.5 and second generations in community rebuilding efforts was universally welcomed by the immigrant generation. In those generations, the immigrant generation saw powerful advocates who could use their English language skills and personal networks to advocate on behalf of the embattled immigrant community. As the post–immigrant generation provided key leadership and resources in the aftermath of the civil unrest, Professor Eui-Young Yu, a longtime observer of the community and a respected sociologist from California State University in Los Angeles, commented in May 1992 to the *Los Angeles Times,* "I was surprised and moved that all generation and sectors are united. Especially the second and first generation: they were pretty much apart. Now they realize they need each other."[55] This sentiment was echoed by post–immigrant generation leaders. In announcing an initiative by the Korean American Coalition to establish a national advocacy organization for Korean Americans (akin to the Japanese American Citizen's League or the Jewish Federation), Jerry Yu declared confidently that since the civil unrest Korean Americans had become politically sophisticated enough to overcome generational divisions and united in addressing "a wide range of issues that affect us as Korean Americans."[56]

This unity across generational lines, however, became quickly strained. Initially, and perhaps predictably, the strain stemmed from competition between social service agencies. In particular, the Korean Youth and Community Center and its 1.5-generation executive director, Bong Hwan Kim, became a target for criticism by a segment of the immigrant generation leadership. As KYCC celebrated the opening of its $4.6 million office and low-income residential complex, the Reverend Hyun Seung Yang, a United Methodist minister and the head of Shalom Community Center, criticized KYCC for enjoying "a lot of privileges" because of its ability to work with mainstream politicians. Moreover, he argued that KYCC was unwilling to share its resources with immigrant generation organizations and that KYCC had staffers who were too Americanized and, in some cases, did not even speak Korean.[57] The same *Los Angeles Times* article that carried Yang's remarks also raised the issue of KYCC's implementation of City Hall's $260,000 liquor store conversion program. While popular among the elected politicians and community activists, the program was condemned by KAGRO as well as by a wide spectrum of Korean American organizations who viewed it as a way to prevent Korean Americans from reopening their businesses.[58]

These issues became a public spectacle when Kapson Yim Lee, the English editor of the *Korea Times*, published an editorial on April 1997 to coincide with the First Korean American Studies Conference. Co-sponsored by KYCC, the Korean Immigrant Workers Advocates (another organization closely identified with post–immigrant generation leadership), and UCLA's Asian American Studies Center, the conference was held to commemorate the fifth anniversary of the civil unrest. Pulling no punches, Lee charged the "English-speaking" community leaders and academics with "continuing to make fame and money on the backs of nameless victims, whose knowledge of English is limited" and of using the community's "tragedy to enhance their personal and organizational agendas." She reserved her harshest criticism for Bong Hwan Kim and KYCC, arguing that during the liquor store controversy they "were on the other side, holding hands with black leaders." She made the intensity of her anger clear with the following advice for the new generation: "Stay away from us. With friends like you, who needs enemies."[59]

At the conference, Lee's charge was met by Angela Oh who had faced similar charges throughout her involvement in the Korean American community. In an emotionally charged speech that began with her claim that she and other members of the post–immigrant generation were an integral part of the "us" in Lee's editorial, she declared that her politics would not be compromised by specious claims of ethnic authenticity and charges of opportunism. She concluded with a promise that she and the thousands in the new generation of Korean Americans would not go away but would continue to participate in the community's political process, including representing its interests in the mainstream political system. By not setting out to narrowly defend liberal politics, but rather to broadly defend the right of the 1.5 and second generations to participate in the community's politics, she was able to take the moral high ground of inclusion rather than appearing as either a community gatekeeper or a partisan advocate. While her defense of inclusion left even the 1.5- and second-generation conservative activists cheering, this exchange served as a powerful message that generational politics would not go away. Rather, the exchange affirmed that Korean American political leaders and their actions—in whatever form—must first gain political legitimacy from the community, including the newer immigrants who are the least able to hold leadership accountable. In this way, Lee's editorial had the effect of disciplining the political activities of the post–immigrant generation. One 1.5-generation Korean American conservative activist observed:

> Even though Mrs. Lee failed to see that not all young Korean Americans are liberals trying our best to appease blacks, her attack was very significant. She made it clear that the first generation will not simply play dead while the young people run circles around them. She essentially stated that the first generation will hold us accountable. In some ways, I agree with her. If we are not accountable to the first generation, how can we claim to represent the Korean American community?[60]

Another second-generation Korean American who works at KYCC recalled that

> the day after the editorial was published, I was very angry and went into the office and wrote down how KYCC's resources were spent on programs that

helped the first generation. I wanted to prove that we weren't so selfish as Kapson suggested in her piece. While I was doing this, I realized that she had made her point: we need to think about generation equity, and we need to be fair.[61]

Lee's editorial and the discussion it generated serve as a powerful statement that generational conflict will play an important role in the evolution of Korean American politics.

CONCLUSION

The civil unrest of 1992 marked a fundamental change in Korean American politics. Clearly, it has resulted in the community's commitment to engage the mainstream political process and to find political empowerment. This new commitment has resulted in shifts within the Korean American political leadership. For example, new leaders have emerged who can participate in the mainstream political process and work in multiracial and multiethnic settings. While Korean Americans are united in their commitment to collective empowerment, they are profoundly divided along partisan lines. At the center of this division lie conflicting "racial visions" of where Korean Americans fit into America's racial landscape as well as conflicting assessments of the civil rights coalition. Liberals have argued that Korean Americans are an oppressed racial minority group and that their rights and interests can be best protected by joining the civil rights coalition and the Democratic Party. By contrast, conservatives have insisted that Korean Americans have fundamental economic and political differences with key members of the civil rights coalition and that they can better meet their interests through the Republican Party and its commitment to fiscal conservatism, law and order, and the dismantling of the welfare state. The emergence of KADC and KARA has put in place a well-defined institutional base for the community's partisan politics at the very inception of Korean American politics. It is too early to tell, though, which one of these partisan efforts will succeed in having a lasting impact on Korean American political formation.

As Korean Americans struggle with partisan divisions whose terms are defined from outside the community, they also find themselves embattled by a generational conflict within the community. While the immigrant generation initially welcomed the participation of the post–immigrant generation, its successful inclusion has brought new anxieties over sharing resources and leadership. On the one hand, the immigrant generation fears that the new generation will monopolize community resources and "sell out" the needs of the immigrant community for the sake of multiracial coalition building. On the other hand, the post–immigrant generation feels that the immigrant community is unwilling to share the responsibility of leadership. In the end, the future success of Korean American (and Asian American) political mobilization will depend not only on the community's relationship with the mainstream political institutions, but also on how the community deals with its important internal divisions.

NOTES

1. For more on the Los Angeles civil unrest of 1992, see Mark Baldassare, ed., *The Los Angeles Riots: Lessons for the Urban Future* (Boulder: Westview Press, 1994); and Robert Gooding-Williams, ed., *Reading Rodney King/Reading Urban Uprising* (New York: Routledge, 1993).

2. Youngbin Kim, interview by author, Los Angeles, March 16, 1999.

3. Ha Chun-shik, "Need for a Unified Organization that Represents Korean American Community," *Korea Times*, May 30, 1992.

4. See Edward J. W. Park, "Competing Visions: Political Formation of Korean Americans in Los Angeles, 1992–1997," *Amerasia Journal* 24 (1998): 41–57.

5. Youngbin Kim, interview.

6. See Paul Ong and Don T. Nakanishi, "Becoming Citizens, Becoming Voters: The Naturalization and Political Participation of Asian Pacific Immigrants," in *The State of Asian Pacific America: Reframing the Immigration Debate*, ed. Bill Ong Hing and Ronald Lee (Los Angeles: LEAP Asian Pacific American Public Policy Institute and UCLA Asian American Studies Center, 1996), 275–305; Harold Brackman and Steven P. Erie, "Beyond 'Politics by Other Means'? Empowerment Strategies for Los Angeles' Asian Pacific community," in *The Bubbling Cauldron*, ed. Michael Peter Smith and Joe R. Feagin (Minneapolis: University of Minnesota Press, 1995), 286–287; Leland T. Saito, *Race and Politics: Asian Americans, Latinos, and Whites in a Los Angeles Suburb* (Urbana: University of Illinois Press, 1998); and L. Ling-chi Wang, "Race, Class, Citizenship, and Extraterritoriality: Asian Americans and the 1996 Campaign Finance Scandal," *Amerasia Journal* 21 (1998): 1–21.

7. Pyong Gap Min, *Caught in the Middle: Korean Merchants in America's Multiethnic Cities* (Berkeley: University of California Press, 1996), 1.

8. Sang Ho Ahn, "Problems of Korean American Community: No Leadership," *Korea Times*, April 10, 1992.

9. Ibid.

10. See Melvin L. Oliver, James H. Johnson, and W. C. Farrell, "Anatomy of a Rebellion," in *Reading Rodney King/Reading Urban Uprising,* ed. Robert Gooding-Williams (New York: Routledge, 1993); and Peter A. Morrison and Ira S. Lowry, "A Riot of Color: The Demographic Setting," in *Los Angeles Riots: Lessons for the Urban Future,* ed. Mark Baldassare (Boulder: Westview Press, 1994).

11. This incident involved a Korean American store owner—Soon Ja Du—who shot and killed a thirteen-year-old African American girl—Latasha Harlins—in a dispute over a bottle of orange juice. When Superior Court judge Joyce Karlin fined Du $500 and sentenced her to probation and 400 hours of community service, the decision was met with profound dismay and protest from the African American community. It also inflamed the existing tension between Korean American merchants and African American community activists. See Raphael J. Sonenshein, "The Battle over Liquor Stores in South Central Los Angeles: The Management of an Interminority Conflict," *Urban Affairs Review* 31 (1996): 716.

12. Morrison and Lowry, "Riot of Color," 34; Oliver et al., "Anatomy of a Rebellion," 121; and Min, *Caught in the Middle,* 84–86.

13. Min, *Caught in the Middle,* 91.

14. Sumi K. Cho, "Korean Americans vs. African Americans," in *Reading Rodney King/Reading Urban Uprising,* ed. Robert Gooding Williams (New York: Routledge, 1993); and K. Connie Kang, "Understanding the Riots—Six Months Later: Touched by Fire," *Los Angeles Times,* November 19, 1992, J3.

15. Edward T. Chang, "America's First Multiethnic 'Riots,' " in *The State of Asian America,* ed. Karin Aguilar-San Juan (Boston: South End Press, 1994), 114.

16. Thomas Lee, interview by author, Los Angeles, May 7, 1996.

17. Park, "Competing Visions," 41.

18. Sookyoung Choi (pseudonym), interview by author, Los Angeles, March 8, 1996.

19. James A. Regalado, "Community Coalition-Building," in *Los Angeles Riots: Lessons for the Urban Future,* ed. Mark Baldassare (Boulder: Westview Press, 1994), 207.

20. K. Connie Kang, "Asian-Americans Seek Role in L.A. Renewal," *Los Angeles Times,* May 29, 1993, B3.

21. Don Lee, "Korean Americans See Need for Political Power," *Los Angeles Times,* May 17, 1992, A1.

22. Winnie Park, "Political Mobilization of the Korean American Community," in *Community in Crisis: The Korean American Community after the Los Angeles Civil Unrest of April 1992,* ed. George O. Totten and H. Erick Schockman (Los Angeles: Center for Multiethnic and Transnational Studies, University of Southern California, 1994), 199.

23. Ibid., 200.

24. The 1.5-generation immigrated to the United States as young children.

25. Regalado, "Community Coalition-Building," 226–227.

26. E. Park, "Competing Visions," 46.

27. Kang, "Asian Americans Seek Role in L.A. Renewal"; and Lydia Chavez, "Crossing the Culture Line," *Los Angeles Times Magazine,* August 28, 1994, 286–287.

28. Edward Park, "Our L.A.? Korean Americans in Los Angeles after the Civil Unrest," in *Rethinking Los Angeles,* ed. Michael J. Dear, H. Erick Schockman, and Greg Hise (Thousand Oaks, Calif.: Sage Publications, 1996), 158; and Brackman and Erie, "Beyond 'Politics by Other Means'?" 286–287.

29. See Manning Marable, *Beyond Black and White: Rethinking Race in American Politics* (New York: Verso, 1995); and Raphael J. Sonenshein, "Los Angeles Coalition Politics," in *Los Angeles Riots: Lessons for the Urban Future,* ed. Mark Baldassare (Boulder: Westview Press, 1994).

30. Lee, "Korean Americans See Need for Political Power."

31. W. Park, "Political Mobilization of the Korean American Community"; and Angela E. Oh, "Rebuilding Los Angeles: Why I Did Not Join RLA," *Amerasia Journal* 19 (1993): 157–160.

32. Sarah Chee, interview by author, Los Angeles, May 22, 1998.

33. Hyesoon Yun (pseudonym), interview by author, Los Angeles, April 9, 1998.

34. Hyunsik Moon, interview by author, Los Angeles, March 12, 1996.

35. E. Park, "Our L.A.?" 164.

36. Hoon Lee, "4.29 Displaced Workers Justice Campaign," *KIWA News* 1 (1994).

37. E. Park, "Our L.A.?" 163.

38. Regalado, "Community Coalition-Building," 226–227.

39. K. Connie Kang, "L.A. Hilton Owner Will Keep Service Workers," *Los Angeles Times* January 10, 1995.

40. Chavez, "Crossing the Culture Line"; and Sonenshein, "Battle over Liquor Stores."

41. E. Park, "Our L.A.?" 160–161; and W. Park, "Political Mobilization of the Korean American Community," 214–216.

42. Gerdeen Dyer, "Build Your Political Clout, Asian-Americans Urged," *Atlanta Constitution,* April 11, 1993.

43. Laura Jeon, interview by author, Los Angeles, March 24, 1999.

44. Min, *Caught in the Middle;* and Sonenshein, "Battle over Liquor Stores," 722.

45. Sonenshein, "Battle over Liquor Stores," 729.

46. E. Park, "Our L.A.?" 161–162.

47. Sonenshein, "Battle over Liquor Stores," 722.

48. K. Connie Kang and Marc Lacey, "Court Rejects Appeal of Rules for Liquor Stores," *Los Angeles Times,* July 15, 1994.

49. Shawn Steel and Michelle E. J. Park-Steel, "Outcome of AB 1974: Korean-Americans Strangled Again," *Korea Times* (English edition), September 7, 1994.

50. K. Connie Kang, "Store Owners Fight Restrictions on Reopening," *Los Angeles Times,* July 21, 1994.

51. Craig Chang (pseudonym), conversation with author, Cerritos, Calif., March 5, 1996.

52. Mark C. Kim, conversation with author, Los Angeles, April 3, 1996.

53. D. Yi, "From NAFTA to Immigration: Rep. Kim Speaks Out before KA Republicans," *Korea Times* (English edition), October 6, 1993, and E. Park, "Our L.A.?" 161. For information on Jay Kim's fund-raising scandal, see Faye Fiore, "Kim Loses to Miller in Bid to Keep Seat," *Los Angeles Times*, June 3, 1998; and David Rosenzweig, "House Ethics Panel Says Kim Violated Code of Conduct," *Los Angeles Times*, October 10, 1998.

54. See Dana Y. Takagi, *The Retreat from Race: Asian-American Admissions and Racial Politics* (New Brunswick, N.J.: Rutgers University Press, 1992); and articles in Bill Ong Hing and Ronald Lee, eds., *The State of Asian Pacific America: Reframing the Immigration Debate* (Los Angeles: LEAP Asian Pacific American Public Policy Institute and UCLA Center for Asian American Studies, 1996).

55. Lee, "Korean Americans See Need for Political Power," A1.

56. Jake Doherty, "Korean American Group to Unite," *Los Angeles Times*, December 6, 1992.

57. K. Connie Kang, "A Cause for Korean American Celebration—and Controversy," *Los Angeles Times*, May 13, 1994, B3.

58. Kang, "Store Owners to Fight Restrictions on Reopening," B3.

59. Kapson Yim Lee, "Sa-ee-gu (April 29) Was a Riot, Not 'Civil Unrest,' " *Korea Times* (English edition), March 26–April 29, 1997.

60. Mary Chung (pseudonym), interview with author, Los Angeles, May 13, 1997.

61. Do Kim, conversation with author, Los Angeles, May 13, 1997.

PART FOUR

TOWARD THE FUTURE

PEOPLE FROM CHINA CROSSING THE RIVER: ASIAN AMERICAN POLITICAL EMPOWERMENT AND FOREIGN INFLUENCE

FRANK H. WU
FRANCEY LIM YOUNGBERG

Why should we think of people from China as fellows the minute they dwell in a certain place, namely the United States, but not when they dwell in a certain other place, namely China?

—Martha Nussbaum, *For Love of Country*

But two-thirds of Asian Americans haven't crossed the river and they can't say, "I'm in the promised land. . . ." We still have to take care of the people on the other side.

—Democratic National Committee fund-raiser John Huang, March 1996 interview

We've got to remember the Chinese are everywhere, as far as our weapon systems, not only in our labs that make our nuclear weapons and development, but also in the technology to deliver them. They're real. They're here. And probably in some ways, very crafty people.

—Sen. Richard Shelby, NBC's *Meet the Press*, March 28, 1999

In late 1996 Asian Americans reached a turning point in their political empowerment. They were transformed from invisible to infamous. A parade of Asian faces showed up on the television news and a lengthy list of Asian names appeared in the newspaper headlines, as the so-called "Asian Connection" raised claims of foreign influence arising from their campaign contributions to the Democratic National Committee (DNC). Together, the scandal and the responses offer a case study of the problems of organizing communities based on ethnic identity within the political process. Minority groups may have distinct political concerns—in some instances as a direct result of racial discrimination—yet their efforts to advance their interests may lead to further backlash.[1]

This chapter analyzes the fund-raising scandal. It argues that whatever the merits of allegations about individual wrongdoing or Chinese government intentions, the Asian Connection affair incorporated racial stereotyping. The allegations, the investigation, and the treatment of Asian American complaints all raise troubling implications about the acceptance of Asian immigrants as U.S. citizens and their ability to participate as equal stakeholders in shaping public policy.[2] Indeed, it is important to emphasize at the outset that it is possible both for an individual to be guilty of wrongdoing and for a racial group to be affected by racial stereotyping.

This chapter is divided into five sections. The first covers the background of the scandal, and the second describes the scandal itself, including the allegations made, and gives examples of the racial aspects of the fund-raising inquiries and media coverage. The third section is an analysis of the protests articulated by Asian Americans and the responses to them; the fourth considers the legitimacy of Asian Americans' influence on immigration issues. The final section raises issues that Asian American community leaders might consider in striving for political participation.

BACKGROUND

The affair called the "Asian Connection"—given that name by the highly influential *New York Times* columnist William Safire[3]—introduced the general public to Asian Americans as political actors. Because of the activities of a handful of individuals in the months leading up to the 1996 presidential election, most notably DNC fund-raiser John Huang, the approximately ten million U.S. citizens and permanent residents of Asian ancestry came to be regarded as a foreign influence over the White House. The extraordinary attention to Asian Americans ended only as independent counsel Kenneth Starr shifted the Whitewater investigation toward President Bill Clinton's relationship with White House intern Monica Lewinsky. Thus the Asian Connection was the dominant political controversy in the nation's capital until it was displaced by the possibility and then the reality of a historic impeachment and trial.[4]

For more than a year, however, Asian Americans were at the center of arguments over the corruption of government institutions. The change in perceptions of Asian Americans was as sudden as it was negative. This section describes the coincidental background of the Asian Connection: first, the emerging Asian American political involvement, and, second, the high-stakes fund-raising of partisan politics. More than either factor alone, this unfortunate coincidence caused the fund-raising fiasco.

Asian American Political Involvement

Before 1996 Asian Americans had been widely regarded as politically "apathetic."[5] They and independent observers offered a multitude of explanations for the apparent absence of political interest, ranging from a tendency of immigrants to concentrate their energies on establishing themselves economically to cultural aversions to electoral campaigns to greater interest in homeland politics.[6] Significantly, even those variables that correlate with higher civic involvement for other racial groups, such as educational level, have not predicted behavior as well for Asian Americans.[7]

Despite their relative low voter turnout, Asian Americans have always contributed money to political candidates. Well before the fund-raising matter developed, empirical evidence and anecdotal reports suggested that Asian Americans were financially involved in electoral politics—although no scholarly study appears to have established, as was often reported in the popular press, that Asian Americans were second only to Jewish Americans in per capita campaign contributions. Typical of the research is Carole Uhlaner's finding that Asian Americans are more likely to make political contributions if they are foreign-born.[8] Prior to the Asian Connection, numerous Asian Americans also remarked on the tendency to emphasize political donations over electoral participation as a means of expressing their political preferences. In 1990 in California—the site of the heaviest concentration of Asian Americans on the mainland, but the Asian American political consciousness was still forming—an Asian American Republican Party leader stated, "A lot [of Asian Americans] are not active in the party. . . . They don't like to rally or anything, but if you knock on their doors they will comply with a donation."[9]

Their generosity, coupled with their growing presence and prominence, made Asian Americans an attractive voting bloc to win over. Both major political parties had begun to pursue Asian Americans as a racial group as early as the 1988 presidential campaign.[10] Consistent with their overall agendas, especially with respect to people of color, the Democrats and the Republicans developed different messages. Both parties made color-conscious efforts—that is, actions that took into account ethnic heritage—in their interactions with Asian Americans.

The Democratic Party appealed to Asian Americans as supportive of diversity. It characterized its political opposition as anti-immigrant. As Huang himself remarked in an interview, "Asian Americans should be natural born Democrats. Without a Democratic President and a Democratic Congress, many of us would not even be here today, because the Democrats were the ones who changed the immigration policies."[11]

The Democratic Party assigned staff to "outreach" and "fund-raise" for various constituencies. Alongside African Americans, Hispanics, "white ethnics," and labor unions, Asian Americans were included within the "base" vote that the Democrats anticipated they would need for victory. An outreach plan, written by the DNC Asian American desk, outlined a goal of raising $7 million from Asian Americans for the 1996 election.[12]

The Republican Party based its appeal to Asian Americans on its anti-communist and pro-business stances, shifting from the former to the latter in response to global political transitions. To appeal to ethnic voters, the party even went so far as to produce foreign language materials that discussed foreign policy issues related to their homelands.[13] It also began to describe its political opposition as favoring affirmative action for African Americans, which, it asserted, was harmful to Asian Americans. During the 1996 election, Republican presidential candidate Bob Dole delivered the lengthiest speech of his campaign on California's Proposition 209, a ballot measure that would have abolished the racial remedies, to a predominantly Vietnamese American audience in Orange County, California.[14] That speech identified him as a supporter of Proposition 209, making explicit a position that until then had only been implicit.

Although the Republican Party had formally abandoned ethnic organizations within its party structure, it retained a "Heritage Group" for Asian Americans, and during the 1996 presidential campaign it designated a coordinator for Asian Americans.[15] Several writers, such as Ron Unz, a California entrepreneur who had briefly challenged Republican incumbent Pete Wilson for the gubernatorial nomination,[16] encouraged the party to recruit Asian Americans as "natural" Republicans. Writing in a publication of the Heritage Foundation, Unz asserted that Republicans and Asian Americans shared traditional values.[17]

On both sides of the aisle, then, Asian Americans' involvement in politics was increasing immediately before the Asian Connection.

High-Stakes Fund-raising

The context for the fund-raising scandal was much larger than it first appeared. The disputed donations were minor elements of a larger nationwide trend toward campaign expenditures of incredible proportions. In anticipation of the possibility of a permanent realignment of the political mainstream and with the 1994 midterm elections having brought Congress under Republican control, both major parties had begun to seek and depend on "soft money," as opposed to "hard money," for their activities.

"Hard money" is extensively regulated by federal law and thus is subject to "hard limits." Some sources of money are prohibited, most sources are subjected to spending limits, and extensive disclosures are required. Corporations and labor unions are prohibited from spending money in federal elections. Post-Watergate reform measures such as the Federal Election Campaign Act of 1974 set maximum ceilings on individual contributions. Even individuals entitled to donate funds are held to a maximum of $1,000 per candidate per election and $25,000 overall per year. To circumvent limits, political action committees, known as PACs, were established to raise voluntary contributions for use in federal elections. Until 1996, PACs—not soft money—were regarded as the primary threat to the substantive equality of individual voters in the electoral process. In 1976 the Supreme Court ruled in *Buckley v. Valeo* that campaign expenditures fall within the scope of the First Amendment protection of free speech.[18]

The Federal Election Commission (FEC) created the "soft money" catchall concept through one of its opinions; it was not authorized to do so explicitly by election statutes or accompanying regulations. Soft money consists mainly of funds given to political parties, instead of individual candidates, ostensibly to support party-related activities rather than specific campaigns. It includes funds for issue advocacy on subjects such as abortion or gun control, but appeals may not be made expressly on behalf of specific candidates. A donor who wishes to exceed hard money limits thus can give soft money to a political party.[19] Because the parties have tended to bundle soft money together with hard money, any given expenditure may blend both forms of funding.

In the 1996 election cycle the Democratic Party raised $123.9 million in soft money and $221.6 million in hard money. The Republican Party raised $138.2 million and $416.5 million, respectively, in the same categories.[20]

Each party's soft money expenditures in 1996 were over 200 percent higher than in the previous election cycle.[21]

This combination—Asian Americans as an emerging voting bloc and the need for soft money—created the circumstances that led to the Asian Connection. Asian Americans sought not only to follow the rules of the game, which they understood to require giving money, but also to gain credit for their donations through centralized record-keeping. They naively believed that after Clinton's reelection they would be recognized with political appointments commensurate with their contributions. They also hoped that they would be able to advocate on issues affecting Asian Americans in particular.

At the center of the allegations was DNC fund-raiser John Huang. But to describe Huang as being at the center of the events, as distinct from the allegations, may be misleading. Because the investigations originated from Huang's work and his DNC files, he appeared to be the focal point of any developments. This was especially true because of the administrative protocol that credited Huang with donations even if, in fact, he had nothing to do with them.

Press reports described Huang's birth in China and later life in Taiwan as unusual, but his career followed a path typical of middle-class Asian immigrants of his generation.[22] After arriving in the United States as a graduate student, Huang pursued a banking career. At one time, he headed the banking operations of the Lippo Group, an Indonesia-based business conglomerate owned by the Riady family, who are ethnic Chinese. Based in Los Angeles, Huang became involved in partisan politics. His objectives appear to have been ambiguous. They ranged from protecting immigration rights to possibly lobbying the federal government on behalf of Lippo for permission to bypass federal regulations on lending to racial minorities.[23]

Although Huang had donated money to candidates of both political parties, he ultimately secured a mid-level appointment in the U.S. Commerce Department during the first term of the Clinton administration. Before the 1996 election Huang joined the DNC fund-raising staff, filling the newly created position of "vice-chair" of finance. There, he was assigned the task of raising money for the DNC from Asian Americans—or, as political operatives have described it, "dialing for dollars."

ALLEGATIONS AND EXAMPLES

As the Asian Connection unfolded, Asian Americans were accused of wrongdoing ranging from common but unseemly campaign finance practices to serious conspiracies verging on treason. Many allegations were credible, and some resulted in admissions of guilt.[24] But the allegations also were accompanied by racial stereotyping, as politicians and pundits charged essentially that Asian Americans were by their very nature likely to engage in bribery, or that their behavior implied that all individuals with Asian-sounding surnames should be suspected of illegal conduct.[25] Many statements issued employed overt racial references; a few resulted in public apologies.

Allegations

The initial assertions concerning improper fund-raising were directed against an Indonesian couple, the Wiriadinatas, lawful permanent residents of the United States who gave $450,000 to the DNC.[26] The Wiriadinata family was associated with the Riady family.

Lawful permanent residents, though technically foreign nationals, are allowed to donate to U.S. political parties under a post-Watergate amendment to the campaign finance statutes. Foreign nationals who are not lawful permanent residents are barred from such donations. The rationale for allowing lawful permanent residents to make donations is that they, as immigrants and taxpayers, are "citizens in waiting" who may (but are not required to) naturalize after five years.[27] This exception to the rule barring donations by foreign nationals was sponsored by Democratic senator Lloyd Bentsen of Texas, and it passed Congress by wide margins. The potential problem developed because lawful permanent residents are not allowed anymore than anyone else to give money on behalf of another individual—operating as a conduit or front.

Accordingly, if the Wiriadinatas had given their own money, their activities would have been well within the applicable law. Moreover, similarly large donations from others had met with minimal objections from the press or the public. However, if the Wiriadinatas had given money on behalf of the Lippo Group or the Riady family, they would have violated the applicable law—even if they had been naturalized citizens. It would have been improper because they would have acted as a conduit or front.

Safire and others suggested such a scenario: the Wiriadinatas had served as a means for the Lippo Group to give money to the DNC that the Lippo Group could not have conveyed directly.

In the fall of 1996, which saw the Clinton-Gore ticket reelected, numerous Asian Americans—most of them Chinese Americans and affiliated with the Democratic Party—were accused of unethical conduct associated with their behind-the-scenes political activities. In addition to Huang, there was Yah Lin "Charlie" Trie, a Little Rock restaurateur who had raised more than a half million dollars for the Whitewater legal defense fund, an unregulated private entity that contributed to those Clinton legal costs not covered by public expenditures. Johnny Chung, a California entrepreneur who had raised hundreds of thousands of dollars for the DNC, was another. He had been given access to the White House for informal tours, on which he was accompanied by Chinese government officials with alleged military agendas. Maria Hsia was a California consultant who organized a visit by Vice President Al Gore to the Hsi Lai Buddhist Temple in suburban Los Angeles, where political donations were made on religious property. And then there was Nora and Gene Lum, a Hawaiian couple who had donated money to both political parties and who were business associates of President Clinton's commerce secretary, Ron Brown, who was killed in an airplane crash in 1996 while on a diplomatic mission.

The allegations against these persons varied, but they can be grouped roughly into several categories.

- political contributions violating campaign finance statutes, because the sources were foreign nationals prohibited from giving such gifts;
- political contributions violating campaign finance statutes, because, regardless of the nationality of the source, they were made through an intermediary;
- contributions violating statutes, regardless of their source, because they were solicited by government officials, with allegations raised against principally Vice President Al Gore;
- perquisites given to large donors, such as exclusive visits to the White House and particularly overnight stays in the Lincoln Bedroom, which, though legal, were criticized as appearing improper;
- quid pro quo favors in the form of alteration of U.S. government policy for political donations—specifically with respect to technology transfers of missile guidance systems to China;
- quid pro quo favors in the form of alteration of U.S. government policy for political donations—specifically with respect to immigration; and
- cover-up(s) related to the original allegations.

These allegations led to numerous official investigations. The DNC itself initiated a voluntary audit after the 1996 elections, resulting in the return of more than $3 million in donations, as described in detail below. The Federal Election Commission also conducted an investigation, and the Justice Department set up a task force that at one point employed 120 attorneys and investigators. Both the Senate and the House held public hearings beginning in the summer of 1997. Criminal prosecutions were initiated against Trie, Chung, Hsia, and the Lums, resulting in plea bargains from all but Hsia.[28]

The most extensive of the responses were the hearings held by the Senate Committee on Governmental Affairs and chaired by Republican senator Fred Thompson of Tennessee—rumored at the outset of the proceedings to be considering a 2000 run for the presidency. The hearings opened with spectacular claims of "hard evidence" of a Chinese scheme to influence the presidential elections. After thirty-three days of hearings, with more than seventy witnesses, over two hundred interviews, about two hundred formal depositions, and some four hundred subpoenas issued, the committee came to a much more modest conclusion. The majority report cited the year-end deadline and the need to protect confidential intelligence data as justification for the investigation not procuring enough information to substantiate the initial claims.[29]

Meanwhile, the House Committee on Government Reform and Oversight held hearings chaired by Republican Representative Dan Burton of Indiana, but as of the summer of 2000 it had not concluded its hearings, which may be postponed indefinitely. The investigations were set back by staff resignations, partisan disagreements, and the chairman's reputation for polemical attacks. While it was in session, the committee issued more than 570 subpoenas, requesting information from a list of individuals with heavy Asian and Asian American representation.[30]

Stereotypes

As the scandal simultaneously became racial, a pattern of investigatory techniques and public perception overtook events. Asian Americans were treated as a single group, presumed guilty by association, by members of both political parties and independent candidate Ross Perot, as well as by leading journalists and news organizations, which were then much less likely to point out the problems they had helped to generate.

The DNC and the popular media engaged in similar strategies for their investigations. Using donor lists compiled by the DNC or appended to filings with the FEC, they contacted individuals in racially determined categories or who had Asian-sounding surnames.[31] The DNC audit exemplified the racial stereotyping of the ensuing investigations. According to the DNC memorandum on its "in-depth contribution review," a leading accounting firm and law firm were retained shortly after the elections to survey 1,200 contributions in seven major categories: (1) any contribution from an individual who gave more than $10,000 in any of the years 1994, 1995, or 1996; (2) contributions in 1996 for which the DNC headquarters in Washington, D.C., was listed as the donor's address; (3) contributions solicited by John Huang, where the donor gave more than $2,500 and "was not well known to the DNC"; (4) contributions made in connection with the April 29, 1996, event at the Hsi Lai Buddhist Temple in southern California; (5) contributions made or solicited by Charlie Trie, his wife, or his company; (6) contributions by Johnny Chung or his company; and, most important, (7) "contributions made in connection with any DNC fund-raising event targeting the Asian Pacific American community."[32] While these categories were admitted by the DNC itself, the interpretation here was disputed by the general counsel to the DNC.[33]

In announcing the audit results, the DNC revealed how its interviewers proceeded. On the script for calls to contributors, question 13 dealt with citizenship status, with follow-up questions about how long a person had been a citizen, and whether he or she held a Social Security card. Other questions were: "What is your annual earned income?" "Who is your employer/supervisor?" "Would you authorize us to obtain a credit report to verify the information you have given us?"[34]

The instructions for the calls to donors were detailed. They advised, for example, that "when possible, the interviewer should be female. Female callers are less threatening and often more successful at getting respondents to cooperate." Interviewers also were told to "anticipate that the person answering may not speak English." Fluent Mandarin and Cantonese speakers were employed to conduct interviews, with translation capabilities for other Asian languages available as well.

Interviewers also were told to "avoid revealing the organization or the purpose of the call until the interviewer is talking to the person he/she is seeking" and not to leave telephone messages or their own phone numbers. But if they had no choice, they were to "obtain the name of the person taking the message and make the message compelling." The suggested message was "Please call the Democratic National Committee to confirm your contribution."

Audit targets were asked to send written confirmation of their phone interviews. Persons who refused to cooperate were threatened: they were informed that their names would be released as individuals suspected of having violated campaign finance laws.

Based on the audit, the Democrats decided to return $1,492,051 in donations (124 contributions) from 77 individuals and corporations. (The DNC had made a series of refunds earlier and would continue with refunds later; the audit produced the largest single set of refunds.) DNC officials confirmed that some of the donations were illegal, but others were deemed inappropriate even if they were permitted by statute.

The Democrats provided a table detailing Huang's accomplishments. He was credited with 424 contributions, of which 88 were refunded. Thus, 336 or approximately 80 percent of the contributions raised by Huang were legitimate and appropriate. Because some contributors donated more than once, and in differing quantities, the 88 contributions raised by Huang and returned accounted for 21.8 percent of the contributions raised by Huang, or 54.8 percent of the dollars returned and 47.4 percent of all dollars raised by Huang. All of the money associated with Trie and Chung also was returned. Eighteen of 46 contributions "connected" with the Hsi Lai Buddhist Temple event were returned as well. The DNC emphasized that all the contributions returned represented 0.001 percent of the total number of contributions, or slightly more than 1 percent of the total dollars received by the DNC between 1994 and 1996.[35]

The DNC later also audited Asian American supporters who had given less than $5,000—indeed even less than $2,500. At the February 28, 1997, press conference at DNC headquarters announcing the results of the initial audit, the DNC's outside legal counsel stated that another audit either had been conducted or would be undertaken. He said, "In addition, you ought to be aware that there are a number of contributions solicited by Mr. John Huang, each under $2,500 in amount, which still have to be reviewed by the DNC. These amount to 171 contributions, and they total $104,000. The results of this review, I am advised, will be made publicly available to you as well."[36] Thus the average donation in the later audit was about $608.

Notwithstanding the wording of category 7 and other indications that the audit was focused on Asian Americans, some might argue that the later audit was appropriate because it was nominally directed at solicitations made by Huang. This argument is belied by the DNC's own accounting practices. It is conceivable that non–Asian Americans contributed through events "targeting" the Asian American community, but the DNC made no references to any such individuals nor has any other observer suggested any such individuals were affected.

As the DNC's outside legal counsel himself conceded, "The more I got into this, the more I looked at the documents at the committee, it's clear that some or all of the attribution of contributors to a specific individual such as Mr. Huang or Mr. Trie or staff of the DNC is sometimes exaggerated and inaccurate. And so there is no precise mathematical way of saying that in the case of any return contributor that this was precisely something solicited by Mr. Huang."[37] The DNC's general counsel made the same admission. He said, "I think, as [outside legal counsel], and particularly when it comes to DNC staff who have solicited contributions, a lot of the attribution is bookkeeping and is not an accurate indication of who solicited the contribution."[38]

Even though the later audit ostensibly was limited to donations "solicited" by Huang, it affected a much larger category of donors. These donors were attributed to Huang by the DNC, even though they may not have had any relationship with him. Most strikingly, for Asian Americans all contributions (above and below the initial $2,500 threshold) were included in the audit; for others, only contributions over $10,000. At an average donation level of $608, Asian Americans were audited even though they gave more than an order of magnitude less than the $10,000 minimum that triggered suspicion of others.

It is reasonable to conclude, then, that the DNC applied different standards to Asian American and non–Asian American supporters. While Asian American donors were audited because of the identity ascribed to them through the crediting to Huang, other donors were audited because of their individual conduct and only if they had contributed large sums. Ironically, the DNC audit was conducted by the beneficiary of the Asian Connection and directed at its own supporters. Moreover, the majority of the individuals who were targeted in an invasive manner turned out to have been exercising their constitutional rights. The DNC, including its co-chairs Roy Romer and Steve Grossman, later apologized for insensitivity in conducting the audit. They personally visited Asian American political leaders throughout the country in an effort to renew these leaders' ties with the party.[39]

Similarly, the public discourse on the fund-raising controversy included repeated references to the race, ethnicity, and national origin of the individuals implicated. The very definition of the scandal as the Asian Connection highlighted its racial element. Much of the description of the matter consisted of expressly racial language, along with racial images. As problematic as the derogatory content of the statements was their general nature, encompassing more than the specific persons who were involved in the controversy and extending to all people of Asian descent. The following are a few examples of statements and situations with racial overtones.[40]

- Reform Party presidential candidate Ross Perot gave two major speeches on the Asian Connection, both of which were so well received that some observers speculated they might have an effect on the electoral college results. In one speech, delivered at the University of Pennsylvania the week before election day, Perot stated, "Now then, Mr. Huang is still out there hard at work for the Democrats. Wouldn't you like to have someone out there named O'Reilly? Out there hard at work. You know, so far we haven't found an American name." Later, after individuals named Middleton and Wood (who were white) were implicated, Perot stated that those were "surnames to which Americans can relate," adding rhetorically, "I wonder if anyone in this country's giving money?"[41]
- On the third day of the Senate hearings, Republican senator Sam Brownback of Kansas, interrogating a white witness who worked with John Huang about the compensation system by which Huang would receive bonuses according to the amounts he solicited, used mock pidgin to describe the system as "no raise money, no get bonus." This was a mocking allusion to the singsong of Chinese laundrymen, who used to be characterized as chiding customers "no tickee, no washee." Brownback later apologized. At a Washington Press Club function prior to the hearings, Brownback also had told a joke with the punch line "Two Huangs Don't Make a Right."[42] White House press spokesperson Michael McCurry had used the same line as well.[43]
- During the investigation, Sen. Robert Bennett, Republican from Utah, stated, "in my opinion, Mr. [Charlie] Trie's activities are classic activities on the part of an Asian who comes out of that culture and who embarks on an activity related to intelligence gathering." Emphasizing that he intended to make a racial reference, Bennett stated that he regretted that one of his colleagues, who had warned against stereotyping, was not present to hear this remark.[44]
- Rep. Jack Kingston, a Georgia Republican, stated and had printed in a revised form in the *Congressional Record*, "Illegal donations are apparently only the tip of the eggroll." [45]
- In the ensuing debate over campaign finance, Rep. Tom DeLay, Republican from Texas, explained how a reform proposal would work. A political candidate would violate the statute if she or he were "aware of a high probability that the contribution originated from a foreign national." De

Lay gave the following example, "if you have a friend by the name of Arief and Soraya, and I cannot even pronounce the last name, Wiriadinata or something like that, who donated . . . and was friends with a guy named Johnny Huang . . . then there's a high probability that it's money from foreign nationals. . . . I could go on with John Lee and Cheon Am, Yogesh Ghandi, Ng Lap Seng, Supreme Master Suma China Hai and George Psaltis." House Republican Christopher Shays of Connecticut responded, "I know the gentleman did not mean it to sound this way, but when I listened to it, it sounded this way. It sounded like if you have a foreign name, there was a high probability they were foreigners." The following day, Rep. DeLay issued a written statement: "In no way did I mean to suggest that Asian Americans should not participate in our democracy."[46]

- After the government adopted extra security measures intended to prevent foreign access to government officials—measures prompted by the Asian Connection matter—U.S. Civil Rights Commissioner Yvonne Lee, while on official business, was initially denied entry to the White House because she was suspected of being foreign, based on her Chinese middle name.[47]
- At the start of the second term of the Clinton administration, Chang Lin Tien, chancellor of the University of California, Berkeley, was being considered for appointment as either secretary of education or secretary of energy. If named, he would have become the first Asian American in the cabinet. Newspapers, however, reported he had received an inquiry from the Riady family about an applicant to the college. University officials confirmed that Tien, in responding, had adhered appropriately to university policies and academic practice. In fact, he had followed the standard operating procedure used for VIP applicants with connections to university officials, a policy that, ironically, benefited mainly white applicants, according to press reports during the affirmative action debate. In part because the articles suggested that Tien had connections with Riady, Tien's prospects were compromised.[48] About the same time, former Democratic House member Norman Mineta of California reportedly was dropped from consideration for a cabinet post because he was Asian American. Subsequent reports indicated that the White House was sensitive about appointing an Asian American for fear of alleged relationships to John Huang.[49] The White House did appoint Asian American Bill Lann Lee to the subcabinet post of assistant attorney general for civil rights. But Larry Klayman, a conservative activist who founded a self-styled public interest group, "Judicial Watch," demanded that Lee be in-

vestigated because, like Huang, he was Asian American, and Huang was a "king maker" among Asian American Democrats.[50]

- While the investigations were under way, U.S. District Judge Denny Chin of New York City, an Asian American appointed by the Clinton administration, was accused by Larry Klayman of bias. Klayman demanded that Chin recuse himself from Klayman's case (unrelated to Huang) simply because of Chin's race and political affiliation. Chin sanctioned Klayman, who had a history of unethical conduct as determined by other courts, and his ruling in the matter was affirmed unanimously by a panel of the Second Circuit Court of Appeals whose three members had diverse racial and political backgrounds.[51]

- The March 24, 1997, cover of the *National Review*, headlined "The Manchurian Candidates," depicted President Clinton, First Lady Hillary Clinton, and Vice President Al Gore with caricatured Asian facial features, including buck teeth and slant eyes, in stereotypical Chinese garments.[52]

- Emmet Tyrell, editor of the *American Spectator*, described the fund-raising controversy as the "Chop Suey connection."[53]

- The *New York Times Sunday Magazine* stated satirically, "This fear of Asians isn't all bad. If riding a few Asians out of Washington on a rail helps generate support for campaign finance reform, well then, hitch up the ponies, giddyap!"[54]

- Some press coverage grouped together reports about the Asian Connection with the case of Republican House member Jay Kim of California, a Korean American and Republican stalwart. Other than ethnicity, Kim had nothing in common with Huang, Trie, or Chung.[55]

- In criticizing the Clinton administration, one writer for the *New Criterion*, a cultural journal, stated, "President Clinton is the final confirmation that we live in an entertainment state: not only because he has reduced the presidency to mere entertainment, or because he sits far more comfortably on the late-night monologues than on the early-evening news, but also because his fellow entertainers are latterly the only folks who can get to see him (apart from interns and Chinamen)."[56]

- Political reporters for a major news magazine asked Matt Fong, a Republican candidate for the U.S. Senate from California, who is fourth-generation Chinese American and a former U.S. military officer, which side he would fight on in the event of war with China.[57]

- One of the few examples of guilt by association that the mainstream media did acknowledge was the case of Democratic House member

Robert Matsui of California and White House staffer Doris Matsui, a husband and wife political duo who were named as connected with Huang, without any factual foundation. After the *New York Times* published damaging articles, a few details of which were later retracted, several commentators observed that the stories appeared to have virtually no news value and that they contained reporting errors.[58]

By contrast, non–Asian Connection campaign finance violations that were proven and for which individuals and corporations received record penalties, were accorded minimal coverage. FEC chairman John Warren McGarry noted that improprieties on the part of Asian Americans had been covered extensively, but violations by others had been given only cursory attention.[59] The many cases comparable to those of Huang and the others implicated in the Asian Connection included: Simon Fireman, a business executive who pleaded guilty and paid $6 million in fines for an elaborate scheme of illegal contributions to the Dole campaign, apparently in an effort to gain appointment as an ambassador;[60] Thomas Kramer, a foreign national, fined $323,000 by the FEC on July 18, 1998, for illegal contributions of $332,600 using conduits;[61] and Empire Sanitary Landfill, a Pennsylvania corporation, fined $8 million by the FEC for illegal contributions of $129,000 to both the Clinton and Dole presidential campaigns.[62]

To use a model from "equal protection" legal doctrines, the stereotyping practiced in the Asian Connection was both over-inclusive and under-inclusive.[63] In terms of conventional legal doctrine, racial stereotypes are applied using proxies. Race is a proxy for behavior; race is used to infer behavior. For example, in the internment of Japanese Americans during World War II, race (Japanese ancestry) became a proxy for behavior (disloyalty). The rationale for prohibiting racial stereotypes that function as a proxy is their combination of over-inclusiveness and under-inclusiveness. Racial stereotypes tend to be both over-inclusive, including too many people based on their race rather than their conduct, and under-inclusive, failing to include too many people because of their race despite their conduct. The Asian Connection displayed both of these problems. It was over-inclusive in the inference from actions by at most a dozen individuals, which were turned into wrongdoing by a racial group. It was under-inclusive in the disregard of other individuals, who had taken similar actions but who were different racially—that is, non-Asians. This inequality is the crux of the matter.

AN ANALYSIS OF THE PROTESTS

Worse than the casual and repeated references to race were the indifferent responses to Asian American protests. This section suggests that the "perpetual foreigner" syndrome explains perceptions of Asian Americans.

In October 1996 in Washington, D.C., Los Angeles, and Chicago, Asian Americans affiliated with both political parties participated in a coordinated series of press conferences criticizing the portrayal of Asian Americans as a racial group.[64] In September 1997 a coalition of more than a dozen Asian American community organizations filed a complaint with the U.S. Civil Rights Commission requesting that it consider the racial aspects of the ongoing investigations and media coverage.[65]

Between those two events, on March 20, 1997, Sen. Daniel Akaka, a Hawaiian Democrat of Asian heritage and a member of the Senate panel investigating the matter, delivered a lengthy floor speech in that most exclusive club.[66] Akaka recounted at length the history of Asian Americans and he noted their contemporary accomplishments. His central themes, however, were paired: "I think I speak for the entire Asian American community in expressing the hope that we can get to the bottom of this whole controversy, wherever the cards may fall." But "let us avoid focusing on such irrelevancies as the ethnicity of the participants in the affair [and] let us cease characterizing individuals by meretricious stereotypes; conversely, let us avoid judging an entire community by the actions of a few individuals." Akaka added that "those responsible for violations of laws or improper conduct should be identified and appropriately dealt with by the relevant authorities." And he implored, "let us keep our attention on matters of substance—the laws that were possibly broken, the processes and procedures that were bent, the individuals who circumvented or corrupted the system, and most of all what we can do to prevent abuses in the future."

On all three occasions, and in written materials the activists prepared, Asian American political leaders took pains to point out that they supported appropriate investigation and that they had asked for Asian Americans to be held accountable under the same standard as any other individuals.[67] They further agreed that it was possible and even plausible that Huang and others were guilty, but they argued that the majority of persons of Asian heritage were innocent of corruption.

Yet as Asian Americans raised these objections, their concerns were dismissed as "playing the race card."[68] Despite their insistence on universal standards and their willingness to entertain credible claims against Asian Americans as individuals, they were charged with presenting self-interested and partisan defenses or offering some sort of special pleading. For example, Senator Akaka's office immediately received a series of faxes, e-mails, and phone calls denouncing him for "playing the race card," with references to the defense strategy in the O. J. Simpson homicide trial.

In an editorial on the Whitewater investigation, the *Washington Post* wrote about the Asian Connection: "The president suggested one day that some of the questioning verged on Asian-bashing. . . . But what a disingenuous defense that is."[69] The *Post* later devoted an entire editorial to refuting an "Asian-bashing defense" that it imputed to defenders of Huang, who, at least among Asian Americans speaking publicly, were nonexistent. The editorial read in full:

> While the Senate committee investigating campaign finances is considering whether to grant some kind of selective legal immunity to John Huang, former Commerce and Democratic National Committee official and key figure in the Democratic fund-raising scandals, there is another kind of immunity that is being sought on his behalf by various friends and backers. It is a kind of immunity by reason of his ethnic background. From the earliest days of Mr. Huang's notoriety, back when the White House was saying it was not even entirely clear who he was, the idea of "Asian bashing" has been floated in his defense. This was then and still is a variant on what is otherwise often know as "playing the race card." The immunity it is meant to afford comes from presumably shaming those who are pursuing Mr. Huang's alleged violations of the law by suggesting that they are acting out of racial bias, not a desire to get to the bottom of scandal.
>
> Americans have faced the situation many times before in which members of a particular ethnic group have been associated with a particular breach of law, whether organized crime, drug crime, stock manipulation or any of a variety of other misconduct. It is true that there is always the danger of generalizing from these few cases so as to smear an entire group that had nothing to do with their behavior. And it is equally true that there is always the danger of sliding sloppily into the false and offensive conclusion that the person charged was acting out of some characteristic ethnic defect. Undoubtedly some of that has seeped into the dialogue about Mr. Huang and other Asians and Asian Americans who are involved in the current fund-raising scandals. But to say that and condemn such thinking where it occurs is not to settle the case. It does not say anything about Mr. Huang's innocence or guilt.
>
> John Huang is accused of very serious misconduct. The administration in which he gained so much access and influence beyond that normally ac-

corded someone in his different jobs has much to answer about his activities. It is not "racist," "Asian bashing" or any other such loathsome practice to seek vigorously to find out the truth about what he did and how he was able to do it.[70]

Likewise, the *Boston Globe* wrote:

It is sad indeed to see President Clinton, as he enters his second term in office, and the Democratic National Committee playing the race card in order to deflect attention from the rising scandal of improper and illegal campaign contributions. . . . Asian-Americans can be sensitive to criticism of their fundraising. . . . It may be painful for Asian-American contributors, the vast majority of whom are innocent of any wrongdoing, to get inquiring telephone calls from reporters because their names are Asian. . . . Most Asian-Americans will see through this shabby maneuver to avoid scrutiny. The president and the Democratic National Committee bring shame on themselves when they employ this divisive and ultimately self-destructive tactic.[71]

This rejection of Asian American complaints as a cynical political ploy, with only cursory consideration of their merits, is aberrational if evaluated against the societal standards that have been accepted for black-white racial interaction. Social scientists have consistently reported in recent years that black and white Americans affirm their belief in antidiscrimination principles.[72] A consensus appears to agree that it is both wrong to make assumptions about a person based on race or to infer from individual conduct any group tendencies associated with race. It was these norms that were violated by, for example, the characterizations of the individuals under investigation, as in Senator Bennett's remarks about "classic activities on the part of an Asian who comes out of that culture," and the generalizations by which all Asian Americans come to be suspected of illicit conduct, as in the DNC audit.

The tendency toward reciting antidiscrimination principles, with solicitude toward Asian Americans, but then engaging in additional violations of those same standards, is puzzling if treated within contemporary conventions of black-white race relations. Perhaps an explanation lies in the "perpetual foreigner" syndrome. Neil Gotanda and others have suggested that the image of Asian Americans is that of the "perpetual foreigner."[73] As Gotanda articulates the thesis, in a literally black and white paradigm of racial dynamics, individuals who are neither black nor white are excluded. They are assumed to be foreigners and take the position of outsiders. Thus it is easy to dismiss a claim by an Asian American that she faces racial discrimination. The different treatment accorded a white individual and an Asian American individual in similar situations can be rationalized as a permissible distinction between citizens and foreigners rather than a problematic distinction based on race. Of course, the confusion of Asian Americans as aliens is the very racial discrimination at issue.

The "perpetual foreigner" is an individualized version of the "Yellow Peril," the notion of Asian immigrants as an invading force. It recalls the "sojourner" thesis of anti-Asian discrimination: that Asians were treated differently than Europeans who settled in the United States because Asians unlike Europeans were expected to return to their homelands and did not establish loyalties here.[74] As FBI director J. Edgar Hoover said in 1969, only a few years after immigration reform finally ended race-based visa preferences, "There are over 300,000 Chinese in the United States, some of whom could be susceptible to recruitment either through ethnic ties or hostage situations because of relatives in Communist China."[75] It did not help Asian Americans that Chinese leaders such as Mao and Deng Xiao Ping casually alluded to Chinese immigration as a threat to be deployed for their advantage in foreign relations. Mao joked with Kissinger about sending ten million Chinese women "so we can let them flood your country with disaster," prompting Kissinger to observe that the wife of his aide Winston Lord was Chinese.[76] Deng famously rebutted American concerns about human rights, and in particular the absolute Chinese emigration restrictions, by stating, "If you want me to release ten million Chinese to come to the United States, I'd be glad to do so."[77]

IMMIGRATION AS THE LINK BETWEEN FOREIGN POLICY AND DOMESTIC POLITICS

Yet Asian Americans do have a connection to Asia through the dynamics of immigration. Influenced by both foreign policy and domestic politics, immigration is a complex issue. Perhaps Americans could assume that other sovereigns and would-be immigrants lack standing to assert moral claims on the United States for admission as immigrants. But such a characterization of immigration as a purely domestic matter shaped by national interest, thereby eliminating interaction with foreign governments and the accompanying foreign policy considerations, would ironically exactly reverse the traditional approach with respect to Asians. After all, the 1882 Chinese

Exclusion Act tested the 1868 Burlingame Treaty and negotiations between the U.S. and Chinese governments.[78]

Asian Americans as citizens presumably have the same right as other citizens—indeed, perhaps all members of a democracy have the responsibility—to develop immigration policies that are just.[79] In some sense, Asian Americans' interest in immigration is just another example of ethnic participation in the political process, regardless of whether the issue is domestic or international.[80] Popular concern with foreign policy signals the "good-bye to the 'wise men,' "[81] or a more democratic and less-elite decision-making structure. In another sense, however, Asian Americans as immigrants have a greater concern with immigration because the issue is fundamental. For the newcomer, permission to immigrate is the threshold test. Everything else, including the very right to remain, much less the political, economic or social rights, turns on immigration policy.

Asian Americans as a community have been shaped more by immigration policies than by any other external force.[82] Historically, Asian immigrants have faced racial discrimination in seeking to join the community. The Chinese Exclusion Act, later expanded to cover an Asiatic barred zone, treated Asian immigrants differently than European immigrants.[83] Asian immigrants were prevented from naturalizing because they were neither "free white persons" nor "of African descent," as the Supreme Court ruled in cases involving a Japanese and an Asian Indian immigrant.[84] The original comprehensive immigration statutes were adopted in an effort to prevent any more than a token number of Asian immigrants from entering the country, but also to limit the numbers of southern and eastern European immigrants, especially from nations more heavily Catholic and Jewish.[85] The openly racial intent of these policies was repudiated only in 1965. (If these statutes and antimiscegenation statutes reflecting similar racial subjugation had been enforced strictly, Asian American communities would have ceased to exist. The former would have prevented further immigration. The latter would have prevented a native-born generation from coming into being due to the skewed gender ratio of early immigration, there having been almost no women within the Chinese American community.)

Even as citizens, naturalized and native-born, Asian Americans continued to face racial discrimination based on the assumption that they were inherently outsiders. The federal law creating the Japanese American internment program during World War II deemed Japanese Americans to be "enemy aliens."[86] The Asian Connection recalls the internment experience in two respects. First, the internment used formal legal categories disingenuously. Although the distinction was explained as one between "citizen" and "enemy alien," it actually was one between Japanese Americans, regardless of citizenship, and others, including the non-Japanese "enemy alien." Second, the circular reasoning that generated racial categories was ignored; because of the racial prerequisites for naturalization, a lawful permanent resident of Japanese ancestry had no choice but to be an "enemy alien."

In the Asian Connection, the distinction of donors who should be doubted correlated neatly to donors of Asian background even though many were Asian Americans and even though many non–Asian Americans also ought to have come under suspicion. The Asian Connection also displayed circular reasoning, though it may be subtler. Unlike most white Americans, Asian Americans were not able to reunite families until recently because of racially restrictive laws. Furthermore, current immigration patterns render Asians seeking to be immigrants disproportionately vulnerable to reductions in levels of available visas. Consequently, while individuals may have become involved in political fund-raising for an assortment of reasons, Asian Americans organized as a group in order to protect immigrant traditions. Legitimate efforts to reform legislation that has racially disparate effects should not be disparaged because they are undertaken by the very groups that face the burden of current policy.

Today, immigration restrictionists such as presidential candidate Pat Buchanan and author Peter Brimelow continue to argue for significantly reducing the prevailing legal limits on immigrants.[87] In his 1995 tract *Alien Nation*, Peter Brimelow warned that "the American nation has always had a specific ethnic core[,] [a]nd that core is white." If Asian Americans have a complaint about assumptions based on race, "there is no cure for that except radically increasing the numbers of minorities and breaking down white America's sense of identity."[88] The arguments of Brimelow and others are based in part on racial differences, because contemporary trends of immigration include many more nonwhite immigrants than in the past, and in part on presumed cultural differences, because newer arrivals are regarded as not assimilating.[89]

Perhaps because of such views, immediately before the 1996 elections Asian Americans' political activities were heavily devoted to immigration issues. In the DNC memo setting a $7 million fund-raising goal for donations from Asian Americans, immigration led the list of issues important to that donor group.[90] History, the factual circumstances surrounding immigration today, and the political possibilities explain this emphasis.

A century ago, immigrants were overwhelmingly of European origin, with the result that from 1901 to 1910, for example, only a little over 3 percent of immigrants were Asian and less than 1 percent were Hispanic in origin. By 1991–1994, the majority of immigrants were either Asian or Hispanic, representing 30 percent and 42 percent of the immigrant flow, respectively.[91] The growth of the Asian American population depends on immigration much more than it does on birthrates; 86 percent of recent increases stemmed from immigration and only 14 percent from birthrates.[92]

Under existing immigration policies, almost all would-be immigrants need a sponsor, typically a prospective employer or a family member. Asian American communities have relied extensively on the family visas, especially the "fourth preference" category that allows adult siblings to serve as sponsors. In fiscal 1996, according to Immigration and Naturalization Service (INS) records, 42,709 or 14 percent of all 307,807 Asian immigrants relied on the fourth preference. More broadly, Asian immigrants account for 42,709 or about 66 percent of the fourth preference allotment of 65,000 visas.[93]

The fourth preference has faced criticism for two reasons. First, as a family-based visa category, it is used to bring in persons who would, because they lack skills, be unable to obtain an employment-based visa. Rational immigrants presumably would prefer an employment-based visa over a fourth preference visa because there are fewer backlogs and thus shorter waiting periods, if any waiting periods at all. For proponents of an immigration policy that would be based on the work skills of the immigrant population, the fourth preference is especially undesirable.

Second, again because of its family-based nature, the fourth preference is believed by some observers to be a key component of "chain migration." Some studies appear to show that individuals sponsor family members, each of whom may bring immediate family members as persons "accompanying or following to join" eligible immigrants. Later, each family member, including those who came only as "accompanying or following to join," may sponsor more immigrants, and so on. The immediate family members are exempt from quotas. As a result, the overall immigration numbers may become much higher than the basic quotas would appear to allow because of chain migration.[94]

The immigration debate in the 1990s threatened the fourth preference. Following passage of California's Proposition 187 in 1994, Rep. Lamar Smith of Texas and Sen. Alan Simpson of Wyoming introduced bills that would have enacted severe cutbacks in the levels of legal immigration.[95] The

Immigration Reform Commission, chaired by former House member Barbara Jordan, recommended similar changes.[96]

The White House position on the fourth preference was ambiguous.[97] As early as July 12, 1995, prior to the Jordan Commission report, the Clinton administration stated its position on pending proposals. Its strategies foreshadowed both its support for family preferences and the strategy of dividing legal and illegal immigration. In a letter from the assistant attorney general for legislative affairs, Andrew Fois, to the chairman of the House Subcommittee on Immigration, Lamar Smith, the administration stated:

> The Administration looks forward to working with Congress to ensure that the Nation maintains a sound legal immigration policy in the national interest. This policy must promote reunification of family members; protect U.S. workers from unfair competition while providing employers with the highly-skilled specialists they need to compete in the international economy; and encourage legal immigrants to become full participants in the national community.
>
> The process to address legal immigration reform is most appropriately conducted outside the context of immigration enforcement legislation. Historically, previous Congresses and Administrations failed, most recently in the early 1980s, when legislative proposals sought to tackle both issues at once. It was not until the 99th Congress with the Immigration Reform and Control Act and the 101st Congress with the Immigration Act of 1990 that landmark reforms on these two distinct issues were enacted. The Administration believes that a similar course in this Congress will best ensure that responsible legislation in each area is enacted.[98]

Furthermore, materials prepared by the DNC's Asian American desk to brief President Clinton for a major fund-raiser (but likely not read by him) noted that "immigration and naturalization" were a top priority for Asian Americans, that the "ability to unify the family unit" is of "grave concern," and that "maintaining the Fourth Preference is of extreme importance." The document set forth the "White House Position" as: "The White House has been silent as to its support of the Fourth Preference."[99]

Persuading the Clinton administration to support the fourth preference, or at least to remain neutral, became the primary goal of Asian Americans interested in immigration reform. Working in coalitions with Latino groups, Jewish groups, and immigrant groups, they also were joined by agricultural and business lobbies interested in the ability to hire foreign workers; antigovernment groups concerned about the proposals for a national identification system; and the Christian Coalition, which supported family-based immigration policies.[100] The Clinton administration eventually endorsed a "split the bill" strategy. It argued that illegal and legal immigration should be split and considered in separate pieces of legislation.[101] That procedural maneuver, common in Congress, ensured that the fourth preference would be saved temporarily.[102]

After their legislative defeat, Representative Smith and Senator Simpson hypothesized that national interests in reducing immigration had been sacrificed because of foreign influence. They identified a fund-raiser organized by John Huang as the crux of the shift. In two articles the *Boston Globe* reported that Smith and Simpson "said they believe Clinton's fund-raising prompted the policy reversal. . . . Smith said he believes Clinton switched course 'because he was more interested in political contributions. It now fits the pattern.' " Simpson was quoted as agreeing. He added, "I never in my 18 years in Congress saw an issue that shifted so fast and so hard."[103]

Immediately after the *Boston Globe* stories appeared, the Federation for American Immigration Reform (FAIR) issued a press statement demanding that the fourth preference be revisited. Its director, Dan Stein, stated, "It is clear to everybody that the White House caved in to special interest pressure on the immigration bill. . . . Beyond serving the narrow interests of people who want to import relatives they chose to leave behind, there is no public policy justification for the fourth preference category."[104]

Representative Smith's and Senator Simpson's assertions that foreigners should not influence immigration policies perhaps should be conceded. Like much of the discourse surrounding the Asian Connection, however, their remarks cover not only Asians but also Asian Americans. The *Boston Globe*, for example, reported that they had formed their opinions based on the DNC memos discussing Asian American political interests in immigration levels; those memos mention nowhere Asian interests (as distinguished from Asian American interests), either on the part of individual foreigners or the Chinese government. Furthermore, the newspapers juxtaposed Smith's and Simpson's comments with an analysis that consistently referred to Asian Americans trying to influence immigration policies. The inaccurate reporting in the popular media has been accepted as the standard account of the legislative consideration of the fourth preference.[105] Some accounts of immigration politics characterize Asian American (not Asian) influence as "corrupt."[106]

But even if Simpson's and Smith's speculation was assumed to be true, their argument suffers. If the fund-raising by Huang indeed caused the

Clinton administration to alter its policies, that may well be troubling—but because of the influence of money, not the influence of Asian Americans. To dismiss Asian American efforts to seek increased immigration (or merely to maintain current levels) would be to disenfranchise individuals selectively because of their racial background. To impugn Asian American participation in the immigration debate, but to condone anti-Asian sentiments to influence the same process, would be even worse. Latinos encountered the same resistance to their efforts to affect immigration policy: marchers in Los Angeles who carried the Mexican flag to oppose California Proposition 187, an anti-immigrant ballot initiative passed in 1994, were blamed for the success of the measure.[107]

In addition to immigration, Asian Americans may have other distinct interests as well. Most of these are defensive reactions to historical or ongoing racial discrimination. For example, they have worked together against hate crimes, which often are perpetrated by assailants who do not distinguish among Asian ethnicities and thus engage in mistaken targeting. Japanese Americans, who had lost their liberty, livelihood, and property during the internment experience of World War II, have successfully sought reparations. Filipino military veterans have tried to gain restoration of the entitlements available to other veterans but not available to them, despite their service, because of U.S. colonial policies. India-trained medical physicians are vulnerable to restrictive licensing policies that threaten to prevent them from practicing their professions. The 1992 Los Angeles riots following the Rodney King verdict also have been cited repeatedly as impetus for increased Asian American, especially Korean American, political participation.[108] The difficulty lies in protecting the rights of political participation, but also ensuring that doing so does not lead to problems such as the Asian Connection matter.

Otherwise, Asian Americans remain in a vicious circle. Immigration policies, with their racial effects, prompt Asian Americans to organize as a group, which in turn leads others to treat Asian Americans negatively as an organized group. Among the adverse consequences are restrictive immigration policies, with additional racial effects, which only give Asian Americans even greater impetus to behave as a group.[109] The implicit premise is pessimistic because, according to some writers, Brimelow and Peter Schuck among them, "demographics are destiny." The resulting situation is bleak: racial groups will pursue self-interested agendas that conflict with one another, without the possibility of coalitions or visions transcending such divisions.

CONCLUSION

The Asian Connection scandal presents a challenge and an opportunity for Asian Americans. The matter underscored the lack of political maturity among Asian Americans and the relative ignorance of the general public and mainstream media about the various communities that are encompassed by the term. The dilemma is how to maintain a level of group political organization that accurately represents the actual communities and allows for protection of civil rights, on the one hand, while allowing individuals to create their own independent identities and avoid racial cycles that perpetuate imposed racial categories, on the other hand. Unlike either Jewish Americans or African Americans, who present the contrasting exemplars of ethnic political success in the United States, Asian Americans have been ambivalent about both their identity as Asian Americans and their ability to influence foreign affairs related to their homelands (ancestral, ascribed, or self-identified). It may even be that the two characteristics are inversely correlated: it is exactly those individuals who are most enthusiastic about the Asian American group identity who are least sanguine about homeland politics.

In speaking metaphorically of the "two-thirds of Asian Americans [who] haven't crossed the river" (see epigraph), politico John Huang erases the distinction based on nationality. Indeed, logically there are no Asian Americans who "haven't crossed the river"—only those Asians who have crossed who may wish as immigrants to become Asian Americans. Huang draws another distinction based on racial identity. In writing idealistically about "people from China" (see epigraph), philosopher Martha Nussbaum almost abandons national identity as well as racial identity. But she does not quite do so, for "people from China" retain that status even after their arrival and whether "people from China" can be born elsewhere is unresolved. The important point is that they can be noted as "people from China." Nussbaum favors an abstract but compelling cosmopolitanism.

Both Huang and Nussbaum address specific audiences, assuming unity and self-awareness with very different conceptions of the "we" among whom they present their thoughts. Their provocative questions contain premises that demand consideration before answers can be hazarded.

As individuals and as communities, Asian Americans should ask themselves about the following sets of issues as they pursue political empowerment:[110]

- *Transnationalism.* Even though trends of globalization and the identity of communities as "diaspora" may be appealing or overwhelming, they also present severe risks of compromised political loyalties and elevation of racial status over citizenship status. A descriptive transnationalism is distinct from a normative transnationalism. It may be possible to recognize that individuals, families, and communities increasingly function without regard to claims of state sovereignty, while being undecided about the desirability of that behavior.[111]

- *Pan-Asian Americanism.* Asian Americans, functioning as a self-consciously constructed category, are vulnerable to divisions along ethnic lines that may weaken their ability to advance their interests but that also may reflect a less-artificial conception of communities. Asian ethnicities in the United States may be able to use pan-Asian Americanism to stress both coalition efforts and their domestic roots. Yet groups who have on average arrived later or whose circumstances differ greatly from native-born, middle-class Asian Americans may have distinct concerns not articulated by ethnic leaders.

- *Generational issues.* The different perspectives of those of immigrant status and those of native-born status create conflicts that are exhibited not only among families but also within organizations in struggles for leadership. These conflicts are exacerbated by the constant influx of newcomers. The formal status of members of the immigrant generation is different from that of their children. Even if the immigrant generation naturalizes, their children acquire their citizenship status automatically through birth. Their cultural perspectives thus are likely to be dissimilar.

- *Class differences.* The fund-raising controversy revealed the potential divergence of interests within Asian American communities based on socioeconomic status. It should be noted that some Asian American critics of John Huang argued forcefully that the progressive civil rights advances of community movements had been compromised by the self-interested political ambitions of individuals.

- *Religious differences.* The religious differences among Asian Americans are similar to those within the public at large, but they assume greater significance because of the influential role of clergy and faith in constituting the community among Asian immigrants. Moreover, Asian Americans are predominantly followers of Western, not Eastern, sects.

- *National versus grass roots.* The widely varying experiences of Asian Americans in different geographic areas of the United States, especially Hawaii and California, compared with the rest of the country, have produced differences in the agendas of groups depending on their geographic base and scope.

- *Homeland politics.* Homeland politics has always affected Asian Americans, but globalization and immigration have increased its divisiveness.
- *Political diversity.* Partisan politics in a traditional sense has prevented Asian Americans from working together even on issues in which they may share interests.
- *"Asian" values.* Assertions of cultural identity, especially if strongly equated with racial identity, may produce beliefs that are incompatible with liberal democratic systems.

Above all, Asian Americans—like all citizens—should pursue political goals that are principled. Whatever course they choose, Asian Americans should continue pursuing political empowerment.

NOTES

1. A vast literature has appeared in the past decade on the subjects of cultural pluralism, racial diversity, and minority rights within liberal societies, both descriptive and normative. The work of Charles Taylor and Will Kymlicka are among the most important contributions. For an overview, see Charles Taylor, *Multiculturalism and "the Politics of Recognition": An Essay,* ed. Amy Gutmann (Princeton: Princeton University Press, 1992); and Ian Shapiro and Will Kymlicka, *NOMOS XXXIX: Ethnicity and Groups Rights* (New York: New York University Press, 1997). Also see Charles Taylor, *Multiculturalism: Examining the Politics of Recognition,* ed. Amy Gutmann (Princeton: Princeton University Press, 1994); Will Kymlicka, *Multicultural Citizenship: A Liberal Theory of Minority Rights* (New York: Oxford University Press, 1995); and Will Kymlicka, ed., *The Rights of Minority Cultures* (New York: Oxford University Press, 1995).

2. For other scholarly discussions of the Asian Connection, see L. Ling-chi Wang, "Race, Class, Citizenship, Extraterritoriality: Asian Americans and the 1996 Campaign Finance Scandal," *Amerasia Journal* 24 (1998): 1–22; and Frank H. Wu and May Nicholson, "Have You No Decency? An Analysis of Racial Aspects of Media Coverage on the John Huang Matter," *Asian American Policy Review* 7 (1997): 1–37.

3. William Safire, "The Asian Connection," *New York Times,* October 7, 1996, A17. He later explained the title was an allusion to the Watergate era espionage movie *The French Connection.* For book-length studies, see Elizabeth Drew, *The Corruption of American Politics: What Went Wrong and Why* (Secaucus, N.J.: Carol Publishing Group, 1999); Drew is a veteran writer for the *New Yorker.* Also see Edward Timperlake and William C. Triplett, *Year of the Rat: How Bill Clinton Com-*

promised U.S. Security for Chinese Cash (Washington, D.C.: Regnery Publications, 1998), a sensationalistic account that claims the Clinton administration was part of a Chinese conspiracy.

4. After the impeachment, Asian Americans and Asian immigrants appeared again in the news as potential foreign agents. The investigations into the loss of nuclear weapons technology data focused on Wen Ho Lee, a scientist at the U.S. government's Los Alamos National Laboratory. The investigations, including the "Cox Report" issued by the U.S. House committee that held special hearings into the matter, and the accompanying media coverage featured the same racial stereotyping that had plagued the campaign finance matter. For discussions, including admissions by government officials that Lee was singled out for suspicion because of his racial ancestry, see Vernon Loeb and Walter Pincus, "Allegations of Bias Hurt Case against Spy Suspect," *Washington Post*, August 26, 1999, A1; Vernon Loeb and Walter Pincus, "Espionage Whistleblower Resigns," *Washington Post*, August 24, 1999, A1; and Vernon Loeb, "Ex-Official: Bomb Lab Case Lacks Evidence," *Washington Post*, August 17, 1999, A1 (describing Lee's ethnicity as "a major factor" in triggering suspicion). Also see Nick Anderson, "Spy Scare Taints Labs' Atmosphere," *Los Angeles Times*, May 21, 1999, A12; Bob Drogin, "Asian American Lab Employees Fear Repercussions of Spy Inquiries," *Los Angeles Times*, June 12, 1999, A10; Vernon Loeb, "Espionage Stir Alienating Foreign Scientists in U.S.," *Washington Post*, November 25, 1999, G1; and Vernon Loeb, "Spy Probe Worries Chinese Americans," *Washington Post*, August 14, 1999, A5. For analysis, see Lars-Erik Nelson, "Reports of the Select Committee on U.S. National, Security and Military/Commercial Concerns with the People's Republic of China," *New York Review of Books*, July 15, 1999, 6. Also see Ted W. Lieu, " 'Are You in the Chinese Air Force?' " *Washington Post*, June 19, 1999, A19; Angela E. Oh, "Spy Charges Fueled Search for Scapegoats," *Los Angeles Times*, June 21, 1999, B5; and Hoyt Zia, "Well, Is He a Spy—Or Not?" *New York Times*, May 16, 1999, A33.

The right-wing periodical *American Spectator* has run numerous articles pointing out the involvement of Chinese Americans in what it alleges is a Chinese government conspiracy of espionage. See, for example, Kenneth R. Timmerman, "Red Star over Washington," *American Spectator* (May 1999): 28; and John B. Roberts II, "Nuclear Secrets and the Culture Wars," *American Spectator* (May 1999): 34.

5. The exceptional episode challenging the prevailing view was the Korean bribery scandal of 1977–1978, in which more than a hundred members of Congress were accused of improperly accepting cash. Yet despite more than a year of official inquiries, "Koreagate" quickly lapsed from collective memory. See Congressional Quarterly, *Inside Congress*, 2d ed. (Washington, D.C.: Congressional Quarterly, 1979), 167–168.

6. Asian American political participation is a burgeoning area of study. The leading academic works include: Bruce E. Cain, "Asian-American Electoral Power: Imminent or Illusory," *Election Politics* 5 (1988): 27–30; Sucheng Chan, *Asian Ameri-*

cans: An Interpretive History (Boston: Twayne, 1991), 171–181; Yen Le Espiritu, *Asian American Panethnicity: Bridging Institutions and Identities* (Philadelphia: Temple University Press, 1992), 53–81; Bob Gurwitt, "Have Asian Americans Arrived Politically? Not Quite," *Governing* 4 (1990): 32–38; Pei-te Lien, *The Political Participation of Asian Americans: Voting Behavior in Southern California* (New York: Garland Publications, 1997); Pei-te Lien, "Ethnicity and Political Participation: A Comparison between Asian and Mexican Americans," *Political Behavior* 16 (1994): 237–264; Don T. Nakanishi and James Lai, eds., *National Asian Pacific American Political Almanac*, 8th ed. (Los Angeles: UCLA Asian American Studies Center, 1998–1999), 121–139; Don T. Nakanishi and James Lai, eds., *National Asian Pacific American Political Almanac*, 7th ed. (Los Angeles: UCLA Asian American Studies Center, 1996–1997), 144–169; Don T. Nakanishi, "The Next Swing Vote? Asian Pacific Americans and California Politics," in *Racial and Ethnic Politics in California*, ed. Bryan O. Jackson and Michael B. Preston (Berkeley: IGS Press, 1991); Don T. Nakanishi, "Asian American Politics: An Agenda for Research," *Amerasia Journal* 12 (1985–1986): 1–27; Don Toshiaki Nakanishi, *In Search of a New Paradigm: Minorities in the Context of International Politics* (Denver: University of Denver Press, 1975); Vincent N. Parrillo, "Asian Americans in American Politics," in *America's Ethnic Politics,* ed. Joseph S. Roucek and Bernard Eisenberg (Westport, Conn.: Greenwood Press, 1982), 89–112; Wendy K. Tam, "Asians—A Monolithic Voting Bloc?" *Political Behavior* 17 (1995): 223–249; Carole J. Uhlaner et al., "Political Participation of Ethnic Minorities in the 1980s," *Political Behavior* 11 (1989): 195–231; and Carole Jean Uhlaner, "Political Participation and Discrimination: A Comparative Analysis of Asians, Blacks, and Latinos," in *Political Participation and American Democracy,* ed. William Crotty (New York: Greenwood Press, 1991), 138–170.

Mass media coverage includes: Stanley Karnow, "Apathetic Asian Americans? Why Their Success Hasn't Spilled Over into Politics," *Washington Post,* September 29, 1992, C16; Dick Kirschten, "Building Blocs," *National Journal,* September 26, 1992, 2173; Seth Mydans, "In Rough World of American Politics, Asian Americans Stand Out as Rare," *New York Times,* June 3, 1996, A16; George Skelton, "Voters of Asian Heritage Slow to Claim Voice," *Los Angeles Times,* August 19, 1993, A3; and Jeff Yang, "Al's Asian Pals: Asian Americans Who Love Politicians Who Mock Asian Americans," *Village Voice,* April 25, 1995, 12.

7. Uhlaner, "Political Participation and Discrimination," 138, 162.

8. Uhlaner et al., "Political Participation of Ethnic Minorities in the 1980s."

9. Quoted in Irene Chang, "Study Finds More Asians Register as Republicans," *Los Angeles Times,* July 8, 1990, J1.

10. See Haynes Johnson and Thomas B. Edsall, "Asian Americans Torn between Two Parties," *Washington Post,* June 2, 1984, A1; Gebe Martinez, "Minorities Asked to the Parties," *Los Angeles Times,* October 4, 1992, B1; and Alison Mitchell, "New York's Political Parties Vie for Votes of Immigrants," *New York Times,* July 4, 1992, A1.

11. See Frank H. Wu, "Grassroots Strategies," *Asian Week*, March 15, 1996, 12. Huang claimed as early as 1992 that immigration issues attracted him to politics and to the Democratic Party; see Kirschten, "Building Blocs." Sen. Daniel Inouye expressed similar sentiments in explaining his membership in the Democratic Party. Frank H. Wu, "Washington Insider," *Asian Week*, April 12, 1996, 12. In interviews, both referred to the 1965 immigration reforms, inspired by the late president John F. Kennedy, that abolished the national origins system instituted a half-century earlier explicitly to maintain the ethnic makeup of the population.

12. Democratic National Committee, Office of Asian Pacific Affairs, "Asian Pacific Americans Coming of Age: DNC Efforts to Assist in the Implementation of the National Asian Pacific American Campaign Plan," internal memo, April 1996 (copy on file with authors). This document was later released to the media by the DNC during its investigation of the campaign finance matter.

General DNC strategies in the 1996 elections are described in Alison Mitchell, "How the President's Team Courted Key Voting Blocs," *New York Times*, January 25, 1997, A8.

13. See, for example, John Mintz, "GOP Gaining Hispanic, Asian Votes," *Washington Post*, October 28, 1984, A1.

14. See Maria L. LeGanga, "Dole Vows Not to Cede California to Clinton," *Los Angeles Times*, March 25, 1996, A1.

15. Like the Democrats, the Republicans wavered on their support for such a group. See William Wei, *The Asian American Movement* (Philadelphia: Temple University Press, 1993), 250, 330, n. 29. They eventually established an Asian American Caucus. See Thomas Massey, "The Wrong Way to Court Ethnics," *Washington Monthly*, May 1986, 21. Julie Rao coordinated Asian American outreach activities for the Dole-Kemp campaign in 1996; see Harry Mok, "Party Woman," *A. Magazine*, October/November 1996, 17. Also see Frank H. Wu, "Driver's Seat," *Asian Week*, December 8, 1995, 11. Another individual worked on a full-time, semi-volunteer basis coordinating "Asian American Republican Headquarters" during the 1988 campaign; see Laura Kurtzman, "From Vietnam to GOP Convention," *Los Angeles Times*, August 4, 1988, B3. The California Republican Party seems to have been more aggressive than the national headquarters about its outreach to Asian Americans; see Johnson and Edsall, "Asian Americans Torn between Two Parties." Also see Sam Fulwood III and Christina Lindgren, "O.C. Asian Americans Hear Bush China Plea," *Los Angeles Times*, June 17, 1991, A1; Evelyn Hsu, "Bush's Good Fortune," *Washington Post*, October 18, 1988, B4; Sarah Jackson-Han, "Fast-Growing Asian Population Confounds Major Political Parties," *Agence France Presse*, August 23, 1996 (available on Lexis-Nexis); Dave Lesher, "GOP Sees Ideological Link to Asian-Americans," *Los Angeles Times*, June 16, 1991, B6; Dave Lesher, "President Bush to Give Speech in Fountain Valley," *Los Angeles Times*, June 11, 1991, B1; Caryle Murphy, "Fearful of Communism, Many New Citizens Lean toward GOP Politics," *Washington Post*, December 18, 1987, A22; and Mike Ward, "Asian Voter

Poll Shows GOP Support," *Los Angeles Times,* July 30, 1988, B18. For an assessment of the GOP strategy toward Asian Americans, see Peter Beinart, "The Lee Rout," *New Republic,* January 5, 1998, 12.

16. See "Election Preview: A Voter's Guide," *Los Angeles Times,* May 29, 1994, Metro B (profile of Ron Unz).

17. See Ron K. Unz, "Immigration or the Welfare State; Which Is Our Real Enemy?" *Heritage Foundation Policy Review* (fall 1994): 33. Also see William McGurn, "The Silent Minority; Asian Americans' Affinity with Republican Party Principles," *National Review,* June 24, 1991, 19; and Stuart Rothenberg and William McGurn, "The Invisible Success Story; Asian Americans and Politics," *National Review,* September 15, 1989, 17.

18. *Buckley v. Valeo,* 424 U.S. 1 (1976).

19. See Elizabeth Drew, *Whatever It Takes: The Real Struggle for Power in America* (New York: Penguin Books, 1998), 116–118.

20. Ibid., 252–253.

21. See Federal Election Commission, "FEC Reports Major Increase in Party Activity for 1995–96" (www.fec.gov/press/ptyye1.htm).

22. For further details on Huang, see Wu and Nicholson, "Have You No Decency?"

23. Compare Dan Morgan and Lena Sun, "Clashing Sketches of Fund-Raiser Begin to Emerge; Huang's Networking Skills Brought Two Worlds Together," *Washington Post,* October 18, 1996, A35 (describing Huang as playing a crucial role in 1988 on immigration issues), with Dan Morgan, "Huang Used Access to Seek Hill Help on Banking Issues," *Washington Post,* March 5, 1997, A1 (suggesting Huang lobbied legislators on fair credit policies). Also see Kirschten, "Building Blocs."

24. John Huang entered a guilty plea in August 1999 as part of a deal with the Justice Department. In exchange for one-year probation, five hundred hours of community service, and a $10,000 fine, Huang agreed to cooperate. Stating "I am very sad and embarrassed by my mistakes that have brought disrepute to my family," Huang admitted criminal violations related to his work on the 1992 and 1994 elections but not the 1996 presidential campaign.

Yah Lin "Charlie" Trie was indicted for illegal donations and obstruction of justice. After his trial began in Arkansas in May 1999, Trie accepted a deal and decided to cooperate. One of those implicated by Trie was Ernie Green, one of the nine black students who integrated the Little Rock Central High School in 1957 in a confrontation that saw federal troops called out to advance civil rights.

Johnny Chung was the first suspect to choose to cooperate. He began to provide information as early as 1997 and then reached a formal agreement with prosecutors in March 1998. He testified that he had served as the conduit for illicit monies from the Chinese military, and he named Chinese general Ji Shengde as his supplier of hundreds of thousands of dollars.

After prevailing on preliminary motions, Maria Hsia was convicted in March 2000 by a D.C. jury on five counts of campaign finance violations for her role in raising $100,000 when Vice President Al Gore appeared among the monks and nuns at the Hsi Lai Buddhist Temple outside of Los Angeles. She could be sentenced to as much as twenty-five years in prison. Later, two nuns were charged with criminal contempt for fleeing the country to avoid having to testify at the Hsia trial.

Yogeshi Gandhi, who claimed to be a distant relative of Mohandas Gandhi, acquiesced to charges of not only breaking campaign finance rules but also committing mail fraud and evading federal taxes. Pauline Kanchanalak, a Thai business executive, continues to await trial.

25. Examples of the kinds of Asian American behavior that were attributed to Asian culture are beyond the scope of this article, but they are described at greater length in Wu and Nicholson, "Have You No Decency?"

26. Safire, "Asian Connection."

27. See *Congressional Record*, 94th Cong., 1st sess., March 28, 1974, 87882–87886.

28. See Roberto Suro, "As Campaign Fund Probe Winds Down, Major Charges Unlikely," *Washington Post*, May 30, 1999, A5. Also see George Lardner Jr., "Fundraiser Set Up Fake Firms for Chinese," *Washington Post*, September 21, 1998, A2; Roberto Suro, "Clinton Fund-raiser to Plead Guilty," *Washington Post*, May 22, 1999, A9; and Edward Walsh, "Huang Pleads Guilty; Gets Probation, Fine," *Washington Post*, August 13, 1999, A9.

29. See Senate Committee on Governmental Affairs, *Final Report: Investigation of Illegal or Improper Activities in Connection with the 1996 Federal Election Campaigns*, 6 vols., 105th Cong., 2d sess., March 10, 1998. The committee set up a dedicated Web site that contains the official records of its hearings <www.senate.gov/~gov_affairs/investig.htm>. See Guy Gugliotta, "Senate Campaign Probers Release Findings," *Washington Post*, May 6, 1998, A6.

30. See, for example, Lloyd Grove, "A Firefighter's Blazing Trail: David Bossie Is Throwing Sparks on the GOP Campaign Finance Probe," *Washington Post*, November 13, 1997, C1; George Lardner Jr., "Democrats Push for Burton Removal," *Washington Post*, May 8, 1998, A16; Susan Schmidt, "Democrats Renew Attacks on House Panel after Staff Turmoil in Political Funds Probe," *Washington Post*, July 3, 1997, A4; George Stuteville, "Alleged Leak Leads Burton Aide to Quit," *Indianapolis News*, July 2,1997; Edward Walsh, "House Democrats May Ask for Discipline for Burton," *Washington Post*, April 24, 1998, A7; and Edward Walsh, "Campaign Probe Panel's Leaders Clash," *Washington Post*, April 1, 1998, A6.

31. The media engaged in the same conduct as the DNC, according to individuals who received calls from reporters. See Angelo Ragaza and Frank Wu, "Damned If We Do, Damned If We Don't," *A. Magazine*, February 1997, 56. Also see U.S. Commission on Civil Rights, "Briefing on Civil Rights Implications in the Treatment of Asian Pacific Americans during the Campaign Finance Controversy," October 1998.

32. See Federal Document Clearing House transcript of the February 28, 1997, DNC press conference (on file with authors). Note that some references to category 7 describe it as events "embracing" rather than "targeting" Asian Americans. One of the authors (Wu) attended the press conference in a reportorial capacity.

33. See Joseph E. Sandler letter to Stephanie Y. Moore, January 28, 1998, reproduced in U.S. Commission on Civil Rights, "Briefing on Civil Rights Implications in the Treatment of Asian Pacific Americans."

34. One of the authors attended the DNC press briefing announcing the results of its audit. The information presented here is based on a review of DNC materials released at that press briefing. The DNC audit script was excerpted by *Harper's* magazine. See "Thank You for Your Contribution," *Harper's*, June 1997, 17.

35. Its memo on the subject stated, "The DNC's actions are not intended to reflect in any way on the character, or motivation of the people who made these contributions."

36. See Federal Document Clearing House transcript of the February 28, 1997, DNC press conference (on file with authors).

37. Ibid.

38. Ibid.

39. See Frank H. Wu, "Better Late Than Never," *Asian Week,* April 25, 1997, 11. Also see "The DNC: Reaching Out to Asian Americans" (letters to the editor), *Washington Post,* September 28, 1997, C6; and Terry M. Neal, "Asian American Donors Feel Stigmatized," *Washington Post,* September 8, 1997, A1.

40. An extensive analysis of media coverage is presented in Wu and Nicholson, "Have You No Decency?"

41. See "In His Own Words," *New York Times,* November 1, 1996, B8; Ernest Tollerson, "Perot Keeps Up Attacks on Clinton's Integrity," *New York Times,* November 5, 1996, A19; and Donald Baker, "Perot Lambasts Both Foes," *Washington Post,* October 25, 1996, I 32.

42. See Federal Document Clearing House transcript of the July 10, 1997, hearing of the Senate Committee on Governmental Affairs. Also see "Senator Apologizes for Mimicry of Asians in Reference to Huang," *Los Angeles Times,* July 11, 1997, A14; and James Warren, "In D.C., Cleveland's 'Dennis the Menace' Has Last Laugh," *Chicago Tribune,* February 2, 1997, C2. The line has its origins in a joke about miscegenation.

43. See Peter Baker and Howard Kurtz, "McCurry Exit: A White House Wit's End," *Washington Post,* July 24, 1997, A1.

44. See Federal Document Clearing House transcript of the July 30, 1997, hearing of the Senate Committee on Governmental Affairs.

45. See *Congressional Record* (House), 105th Cong., 1st sess., July 7, 1997, 143: 5500.

46. See *Congressional Record* (House), 105th Cong., 2d sess., July 14, 1998, 144: 5485; and Alison Mitchell, "After Hours, Debate on Fund-Raising Rages," *New York Times,* July 20, 1998, A1.

47. See Lena H. Sun, "Asian Names Scrutinized at White House," *Washington Post,* September 11, 1997, A1.

48. See Peter S. Goodman, "Riady Helped Kin Enter UC-Berkeley," *Washington Post,* December 14, 1996, A17; and Frank H. Wu, " 'Asian Connection' Controversy Won't Quit," *Asian Week,* December 20, 1996, 8. The authors have copies of the actual documents on which the *Washington Post* report was based, along with responses from the University of California press office.

49. See Hanna Rosin, "FOR E.G.G. HEADS," *New Republic,* December 2, 1996, 13; and "Riady's Shipping Agenda," *Journal of Commerce,* December 16, 1996, A6.

50. See Frank H. Wu, "Slurs on Judge Warrant Sanctions," *Asian Week,* March 5, 1998, 11.

51. *MacDraw, Inc. v. CIT Group Equipment Financing, Inc.,* 138 F.3d 33 (2d Cir. 1998); and Deborah Pines, "Slurs on Judge Require Penalties," *New York Law Journal,* February 4, 1998, 1.

52. "Manchurian Candidates," *National Review,* March 24, 1997.

53. R. Emmett Tyrrell Jr., "Witnesses In and Out of the Hearing Room," *Washington Times,* July 18, 1997, A18.

54. Michael Lewis, "The Asian Con, Part 2," *New York Times Sunday Magazine,* May 4, 1997, 28.

55. See Jill Abramson and Michael Moss, "World of Money: Fund-Raisers Tap Their Ethnic Roots for Political Parties," *Wall Street Journal,* October 22, 1996, A1.

56. Mark Steyn, "The Entertainment State," *New Criterion,* September 1998, 24, 28.

57. Fong related this incident in a public speech given at the Congressional Asian Pacific American Caucus "Washington Briefing" session, Yerba Buena Conference Center, San Francisco, July 21, 1997.

58. See Howard Kurtz, *Spin Cycle: How the White House and the Media Manipulate the News,* rev. ed. (New York: Simon and Schuster, 1998), 58–62; Thomas Oliphant, "Another Victim Is Caught in the Scandal Machine," *Boston Globe,* September 16, 1997, A17; and Robert Wright, "Slanted," *Slate,* January 1, 1997 <slate.msn.com/Earthling/97-01-01/Earthling.asp>.

59. See Julie Chao, "Campaign Finance Coverage Unfair," *San Francisco Examiner,* November 16, 1997, B1.

60. See Fox Butterfield, "Ex-Aide to Dole Campaign Admits Illegal Contributions," *New York Times,* July 11, 1996, B10.

61. See Leslie Wayne, "F.E.C. Fines German Citizen for U.S. Campaign Donations," *New York Times,* July 19, 1997, A8.

62. See David Stout, "Largest Fine to Be Paid for Donation," *New York Times,* October 9, 1997, A27.

63. This logical analysis of the Fourteenth Amendment was proposed by two scholars interpreting the Japanese American internment decisions by the Supreme Court. See Joseph Tussman and Jacobus ten Broek, "The Equal Protection of the Laws," *California Law Review* 37 (1949): 341.

64. See, for example, Michael A. Fletcher, "Coalition Says DNC Fund-Raising Flap Is Generating 'Asian-Bashing,' " *Washington Post,* October 23, 1996, A16; and K. Connie Kang, "Asian Gifts Coverage Called Stereotyping," *Los Angeles Times,* October 23, 1996, A11.

65. See Steven A. Holmes, "Asian American Groups File a Complaint of Bias in Inquiries and Coverage," *New York Times,* September 12, 1997, A32. The complaint itself is reprinted in *Asian Law Journal* 5 (1998): 357. The authors participated in the drafting of the complaint and accompanying materials. The U.S. Civil Rights Commission held a "briefing" in December 1997; see Marc Lacey, "Parties Exchange Charges at Hearing on Anti-Asian Bias," *Los Angeles Times,* December 6, 1997, A20. One of the authors (Wu) testified at the session; see U.S. Commission on Civil Rights, "Briefing on Civil Rights Implications in the Treatment of Asian Pacific Americans during the Campaign Finance Controversy," October 1998.

66. An edited version appears as Sen. Daniel Akaka, "From the Senate Floor: Asian Americans and the Political Fund-raising Investigation," in *National Asian Pacific American Political Almanac,* 8th ed., ed. Don T. Nakanishi and James Lai (Los Angeles: UCLA Asian American Studies Center, 1998–1999), 22–28.

67. See "A Call to Action: Briefing Package on Asian Pacific Americans and the Campaign Finance Controversy," prepared by an Ad Hoc Coalition of National Asian Pacific American Groups Based in D.C., undated document. The authors participated in the drafting of this brochure, which was printed and distributed by five Asian American community organizations.

For an early articulation of these viewpoints, see Stewart Kwoh and Frank H. Wu, "Don't Build Reform on a Scapegoat," *Los Angeles Times,* October 24, 1996, B9. Asian American community activists also warned against defending Huang; see Ling-chi Wang, "Asians Shouldn't Jump to Defend Huang," *Newsday,* October 25, 1996, A43.

68. For an overview of "playing the race card" by critics of this supposed strategy, see Peter Collier and David Horowitz, eds., *The Race Card: White Guilt, Black Resentment, and the Assault on Truth and Justice* (Rocklin, Calif.: Prima Publications, 1997).

69. "Whitewater (and Related) Basics" (editorial), *Washington Post,* November 22, 1996, A30.

70. "The 'Asian Bashing' Defense" (editorial) *Washington Post,* July 10, 1997, A18.

71. "The Asian Affair" (editorial), *Boston Globe,* January 21, 1997, A12.

72. See, for example, Howard Schuman et al., *Racial Attitudes in America: Trends and Interpretations,* rev. ed. (Cambridge: Harvard University Press, 1997); Alan Wolfe, *One Nation, After All: What Middle-Class Americans Really Think About: God, Country, Family, Racism, Welfare, Immigration, Homosexuality, Work, The Right, The Left, and Each Other* (New York: Viking, 1998); Tom W. Smith, "Intergroup Relations in Contemporary America: An Overview of Survey Research," in

Intergroup Relations in the United States: Research Perspectives, ed. Wayne Winborn and Renae Cohen (New York: National Council of Women of the United States, 1959); and Richard Morin, "A Distorted Image of Minorities," *Washington Post,* October 8, 1995, A1 (summary of results of telephone survey conducted by the *Washington Post,* Kaiser Foundation, and Harvard University). Much survey research, however, continues to exclude Asian Americans.

73. See, for example, Neil T. Gotanda, " 'Other Nonwhites' in American Legal History: A Review of Justice at War," *Columbia Law Review* 85 (1985): 1186; and Neil T. Gotanda, "Asian American Rights and the 'Miss Saigon Syndrome,' " in *Asian Americans and the Supreme Court: A Documentary History,* ed. Hyung-Chan Kim (New York: Greenwood Press, 1992), 1087.

74. See Ronald Takaki, *Strangers from a Different Shore: A History of Asian Americans* (Boston: Little, Brown, 1989), 10–11. This view is exemplified by Gunther Barth, *Bitter Strength: A History of the Chinese in the United States, 1850–1870* (Cambridge: Harvard University Press, 1964).

75. See Helen Zia, *Asian American Dreams: The Emergence of an American People* (New York: Farrar Straus Giroux, 2000), 45.

76. See William Burr, ed., *The Kissinger Transcripts* (New York: New Press, 1999), 94–95.

77. James Mann, *About Face: A History of America's Curious Relationship with China, From Nixon to Clinton* (New York: Knopf, 1999), 107.

78. See Joan Fitzpatrick and William McKay Bennett, "A Lion in the Path? The Influence of International Law on the Immigration Policy of the United States," *Washington Law Review* 70 (1995): 589.

79. See generally Alexander DeConde, *Ethnicity, Race, and American Foreign Policy* (Boston: Northeastern University Press, 1992). Also see Louis L. Gerson, *Hyphenate in Recent American Politics and Diplomacy* (Lawrence: University of Kansas Press, 1964); "New Ethnic Voices" (symposium), *Foreign Policy* (1985): 3–39 n. 60; Charles McC. Mathias Jr., "Ethnic Groups and Foreign Policy," *Foreign Affairs* 59 (1981): 975–998; and Yossi Shain, "Multicultural Foreign Policy," *Foreign Policy* (1995): 69–87 n. 100.

For an overview of the current debate on immigration policy, see Owen Fiss, *A Community of Equals: The Constitutional Protection of New Americans* (Boston: Beacon Press, 1999); Nicolaus Mills, ed., *Arguing Immigration* (New York: Simon and Schuster, 1994); Noah M. J. Pickus, *Immigration and Citizenship in the Twenty-First Century* (Lanham, Md.: Rowman and Littlefield, 1998); and Warren F. Schwartz, ed., *Justice in Immigration* (New York: Cambridge University Press, 1995). For analysis of Asian immigration to the United States, see Elliot Robert Barkan, *Asian and Pacific Islander Migration to the United States: A Model of New Global Patterns* (Westport, Conn.: Greenwood Press, 1992); James T. Fawcett and Benjamin V. Carino, eds., *Pacific Bridges: The New Immigration from Asia and the Pacific Islands* (Staten Island: Center for Migration Studies, 1987); and Paul Ong et al., eds., *The*

New Asian Immigration in Los Angeles and Global Restructuring (Philadelphia: Temple University Press, 1994).

80. For excellent selections of essays on the relationship of immigration, domestic politics, and foreign policy, including with respect to national security, see Michael S. Teitelbaum and Myron Weiner, eds., *Threatened Peoples, Threatened Borders: World Migration and U.S. Policy* (New York: Norton, 1995); Robert W. Tucker et al., eds., *Immigration and U.S. Foreign Policy* (Boulder: Westview Press, 1990); and Myron Weiner, ed., *International Migration and Security* (Boulder: Westview Press, 1993). The Council on Foreign Relations held a 1996 conference on minorities and foreign policy, summarized in David J. Vidal, *Defining the National Interest: Minorities and U.S. Foreign Policy in the 21st Century* (New York: Council on Foreign Relations, 1997). For a disapproving view of the role of ethnicity in global politics, see Daniel Patrick Moynihan, *Pandaemonium* (New York: Oxford University Press, 1993). Also see Michael Walzer et al., *The Politics of Ethnicity* (Cambridge: Harvard University Press, 1982).

81. See Michael Clough, "Grass-Roots Policymaking: Say Good-Bye to the 'Wise Men,' " *Foreign Affairs* (January/February 1994): 2–7.

82. See Bill Ong Hing, *Making and Remaking Asian America through Immigration Policy, 1850–1990* (Stanford: Stanford University Press, 1993); and Lisa Lowe, *Immigrant Acts: On Asian American Cultural Politics* (Durham: Duke University Press, 1996). Also see Ignatius Bau, "Immigrant Rights: A Challenge to Asian Pacific American Political Influence," *Asian American Policy Review* 5 (1995): 7; Bill Ong Hing and Ronald Lee, eds., *The State of Asian Pacific America: Reframing the Immigration Debate* (Los Angeles: LEAP Asian Pacific American Public Policy Institute and UCLA Asian American Studies Center, 1996); Larry Hajime Shinagawa, "The Impact of Immigration on the Demography of Asian Pacific Americans," in *National Asian Pacific American Political Almanac*, 8th ed., ed. Don T. Nakanishi and James Lai (Los Angeles: UCLA Asian American Studies Center, 1998–1999), 56; and Bill Tamayo, "Broadening the 'Asian Interests' in United States Immigration Policy," *Asian American Policy Review* (spring 1991): 65.

83. See generally Hing and Lee, *State of Asian Pacific America*; Jan C. Ting, " 'Other than a Chinaman': How U.S. Immigration Law Resulted From and Still Reflects a Policy of Excluding and Restricting Asian Immigration," *Temple Political and Civil Rights Law Review* 4 (1995): 301.

84. The requirement was adopted in 1790. The Supreme Court decided two prerequisite cases holding that Asians were neither white nor Caucasian. *Ozawa v. United States*, 260 U.S. 178 (1922); and *United States v. Thind*, 261 U.S. 204 (1923). See generally Ian Haney Fidencio Lopez, *White by Law: The Legal Construction of Race* (New York: New York University Press, 1996).

85. See generally John Higham, *Strangers in the Land: Patterns of American Nativism, 1860–1925* (New Brunswick, N.J.: Rutgers University Press, 1988).

86. See *Personal Justice Denied: Report of the Commission on Wartime Relocation and Internment of Civilians* (reprint) (Seattle: University of Washington Press, 1997); and Roger Daniels, *Concentration Camps: North America Japanese in the United States and Canada during World War II* (Malabar, Fla.: Krieger Publishing, 1993).

87. Peter Brimelow, *Alien Nation: Common Sense about America's Immigration Disaster* (New York: Random House, 1995). Brimelow is not alone; also see Roy Beck, *The Case against Immigration: The Moral, Economic, Social, and Environmental Reasons for Reducing U.S. Immigration Back to Traditional Levels* (New York: Norton, 1996); and Chilton Williamson Jr., *The Immigration Mystique: America's False Conscience* (New York: Basic Books, 1996).

88. Brimelow, *Alien Nation*, 10, 271–272.

89. Several writers have argued that immigration would be acceptable, but for failure to assimilate. See, for example, Peter D. Salins, *Assimilation, American Style* (New York: Basic Books, 1997). Also see Georgie Anne Geyer, *Americans No More: The Death of Citizenship* (New York: Atlantic Monthly Press, 1996); and John J. Miller, *The Unmaking of Americans: How Multiculturalism Has Undermined the Assimilation Ethic* (New York: Free Press, 1998).

90. Democratic National Committee, Office of Asian Pacific Affairs, "Asian Pacific Americans Coming of Age: DNC Efforts to Assist in the Implementation of the National Asian Pacific American Campaign Plan," internal memo, April 1996, 6, 7, 19, 32 n. 42 (copy on file with authors). Few texts on interest group politics even mention Asian Americans, other than in the context of organizing on immigration issues. See Ronald J. Hrebenar, *Interest Group Politics in America*, 3d ed. (New York: M. E. Sharpe, 1997), 11.

91. See National Research Council, *The New Americans: Economic, Demographic, and Fiscal Effects of Immigration* (Washington, D.C.: National Academy Press, 1997), 2-1–2-25.

92. Shinagawa, "Impact of Immigration on the Demography of Asian Pacific Americans."

93. This information is available from the INS Web site <www.ins.usdoj.gov/> or from its 1996 *Statistical Yearbook*. It is possible that some immigrants were from Asia in terms of nationality or birth, but that they would not identify themselves as Asian in terms of race.

94. See, for example, Brimelow, *Alien Nation*, 80, 141–42; Beck, *Case against Immigration*, 40–41; and Geyer, *Americans No More*, 251–254.

95. H.R. 2002, 104th Cong., 1st sess. (1995); S. 1394, 104th Cong., 1st sess. (1995).

96. U.S. Commission on Immigration Reform, *U.S. Immigration Policy: Restoring Credibility* (1994); and *Legal Immigration: Setting Priorities* (1995), 70–72. Its final report was U.S. Commission on Immigration Reform, *Becoming an American: Immigration and Immigrant Policy* (1997). For press coverage, see Bill McAllister,

"Commission to Propose Lowering Number of Immigrants Let into U.S.," *Washington Post,* June 6, 1995, A4.

97. See John F. Harris, "Clinton Backs Call to Reduce Immigration," *Washington Post,* June 8, 1996, A1; Janet Hook, "Immigration Cutback Urged by U.S. Panel," *Los Angeles Times,* June 8, 1996, A1; Robert Pear, "Clinton Embraces a Proposal to Cut Immigration by a Third," *New York Times,* June 8, 1996, B10; and M2 Presswire, "Daily Press Briefing by Mike McCurry at White House," June 8, 1995 (available on Lexis-Nexis). Also see Paul Richter, "Clinton, Zedillo Meet as Immigration Tension Grows," *Los Angeles Times,* October 10, 1995, A9.

For an after-the-fact account of the matter, see Lanny J. Davis, *Truth to Tell: Tell It Early, Tell It All, Tell It Yourself: Notes From My White House Education* (New York: Free Press, 1999), 137–157. Davis categorically denied that the Huang fundraiser contributed to any change in Clinton administration immigration policy. He described strategic reasons for the "split the bill" decision.

98. Andrew Fois, letter to Lamar S. Smith, July 12, 1995, 4–5 (on file with authors).

99. Democratic National Committee, "Briefing for the President of the United States," prepared for the Asian Pacific American Leadership Council Dinner, February 19, 1996, Hay-Adams Hotel, Washington, D.C., credited to John Huang (copy on file with authors). This document was later released to the media by the DNC during its investigation of the campaign finance matter. It most likely was written by the Asian American outreach office and not John Huang.

100. See, for example, Stephen A. Holmes, "Anti-Immigrant Mood Moves Asians to Organize," *New York Times,* January 3, 1996, A1. Also see William Branigan, "Unusual Alliance Transformed Immigration Debate," *Washington Post,* March 23, 1996, A8; Stephen A. Holmes, "The Strange Politics of Immigration," *New York Times,* December 31, 1995, D3; Jeffrey L. Katz, "An Unusual Immigration Alliance," *Congressional Quarterly Weekly Report,* March 16, 1996, 700; Holly Idelson, "Ethnic Groups Add Voices to Critics of GOP Plans," *Congressional Quarterly Weekly Report,* January 13, 1996, 92; and Dick Kirschten, "An Old Debate, Strange New Alliances," *National Journal,* November 18, 1995, 2871. Also see John Heilemann, "Do You Know the Way to Ban Jose," *Wired,* August 1996, 45.

101. See Holly Idelson, "Immigration: Senate Rejects Two Attempts to Cut Legal Immigration," *Congressional Quarterly Weekly Report,* April 27, 1996, 1173; Holly Idelson, "House Votes to Crack Down on Illegal Immigrants," *Congressional Quarterly Weekly Report,* March 23, 1996, 79; and David Masci, "Odds for Curb on Legal Immigrants Grow Longer as Senate Splits Bill," *Congressional Quarterly Weekly Report,* March 16, 1996, 698. See also Philip G. Schragg, *A Well-Founded Fear: The Congressional Battle to Save Political Asylum in America* (New York: Routledge, 2000).

102. Three bills ultimately passed on immigration issues, none of them altering overall levels of legal immigration: Antiterrorism and Effective Death Penalty Act of

1996, Public Law 14-132, 110 Stat. 1214 (enacted April 24, 1996); Personal Responsibility and Work Opportunity Reconciliation Act of 1996, Public Law 104-193, 110 Stat. 2105 (August 22, 1996); and Illegal Immigration Reform and Immigrant Responsibility Act of 1996, Public Law 104-207, 110 Stat. 3009 (October 1, 1996).

103. Michael Kranish, "Clinton Policy Shift Followed Asian-American Fund-Raiser," *Boston Globe,* January 16, 1997, A1; and Michael Kranish, "Policy Shift over Fund-Raiser Is Denied," *Boston Globe,* January 17, 1997, A1.

104. See R. Newswire, "Hollow Denial from White House about Immigration About-Face," January 17, 1997 (available on Lexis-Nexis).

105. See James G. Gimpel and James R. Edwards Jr., *The Congressional Politics of Immigration Reform* (Boston: Allyn and Bacon, 1999), 261; and David M. Reimers, *Unwelcome Strangers: American Identity and the Turn against Immigration* (New York: Columbia University Press, 1998), 139–140.

106. Nicholas Laham, *Ronald Reagan and the Politics of Immigration Reform* (Westport, Conn.: Praeger), x, xiv, 26–27, 213, 216.

107. See Sand Banks, "Why Did Some Protesters against Proposition 187 Carry the Red, White and Green Instead of the Red, White, and Blue?" *Los Angeles Times,* November 10, 1994, B1; and Leslie Berger and Jocelyn Stewart, "Many Angered by Pro 187 Demonstrations," *Los Angeles Times,* November 4, 1994, A1.

108. See Stewart Kwoh and Mindy Hui, "Empowering Our Communities: Political Policy," in LEAP Asian Pacific American Public Policy Institute, *The State of Asian Pacific America: Policy Issues to the Year 2020* (Los Angeles: LEAP Asian Pacific American Public Policy Institute and UCLA Asian American Studies Center, 1993), 189–197.

109. See, for example, James Sterngold, "For Asian-Americans, a New Political Resolve," *New York Times,* September 22, 1999, A1; and Will Van Sant, "One Step Forward, Two Steps Back," *National Journal,* May 8, 1999. Also see Gregory Rodriguez, "Minority Leader," *New Republic,* October 19, 1998, 21; and Romesh Ratnesar, "A Place at the Table," *Time,* October 12, 1998, 38.

110. See Paul Ong and Karen Umemoto, "Diversity within a Common Agenda," in *The State of Asian America: Economic Diversity, Issues and Policies,* ed. Karin Aguilar-San Juan (Boston: South End Press, 1994), 271–276.

111. See Yasemin Nuhoglu Soysal, "Toward a Postnational Model of Membership," in *The Citizenship Debates,* ed. Gershon Shafir (Minneapolis: University of Minnesota Press, 1998). For an explicitly Asia-Pacific conception of Asian American identity, see Arif Dirlik, "The Asian-Pacific in Asian American Perspective," in *What Is in a Rim? Critical Perspectives on the Pacific Region Idea,* 2d ed., ed. Arif Dirlik (Lanham, Md.: Rowman and Littlefield, 1998), 283–308; and Evelyn Hu-DeHart, ed., *Across the Pacific: Asian Americans and Globalization* (New York: Asia Society; Philadelphia: Temple University Press, 1999). For a recent analysis of the Chinese diaspora in capitalistic ventures, see Aihwa Ong and Donald Nonini, eds., *Un-*

grounded Empires: The Cultural Politics of Modern Chinese Transnationalism (New York: Routledge, 1997). Also see Robin Cohen, *Global Diasporas: An Introduction* (Seattle: University of Washington Press, 1997); Gabriel Sheffer, ed., *Modern Diasporas in International Politics* (London: Croom Helm, 1986); and L. Ling-chi Wang, "The Structure of Dual Domination: Toward a Paradigm for the Study of the Chinese Diaspora in the U.S.," *Amerasia Journal* 21 (1995): 149–170 n. 1–2.

Some Asian Americanists have been critical, however, of works that situate Asian immigrants as the overseas diaspora. One leading work in that vein is Lynn Pan, *Sons of the Yellow Emperor: A History of the Chinese Diaspora* (Boston: Little, Brown, 1990). Also see Lynn Pan, *The Encyclopedia of the Chinese Overseas* (Cambridge.: Harvard University Press, 1999).

The literature of transnationalism is developing. For representative works, see Mohammed A. Bamyeh, "Transnationalism," *Current Sociology* 41 (1993): 1–95 n. 3; Linda Basch et al., *Nations Unbound: Transnational Projects, Postcolonial Predicaments, and Deterritorialized Nation-States* (Langhorne, Pa.: Gordon and Breach, 1994); Rainer Baubock, *Transnational Citizenship: Membership and Rights in International Migration* (Brookfield, Vt.: E. Elgar, 1994); Leo Chavez, "Immigration Reform and Nativism: The Nationalist Response to the Transnationalist Challenge," in *Immigrants Out! The New Nativism and the Anti-Immigrant Impulse in the United States,* ed. Juan F. Perea (New York: New York University Press, 1997); Robert O. Keohane and Joseph Nye Jr., *Transnational Relations and World Politics* (Cambridge: Harvard University Press, 1972); John F. Stack, ed., *Ethnic Identities in a Transnational World* (Westport, Conn.: Greenwood Press, 1981); Nina Glick Schiller et al., eds., *Toward a Transnational Perspective on Migration: Race, Class, Ethnicity, and Nationalism Reconsidered* (New York: New York Academy of Sciences, 1992); Nina Glick Shiller, "From Immigrant to Transimmigrant: Theorizing Transnational Migration," *Anthropological Quarterly* 68 (January 1995): 48 n. 1; and Michael Walzer, *Toward a Global Civil Society* (Providence: Berghahn Books, 1995).

CHAPTER THIRTEEN

LESSONS LEARNED FROM THE "LOCKE FOR GOVERNOR" CAMPAIGN

JUDY YU
GRACE T. YUAN

Increasing the number of Asian American elected officials has been, and continues to be, an important objective of the Asian American political movement. The result thus far—a growing number of Asian American officeholders—is a sign that the community has become an integral part of the American political and decision-making infrastructure. In fact, in gaining access to the political system, these Asian American elected officials are making a statement about equality in America.

Another goal of the Asian American community is to elect officials who will be sensitive to the concerns of the community. Topics such as immigration, civil rights, economic development, foreign trade, welfare, and bilingual education are likely to be championed by Asian Americans and members of other communities of color. In seeking to garner support for issues, Asian American elected officials can point to their personal experiences. Officeholders with such experiences and a history of commitment to these issues often bring credibility and passion to the public dialogue.

Finally, by electing one of its own to public office, the Asian American community creates a bridge to legislators who are not members of the community. The bridge is an important tool for community members who seek to participate in all areas of government and to affect the outcome of the political process.

Although the Asian American political movement can point to its successes in different parts of the United States, Washington State, because of its unique geographical position in the Pacific Rim and its ability to attract talented Asian immigrants, has had a larger number of Asian American elected officials than other states relative to the size of the state's Asian American population. No single political campaign has captured the hopes and imaginations of Asian Americans more than Gary Locke's 1996 race for the governorship of Washington State. Now, several years after Locke was elected to the state's highest office, the Asian American community and those who support the Asian American political movement continue to discuss the merits of this campaign and whether it can be replicated by other Asian American candidates in local, state, and even national campaigns.

Did Locke's success result from a unique set of circumstances? Are there tangible lessons to be learned from Locke's experience on the campaign trail? Did Locke's Asian American identity work to his advantage or disadvantage? In addition to the victory on election day, what were the other outcomes of the Locke campaign? Are there long-term effects from the positive campaign Locke ran? How can other candidates, whatever their ethnic background, apply these lessons to their own campaigns? This chapter will address and discuss these questions.

THE POLITICAL LANDSCAPE IN WASHINGTON STATE IN 1996

In February 1996 the Democratic governor of Washington, Mike Lowry, announced unexpectedly that he would not seek reelection after serving one term in office. Many Democrats were surprised by the decision and the timing of his announcement; several Republicans had already declared their candidacies. In the days and weeks that followed, potential Democratic candidates held a flurry of meetings, each assessing their strengths and weaknesses, and analyzing their ability to raise the funds needed to run a statewide campaign.

Four days after Lowry decided not to seek reelection, Locke announced that he would enter the governor's race. No one was surprised by the announcement given Locke's political résumé. He was then serving as the executive of King County, the largest county in the state of Washington and the thirteenth largest county in the United States. He also had represented south Seattle in the state legislature for eleven years. During his tenure in the legislature, Locke had served as chair of the powerful House Appropriations Committee. In view of his experience, his familiarity with state politics, the policy-making process, and the state budget, Locke had an immediate advantage vis-à-vis the other candidates.

When the dust settled, five Democratic and six Republican candidates began to campaign—and to fund-raise—in earnest for their respective party's nomination. The mayor of Seattle, Norm Rice, was a prominent contender in the Democratic primary. A popular African American, he was known for his liberal policies in the health and human services area. Another strong candidate was Nita Reinhart, a high-ranking woman in the Democratic Party and a longtime state senator from Seattle, also known for her liberal political philosophy. Jay Inslee, yet another candidate in the gubernatorial primary, had previously served one term in the U.S. House of Representatives and had name recognition in eastern Washington.[1]

On the Republican side were several well-known moderates from the Seattle area and one state representative, Ellen Craswell, who was a member of the conservative Christian Coalition. At the time, Craswell was one of the least known of the Republican candidates because she represented a legislative district outside of the Seattle area. As the campaign unfolded, however, she proved to be the strongest Republican candidate; her clear message targeted conservative voters. Craswell eventually advanced to the general election by a narrow margin.

In 1996 Washington State held open primaries—that is, all candidates are listed on the ballot, and the top vote-getter from each party advances to the general election. Open primaries can result in interesting voting patterns and unpredictable outcomes.

Based on experience, some political consultants believe that very liberal candidates in Washington garner close to 30 percent of the vote in a primary election. While this is generally not sufficient to win the primary, it is enough to cause other candidates to lose. Very conservative candidates might expect to poll another 30 percent, with the remaining votes veering toward the moderate middle. Thus, from the beginning it was important not only to assess how Locke should position himself relative to the other Democrats, but also to anticipate how the campaign would unfold in the general election if Locke emerged as the winner of the primary.

Because Locke had extensive experience with welfare reform, fiscal management, and higher education issues, he could have positioned himself as a liberal, a moderate, or a conservative in the Democratic primary. He knew, however, that Washington State had a history of voters tending to support moderate Republicans or moderate Democrats in major elections. Therefore, the Locke campaign decided to position Locke as a moderate Democrat. The campaign also hoped that a moderate Republican would not emerge from the primary, leading to a tougher general campaign.

As for Locke's Asian American heritage, early polling by the Locke campaign indicated that certain positive stereotypes were associated with this community: hardworking, family-oriented, strongly supportive of education, and possessing fiscal management skills. This image of Asian Americans proved to be an advantage to Locke because it placed him solidly in line with middle-class values. The alignment of these values with Locke's political ideology positioned him squarely in the center of the political spectrum, allowing him to appeal to a broad range of voters. Yet it is important to note that prior to the governor's race, Locke's Asian American identity and his family's long ties to the Chinese American community were never a major focus of political attention. To most voters he was just "Gary." Furthermore, the media did not seem to place any importance on his ethnic heritage. In a way, the local media appeared to be colorblind.

Over the next six months, the Locke campaign concentrated on appealing to the values of the moderate and middle-class voter. In addition to his "tough on crime" and "high on education" messages, Locke's personal story of achieving the "American Dream" was promoted, both with Washington voters and within the Asian American community. It was a message that resonated with the residents of the state and clearly set Locke apart from the other candidates as an immigrant success story. In fact, historically Washington has recognized the contributions of immigrants to the development of this state. European groups, as well as Asian Americans, have worked to preserve their distinct ethnic heritage. The Nordic Museum in Seattle, for example, captures the history of Scandinavians in the fishing industry. Hundreds of cultural events around Washington each year celebrate immigrant traditions and the contributions of each community and remind Washingtonians of the diversity of the population.

On election day, the campaign messages and hard work paid off. Locke won with 58 percent of the vote, capturing along the way twenty-five of the state's thirty-nine counties. His margin of victory was the fourth largest ever achieved in a Washington State gubernatorial race.

HISTORY OF ASIAN AMERICAN ELECTED OFFICIALS IN WASHINGTON STATE

Gary Locke's victory continued Washington State's long tradition of electing Asian Americans to public office. For example, Wing Luke was elected to the Seattle City Council in 1962 and was touted as a mayoral hopeful until his tragic death in a 1965 airplane accident. Wing Luke touched many during his years of public service and inspired a future generation of Asian Americans in politics, many of whom worked on his campaign. As teen-agers, when they were making decisions about their own futures, both Gary Locke and Cheryl Chow, a former Seattle City Council member, were in-troduced to politics by Wing Luke.

In 1973 John Eng became the first Asian American elected to the state legislature, serving until 1981. Dolores Sibonga was appointed in 1978 to fill a vacancy on the Seattle City Council. She was elected to the council in 1979 and served until 1991. Another legend in King County is Ruby Chow, who became the first Asian American elected to the King County Council, where she served from 1979 to 1985. Chow was a role model and mentor to her daughter, Cheryl, who was elected to the Seattle City Council and served from 1990 to 1998, and to her son, Mark, a King County District Court judge who was elected in 1991 and continues to serve on the bench.

Another high-water mark was the 1992 legislative session, when five Asian Americans held seats in the Washington state legislature. This may have been one of the largest Asian American delegations in a state legisla-ture in the continental United States. Stan Fleming, Gary Locke, Paull Shin, Velma Veloria, and Art Wang all served together on the floor of the House of Representatives. They were instrumental in raising the visibility of Asian Americans in politics in Washington State and around the country. Then, in 1996, while Gary Locke was running for governor, another landmark was achieved: three of the nine members of the Seattle City Council were Asian Americans—Martha Choe, Charlie Chong, and Cheryl Chow.

This history of Asian Americans in Washington State politics has paved the way for others to follow. Gary Locke was one such candidate who fol-lowed that path to elected office, who worked hard to build his experience and visibility, and whose timing was perfect.

LOCKE THE CANDIDATE

In 1996 Gary Locke was a candidate who was considered eminently electable by those observing electoral politics. He was a graduate of Yale University and Boston University Law School and a former King County prosecutor. In 1996 he was serving as the King County executive, the high-est elected office in the county and one of the highest offices in the state. In the 1994 executive's race, he received over 70 percent of the vote in the general election, which at that time was the largest margin of victory ever achieved for his position. Because King County is the largest county in the state, Locke's popularity and name recognition in the county was a good indicator of his potential strength in a statewide election.

Locke's background in politics was solid. As noted, he had served for eleven years in the state legislature, and he had a reputation as a hard worker and a wizard with the state budget during his tenure as chair of the House Appropriations Committee. As the King County executive, Locke solidified his reputation as a leader and developed his skills.

Within the Asian American community, Locke was a well-known figure who had played a key role in aiding the development of major projects. As a result, he had broad support within the community. In short, Locke was perceived to be a solid candidate capable of generating enthusiasm and support in his bid for the governor's office.

THE CAMPAIGN THAT TOUCHED THE ASIAN AMERICAN COMMUNITY

Prior to the Locke for Governor campaign, several Asian American elected officials and candidates had sought the support of the national Asian American community by conducting fund-raising campaigns across the country. Notable among these candidates were Michael Woo, who ran for the mayor of Los Angeles in 1993, and S. B. Woo, who served as the lieutenant governor of Delaware from 1985 to 1989, and ran for the U.S. Senate in 1988, and the U.S. House of Representatives in 1992.

Nationwide fund-raising efforts targeting the Asian American community are not a new phenomenon.[2] In the mid-1970s, the Democratic National Committee (DNC) focused on identifying Asian American financial supporters. Then, in the early 1980s, the DNC established the Asian Pacific Caucus with the goal of generating political and financial support from Asian Americans for Democratic candidates.

One of the first candidates to place a substantial emphasis on national fund-raising within the Asian American community was Michael Woo. Woo had served as a Los Angeles City Council member for eight years when he decided to enter the mayoral race. During his tenure on the City Council, Woo had successfully built a solid base of financial support, and many Asian Americans were on his donor list. When he decided to run for mayor, Woo embarked on a fund-raising tour around the country, targeting Chinese Americans in cities such as San Francisco, Seattle, Detroit, New York, and Washington, D.C. His focus on the Asian American community was strategic and productive. Although some Asian immigrants may not have participated in the process, Woo inspired many to make their first political contributions. With expenditures of over $12 million, Woo's campaign set a new benchmark for fund-raising by an Asian American candidate.

During and prior to this period, S. B. Woo also attempted to leverage his popularity in the Chinese American community with fund-raising tours conducted much like Michael Woo's. (The two candidates are not related.) Many Asian Americans who contributed to the campaigns of Michael Woo and S. B. Woo were disappointed when neither candidate was elected to office that year. This sense of disenchantment lingered within the community until the Locke campaign in 1996. Many were frustrated with the political process and did not believe that supporting Asian American candidates from other parts of the country had any value.

In this atmosphere, the Locke gubernatorial campaign was launched. Locke asked Grace Yuan, who has been active in politics and involved in the Asian American community, to lead the national effort. As the director of national outreach, Yuan systematically developed a program that generated contributions from around the country and helped to establish Locke as a national figurehead in the Asian American community. This program was supported by a media campaign that targeted the U.S. and overseas Asian media on Locke's behalf. Judy Yu, a media consultant with expertise working with the Asian American community and celebrity clients, led this initiative in support of the national fund-raising campaign. Asian Americans needed to be educated about Locke, his campaign, and the importance of supporting him in Washington State.

Washington State law places many restrictions on individual campaign donations. One restriction is that each donor can contribute only $1,100 per election cycle (adjusted for inflation), which makes influence-peddling by large donors virtually impossible. Effectively, the campaign finance law forces candidates to seek contributions from a large number of donors rather than secure a few large contributions. Candidates who are able to raise a portion of their funds from out-of-state sources have an advantage. Such efforts must be balanced, however, so that only a small proportion of funds are generated from out of state to avoid the appearance that a campaign is being influenced by outsiders.

In 1996 both Norm Rice and Gary Locke sought financial support from communities outside of Washington State. Many mayors, particularly African American mayors, hoped to see an African American elected governor. They helped Rice and arranged fund-raising events in their own cities such as San Francisco, Detroit, and Cleveland. Many mayors even made their own donor lists available to him.

By contrast, Locke relied on community networks, Asian American organizations, and Chinese family associations. His campaign worked with local Asian American communities around the country to connect with their leadership and with their personal contacts. Many supported Locke out of a sense of ethnic pride, others out of a sense of duty. As a result, Locke was able to generate early financial support for his campaign from donors around the country.

Although several postelection news stories focused exclusively on Locke's out-of-state fund-raising efforts, other candidates adopted similar fund-raising strategies. They were used by the Rice campaign and by several Washington State congressional candidates who, through family connections, generated substantial contributions from the Washington, D.C., area and from the Midwest. Out-of-state fund-raising continues to be a factor in many campaigns.

In the end, Asian American communities around the country and within the state contributed significantly to the success of the Locke for Governor campaign. Accurate statistics on the total amount of the Asian American contributions are not available because the tracking mechanisms do not monitor these statistics based on ethnicity. Even a methodology that predicts the ethnicity of the donor based on known Asian American surnames such as Ng or Lee would be inaccurate and would yield misleading results. It is possible, however, to determine precisely the donations received from outside the state of Washington. Of the $2.2 million raised by the Locke campaign for the primary and general elections, 18 percent, or $396,000, was donated by those living outside the state. Thirty-seven percent of the out-of-state contributions were made by donors living in the state of California. Because almost all out-of-state contributions were made by Asian Americans, these figures provide a general indication of the contributions by the national Asian American community (outside Washington state).

The average size of the donations was roughly the same for donors out-of-state ($226 per donor) and in-state ($207 per donor), but the timing of the donations differed significantly. Because of the crowded 1996 primary, the candidates were competing for a limited pool of donors. Many of the donors who historically had supported Rice, for example, also historically had supported Locke. Some of these donors decided not to contribute to either campaign until after the gubernatorial primary. Thus, early money was critical.

Contributions received in the early days of a campaign give a candidate credibility and stature, and often generate more money—that is, a candidate who successfully raises money is more likely to be viewed as a serious contender. The press also uses total dollars raised as an indicator of a candidate's viability. In this situation, the national Asian American community played a critical role. The Locke campaign hosted successful fund-raising events in Washington, D.C., New York, and northern California during the first few months of the campaign that were extremely important in bringing in early donations.

In a July 16, 1996, article entitled "Locke's Asian Roots May Be Big Asset in Bid for Governor," the *Seattle Post-Intelligencer* commented on this phenomenon. The article reported that as of May 1996 Locke had raised 43 percent of his contributions through out-of-state Asian American community fund-raisers. In fact, during the first three months of the campaign 20 percent of the contributions came from out of state, mostly from Asian Americans in California and New York. Thus, the early support of the Asian American community gave the Locke campaign a strategic and critical advantage.

ROLE OF THE ASIAN AMERICAN MEDIA

In 1996 candidate Gary Locke was virtually unknown to the national Asian American community. His involvement had been limited because he had tended not to travel out of state and had only attended a limited number of national Asian American conferences. His public relations strategists found it a challenge, then, to create awareness in the Asian American community about his candidacy and to generate enthusiasm for the Washington State governor's race. The media relations campaign was conducted in tandem with a fund-raising campaign that broke new ground in the Asian American community. The public relations effort sought to create positive media support for short-term fund-raising goals, to anticipate future needs, and to focus on the long-term goals of building Locke's image as a celebrity in the Asian American community and in Asia.

The Asian American media have developed a strong infrastructure of print, radio, TV, and now Internet communications. Many Asian American media organizations also are connected to foreign media outlets in Asia through business ties or through ownership. Through Locke's Asian American publicist, who had developed relationships with many of these media contacts, the Asian American media were provided with a stream of information from the campaign. As with any campaign, a communications strategy, based on the goals defined for the Asian American component of the Locke campaign, was developed and implemented.

And what were those goals? Most Asian American candidates, regardless of the number of generations their families have lived in the United States or the ethnic composition of their districts, have continued to be perceived as Asian by the community and by the voters. The issue can become complicated and a challenge to manage, but a review of the history of other Asian American elected officials suggests that a pattern has emerged.

Asian Americans, like some other minorities in leadership positions, must define and present themselves in two ways—to their specific communities and to the general public. Those involved in public relations often say that "it's not what people are seeing that's important, it's what you make them believe they're seeing that's important." For example, an actor such as Eddie Murphy can play the comic yet conservative role of a Dr. Doolittle one moment, and the jive-talking role of a black police officer the next. He "morphs" between the two and creates different impressions of himself, depending on the role he is playing. Asian American candidates, in some ways, must do the same—walk in and out of several communities. Eventually, the two or more personas begin to converge.

Some candidates are more successful at being multicultural or having their "feet firmly planted in two cultures" than others. Gary Locke clearly appealed to the Asian American community with his good looks and serious demeanor, and his speeches articulated his desire to bring more Asian Americans "to the table where decisions are made." He promised to advocate issues such as welfare reform and affirmative action. He also paid a great deal of respect to his wife, Mona Lee Locke, and to his parents, who as immigrants to this country struggled to make life better for their children. For mothers and fathers in the Asian American community, he was a "favorite son" who represented the hope that their sons and daughters could one day become a person of such stature.

Locke's immigrant story and his qualifications in state and county government began to draw media attention from around the world. In a landmark speech in San Francisco that was a part of his West Coast trip, Locke explained how his grandfather had worked as a houseboy in a home less than one mile from the governor's mansion, where he, Locke, hoped to live. He described growing up in public housing and working long hours in a store as a child. In a sense, the family had traveled less than one mile in a hundred years—but what a change!

Eventually, national media such as the *New York Times* and *Washington Post* began to notice that the Asian American community was showing interest in candidate Locke. The story of the American Dream and the excitement in the Asian American community nationwide about the Locke campaign became a focal point for the media. The story was new, the story was fresh, and Locke's popularity became a phenomenon.

Press releases and press conferences, one-on-one visits with journalists and publishers, editorials submitted to newspapers around the country, feature story interviews with radio and television, and publicity events, such as visits to the offices of a family association or social service organization, were just a few of the ways in which the hearts and minds of the Asian American community became focused on the Locke campaign. In addition, the campaign developed media relations with foreign press representatives from Hong Kong, Japan, China, and Taiwan in order to build on Locke's popularity and to promote his potential in the international arena.

Quickly, the Asian American and general media attention to Locke focused on Locke's value as a potential governor with strong Pacific Rim ties. This recognition was even extended from the White House when Locke, while only a candidate for governor, was invited to a high-profile dinner attended by trade and economic development leaders. The media efforts focused on Locke's abilities to serve as a bridge to the state's trading partners. In a state where three out of five jobs are related to trade, this image was attractive to the electorate.

LESSONS FOR OTHER CANDIDATES

Future Asian American candidates may find lessons from the Locke campaign useful as they forge new paths in the areas of fund-raising, public relations, and policy development, and as they involve the Asian American community in different activities. Meanwhile, the Asian American political movement, which has been spurred by victories and successes, also is facing setbacks resulting from allegations about campaign finance irregularities.

While there have been gains in the number of Asian American elected officials, the numbers need to be sustained and the base of political support must be expanded. For example, in contrast to the Latino community whose representation in areas like Los Angeles has grown to over 30 percent, Asian Americans are still underrepresented in electoral politics. For those seeking to address this situation, here are some specific lessons from the Locke campaign:

- Fund-raising will always be one of the most important factors in a successful campaign. The cloud of negative publicity in 1996 and 1997 associated with certain donors to the Democratic National Committee should not deter Asian Americans from making legal contributions to the candidates of their choice. Many Asian Americans have the means to participate in the political process by making donations, and they should continue to be involved in the democratic system at the local, state, and national levels.
- Successful fund-raising early in the campaign from the national Asian American community can signal strong support and generate additional donations. Fund-raising efforts must be approached systematically and supported by a strong public relations campaign.
- Asian Americans in politics should consider a multipronged approach to their public image. Although it can be a challenge, a multicultural approach is a key asset. Investing in a public relations effort can build celebrity identity that will continue to be valuable in the years to come.
- A strong image of inclusion and doing what is best for the American public is a critical message. Asian American elected officials must represent their constituents, most of whom will not be of Asian heritage. These officials must maintain the delicate balance between responding to local issues and needs versus demands at the national level.

The Asian American community continues to celebrate the victory of Gary Locke in reaching the governor's mansion. The Locke campaign was one of the most visible elections to date in the Asian American community. It created a celebrity who represents the ideals and values of Americans everywhere. In one of Governor Locke's first speeches to the Asian American community after his election, he said that "the best thing he could do for the community is to be the best Governor possible." By becoming a great governor, he will prove to the voters that their confidence is well deserved.

For future Asian American political leaders, Locke will be one of the key role models of his generation. It is unknown what path Locke will take in his political future. What is known, however, is that with a leader such as Governor Locke, Asian Americans can stand together to decide where to go and where others may follow.

NOTES

1. In 1998 Inslee was elected to the U.S. House of Representatives from Washington's First Congressional District.

2. As early as the 1960s, several elected officials organized successful fund-raising efforts focused on the Japanese American community. Among the early leaders were Daniel Inouye, Spark Matsunaga, and Patsy Mink, followed by Norman Mineta in 1974 and Robert Matsui in 1978.

CHAPTER FOURTEEN

BUILDING ON THE INDIGENOUS BASE: THE FUND-RAISING CONTROVERSY AND THE FUTURE OF ASIAN AMERICAN POLITICAL PARTICIPATION

PAUL Y. WATANABE

More than thirty years ago, G. William Domhoff first published his provocative book *Who Rules America?*[1] In that edition there was no index entry for Asian Americans. The latest edition of *Who Rules America?* was published recently.[2] Under "Asian Americans" there is now a single reference.

Perhaps this means that Asian Americans have progressed, albeit glacially, in taking a hand in ruling the United States. Certainly, anyone who has followed in recent years the extensive media coverage and political intrigue surrounding Asian American fund-raising and donations might have the impression that Asian Americans do indeed rule America. Johnny Chung, Maria Hsia, John Huang, Yah Lin "Charlie" Trie, and countless others, it seems, were in charge, with President Bill Clinton, members of Congress, and the Democratic National Committee in their hip pockets.

Of course, these imaginative portrayals of Asian Americans as political behemoths have been wildly, almost laughably, overdrawn. But, as several contributions to this volume suggest, the preoccupation of the press, politicians, and the public with Asian Americans bearing gifts reflects a perpetuation of attitudes toward and characterizations of Asian Americans with decidedly important consequences for their societal and political roles.

This chapter begins with a brief examination of the political meaning of the fund-raising controversy without offering a meticulous cataloging of the events and activities manifested throughout the fund-raising experience. (In this volume Chapter 12 by Frank Wu and Francey Lim Youngberg ably offers this more detailed account.) This controversy is best understood in a much broader context that both illuminates and reflects fundamental aspects of the historical, social, cultural, and political lives of Asian Americans. An understanding of this context is critical to the development of effective strategies for Asian American political activism. Most of this chapter, then, is devoted to outlining a particular direction and location for Asian American political involvement. It is less, therefore, about what has been done to or said about Asian Americans and more about the ways Asian Americans should organize themselves in order to maximize and sustain their political influence.

RACE AND POLITICS

Frank Wu and May Nicholson, in an article in the *Asian American Policy Review,* examined media coverage of the fund-raising controversy, including "the number of troubling themes implicating race."[3] Their review of newspaper articles nicely summarized the dominant tendencies of most media venues and the attitudes of many political operatives:

> Many articles imply that Huang represents all Asian Pacific Americans, that race is directly relevant, that Asians and Asian Americans are indistinguishable, that Asian culture can explain the conduct of Asian American individuals, and that all Asian Americans who participate in politics are somehow linked to the scandal.[4]

These familiar depictions of Asian Americans are enormously meaningful in assessing the place of and prospects for Asian Americans in political life. As the articles in this volume by Claire Jean Kim (Chapter 2) and Neil Gotanda (Chapter 3) amply illustrate, the language and images that accompanied press and political commentaries related to Asian Americans were not new. They did not commence nor will they end with the fund-raising affair. Following close on the heels of the fund-raising controversy, for example, dramatic charges of Chinese espionage allegedly aided and abetted by Asian American accomplices such as scientist Wen Ho Lee emerged. Rather than limiting scrutiny to a few Asian Americans at a few locations, some members of the press, public, Congress, and government officials broadly invoked the specter of blanket suspicion and questionable loyalties.

Although there appeared to be no evidence that the activities of any Asian American scientists were linked to illegal fund-raising contributions, commentators such as William Safire of the *New York Times* were quick to "connect the dots."[5]

In short, the stereotypical portrayals of and assumptions about Chung, Hsia, Huang, Trie, and others involved in the contributions scandal and scientist Wen Ho Lee in the Los Alamos National Laboratory case really had little to do with them specifically. These images and ideas had everything to do, however, with the treatment of Asian Americans in general over many decades, reliably reinforcing racial prejudice and political subordination.

This treatment did not go unchallenged. During the fund-raising controversy, numerous individuals and organizations in the Asian American community registered sustained and careful criticism of the worst aspects of the behavior manifested by the press and politicians. In numerous demonstrations, petitions, press conferences and releases, forums, and commentaries, Asian Americans took issue with the often-unwarranted allegations, demeaning stereotypes, and sweeping condemnations.

Asian American criticism, in turn, did not go unanswered. Indeed, the nature of the counterattacks aimed at activist critics was just as instructive in exposing ideas about the role of Asian Americans in politics as was the treatment of the alleged wrongdoers themselves. For the most part, Asian American complaints were ignored or dismissed or those who dared protest were themselves discredited.[6] Race and other elements played prominent roles in the construction of some responses by U.S. senators and members of Congress, decision makers at the Democratic National Committee and the White House, and editorial writers and reporters at the *Washington Post, Washington Times, Boston Globe, Wall Street Journal,* and *National Review,* among others.

Vast experience supports the notion that racial factors influence the participation of and receptivity toward certain groups in American society. The unfulfilled struggle of nonwhites, including Asian Americans, for political parity has been part of the nation's history since its inception. Although many formal impediments have been steadily chipped away, formidable resistance remains. In consistent and obvious ways, racially charged elements with political consequences have been central considerations in the treatment of nonwhites and Asian Americans generally and in the handling of the recent fund-raising matter specifically. Reporters, columnists, commentators, and politicians and their staffs have fed the public a steady diet of racially tinged messages.

Although the relationship between race and politics is familiar and applies to most nonwhites, the treatment of Asian Americans both reflects and transcends race. Asian Americans must confront barriers of nativism as well as racism, which pose a formidable double challenge with significant political implications.

BEYOND RACE: 'FOREIGNERS' FOREVER

The sting of nativism has been felt by most immigrant groups and not only those from Asia. For most European immigrants, however, after the burdens of nativist suspicions were thrust aside, political assimilation followed. For Asian Americans, despite having resided in the United States for over a century and a half, the nativist prejudices have persisted. Cast as foreigners and outsiders throughout their history, they have been pressed upon legally and attitudinally. The racial stigmas have remained as well, meaning that Asian Americans have undergone a process Angelo Ancheta calls "outsider racialization."[7]

The pervasive persistence during the fund-raising crisis of the themes of Asian Americans as foreigners or as Americans with undiluted foreign attachments illustrates what Asian Americans have encountered in diverse dimensions of American life. As was clearly apparent in the recent Los Alamos nuclear espionage allegations, the idea of Asian Americans as spies is one that comes easily. This attribution of foreignness lies at the heart of the racialization of Asian Americans vis-à-vis politics. Whether held consciously or unconsciously, it drives the attitudes and actions related to Asian American political empowerment. Nothing is more direct, reliable, or imbedded—and thus more devastating—in cutting the legs out from under Asian American political strength than invoking the specter of foreign attachments. Lisa Lowe ably summarizes this dynamic:

> Immigration regulations and the restrictions on naturalization and citizenship have thus racialized and gendered Asian Americans, and this history has situated Asian Americans, even as citizens, in a differential relationship to the political and cultural institutions of the nation-state. The racialization of Asian Americans in relation to the state locates Asian American culture as a site for the emergence of another kind of political subject, one who has a historically 'alien-ated' relation to the category of citizenship. That historical alienation situates the Asian American political subject in critical apposition

370

to the category of the citizen, as well as to the political sphere of representative democracy that the concept of citizen subtends.[8]

Full and unfettered political activism is fundamentally about membership in the society, about equal worth and opportunity. To be counted outside of the society is to be marginalized. "Once they are racialized as foreign-born outsiders," Ancheta has observed, "Asian Americans can be racially subordinated by any action that distinguishes between citizens and noncitizens, between Americans and foreigners."[9] Reminded of their proper "place," Asian Americans may be in this country, but they are not of it.

Although the depiction of the racialization of Asian Americans as outsiders is broadly embraced as reflective of behavior toward Asian Americans, few commentators carefully consider its implications for the political behavior of Asian Americans. Logic suggests that if, as it seems, Asian Americans are regarded differently and often to their detriment, then they must develop correspondingly different responses. Valuable time and energy can best be applied to searching for optional strategies and departures from what may have been done previously rather than on often fruitless political mimicry.

These political strategies could be alternatives to mainstream political participation, which often takes the form of working in major national and state campaigns, giving money to candidates in these races and to the major political parties, and concentrating on voting in elections and other political activities at these levels. The fund-raising experience and the prevailing context clarified many of the limitations of mainstream involvement. An examination of these limitations will help to structure the full range of reasonable options.

LIMITATIONS OF MAINSTREAM PARTICIPATION

Some observers have viewed the fund-raising experience as a painful but perhaps necessary trial by fire for Asian Americans, a "rite of passage," to use Wu and Nicholson's terminology, for those aspiring to play in the political big leagues. Time and patience, it is argued, will be rewarded with clout and influence for Asian Americans. Their day will come. In the meantime, as political neophytes Asian Americans will find many suitors willing to take advantage of their alleged naivete. This view is reflected in the observations of Joel Kotkin writing in the *Wall Street Journal*:

This proclivity to seek influence has made Asian-Americans exceedingly liable to the kind of suggestive wooing that is hallmark of the Democratic Party under Clinton. But this should not shock anyone, since newcomers to America—such as the Irish in the 19th century—also often gravitated to unscrupulous politicians who promised them both respect and influence for money. Wealthy Jews, for example, often found the Democrats attractive because, in large part, they felt unwelcome in the WASP-dominated GOP.

Ultimately, these same immigrants later learned more about how to use and, in some places, dominate the political system, as the Italians did in much of New York state or as the Irish did in Massachusetts. A similar maturation will likely also occur among Asians, whose numbers and economic power are increasingly palpable, and not only in California.[10]

In a similar vein, John Miller has written:

Harvard sociologist David Riesman once noted that when a daughter comes home from college with her Japanese American boyfriend who is majoring in physics, her parents see the physicist rather than the Asian. Something similar could be said for voters. Asians will probably continue to make inroads locally and nationally—their growing numbers dictate that—and they will do so without relying on a grassroots ethnic base. . . . Asian Americans will increasingly be seen as indistinguishable from whites.[11]

The ways in which Asian Americans were portrayed before and throughout the donor controversy make it amply clear that for many people Asian Americans remain readily distinguishable from whites. The "Asian" is "visible" in individuals when it comes to their political participation. Consequently, utilizing Miller's logic, the ability of Asian Americans to mature and to make "inroads" may be compromised. And, most important, a strong ethnic base may not be as dispensable as he suggests.

Involvement at the national level, particularly in the manner in which it was so prominently portrayed during the 1996 national election season, also may be problematic for other reasons. Individual efforts or those bundled through select intermediaries, such as John Huang, often carry little influence as far as promoting a community agenda. The volume of money delivered may be impressive, but the payoffs are likely to be small.

A second problem arises even in those cases where there is some payback, because the beneficiaries are commonly those pursuing primarily narrow, selective interests. "Since money has become the lifeline of American democracy and politicians are always hungry for cash, some Asian Americans go along with these opportunists, pretending they are responding to grass-roots concerns," Ling-chi Wang has asserted. "But the opportunists could care less about the community. We have to be fools to think that [James] Riady contributed up to $1 million to promote Asian American political power."[12]

In a similar vein, Henry Der, in an article in the *Los Angeles Times* entitled "Don't Play the Money Game to Be Heard," offered this assessment of donors such as Johnny Chung and Charlie Trie:

> Did Asian Americans talk about welfare reform, human rights, bilingual education, student loans, housing and health insurance for the poor with the president? Or is it even realistic to expect Asian Americans who can afford to donate large sums of money to political parties to act differently from other well-heeled donors who, more often than not, pursue private interests?[13]

The sentiments of Wang and Der are, for the most part, sensible. As the title of Der's article suggests, playing the money game has serious drawbacks. To the extent that they can be detected, the agendas of many big money players (Aihwa Ong describes them as "equal opportunity opportunists")[14] seemed to be decidedly more personal than communal, and their actions in some cases were illegal. Consequently, Wang and Der appropriately argue that it would be foolish for Asian Americans to blindly come to the defense of large donors just because they are of Asian descent.

Most of the Asian American activists who raised their voices during the controversy, however, were not fools. They were well aware that rank-and-file Asian American interests were not the prime motivations behind much of the controversial fund-raising and contributions. Furthermore, their criticism of the press and politicians did not automatically constitute an embrace of potential wrongdoers. One thing they did realize with great clarity, however. Although these individuals and countless others may not have acted differently than non–Asian American donors, they were treated differently. For example, the Democratic National Committee conducted a special audit of contributors with Asian surnames.[15] Without sharing either the interests or agenda of the individuals accused of wrongdoing, those who were critical of the handling of the controversy could recognize and oppose the fact that ancestry and race were significant factors in how some Asian Americans were portrayed and dealt with, which had consequences for Asian Americans broadly.

Other factors affecting Asian American political involvement are the size and scope of the terrain on which they choose to battle. In many large political arenas, for example, the effectiveness of Asian Americans may be substantially diluted. Carole Uhlaner has observed that "they [Asian Americans] aren't big enough to make politics worth pursuing on an ethnic basis."[16] Therefore, to those who were inclined to characterize the 1996 victory of Gary Locke as governor in Washington as a victory by Asian Americans, prudent analysts would respond by describing Locke's success as the political triumph of an Asian American rather than of Asian Americans. Locke certainly generated a strong political response from the Asian American community, but, in truth, if every Asian American who voted for Locke had stayed home, Locke still would have won handily. This has generally been the case as well in other instances, at least outside of Hawaii, where Asian Americans have captured major electoral offices.

In some smaller jurisdictions, a concentration of Asian Americans can markedly enhance the potential impact of Asian American participation, resulting in the election of Asian Americans to political offices. For example, in San Francisco and Monterey Park, California, political successes have been achieved by building on determined community activism and organizing and adequate numbers. Recently in Lowell, Massachusetts, Asian American involvement was a key factor in the election of the first Cambodian American to the city council.

Beyond sheer numbers in most jurisdictions, Asian Americans may be hampered by low naturalization and voter registration rates and limited voter turnout.[17] Many of these impediments to participation reflect structural, legalistic, and cultural factors that weigh heavily on Asian Americans desiring to engage in certain political pursuits.[18] As a practical matter, limited English language competency also can restrict mainstream participation.

Asian Americans, as a result, are not in the main generally responsible for electing high-level public officials and formulating and implementing sweeping public policies. But whether "politics" is worth pursuing, as Uhlaner suggests, depends on how narrowly "politics" is defined and how broadly participation is considered. At the community level Asian Americans can be "big enough" to make a difference. There, the abilities and prospects of concentrated and organized minorities, including Asian Americans, to influence policies and programs are enhanced. In addition, Asian Americans are often responsible for running and advocating for community programs dealing, for example, with day care, literacy, legal assistance, public health, and workers' and tenants' rights.

Political activism at the local or community level may minimize apparent liabilities and, indeed, turn them into assets. On this terrain, the attribution of Asian Americans as foreigners has less meaning. Here alternatives might be found to what is often the too large, costly, impermanent, and ineffectual focus on mainstream politics. At the very least, a more solid foundation can be constructed for supporting forays into politics at any level—a base that can serve as well as a refuge during the inevitable political storms.

STRENGTHENING THE INDIGENOUS BASE

An inescapable lesson of the recent fund-raising experience—and, indeed, a thread running throughout the history of Asian Americans—is that their political fates are often inextricably linked. When white Americans act as individuals, they are seldom judged as a group. That is not true for Asian Americans and nonwhites in general. Their individual actions are often accounted for and judged collectively.

Since it is as a group that Asian American participation has been assessed, a prudent response to this dynamic is to establish a strong, collective presence. The most enduring impact is likely to be achieved through collective efforts in pursuit of shared interests. Lani Guinier has observed that "people participate 'where, when and how' they think it matters."[19] It is at the local level that politics matters a great deal and where collective purposes can be most effectively pursued.

In American culture, William Flanigan and Nancy Zingale have noted, "The role of the individual in influencing government is stressed; the role of organized activity in politics is downgraded."[20] The community-grounded approach advocated here runs counter to this notion. Despite the strenuous attempts made to find a pattern of widespread collusion in the fund-raising activities of Asian Americans, the evidence indicates that individual desire and specific interests rather than larger, group-oriented goals and behavior were behind the efforts of most of the notorious contributors. Their actions were perfectly consistent with the dominant individualistic approach to political participation. This approach in the long run, however, is inconsistent with the establishment of a sustained and effective role for Asian Americans—and, indeed, for other minority groups—in the political life of their nation and their communities.

By focusing even more sharply on the community level, Asian Americans can increase their political resources and achieve meaningful political outcomes. In doing so, their activism may become less episodic and more durable, firmly grounded, and respected. Wads of cash dropped off by a few individuals cannot in the end match the potential clout of cadres of individuals joined together with demonstrated organizational, strategic, and political strengths and in support of community-focused agendas. The impression that this organizational muscle can convey to politicians, public officials, and the media should not be underestimated.

Consistent with the desire to increase and maintain political influence and involvement at all levels, a refocusing at the community level is important not only because of its impact on local outcomes but also because it can prepare individuals, organizations, and communities for maximum political effectiveness in other arenas. Efforts by organizations such as the Coalition of Asian Pacific Americans for Fair Reapportionment in California serve a vital enabling function by addressing the need to prevent the fragmentation of Asian Americans among electoral districts. The Chinese American Voters Education Committee in the San Francisco Bay Area, the Asian Pacific Policy and Planning Council in Los Angeles, and the Asian American Legal Defense and Education Fund in New York City have helped to lay the groundwork for political participation by promoting naturalization, voter registration, and voting. An enhanced indigenous base contains resources—individual, organizational, financial, experiential—that are crucial in support of expeditions into the larger political milieu. It offers sustenance through the battles that may be waged. And it may provide shelter and strength when opposition emerges and attacks commence as they did in the turbulent fund-raising experience.

An additional virtue of the community-focused strategy is that even if it does not result in winning friends and influencing people in high places in the press and political establishment, the process of building community capacity continues and is assuredly strengthened. A broader political influence, therefore, is more than just a spillover effect of community capacity building. It is a central reason for involvement at this level. However, if influence in other domains is in fact not strengthened by this strategy, the gains in other ways remain considerable.

Research indicates that, for most people, involvement at the community level intensifies their positive group identification, which in turn affects their proclivity to engage in a variety of politically meaningful endeavors. For example, Pei-te Lien has found that heightened Asian American ethnic group identification can significantly strengthen a person's involvement in most political activities, including working with others in a group.[21] In their study of Japanese Americans, Stephen Fugita and David O'Brien found that ethnic community involvement had a positive effect on mainstream political participation.[22]

Among the challenges confronting activists and organizers interested in enhancing the effectiveness of mainstream participation is the need to transform resources held and honed in the community base into support for effective interventions in the broader political environment. If neighborhoods can be mobilized to engage local political units and interests in the fight against crime and unchecked institutional expansion, for example, then Asian Americans can improve their chances for success in larger arenas. Boston's Coalition to Protect Chinatown is a good example of a neighborhood effort aimed at softening the negative consequences of (or redirecting altogether) urban development projects that are not consistent with the interests of Chinatown residents. One of the explicit objectives of Asia Women United of Minnesota is to build on its advocacy in behalf of services and programs to address domestic violence in order to "empower Asian women and girls." Viewed in this way, involvement in the community and neighborhood is not the abandonment of politics and political participation but a prioritization of its locus.

Many other reasons for concentrating at the community level are evident as well. Some factors that may exclude or weaken involvement in mainstream political pursuits may be irrelevant or even assets in other arenas. The multilingualism of many Asian Americans, for example, is perceived in some contexts as a political liability. This enhanced language capability, however, if appropriately applied can be a source of strength and a valuable resource facilitating political endeavors at the community level.

As noted earlier, a substantial number of Asian Americans are foreign-born and remain unnaturalized and are thus locked out of certain political activities such as voting in most jurisdictions in the United States. In some local jurisdictions, however, noncitizens are eligible to vote in community and school board elections. Somerset, Barnesville, Takoma Park, Chevy Chase, and Martin's Additions, Maryland, for example, allow noncitizens to participate in local elections. Amherst, Massachusetts, recently voted as well to allow noncitizen suffrage at the local level. The school boards in New York City and Chicago also grant noncitizens the right to cast a ballot in school board elections. Certainly in these locales the potential electoral influence of native-born Asian Americans, when augmented by the participation of adult immigrants, citizen and noncitizen, is significantly expanded.[23]

Another way in which Asian Americans can counteract the attribution of foreignness toward most and the reality of noncitizenship status for many is through participation in local community-based groups, very few of which require citizenship as a precondition for involvement and the right to vote for boards and such. In Boston's Chinatown, for example, the elections of the influential Neighborhood Council are open to all adult residents of Massachusetts of Asian ancestry. In short, almost anyone can participate politically at the community level. There are virtually no formal restrictions related to citizenship status and age and few informal barriers such as language limitations.

"A participatory polity," Sidney Verba and Norman Nie observed in their landmark work, *Participation in America,* "may rest on a participatory society."[24] The process of developing and sharing experiences and traditions is vitally important in sustaining effective participation. It is at the local level where the greatest opportunities for cross-generational learning can take place and where memory resides. Aldon Morris communicates the flavor of this phenomenon in the African American community:

> The tradition of protest is transmitted across generations by older relatives, black educational institutions, churches, and protest organizations. Blacks interested in social change inevitably gravitate to this "protest community," where they hope to find solutions to a complex problem. Once the contact is made the newcomer becomes a link in the tradition. Thus, the tradition is perpetually rejuvenated by new blood.[25]

In urban centers with heavy concentrations of Asian Americans, Latinos, and African Americans, individuals and groups, by working together at the community level, increase the likelihood of interracial contacts and productive collaborations. They can address mutual concerns about economic and political empowerment through transracial structures. Coalition building and racially united blocs that include Asian Americans will enhance individual and collective clout. This close proximity, however, does not guarantee positive interactions, as some troubling experiences from New York to Los Angeles have demonstrated. Yet benefits will emerge from reaching across racial lines for shared political purposes at the community level.

Finally, a lesson learned from the fund-raising fiasco is that Asian American money contributed for political purposes can, with substantially less pain and most likely greater impact, be invested directly in Asian American causes and organizations. While it is unrealistic to expect all Asian Americans to forego what Der has described as the big time "money game," the redirection to Asian American communities of even a small fraction of the money spent on major candidates and political parties would greatly affect policies, programs, and political capacity-building and advocacy efforts. With more contributions, financially strapped organizations and individuals engaged in productive political work in Asian American communities could be strengthened enormously.

Undoubtedly, there are potential pitfalls in pursuing this indigenous-based strategy. Some people, for example, might contend that a refocus on building Asian American consciousness and structures might bolster familiar accusations of clannishness and unassimilability. Political resources focused back on the community might mean in some sense that Asian Americans are setting themselves apart.

To the extent that some degree of separation does occur, however, it must be remembered that this regrouping is largely a response to group-directed, collective portrayals and blanket mistreatment such as that manifested to an extraordinary degree in the fund-raising fiasco. Indeed, the search for alternative sites in which Asian Americans can construct meaningful political, social, and cultural identities is principally the product of the stifling contradictions of race and citizenship that often force Asian Americans to the margins of the political system and together as a group. While necessity is regularly invoked as a reason for assimilation, experiences of racism and prejudice also may necessitate the strengthening of ethnic-based identities and institutions. It is disturbingly ironic, and indeed disingenuous, that Asian Americans, who have been wrongly characterized as permanent foreigners, outsiders, political pariahs, and spies, would be condemned for seeking refuge and strength in their communities. This is a classic case of blaming and disempowering the victims.

By refocusing their energies on community-related structures and issues, Asian Americans may further racialize political issues and agendas. What may be different, however, is that nonwhite communities could be more consciously directed toward transcending the confines of reaction. Rather than following the usual course, in which initiatives emanate from the dominant power structure supported by strategies often built on the exploitation of racial fears and tensions, communities of color themselves may attempt to take the initiative and help to shape the boundaries of racial discourse. In other words, the burden of response, at least initially, could be shifted away from the shoulders of nonwhites. Although there is nothing either automatic or easy about the fulfillment of this dynamic, its realization, with the newly racialized politics emanating at least in part from empowered communities, would profoundly transform many contours of the political landscape.

CONCLUSION

In a hopeful parting thought as she concludes her analysis of mainstream Asian American political participation, Wendy Tam observes: "Asian American politics is at an exciting and critical time. The ensuing decades will see their [Asian Americans'] full emergence into the political process. The numbers are there. Apathy is now their last and greatest barrier."[26]

On the heels of the turbulent fund-raising experience, this is indeed an exciting and critical period for Asian Americans. Unfortunately, that experience offers ample evidence that barriers more formidable and more longstanding than just apathy may continue to retard the full emergence of Asian Americans in the political process. Despite the considerable sound and fury over claims that Asian Americans in various ways "took over" the political system during the 1996 elections, Asian Americans are far from "ruling" America, to use Domhoff's language. By heeding important lessons learned from the campaign finance scandal, however, Asian Americans can find some answers to the question: What must be done if Asian Americans ever wish to participate as they should in ruling America?

A solid and properly tended community base can be the crucial element in preparing for and sustaining political participation, including mainstream political interventions. Individuals and groups intent on strengthening their abilities to engage successfully in meaningful political pursuits at whatever level are well advised to recognize and, it is hoped, to build on the resources cultivated and experiences shared at the community level. Mobilizing their communities to address matters of health care, land development, housing, civil rights, social welfare, immigration, and a host of other areas is the responsibility of Asian Americans. Much of this activity at the community level is explicitly political and much, although less obviously so, is still immensely politically relevant—a reflection of what Sidney Verba, Kay Lehman Schlozman, and Henry Brady appropriately describe as "the embeddedness of political activity in the non-political institutions of civil society."[27]

In short, the primary lesson to be learned from the troubling fund-raising and related experiences is that Asian Americans intent on enhancing their political power and overall well-being must reenergize and refocus their attention on those parts of America—Asian American communities—that many of them are especially equipped by interest, skill, and experience to maintain, build, and protect.

NOTES

1. G. William Domhoff, *Who Rules America?* (Englewood Cliffs, N.J.: Prentice-Hall, 1967).

2. G. William Domhoff, *Who Rules America? Power and Politics in the Year 2000*, 3d ed. (Mountain View, Calif.: Mayfield Publishing, 1998).

3. Frank H. Wu and May Nicholson, "Have You No Decency? An Analysis of Racial Aspects of Media Coverage on the John Huang Matter," *Asian American Policy Review* 7 (1997): 1–37.

4. Ibid.

5. William Safire, "Follow Up the Cox Report," *New York Times*, May 27, 1999, A31.

6. See Paul Y. Watanabe, "Dismissed and Discredited: The Media's Response to Asian Pacific American Criticism," *Asian American Policy Review* 8 (1998): 64–67.

7. Angelo N. Ancheta, *Race, Rights, and the Asian American Experience* (New Brunswick, N.J.: Rutgers University Press, 1998), especially chap. 3.

8. Lisa Lowe, *Immigrant Acts: On Asian American Cultural Politics* (Durham: Duke University Press, 1996), 12.

9. Ancheta, *Race, Rights, and the Asian American Experience*, 47.

10. Joel Klotkin, "Asian-Americans Left Holding the Bag," *Wall Street Journal*, January 23, 1997.

11. John J. Miller, "Asian Americans Head for Politics: What Horse Will They Ride?" *American Enterprise* (March/April 1995): 58.

12. Quoted in Annie Nakao, "Asians' Political Image Marred," *San Francisco Examiner*, November 17, 1996.

13. Henry Der, "Don't Play the Money Game to Be Heard," *Los Angeles Times*, September 17, 1997.

14. Quoted in William Wong, "Asian-American Politics Complex," *Patriot Ledger*, December 12, 1997.

15. See Daphne Kwok and Robert Sakinawa, "How's This for Gratitude?" *New York Times*, March 21, 1997.

16. Quoted in Bruce Stokes, "Learning the Game," *National Journal*, October 22, 1988, 2653.

17. For a detailed discussion of these matters, see Paul Ong and Don T. Nakanishi, "Becoming Citizens, Becoming Voters: The Naturalization and Political Par-

ticipation of Asian Pacific Immigrants," in *The State of Asian Pacific America: Reframing the Immigration Debate,* ed. Bill Ong Hing and Ronald Lee (Los Angeles: LEAP Asian Pacific American Public Policy Institute and UCLA Asian American Studies Center, 1996), 275–305.

18. For a discussion, see Su Sun Bai, "Affirmative Pursuit of Political Equality for Asian Pacific Americans: Reclaiming the Voting Rights Act," *University of Pennsylvania Law Review* 139 (1991): 731–767.

19. Lani Guinier, "Keeping the Faith: Black Voters in the Post-Reagan Era," *Harvard Civil Rights Civil Liberties Law Review* 24 (1989): 393, 417.

20. William H. Flanigan and Nancy H. Zingale, *Political Behavior of the American Electorate,* 9th ed. (Washington, D.C.: CQ Press, 1998), 21.

21. Pei-te Lien, "Ethnicity and Political Participation: A Comparison between Asian and Mexican Americans," *Political Behavior* 16 (1994): 237–264.

22. Stephen S. Fugita and David J. O'Brien, *Japanese American Ethnicity: The Persistence of Community* (Seattle: University of Washington Press, 1991), 150–164.

23. For a discussion of "alien suffrage," see Jamin B. Raskin, "Legal Aliens, Local Citizens: The Historical, Constitutional and Theoretical Meanings of Alien Suffrage," *University of Pennsylvania Law Review* 141 (1993): 1391–1470; Gerald M. Rosburg, "Aliens and Equal Protection: Why Not the Right to Vote?" *Michigan Law Review* 75 (1977): 1092–1136; and Paul Tiao, "Non-citizen Suffrage: An Argument Based on the Voting Rights Act and Related Law," *Columbia Human Rights Review* 25 (1993): 171–218.

24. Sidney Verba and Norman H. Nie, *Participation in America: Political Democracy and Social Equality* (New York: Harper and Row, 1972), 3.

25. Aldon D. Morris, *The Origins of the Civil Rights Movement: Black Communities Organizing for Change* (New York: Free Press, 1984), 4.

26. Wendy K. Tam, "Asians—A Monolithic Voting Bloc?" *Political Behavior* 17 (1995): 247.

27. Sidney Verba, Kay Lehman Schlozman, and Henry E. Brady, *Voice and Equality: Civic Voluntarism in American Politics* (Cambridge: Harvard University Press, 1995), 40.

CHAPTER FIFTEEN

ASIAN AMERICANS AND MULTIRACIAL POLITICAL COALITIONS: NEW YORK CITY'S CHINATOWN AND REDISTRICTING, 1990–1991

LELAND T. SAITO

Asian Americans are the fastest-growing group in the United States, but even the major Asian American urban concentrations (outside of Hawaii) are too small to form a majority of voters within electoral districts and elect their own candidates without crossover votes. Developing alliances with other groups is a crucial issue for Asian American political power, which raises the question: What forms the foundation for political alliances with other racial minorities, whites, or both? Elevating the importance of this issue, the populations of major U.S. urban areas—such as Los Angeles, New York, and Houston—have changed dramatically over the last few decades because of immigration from Asia, Latin America, and the Caribbean. This demographic restructuring—from white majority to "majority-minority" cities—has created new possibilities for the construction of multiracial alliances and enhanced power for disenfranchised minorities. Yet as voters and elected officials whites continue to be the major political force in these areas, although that position is shifting with the growing power of minorities.

Using a case study of the redistricting that faced New York City's Chinatown in 1990–1991 and the elections that followed, this chapter examines the dialogue among community activists as they debated their options when faced with the need to add neighboring areas to fulfill district population requirements. The proposals that emerged offered two distinct scenarios: linking Chinatown with middle-class whites to the west and south and taking advantage of past electoral support for Asian American candidates, or joining with predominantly working-class Latinos and African Americans to the east and north based on a history of multiracial, grassroots political alliances.

Alliances among racial minorities have a long history in which the "politics of prejudice"[1] and explicitly racialized government policies became embedded in economic, political, and social relations and channeled Asian Americans, Latinos, African Americans, and Native Americans into similar occupational, residential, and political urban spaces, creating common interests and concerns.[2] In 1949, for example, Mexican American Edward Roybal utilized a grassroots alliance composed of Latinos, African Americans, Asian Americans, and whites to become the first Latino Los Angeles City Council member in the twentieth century.[3]

Racial minorities joining with whites to gain political incorporation is one of the dominant themes of contemporary urban politics.[4] Such efforts have been based on a shared ideology of social justice such as the civil rights movement,[5] or a convergence of interests such as when Jews and African Americans joined together to supplant entrenched white conservatives by electing African American Tom Bradley mayor of Los Angeles in 1973.[6]

The New York City redistricting process was documented through transcripts of public hearings, Districting Commission reports, city newspaper articles, and, after its completion, written reports by city and community participants. These detailed and contrasting accounts of the process, as well as interviews with community activists, are used here as a way of examining the participants' understandings and characterizations of race, politics, and government policies.

The dialogue reveals the complexity of local politics rooted in neighborhood history and issues, such as the gentrification of Chinatown, and the linkage of local politics to larger political and economic processes, such as international capital investment and deindustrialization supported by city policies. Moreover, it reveals that even though ethnically Chinatown is predominantly Chinese, participants spoke of themselves more broadly as "Asian Americans," linking their experiences and political analysis to local and national narratives of the political exclusion faced by Asian Americans. The redistricting conflict, however, also illuminates the heterogeneity of the Chinatown community, especially in terms of class and political ideology. A closer look at the view that Chinatown residents constitute a unified "community of interest" is thus required.

The spatial representation of race in the form of residential segregation and the use of race as a factor in creating districts stem directly from the history of economic, political, and social discrimination faced by racial minorities. Discriminatory practices were assisted by the massive government subsidies and support for the zoning and financial policies that generated and supported segregated communities.[7] Asian Americans, Latinos, and African Americans faced greater levels of segregation in that order,[8] with the result that Asian Americans were literally positioned between whites and other racial minorities in metropolitan areas throughout the United States, such as Los Angeles and New York.

In the redistricting deliberations, the dominant issues were, first, how to craft a district while taking into account the heterogeneity of Chinatown and, second, how to incorporate into the process the varied relations that Asian Americans have with other racial minorities and whites. In view of the fact that, as Joe Feagin and Hernan Vera suggest, white-on-black oppression established the U.S. racial framework, that it forms the foundation for the incorporation of other minority groups into U.S. society,[9] and that it dominates the present national conversation on race,[10] a growing debate has developed over the position of Asian Americans within that framework.[11] One scholar, in his discussion of Asian Americans as "between black and white," suggests that Asian Americans might become the next "whites" in order to preserve and maintain the cultural and political primacy of whites,[12] or in recognition of the impressive economic gains made by Asian Americans and their depiction as a "model minority." By contrast, other scholars maintain that historic and contemporary patterns of discrimination continue to position Asian Americans as a racialized minority, generating shared experiences with other minorities.[13]

Clearly, the shared history of issues such as residential segregation, political disenfranchisement, and discrimination in the labor market reveals the fundamental and central forces generating for racialized minorities the common experiences that transcend group boundaries. Discussions of the "relative" position of Asian Americans vis-à-vis whites and African Americans, however, obscure the historical and contemporary circumstances that generate significant differences in the experiences of racial minorities. For example, beyond the U.S. government practices that disenfranchised and subjugated all minorities, African Americans experienced the power of the state through such policies as slavery and Jim Crow laws, Mexican Americans in the Southwest bore the loss of land following the Mexican American War and forced repatriation in the 1930s and 1950s, Native Americans suffered genocide, and Asian Americans were denied the right to naturalization and were incarcerated during World War II. In addition, within the context of the U.S. black/white racial framework and the fundamental ways in which racialization as minorities links the experiences of minorities, factors such as nativism and U.S. military incursions in Asia have produced meaningful differences in the lived experiences of individuals at the neighborhood level for particular groups.[14]

This chapter focuses on relations between Latinos and Asian Americans, the two largest minority groups in lower Manhattan. These groups share factors—recent large immigrant populations, a history as laborers in the United States, their status as language minorities, among other things—that have generated common experiences. Relations between Asian Americans and Latinos have been marked both by alliances, such as in labor and the formation of the United Farm Workers by Filipinos and Mexicans,[15] and by conflict, such as the 1992 outbreak of civil unrest in Los Angeles and the destruction of Korean-owned businesses by Latinos (see Chapter 11).[16]

Redistricting exemplifies the way government policies have defined and reflected racial categories and the tremendous social, political, and economic implications of such policies.[17] In the redistricting case of New York City, the process was framed by lawsuits charging racial discrimination and violation of the U.S. Constitution in the city's electoral system, a single-member district electoral system (as compared with cumulative voting as one alternative), number of districts and the resulting population requirements, the U.S. Census undercount, and the process in which the Districting Committee created the boundaries.[18] These structural factors are important, but because of space limitations this chapter focuses on the discussion and activities generated and framed by these factors.

REDISTRICTING: CHINATOWN AND THE LOWER EAST SIDE

The Lower East Side of New York has historically housed the city's immigrants and working classes. The Irish and Germans employed in the shipbuilding industry in the mid-1800s were followed by Italians and Eastern European Jews in the garment industry in the 1920s. In the post–World War II industrial expansion, labor recruiters encouraged large-scale Puerto Rican migration to New York City.[19] From the 1820s to the 1870s, Chinese men trickled into New York City, by land from the west and by sea as ship crew members. Official counts list nineteen Chinese in 1870, and the population expanded rapidly over the next several decades, concentrating in what is now the Chinatown area.[20] Beginning in the late 1880s, a series of U.S. immigration quotas and exclusionary policies targeting Asians slowed population growth. The Chinese population totaled 6,000 in 1900 and 33,000 in 1960.[21] Chinese immigration rapidly increased after the Immigration and Nationality Act Amendments of 1965 (also known as the Hart-Cellar Act), which eliminated the restrictive policies, and the New York and Los Angeles metropolitan regions topped the list of favorite destination points.[22]

Considering the extreme scarcity of land in lower Manhattan and Chinatown's proximity to the financial district, civic center, and increasingly popular residential and entertainment districts such as SoHo, it is an invaluable site for new, up-scale development. With the growing local and international capital investment by both Chinese and non-Chinese in Chinatown, the struggle has intensified between those who view urban centers as "growth machines" and seek to maximize their real estate investments and those who rely on these areas as places of residence, work, recreation, and services which are threatened by such investment.[23] Economic development strategies directed at transforming downtown areas into "corporate centers" based on advanced services and entertainment proceed not simply through free market forces, but also with major support from local and federal government policies.[24]

Because low-income racial minorities have long absorbed a disproportionate share of the negative effects—loss of affordable housing and living wage jobs—of federal urban renewal programs, interstate highway construction, and local infrastructure projects,[25] Asian Americans in New York City clearly understood the need to gain political power to influence government policies that directly affect economic development, housing, and employment opportunities. In contemporary Chinatown, however, Chinese Americans were on both sides of the debate—as investors and developers and as working-class residents.[26]

In 1989, prompted by lawsuits charging racial discrimination and violation of the U.S. Constitution, the New York City charter was amended to increase the number of City Council districts from thirty-five to fifty-one, a change intended to increase the political representation of minorities.[27] From 1990 to 1991 the New York City Districting Commission created new council districts. At that time, no Asian American had ever been elected to the City Council or any citywide office. Because Chinatown and the neighboring Lower East Side contained the city's largest concentration of Asian

Americans, the area offered the greatest opportunity for Asian American representation.

A unique confluence of national and local events created a historical moment in which significant political change appeared likely. The judicial climate seemed to favor minority interests, if the recent landmark Voting Rights Act court cases won by racial minorities were any indication.[28] Also, New York City had to submit its plans to the U.S. Justice Department for preclearance because in the past it had employed procedures, such as the literacy tests the state had used in the 1960s, to circumscribe the political participation of racial minorities.[29] Practical matters favoring minorities included the increase in the number of council districts and the tremendous growth of the Asian American and Latino populations in the 1980s. Advances in computer hardware and software and the availability of demographic and political data (including a Public Access Terminal provided by the Districting Commission) allowed nongovernmental groups to carry out sophisticated data analysis.

Asian Americans in New York City directly linked efforts for political representation to local and national narratives of racial exclusion and hierarchy. Since the earliest history of the United States, political practices have had racial consequences. Such practices have been rooted in whites' privileged access to power, rewards, and opportunities.[30] During public hearings, Asian Americans enumerated the federal policies and practices that had specifically disenfranchised and discriminated against Asian Americans, such as exclusionary immigration laws, the denial of naturalization to early immigrants, the incarceration of Japanese Americans during World War II, and gerrymandered districts. Community activists used the panethnic label *Asian American* when recognizing the common racialization of the diverse Asian ethnic groups and the ethnic-specific term *Chinese American* for particular individuals or events.[31]

During the redistricting process, Rosa Koo, vice president of the New York City Chapter of the Organization of Chinese Americans, stated, "Historically, Chinese and Asian Americans have been ignored, misunderstood, discriminated, and denied the right to citizenship. WE are often the forgotten 'other' in statistics, and, left UNHEARD outside the door by elected officials and other policy-makers."[32] Margaret Chin, City Council candidate, administrator of the F. H. LaGuardia Community College Chinatown Center, and member of Asian Americans for Equality (AAFE, a Chinatown social service provider) expressed her hopes that the redistricting efforts would end exclusion:

You have the power in your hand to make the dreams of thousands of . . .
Asian American New Yorkers, to come true. . . . These new seats are like sixteen doors of opportunity swinging open for the minority communities of
the City. . . . It is the opportunity for real representation for communities that
have too long been under represented.[33]

Community activists agreed that uniting Chinatown within one district
was the principal goal, ending the spatial fragmentation and dilution of political power that had characterized past redistricting plans. Margaret Fung,
executive director of the Asian American Legal Defense and Education
Fund (AALDEF, a New York City legal advocacy organization), explained
that "the voting strength of Chinese Americans has been diluted because
Chinatown was divided into two state assembly districts. Moreover, Chinatown has also been split between two community board districts and two
school board districts. This . . . has merely reinforced our community's inability to organize and develop a political cohesiveness."[34]

The studies undertaken by the New York Chinatown History Project and
AAFE to develop the criteria needed to define Chinatown were presented to
the Districting Commission. The studies focused on population, housing,
schools, social services, employment, industry, organizations, and commercial enterprises.[35] It was determined that the "core of Chinatown" was contained in eight contiguous census tracts (6, 8, 16, 18, 25, 27, 29, 41) and that
Asian Americans made up about 80 percent of the population of that area.[36]
AALDEF outlined a similar area.[37]

The 1990 U.S. Census placed the city's population at 7,322,564 (6.7 percent Asian American, 24.4 percent Latino, 25.2 percent African American,
and 43.2 percent white). Thus each of the fifty-one new districts would require a population of approximately 143,579 (compared with 212,000 for
thirty-five districts). The eight census tracts containing Chinatown had a
population of 62,895, which fell short of the district requirement by approximately 80,000. Before the release of the 1990 census data, community
organizations had estimated that Chinatown was home to between 100,000
to 150,000 inhabitants based on the number of housing units and average
occupancy.[38] One Districting Commission member reported that the U.S.
Census Bureau suggested that New York City's Asian Americans were un-
dercounted by about 18 percent.[39] One other factor in the redistricting process: the Charter Revision Commission's decision in 1989 to increase the
number of council districts from thirty-five to fifty-one had disregarded
AALDEF's proposal to increase the number of districts to a minimum of

sixty.[40] While the impacts of the undercount and the number of districts may have been minimal taken separately, they added to the sedimentation of political inequality faced by Asian Americans.

The Two Competing Plans

The decision over which areas should be added to Chinatown to meet the population requirement was the fundamental issue that divided Chinatown activists. Two competing plans emerged in the debate, offering contrasting alternatives for Chinatown and its relation to the predominantly Puerto Rican neighborhood to the north and east and the white areas to the west and south. One plan emphasized "descriptive representation"[41] and the historic opportunity to elect an Asian American; the other supported a multiracial district based on similar political interests generated by the intersection of race, class, and neighborhood conditions. These appeals to the commission went beyond the traditional definitions of enfranchisement for racial minorities that focused on citizenship, voter registration, and voter turnout.[42] They defined political power as the ability to elect officials who could enact policies on behalf of their constituents.[43]

Members of AAFE led the effort for a district based on descriptive representation. Election of an Asian American to the City Council represented a genuine and concrete political gain, not merely a symbolic gesture such as a city festival for diversity. Members of AAFE characterized redistricting and the upcoming election jointly as a pivotal moment that could mark the end of political exclusion.

For advocates of the AAFE plan, an Asian American elected official signified representation—that is, a co-ethnic whose background was similar to those of his or her constituents, who was knowledgeable about and supportive of community issues, who had political mobility into the mainstream, and who would serve as a role model. Virginia Kee, president of the Chinese American Planning Council, stated at a public hearing, "As a teacher, I can tell you that our young people must see their own faces in their government. If, in this decade, we are still without representation, then how can this city government work for us?"[44]

Members of AAFE, using data from elections in which Asian Americans had participated, crafted a district in which they believed an Asian American could win. Because Asian Americans did not have the numbers to elect a candidate on their own, AAFE understood that a successful campaign would require the support of a multiracial coalition of voters, and it considered areas where such efforts have succeeded. The AAFE plan, then, built on the strengths of Margaret Chin, who was a member of Community Board 1 and who had been elected twice in the 1980s to the Democratic State Committee in that area. As Koo observed: "For an Asian American to win, he or she must build on the strength of a coalition of voters supportive of, and proven to have elected, minority candidates in the past. . . . Our objective is not to look for districts where Asians did well. Our objective is to look for districts where Asians have *won*."[45]

With this in mind, AAFE proposed that the core of Chinatown be joined with areas to the west and south—that is, SoHo, City Hall, Tribeca, and Battery Park City. It pointed out that "Asian candidates have done better than white candidates in the area West of Core, where one would assume white candidates with a liberal agenda would traditionally be at their best."[46] AAFE ruled out the areas to the east of Chinatown because its data analysis showed that Asian American candidates did poorly there in local elections.[47] Describing the social networks that linked the neighborhoods in the proposed district, Doris Koo pointed out that in areas beyond Chinatown schools had high percentages of Asian American students, neighborhood services were available such as a senior citizen center and hospitals, and a growing number of Asian-owned businesses and manufacturers were providing employment for Chinatown residents.[48]

An alternative to AAFE's plan was developed by a variety of community activists and organizations, including AALDEF, the Community Service Society, and the Puerto Rican Legal Defense and Education Fund (PRLDEF). Recognizing that no single ethnic or racial group in the area was large enough to constitute 50 percent or more of a district, residents formed an organization—Lower East Siders for a Multi-racial District—which proposed a plan that would create a majority Latino, Asian American, and African American district based on the needs and interests of low-income and working-class residents.[49] The proposed district incorporated the bulk of the minorities' communities in the area and took into account population growth trends. The Multi-racial District group described the new district:

> The ethnic breakdown is as follows: Asians: 37%, Latinos: 34% and African-Americans 13% (total 84%). The district includes over 94% of the total Latino population below 14th Street, 96% of the Asian and 91% of the African-American population. In addition, it seeks to incorporate areas in which both Asian and Latino populations will continue to grow and expand.[50]

Elaine Chan, a member of the Multi-racial District organization, a City Council candidate who withdrew from the race, and the coordinator of the Lower East Side Joint Planning Council, a housing advocacy group, explained that "Asians, Latinos, and African Americans have had a historic working relationship on issues of common concern: housing, health care, immigration, day care, bilingual education, affordable commercial space, job training, and general quality of life issues."[51] Chan also stressed the long history of multiracial activism in the area and how that defined and reinforced a tightly knit political community: "We represent more than thirty organizations on the Lower East Side that advocate for decent and affordable housing. Our plan, the United District, calls for a council district that closely resembles traditional Lower East Side boundaries as delineated by the parameters of Community Board 3."[52] In addition, Chan refuted the assumption that Latinos would not vote for Asian Americans, noting that Latinos supported two Asian American candidates in the 1987 judicial race.[53]

Offering her interpretation of descriptive representation versus community empowerment, Mini Liu, a member of the Multi-racial District group, stated, "Yes, we want minority representatives. But we want minority representatives who are accountable to the Asians and Latinos on the Lower East Side, not just Asian and Latino faces in City Council, representing white middle and upper class interests."[54]

Margarita Lopez, a housing activist since she moved to the Lower East Side in 1978 from her native Puerto Rico and a member of the Multi-racial District group, identified the battle over real estate and gentrification (the movement of higher-income residents into low-income neighborhoods with a concomitant increase in property values)[55] as one of the community's critical issues: "The Lower East Side has a key geographic position in Manhattan. [It is next to] the financial center of the world. The Lower East Side is as close to Wall Street as you walking there with your own feet and you don't have to pay for transportation. . . . It's not just prime real estate, it's the dream of anyone who is a high executive."[56]

Wing Lam, a member of the Chinese Staff and Workers Association and a supporter of the Multi-racial District plan—underscored the importance of housing as a factor uniting the residents of Chinatown and the Lower East Side. Lam explained that the "Lower East Side people know that if the developers can gentrify us (Chinatown), they can go east, we are the front line."[57] Signs of the transformation and diversification of the economy in Chinatown were the increasing numbers of overseas and local Chinese banks, the construction of office buildings, and the opening of professional offices—such as law and accounting firms.[58] Rather than arising simply from free-market processes, gentrification in the Lower East Side and Chinatown had progressed with the aid of city government policies that favored and subsidized development, such as tax incentives, zoning variations, loans, and city staff assistance.[59]

To receive public input on the redistricting, the Districting Commission held twenty-seven well-attended public hearings throughout the city in 1990 and 1991, and the commission outreach staff claimed to have organized more than four hundred meetings. At the hearings, Antonio Pagan, director of Coalition Housing which built low- and moderate-income housing and a Puerto Rican candidate for City Council in the Lower East Side, supported separate Asian American and Latino districts, stating that he was "emphatically in favor and supportive of the creation of a Chinese seat or Asian seat at this moment . . . but we want to be able to elect our own."[60]

Later, in 1993, Latinos and Asian Americans would work together successfully in Oakland, California, to support the creation of separate Asian American and Latino influence City Council districts. Meanwhile, in 1991 they were working together in the San Gabriel Valley of Los Angeles County to create state assembly and senate districts that joined their populations.[61] In contrast with New York, in the San Gabriel Valley Latinos had supported Asian American candidates, whereas whites in the prospective areas had not. In fact, the white areas were marked by hate crimes against Asian Americans. The San Gabriel Valley Latino and Asian American populations varied greatly, especially in terms of class and political ideology, but the two groups had large, professional middle classes that had forged a common political agenda, in contrast to the more heavily working-class and low-income Asian American and Latino populations on New York's Lower East Side.[62]

According to Districting Commission executive director Alan Gartner, when the commission finally created the boundaries of the new district, they considered what they believed the majority of the Asian American community favored—that is, they disengaged the Asian American and Latino populations.[63] The commission stated that there was little statistical evidence that Asian Americans and Latinos would jointly support a candidate. Judith Reed, general counsel to the Districting Commission, wrote in a July 17, 1991, letter to the Department of Justice: "Statistical analyses concerning political cohesion were inconclusive. The issue came to rest squarely in the realm of judgment." In Gartner's judgment, AAFE had become "the dominant player in the Asian American community. . . . The careful and comprehensive presentations of AAFE's executive director, Doris Koo, impressed the Commission and staff." As a result, the commission gave serious consideration to AAFE's data showing white support for Asian American candidates.[64]

Having considered the local dynamics, as Gartner explained, "Ultimately, the Districting Commission opted to craft a district designed to offer the only opportunity in the city to the Asian-American community to elect a candidate of its choice." The Districting Commission joined Chinatown with areas to the west. Gartner went on to note that "the Commission hoped that a strong Asian-American candidate, with the support of the white, liberal areas surrounding Chinatown, could be elected."[65]

According to Judith Reed, however, others affiliated with the commission believed that public testimony clearly favored a multiracial district, contradicting Gartner's interpretation of events.

> Indeed, the commission's deputy counsel, Joseph Diaz, was so convinced that the public had indicated a preference for a lower Manhattan district that combined Latinos of the lower east side and Asians of Chinatown, that after one public hearing dedicated primarily to district 1, he mused: "Well, we know what the public wants, I wonder how the commissioners will respond?"[66]

Margarita Lopez asserted that the Districting Commission ignored evidence presented by the Multi-racial District organization that clearly demonstrated Latino support for Asian Americans, such as the successful efforts of Latinos to increase the number of Asian Americans on Community Board 3.[67]

Approved by the U.S. Justice Department on July 26, 1991, the districting plan joined Chinatown with areas to the west and created District 1 in which Asian Americans were the largest group with 39.2 percent of the population, but made up only 14.2 percent of registered voters. By contrast, whites made up 37.2 percent of the population but 61.5 percent of registered voters, Latinos 17.4 of the population and 15.5 percent of voters, and African Americans 5.8 percent of the population and 8.8 percent of voters. In new District 2 on the Lower East Side, Latinos made up 25.2 percent of the population and 18.4 percent of registered voters, whites 59.3 percent of the population and 71 percent of registered voters, African Americans 8.0 percent of the population and 8.1 percent of voters, and Asian Americans 7.1 percent of the population and 2.3 percent of voters.[68]

CITY COUNCIL ELECTIONS

In District 2, Antonio Pagan, by narrowly defeating incumbent Miriam Friedlander, emerged as the victor in the 1991 elections. During his campaign, he advocated community safety, Puerto Rican empowerment, and his work promoting affordable housing. His detractors argued that his efforts were intended to support the interests of real estate developers.[69] Pagan's election increased minority representation on the City Council, a major goal of the commission.

Divisions in Chinatown did not run neatly along racial or class lines, but originated from a complex and often contradictory mixture of group and personal interests and histories that carried over into the redistricting dialogue and the elections that followed. From the perspective of many Asian Americans, District 1 was inextricably linked with AAFE and its council candidate, Margaret Chin. After all, the organization had created and supported the general guidelines for the formation of the district.

AAFE was born in 1974 out of efforts to force contractors to comply with city policies on minority employment and hire Asian Americans for the construction of Confucius Plaza in Chinatown. Since then, it had provided a range of community services, such as building and renovating affordable housing, filing the *AAFE v. Koch* lawsuit (1983) to counter gentrification, offering information and training to small business owners, and enforcing tenant rights.[70] Critics of AAFE charged that, from its indisputable progressive and community roots, the organization had become a developer intent on following its own agenda[71] and that it had unilaterally put forth its redistricting plan reinforcing that image. AAFE's support in 1982 of Chinatown garment subcontractors against workers and the charges it had used a subcontractor who paid below the minimum wage supported the view that the organization had strayed from its original mission.[72] Chin also was criticized for accepting campaign contributions from developers and garment manufacturers and for crossing a labor picket line in 1991.

Kathryn Freed, Chin's major opponent for the District 1 City Council seat, was the former chair of Community Board 1 and an attorney with a history of working for tenants' rights and affordable housing. Yet Wayne Barrett of the *Village Voice* contended that Freed also had attended a dinner sponsored by the group that Chin was criticized for supporting because of its labor problems and that Freed also received contributions from real estate interests and garment manufacturers.[73]

During the election campaign, opponents of the AAFE plan asserted that the low-income inhabitants of Chinatown had little in common with the affluent whites to the west. Wing Lam of the Chinese Staff and Workers Association claimed that "by merging with the west, AAFE essentially sold the poor and working class of Chinatown down the drain."[74] In recent decades, economic restructuring and deindustrialization, characterized by a shift from the production of goods to the production of services, have transformed major U.S. urban areas, including a loss of unionized manufacturing jobs which provided living wages and benefits, contributing to increasing income inequality and poverty.[75] New York City's manufacturing employment decreased by two-thirds from 1950 to 1989, a reduction of 680,000 jobs, and dropped from 30 to 10 percent of the city's employment.[76] Deindustrialization, which has had a substantial impact on Puerto Ricans because of their historically high participation rates in manufacturing, has created a range of both problems and opportunities for Chinatown's more heterogeneous population.[77] In Lower Manhattan, garment factories and restaurants are the major employers of working-class Chinese Americans.[78] The exodus of manufacturing left empty buildings and lowered rents which benefited garment manufacturers.[79] The Chinatown Land Use and Planning Study (1992) cautioned, however, that increased office development threatened both restaurants and garment factories by driving rents up.[80]

Margaret Chin strongly disagreed with the characterization of Chinatown and the West Side, suggesting that the residents were joined by real material interests:

> A lot of them (on the West Side) send their kids to Chinatown schools. There is also a natural connection in terms of traffic problems and sanitation. When you talk about housing, everybody thinks that people on the West Side all live in luxury housing. Not true. There is government subsidized housing which have the same tenant issues as Chinatown.[81]

Although racial minorities have formed alliances with white liberals to elect minority candidates a convergence of interests, the driving force of such coalitions,[82] did not frame District 1 events. Chin was unable to gain crucial West Side support for her candidacy.[83] The influential Soho Alliance argued that "problems on the West Side—overdevelopment, the waterfront, the West Side Highway, loft laws, historic districts . . . have little in common with the Chinatown community's woes, such as the need for affordable housing, jobs and education programs."[84]

The rapid growth of Chinatown received little campaign attention, although the long, and often heated, history of negotiations over the preservation of Little Italy continued as a major dividing issue. The Committee Against Anti-Asian Violence (CAAAV), a community advocacy group located on the Lower East Side, reported that white residents, merchants, and real estate developers in Little Italy and SoHo had employed complaints to the police and city agencies and lawsuits to harass and close down Asian wholesale vegetable and fish merchants to restrict the growth of Chinatown.[85]

Although it was not a major campaign issue, police brutality further divided whites and Asian Americans. Asian Americans were concerned about crime, but they wanted crime control without biased harassment. CAAAV was formed in 1986, working with Latinos and African Americans, to address this issue, including investigations of Asian Americans killed, beaten, or verbally abused with racial epithets by police.[86] Data in a 1994 national report revealed that in New York City "the main perpetrator of suspected and/or racially motivated violence against Asian Pacific Americans is the police."[87]

Although New York City's Democratic Party had declined in power and its local structure was highly fragmented, it continued to exert a strong influence on community politics, unlike politics in California shaped by the reform movement.[88] Considering the way ethnic and racial groups had used the party historically to gain power while keeping others out,[89] or the way the Democratic Party had granted limited concessions to African Americans and Latinos,[90] it may have been unrealistic to expect West Side whites to forego power to help Asian Americans in Chinatown. Freed gained the endorsement of several key Democratic groups, including the Downtown Independent Democrats with its critical base in the West Side and the Democratic leaders of the Assembly district in the area; Chin received support primarily from the Village Independent Democrats.[91] Because of Freed's support for low-income housing, employment issues, and multiracial coalition building, she received the backing of the Asian American Union for Political Action, whose members included supporters of the multiracial district.[92]

In the Democratic primary, Freed emerged the victor with 42 percent of the vote to Chin's 31 percent. Freed was elected with 53 percent of the vote in the 1991 general election, Chin received 24 percent running on the Liberal Party ticket, and Republican Fred Teng received 23 percent. Teng, former board president of the Chinatown Planning Council, received support from segments of the Chinatown business community. Although Asian Americans in Chinatown voted overwhelmingly for Asian American representation, an exit poll conducted by AALDEF revealed the heterogeneity of the community.[93] According to its survey of 507 Asian Americans (predominantly Chinese) in Chinatown, 43.8 percent voted for Chin, 38.3 percent for Teng, 5.6 percent for Freed, and 12.2 percent declined to state or voted for another candidate.[94]

CONCLUSION

Although the Districting Commission crafted District 1 to support Asian American descriptive representation, the electoral reality was a district dominated by white voters. Margaret Chin attempted to build a campaign that went beyond Asian Americans, recognizing that white voters had supported Asian American candidates in previous local elections. But Chin's campaign apparently had not laid the groundwork needed to gain the endorsement of key West Side community leaders and also failed to generate compelling issues that would win the support of a majority of voters. In hindsight, the Districting Commission's reading of possible white support for Margaret Chin did not adequately consider interests in Chinatown, such as affordable housing and employment, that West Side residents did not share. Also, major concerns divided the two areas, such as the conflict over the expansion of Chinatown into the West Side. Clearly, many whites crossed over and voted for Chin because Chinatown had a low voter turnout and only about 14 percent of the district's electorate was Asian American. Other white voters, however, unlike in 1986 and 1988 when they supported Chin's election wins as Democratic Party State Committee representative, apparently were reluctant to elect her to the much more significant position of council member.

Freed's efforts to gain Asian American backing and her support of working-class issues transcended narrowly defined racial and neighborhood politics and demonstrated the importance of building a larger, more inclusive base and political platform that represented a range of interests. Also, Chinatown was kept intact and not fragmented among different districts, a key goal of the multiracial district advocates and AAFE. On the other hand, Freed's election was not a complete victory for backers of the multiracial district, even though some of its supporters had endorsed Freed.

The central concern that had driven their plans was the preservation and reinforcement of the political community generated from the history of alliances in the Chinatown/Lower East Side region—a community now fragmented by the boundaries of Districts 1 and 2.

The members of the Districting Commission emphasized racial boundaries, labels for Asian Americans and Latinos, and past white support for Asian American candidates. Implied in the commission's analysis was that whites would recognize the merits of Asian American political representation and would support a qualified Asian American candidate. This viewpoint, however, did not adequately consider the "racial" identity of whites and the active support of white racial privilege through the historic and contemporary practices of political exclusion employed by whites against racial minorities.[95] Certainly whites have joined with racial minorities to elect minorities, but they have done that primarily when progressive whites need allies to supplant an entrenched group,[96] not when they are a voting majority such as in District 1.

Any suggestion that Asian Americans will be the "next whites," following the pattern of acceptance of formerly nonwhite groups, such as southern and Eastern Europeans,[97] favors an assimilation model of political integration[98] that ignores the "color line" and the fundamentally different racial experiences of Native Americans and groups from Asia, Latin America, and Africa. While white voters have elected Asian Americans—such as California members of Congress Robert Matsui and Norman Mineta, and Washington governor Gary Locke—these politicians generally have run "deracialized" campaigns to attract all voters in areas with low numbers of Asian Americans.[99] I suggest, however, that the racial identity of candidates gains added importance when a minority population becomes significant. At this "tipping point"[100] the political importance of race is amplified when neighborhood interests and race create distinct communities—such as in District 1 where Asian Americans and the Soho Alliance had clear differences over issues. As a result, whites "see" a minority candidate as inextricably linked to his or her ethnic community, whether or not such a connection actually exists, as opposed to a candidate who will represent the entire district. In the case of Margaret Chin, any failings of her campaign to win over white voters may have been unimportant in a council race explicitly framed by race. The history of minority disenfranchisement was in full public view through the lawsuits that generated the charter amendments and the public discussion on the need for City Council minority representation.

Given the increasing heterogeneity of the Asian American community in terms of factors such as class, nativity, and political ideology, is race a viable category for the construction of districts? The explicitly racialized government policies that are embedded in economic, political, and social relations, and thereby negatively affect minorities, are a major basis for the political importance of race, ethnicity, and class.[101] Understanding the history of political and economic exclusion faced by Asian Americans locally and nationally, Asian Americans in Chinatown voted overwhelmingly for Asian American representation. And, while some whites crossed over to support the Asian American candidates, the majority did not.

The racial politics of lower Manhattan demonstrates that what it means to be "Asian American," "Latino," or "white" is highly situational and multilayered. The personal meaning that emerges from the local context is linked with larger social and economic factors, giving racial identities complex material meaning and consequences. Voters in the City Council elections considered neighborhood issues—such as the personal histories of the candidates and the organizations that supported them, changing demographics, efforts to slow the growth of Chinatown, and gentrification—and the connection between these neighborhood issues and large-scale considerations, such as the history of political exclusion faced by Asian Americans, the global flow of capital and economic development, and city policies supporting gentrification in Chinatown.

The debate over what areas to add to Chinatown revealed the complexity and heterogeneity of the Chinatown community. Yet the complex and varied deliberations within Chinatown—such as the delicate negotiation and compromise within a community over which agenda would be supported through the person elected—could not be contested by Asian Americans through the ballot box. Instead, the entire effort was mediated through the dominant political voice, white voters.

Asian Americans joined in their support of a Chinatown united within a district—as did Asian Americans in the San Gabriel Valley and Oakland—but because limitations were imposed by the census undercount and the number of districts, and because the Asian American population was dispersed and relatively small, a majority Asian American district was impossible. The Voting Rights Act of 1965 was primarily designed to enfranchise African Americans in the South. With their much larger and more highly segregated populations compared with Asian Americans, African Americans, Latinos, and whites in New York City have been better served by single-member districts as the New York City Council elections demonstrated. Suggestions for alternative electoral systems that would allow greater opportunity for smaller and more dispersed populations to elect candidates of their choice should be considered. Gaining support, for example, is cumulative voting, in which voters can cast as many votes as there are open seats and can strategically use those votes by spreading them among the candidates or using all of their votes for one candidate.[102]

NOTES

1. Roger Daniels, *The Politics of Prejudice* (Berkeley: University of California Press, 1962).

2. George Lipsitz, *The Possessive Investment in Whiteness: How White People Profit from Identity Politics* (Philadelphia: Temple University Press, 1988).

3. Katherine Underwood, "Process and Politics: Multiracial Electoral Coalition Building and Representation in Los Angeles' Ninth District, 1949–1962," Ph.D. dissertation, University of California, San Diego, 1992.

4. Rufus P. Browning, Dale Rogers Marshall, and David H. Tabb, *Protest Is Not Enough* (Berkeley: University of California Press, 1984).

5. Aldon D. Morris, *The Origins of the Civil Rights Movement* (New York: Free Press, 1984).

6. Raphael J. Sonenshein, *Politics in Black and White: Race and Power in Los Angeles* (Princeton: Princeton University Press, 1993).

7. Kenneth Jackson, *Crabgrass Frontier: The Suburbanization of the United States* (New York: Oxford University Press, 1985); Douglas S. Massey and Nancy A. Denton, *American Apartheid* (Cambridge: Harvard University Press, 1993); and Melvin L. Oliver and Thomas M. Shapiro, *Black Wealth/White Wealth: A New Perspective on Racial Inequality* (New York: Routledge, 1995).

8. John R. Logan, Richard D. Alba, and Shu-Yin Leung, "Minority Access to White Suburbs: A Multiregional Comparison," *Social Forces* 74 (1996): 851–881.

9. Joe R. Feagin and Hernan Vera, *White Racism* (New York: Routledge, 1995).

10. Andrew Hacker, *Two Nations: Black and White, Separate, Hostile, Unequal* (New York: Scribner's, 1992).

11. Edward J. W. Park, "Our L.A.? Korean Americans in Los Angeles after the Civil Unrest," in *Rethinking Los Angeles,* ed. Michael J. Dear, H. Eric Schockman, and Greg Hise (Thousand Oaks, Calif.: Sage Publications, 1996), 153–168; Edward J. W. Park and John S. W. Park, "A New American Dilemma? Asian Americans and Latinos in Race Theorizing," *Journal of Asian American Studies* 2 (1999): 289–309; Kyeyoung Park, "Use and Abuse of Race and Culture: Black-Korean Tension in America," *American Anthropologist* 98 (1996): 492–499; and Mia Tuan, *Forever Foreigners or Honorary Whites?* (New Brunswick, N.J.: Rutgers University Press, 1998).

12. Herbert Gans, "Symbolic Ethnicity and Symbolic Religiosity: Towards a Comparison of Ethnic and Religious Acculturation," *Ethnic and Racial Studies* 17 (1994): 577–592.

13. Lisa Lowe, *Immigrant Acts: On Asian American Cultural Politics* (Durham, N.C.: Duke University Press, 1996).

14. Angelo N. Ancheta, *Race, Rights, and the Asian American Experience* (New Brunswick, N.J.: Rutgers University Press, 1998); and Gary Y. Okihiro, *Margins and Mainstreams: Asians in American History and Culture* (Seattle: University of Washington Press, 1994).

15. Tomas Almaguer, *Racial Fault Lines: The Historical Origins of White Supremacy in California* (Berkeley: University of California Press, 1994); Yuji Ichioka, *The Issei: The World of the First Generation Japanese Immigrants, 1885–1924* (New York: Free Press, 1988); and Craig Scharlin and Lilia V. Villanueva, *Philip Vera Cruz* (Los Angeles: UCLA Labor Center, Institute of Industrial Relations, and Asian American Studies Center, 1992).

16. Armando Navarro, "The South Central Los Angeles Eruption: A Latino Perspective," *Amerasia Journal* 19 (1993): 69–85.

17. Chandler Davidson and Bernard Grofman, *Quiet Revolution in the South* (Princeton: Princeton University Press, 1994); Bernard Grofman and Chandler Davidson, *Controversies in Minority Voting: The Voting Rights Act in Perspective* (Washington, D.C.: Brookings, 1992); and Lani Guinier, *The Tyranny of the Majority* (New York: Free Press, 1994).

18. Alan Gartner, "Drawing the Lines: Redistricting and the Politics of Racial Succession in New York," unpublished monograph, Graduate School and University Center, City University of New York, 1993; Frank J. Macchiarola and Joseph G. Diaz, "Minority Political Empowerment in New York City: Beyond the Voting Rights Act," *Political Science Quarterly* 108 (1993): 37–57; and Judith Reed, "Of Boroughs, Boundaries and Bullwinkles: The Limitations of Single-Member Districts in a Multiracial Context," *Fordham Urban Law Journal* 19 (1992): 759–780.

19. Sherrie Baver, "Puerto Rican Politics in New York City: The Post–World War II Period," in *Puerto Rican Politics in Urban America*, ed. James Jennings and Monte Rivera (Westport, Conn.: Greenwood Press, 1984), 43–59; and Christopher Mele, "Neighborhood 'Burn-Out': Puerto Ricans at the End of the Queue," in *From Urban Village to East Village: The Battle for New York's Lower East Side*, ed. Janet L. Abu-Lughod (Cambridge: Blackwell, 1994), 126–140.

20. Jan Lin, *Reconstructing Chinatown: Ethnic Enclave, Global Change* (Minneapolis: University of Minnesota Press, 1998).

21. Roger Waldinger and Yen Fen Tseng, "Divergent Diasporas: The Chinese Communities of New York and Los Angeles Compared," *Revue Europénne des Migrations Internationales* 8 (1992): 91–115.

22. Timothy P. Fong, *The First Suburban Chinatown* (Philadelphia: Temple University Press, 1994).

23. John R. Logan and Harvey Molotch, *Urban Fortunes: The Political Economy of Place* (Berkeley: University of California Press, 1987).

24. Joe R. Feagin, *Free Enterprise City: Houston in Political Economic Perspective* (New Brunswick, N.J.: Rutgers University Press, 1988); Mark Gottdiener, *The Decline of Urban Politics: Political Theory and the Crisis of the Local State* (Beverly Hills, Calif.: Sage Publications, 1987); Marc V. Levine, "Downtown Redevelopment as an Urban Growth Strategy: A Critical Appraisal of the Baltimore Renaissance," *Journal of Urban Affairs* 9 (1987): 103–123; John H. Mollenkopf, *The Contested City* (Princeton: Princeton University Press, 1983); and John H. Mollenkopf, *A Phoenix in the Ashes: The Rise and Fall of the Koch Coalition in New York City Politics* (Princeton: Princeton University Press, 1992).

25. Martin Anderson, *The Federal Bulldozer: A Critical Analysis of Urban Renewal, 1949–1962* (Cambridge: MIT Press, 1964); Robert A. Caro, *The Power Broker: Robert Moses and the Fall of New York* (New York: Vintage Books, 1975); Robert Fitch, *The Assassination of New York* (New York: Verso, 1993); John M. Levy, *Contemporary Urban Planning* (Englewood Cliffs, N.J.: Prentice Hall, 1991); Raymond A. Mohl, "Race and Space in the Modern City: Interstate-95 and the Black Community in Miami," in *Urban Policy in Twentieth-Century America,* ed. Arnold R. Hirsch and Raymond A. Mohl (New Brunswick, N.J.: Rutgers University Press, 1993), 100–158; and Joel Schwartz, *The New York Approach: Robert Moses, Urban Liberals, and the Redevelopment of the Inner City* (Columbus: Ohio State University Press, 1993).

26. Lin, *Reconstructing Chinatown.*

27. In the early 1980s lawsuits were filed charging the city with discrimination against African American and Latino voters—see Frank J. Mauro, ed., *Restructuring the New York City Government: The Reemergence of Municipal Reform* (New York: Academy of Political Science, 1989). In response, Mayor Ed Koch formed a Charter Revision Commission, and it recommended elimination of the Board of Estimate, the transfer of its authority to the mayor and the City Council, and an increase in the number of council seats. A 1989 citywide vote approved these recommendations.

28. This would quickly change, however. For example, in *Shaw v. Reno* (1993) and *Miller v. Johnson* (1995) the U.S. Supreme Court ruled that the Constitution does not allow for the use of race as the "predominant" factor when drawing up districts, especially odd-looking or "bizarre" configurations (see Levin Sy, "Voting Rights Timeline," in *National Asian Pacific American Political Almanac,* ed. Don T. Nakanishi (Los Angeles: UCLA Asian American Studies Center, 1996), 175–179.

29. New York City Districting Commission, "A Short History of the Reapportionment of the City Council," in Appendix 1, "Submission under Section 5 of the Voting Rights Act for Preclearance of 1991 Redistricting Plan for New York City Council," 1991, p. 8, no. 19. Districting plans were submitted to the U.S. Justice Department on June 17.

30. Ruth Frankenberg, *The Social Construction of Whiteness: White Women, Race Matters* (Minneapolis: University of Minnesota Press, 1993); Lipsitz, *Possessive In-*

vestment in Whiteness; and David Roediger, *The Wages of Whiteness: Race and the Making of the American Working Class* (New York: Verso, 1991).

31. Yen L. Espiritu, *Asian American Panethnicity: Bridging Institutions and Identities* (Philadelphia: Temple University Press, 1992); Leland T. Saito, *Race and Politics: Asian Americans, Latinos, and Whites in a Los Angeles Suburb* (Urbana: University of Illinois Press, 1998); and Linda Trinh Vo, "Asian Immigrants, Asian Americans, and the Politics of Economic Mobilization in San Diego," *Amerasia Journal* 22 (1996): 89–108.

32. Rosa Koo, written testimony delivered to the New York City Districting Commission, November 1, 1990, Appendix 3, Vol. 2.

33. Margaret Chin, oral testimony delivered to the New York City Districting Commission, November 1, 1990, Appendix 3, Vol. 2, 127.

34. Margaret Fung, written testimony delivered to the New York City Districting Commission, November 1, 1990, Appendix 3, Vol. 2.

35. New York Chinatown History Project, written testimony delivered to the New York City Districting Commission, November 1, 1990, Appendix 3, Vol. 2; and Doris Koo, written testimony delivered to the New York City Districting Commission, November 1, 1990, Appendix 3, Vol. 2.

36. Koo, written testimony delivered to the New York City Districting Commission, November 1, 1990, Appendix 3, Vol. 2.

37. With the exception of census tract 18, which is on the northern edge of Chinatown. See Margaret Fung, written testimony delivered to the New York City Districting Commission, March 27, 1991, Appendix 3, Vol. 7.

38. Chinatown Voter Education Alliance (see Nancy Lam, Chinatown Voter Education Alliance, written testimony delivered to the New York City Districting Commission, November 1, 1990, Appendix 3, Vol. 2); New York Chinatown History Project (see New York Chinatown History Project, written testimony delivered to the New York City Districting Commission, November 1, 1990, Appendix 3, Vol. 2); AAFE, *Asian Americans for Equality: 1974–1994* (New York: AAFE, n.d.); and Koo, written testimony delivered to the New York City Districting Commission, November 1, 1990, Appendix 3, Vol. 2.

39. Ken Chin, transcript of New York City Districting Commission meeting, July 25, 1991, 20.

40. Margaret Fung, written testimony delivered to the New York City Districting Commission, March 27, 1991, Appendix 3, Vol. 7. For a discussion of the charter revision process in New York City, see Douglas Muzzio and Tim Tompkins, "On the Size of City Council: Finding the Mean," in *Restructuring the New York City Government: The Reemergence of Municipal Reform,* ed. Frank J. Mauro (New York: Academy of Political Science, 1989), 83–96.

41. Hanna Fenichel Pitkin, *The Concept of Representation* (Berkeley: University of California Press, 1967).

42. Abigail M. Thernstrom, *Whose Votes Count? Affirmative Action and Minority Voting Rights* (Cambridge: Harvard University Press, 1987).

43. Davidson and Grofman, *Quiet Revolution*; and Guinier, *Tyranny of the Majority*.

44. Virginia Kee, oral testimony delivered to the New York City Districting Commission, November 1, 1990, Appendix 3, Vol. 2, 64.

45. Doris Koo, written testimony delivered to the New York City Districting Commission, December 10, 1990, Appendix 3, Vol. 4.

46. Ibid.

47. AAFE used data on the following elections and Asian American candidates: 1985 City Council race, 2d District, Virginia Kee; 1986 judicial race, Democratic primary, Dorothy Chin Brandt; 1987 judicial race, Democratic primary, Peter Tom and Dorothy Chin-Brandt; 1986 and 1988 Senate committeewoman, 61 AD, Democratic primary, Margaret Chin.

48. Doris Koo, written testimony delivered to the New York City Districting Commission, November 1, 1990, Appendix 3, Vol. 2.

49. Sucheng Chan, *Asian Americans: An Interpretive History* (Boston: Twayne Publishers, 1991).

50. Multi-racial District Group, "Lower East Siders for a Multi-Racial District. Redistricting: A Plan for the Redistricting of the Lower East Side/Chinatown Area," March 1991.

51. Elaine Chan, oral testimony delivered to the New York City Districting Commission, March 21, 1991, Appendix 3, Vol. 7, 182.

52. Elaine Chan, oral testimony delivered to the New York City Districting Commission, November 1, 1990, Appendix 3, Vol. 2, 253.

53. Keiko Ohnuma, "Asian Camps Split on District Lines for Lower Manhattan," *AsianWeek*, April 26, 1991, 1.

54. Mini Liu, oral testimony delivered to the New York City Districting Commission, March 21, 1991, Appendix 3, Vol. 7, 290.

55. Frank F. DeGiovanni, *Displacement Pressures in the Lower East Side*, Community Service Society Working Papers (New York: Community Service Society of New York, 1987).

56. Margarita Lopez, interview by Leland T. Saito, April 26, 1996.

57. Wing Lam, interview by Leland T. Saito, April 30, 1996.

58. Hunter College Neighborhood Planning Workshop, "Chinatown: Land Use and Planning Study," Hunter College Neighborhood Planning Workshop, New York, 1992; and Lin, *Reconstructing Chinatown*.

59. William Sites, "Public Action: New York City Policy and the Gentrification of the Lower East Side," in *From Urban Village to East Village: The Battle for New York's Lower East Side*, ed. Janet L. Abu-Lughod (Cambridge: Blackwell, 1994).

60. Antonio Pagan, oral testimony delivered to the New York City Districting Commission, November 1, 1990, Appendix 3, Vol. 2, 213.

61. Timothy P. Fong, "Asian American Redistricting in Oakland, California," paper presented at the 1995 Association for Asian American Studies National Con-

ference, 1995; Tim Fong, "Why Ted Dang Lost: An Analysis of the 1994 Mayoral Race in Oakland, California," *Journal of Asian American Studies* 1 (1998): 153–171; and Saito, *Race and Politics.*

62. In a postscript to that working alliance, however, the Democratic State Assembly primary in 1998 pitted two strong candidates against one another, one Latino, the other Asian American. With Latinos the majority population in the area and with their respective political bases roughly divided along racial lines (despite the history of Asian American–Latino alliances), the Latino won. The race strained the biracial alliances in the area and forms the backdrop as each community contemplates their strategies for the next round of redistricting after the 2000 census.

63. Gartner, "Drawing the Lines," 67, 109.

64. Ibid., 130.

65. Ibid., 67–68.

66. Reed, "Of Boroughs, Boundaries, and Bullwinkles," 777.

67. John Santiago, ed., *Redistricting, Race and Ethnicity in New York City: The Gartner Report and Its Critics* (New York: Institute for Puerto Rican Policy, n.d.).

68. Victor A. Kovner, Joel Berger, and Judith Reed, letter to Richard Jerome, Esq., U.S. Department of Justice, on behalf of the New York City Districting Commission. Re: Section 5 submission for preclearance of 1991 City Council districts: Expedited consideration requested. July 26, 1991.

69. Sarah Ferguson, "Bucking for Realtors," *Village Voice,* September 14, 1993, 14; and Ed Morales, "East Side Story," *Village Voice,* August 20, 1991, 11.

70. AAFE, "Asian Americans for Equality."

71. Andrew Jacobs, "What a Difference Two Decades Make: Asian Americans for Equality Is Attacked as the Establishment It Once Fought," *New York Times,* January 12, 1997, 4.

72. Milyoung Cho, "Overcoming Our Legacy as Cheap Labor, Scabs, and Model Minorities: Asian Activists Fight for Community Empowerment," in *The State of Asian America: Activism and Resistance in the 1990s,* ed. Karin Aguilar-San Juan (Boston: South End Press, 1994), 253–273; and Lucette Lagnado, "Friends in High Places: Margaret Chin's Ties to the Chinatown Elite," *Village Voice,* September 9, 1991, 17.

73. Wayne Barrett, "Anatomy of a Smear: How a Former Reformer Set New Lows in New York City Politics," *Village Voice,* November 5, 1991, 11.

74. Valerie Chow Bush, "Division Street: East Meets West, and the Poor Lose," *Village Voice,* July 23, 1991, 11.

75. Bennett Harrison and Barry Bluestone, *The Great U-Turn: Corporate Restructuring and the Polarizing of America* (New York: Basic Books, 1988); John H. Mollenkopf and Manuel Castells, *Dual City: Restructuring New York* (New York: Russell Sage Foundation, 1991); and Paul Ong (project director), "The Widening Divide: Income Inequality and Poverty in Los Angeles," Research Group on the Los Ange-

les Economy, School of Architecture and Urban Planning, University of California at Los Angeles, 1989.

76. Mollenkopf, *Phoenix in the Ashes*, 53–54.

77. Thomas Bailey and Roger Waldinger, "The Changing Ethnic/Racial Division of Labor," in *Dual City: Restructuring New York*, ed. John H. Mollenkopf and Manuel Castells (New York: Russell Sage Foundation, 1991), 43–78; and Roger Waldinger, *Still the Promised City? African-Americans and New Immigrants in Postindustrial New York* (Cambridge: Harvard University Press, 1996).

78. Peter Kwong, *The New Chinatown* (Toronto: HarperCollins, 1996).

79. Min Zhou, *Chinatown: The Socioeconomic Potential of an Urban Enclave* (Philadelphia: Temple University Press, 1992).

80. Chinatown Land Use and Planning Study, report issued by the Hunter College Neighborhood Planning Workshop, spring 1992.

81. Margaret Chin, interview.

82. Such as whites, Latinos, and African Americans joining to replace Mayor Edward Koch and his divisive policies, in a period marked by heightened racial tension, a political corruption scandal, and economic recession, with African American David Dinkins in 1989. See Mollenkopf, *Phoenix in the Ashes*.

83. Ibid.

84. Jere Hester, "Downtown on the Chopping Block: How Downtown's Political Future Is Being Divided," *Downtown Express*, April 10, 1991, 10.

85. The organization has changed its name from the Committee Against Anti-Asian Violence to CAAAV: Organizing Asian Communities. See *CAAAV Voice* (newsletter of the Committee Against Anti-Asian Violence) 10 (spring 1998): 5.

86. *CAAAV Voice* (newsletter of the Committee Against Anti-Asian Violence) 8 (winter 1996): 3.

87. National Asian Pacific American Legal Consortium, "Audit of Violence against Asian Pacific Americans," NAPALC, Washington, D.C., 1991.

88. Mollenkopf, *Phoenix in the Ashes*; and John H. Mollenkopf, "New York: The Great Anomaly," in *Racial Politics in American Cities*, ed. Rufus P. Browning, Dale Rogers Marshall, and David H. Tabb (New York: Longman, 1990).

89. Steven P. Erie, *Rainbow's End: Irish Americans and the Dilemmas of Urban Machine Politics, 1840–1985* (Berkeley: University of California Press, 1988); and Nathan Glazer and Daniel P. Moynihan, *Beyond the Melting Pot: The Negroes, Puerto Ricans, Jews, Italians, and Irish of New York City*, 2d ed. (Cambridge: MIT Press, 1970).

90. Mollenkopf, "New York: The Great Anomaly."

91. Jere Hester, "Downtown Dems Shun Chin Candidacy," *Downtown Express*, May 1, 1991; Margaret Chin, campaign flyer for 1991 City Council campaign; and Kathryn Freed, campaign flyer for 1991 City Council campaign.

92. Asian American Union for Political Action, letter stating position of the organization on the 1991 City Council elections, August 31, 1991.

93. Asian American Legal Defense and Education Fund, *Outlook* (newsletter) (spring 1992): 5.

94. The political ideology of the voters was wide-ranging: 38.5 percent were Democrats, 21.5 percent were Republicans, 26.4 percent were registered with no party, and 13.6 percent declined to state or registered with another party. Of those who had voted in the 1988 mayoral elections, 28 percent had voted for Democrat David Dinkins and 31.2 percent had voted for Republican Rudolph Giuliani. The range in economic backgrounds is roughly indicated by educational level—28 percent responded that they had less than a high school education, 12 percent had a high school degree or attended a trade/business school, and 33 percent had some college.

95. Lipsitz, *Possessive Investment in Whiteness.*

96. Browning et al., *Protest is Not Enough*; and Sonenshein, *Politics in Black and White.*

97. Karen Brodkin Sacks, "How Did Jews Become White Folks?" in *Race,* ed. Steven Gregory and Roger Sanjek (New Brunswick, N.J.: Rutgers University Press, 1994), 78–102.

98. Robert A. Dahl, *Who Governs? Democracy and Power in an American City* (New Haven: Yale University Press); and Milton M. Gordon, *Assimilation in American Life* (New York: Oxford University Press, 1964).

99. Joseph McCormack and Charles E. Jones, "The Conception of Deracialization: Thinking through the Dilemma," in *Dilemmas of Black Politics,* ed. Georgia Persons (New York: HarperCollins, 1993), 66–84; and Katherine Underwood, "Ethnicity Is Not Enough: Latino-Led Multiracial Coalitions in Los Angeles," paper presented at the 1995 annual meeting of the American Political Science Association.

100. Stanley Lieberson, *A Piece of the Pie: Blacks and White Immigrants since 1880* (Los Angeles: University of California Press, 1980).

101. Edna Bonacich, "A Theory of Ethnic Antagonism: The Split Labor Market," *American Sociological Review* 37 (1972): 547–559; and Richard H. Thompson, "Ethnicity versus Class: An Analysis of Conflict in a North American Chinese Community," *Ethnicity* 6 (1979): 306–326.

102. Guinier, *Tyranny of the Majority*; and Reed, "Of Boroughs, Boundaries and Bullwinkles."

CONTRIBUTORS

Bruce E. Cain is director of the Institute of Governmental Studies and Robson Professor of Political Science at the University of California, Berkeley. His writings include *The Reapportionment Puzzle*, a landmark study of California reapportionment; *The Personal Vote*, written with John Ferejohn and Morris Fiorina; and *Congressional Redistricting*. He has also written numerous articles for professional journals and co-edited several books, including *Developments in American Politics*, vols. 1–3, with Gillian Peele, *Governing California: Politics, Government and Public Policy in the Golden State* with Gerald Lubenow, and *Racial and Ethnic Politics in California*, vol. 2, with Michael Preston and Sandra Bass. He has been a consultant to the *Los Angeles Times* and a commentator for numerous radio and television stations in Los Angeles and the San Francisco Bay area. Cain was elected to the American Academy of Arts and Sciences in April 2000.

Kenyon S. Chan is dean of the Bellarmine College of Liberal Arts and professor of psychology at Loyola Marymount University. His research focuses on social science perspectives on ethnic studies, social policy, and interdisciplinary analyses of race in America. He is recognized as an expert on the effects of race on the emotional development of children and has written extensively on the sociocultural factors that influence motivation, learning, and schooling with particular attention to poor and immigrant children.

Gordon H. Chang is the author of *Friends and Enemies: The United States, China, and the Soviet Union, 1948–1972,* and *Morning Glory, Evening Shadow: Yamato Ichihashi and His Internment Writings, 1942–45,* and many articles on U.S.-East Asian relations and on Asian American history. He was a Guggenheim Fellow in 1999 and is an associate professor in the Department of History at Stanford University.

Wendy K. Tam Cho is assistant professor of political science and assistant professor of statistics at the University of Illinois at Urbana-Champaign. She specializes in issues of race in American politics and in statistical modeling. Her work has appeared in a number of journals including the *American Political Science Review, Political Analysis,* and the *Journal of Politics.*

Manish Desai is completing degrees in economics and public policy at Stanford University. He has worked for various congressional campaigns, and at the Office of Management and Budget and the American Enterprise Institute.

Neil T. Gotanda has written and lectured extensively on issues of racial ideology in American law, focusing on the construction of race in Supreme Court opinions. His writings include "A Critique of 'Our Constitution Is Color-Blind' " in *Stanford Law Review,* and "Comparative Racialization: Racial Profiling and the Case of Wen Ho Lee" in *UCLA Law Review.* A professor at Western State University, he is currently visiting at St. Johns University School of Law.

Sanjeev Khagram is a faculty member at the John F. Kennedy School of Government, Harvard University. In addition to his work on Asian Americans and race in the United States, he specializes in leadership, strategic management, the political economy of development, civil society, and global and democratic governance. He is co-editor of *Restructuring World Politics: The Power of Transnational Norms, Networks, and Social Movements* (forthcoming).

Peter Nien-Chu Kiang is associate professor of education and director of the Asian American Studies Program at the University of Massachusetts, Boston. His research focuses on leadership development with Asian American youth and documenting the experiences of Asian Pacific American Vietnam veterans. Kiang's work with Asian Americans in both K–12 and higher education has been recognized by groups such as the National Academy of Education, the National Endowment for the Humanities, the Massachusetts Teachers Association, the Massachusetts Association for Bilingual Education, the NAACP, and the Anti-Defamation League.

Claire Jean Kim is on the faculty at the University of California, Irvine, where she holds a joint appointment in the Department of Political Science and the Asian American studies program. She is the author of *Bitter Fruit: The Politics of Black-Korean Conflict in New York City* and numerous articles on the social construction of race in the United States.

David E. Lee is the executive director of the nonpartisan Chinese American Voters Education Committee (CAVEC), a private nonprofit corporation. Founded in 1976, CAVEC's mission is to research the causes of low Asian American political participation and to develop and implement remedies. Recent projects include a major survey of Chinese newspaper readers, a conference of California ethnic news organizations, and an ethnic news web-portal (www.ncmonline.com).

Pei-te Lien teaches political science and Asian American studies at the University of Utah. Her primary research interest is the political participation of Asian and other groups of Americans. She is the author of *The Political Participation of Asian Americans: Voting Behavior in Southern California* and *The Making of Asian America Through Political Participation* (forthcoming). She also publishes widely on issues of race, gender, and Asian American politics in professional journals and edited book volumes.

Don T. Nakanishi is the director of the Asian American Studies Center at the University of California, Los Angeles, and a professor in the UCLA Graduate School of Education and Information Studies. A political scientist, he is the author of more than seventy books, articles, and reports on the political participation of Asian Pacific Americans and other ethnic and racial groups in American politics; educational policy research; and the international political dimensions of minority experiences. He has received numerous awards for his scholarly achievements and public service, and has been a member of the board of directors for many national and local organizations.

Paul M. Ong is a professor at the School of Public Policy and Social Research at the University of California, Los Angeles, and director of UCLA's Lewis Center for Regional Policy Studies and Institute of Industrial Relations. His publications include *The New Asian Immigration in Los Angeles and Global Restructuring, Impacts of Affirmative Action: Policies and Consequences in California*, and *Transforming Race Relations: The State of Asian Pacific America*. He has served on advisory committees for the state of California, the South Coast Air Quality Management District, the Getty

Research Institute for the History of Art and the Humanities, the California Wellness Foundation, and the U.S. Bureau of the Census.

Edward J. W. Park is the director of the Asian Pacific American Studies Program at Loyola Marymount University. His research topics include Asian American politics, ethnic economy, and race relations, and he has consulted widely for numerous organizations on racial and immigration issues, including the Social Sciences Research Council, the Russell Sage Foundation, the U.S. Department of Housing and Human Services, the Korean American Museum, and the Getty Research Institute.

Leland T. Saito is associate professor of ethnic studies at the University of California, San Diego. His research focuses on urban politics, economic redevelopment, and race relations in multiracial communities, particularly in Los Angeles, New York City, and San Diego. In addition to articles on these topics, he is the author of *Race and Politics: Asian Americans, Latinos, and Whites in a Los Angeles Suburb.* He is a co-founder of the Southwest Center for Asian Pacific American Law.

Jason Varughese is completing a degree in symbolic systems with a concentration in biomedical informatics at Stanford University. His research interests also include the effects of sleep loss on fatal automobile accidents. He has worked for 3M's Health Information Systems division and Howard Schultz & Associates.

Paul Y. Watanabe is co-director of the Institute for Asian American Studies and associate professor in of political science at the University of Massachusetts. He is vice president of the board of directors of the Massachusetts Immigrant and Refugee Advocacy Coalition and a member of the boards of the Asian Pacific American Agenda Coalition and the Asian Task Force Against Domestic Violence. He is also a member of the Academic Advisory Committee of the John F. Kennedy Library and the National Academic Board of the *Asian American Policy Review.* He is the author of *Ethnic Groups, Congress, and American Foreign Policy* and co-author of *A Dream Deferred: Changing Demographics, New Challenges and Opportunities for Boston.* His research has appeared in *Political Psychology, World Today, Public Perspective, Asian American Policy Review,* and *Business in the Contemporary World.*

Frank H. Wu joined the faculty of the Howard University School of Law in 1995. Currently the clinic director and an associate professor at Howard, he supervises students working on actual cases in the D.C. Superior Court and also teaches traditional courses such as civil procedure and federal courts. His op-ed pieces have appeared in the *Washington Post,* the *Los Angeles Times, Chicago Tribune*, among other newspapers. His *Yellow: Civil Rights Beyond Black and White* is forthcoming. Formerly the Washington correspondent for *Asian Week*, he is a political columnist for *A. magazine*.

Francey Lim Youngberg is the president of Youngberg & Associates based in Washington, D.C. Youngberg, a consultant to numerous national and local organizations serving the Asian Pacific American community, was the founding executive director of the Asian Pacific American Institute for Congressional Studies, formerly named the Congressional Asian Pacific American Caucus Institute. She has been named as one of the Twenty-five Influential Minority Women in Business by the Minority Business and Professional Network, one of the Twenty-five Most Influential Asians in America by *A. magazine* and one of fifteen Washingtonians of the Year by *Washingtonian* magazine in 1996.

Judy Yu, president of AsiaNet Marketing, is a public relations and strategic planning consultant. She specializes in advising clients interested in developing marketing and communications programs targeting the Asian American communities around the country. These clients include politicians, entertainers, and corporations.

Grace T. Yuan is a partner at the law firm of Preston Gates & Ellis. She practices in the areas of municipal, land use, and education law. She authored "Assuring Equal Access of Asian Americans to Highly Selective Universities," 98 *Yale Law Journal* 659 (1989), 135 *Cong. Rec.* § 1146 (daily edition Feb. 2, 1989), and was a senior editor of the *Yale Law Journal.* Yuan also co-authored *Voting in Washington: A Teacher's Reference Guide* for Kids Voting Washington and *The SEPA/GMA Workbook* for the Washington State Department of Community, Trade, and Economic Development. Yuan is the author of a number of local ordinances for county councils and city councils and has assisted in drafting legislation that has been enacted into law by the Washington state legislature.

INDEX

AAFE (Asian Americans for Equality), 388, 390–91, 393–96

AALDEF (Asian American Legal Defense and Education Fund), 376, 389, 391, 398

affirmative action: African Americans and, 59–61, 139, 143, 145; Asian Americans and, 59–61, 75n. 81, 103, 139–40, 142, 144, 165–66, 239, 314, 363, 378; Asian Indian Americans and, 277; in California, 61, 103, 134, 140–41; model minority myth and, 61; Proposition 209 and, 61, 103, 134, 140–42, 145–49, 165; racial retrenchment and, 59; racial triangulation and, 59–62

African Americans: affirmative action and, 59–61, 139, 143, 145, 314; Asian Americans and, 28, 55–56, 59–61, 68n. 6, 71n. 42, 81, 176, 384, 391–92, 397; assimilation of, 45; in California, 44–46, 48, 135–36; campaign donations and, 361–62; Chinese Americans and, 44–49; citizenship and, 48–49, 81–82; community and, 378; cultural values of, 53, 57; December 12th Movement and, 62–63; discrimination against, 44, 48, 60, 62, 385; electoral involvement of, 48–49, 179–88, 394; Flatbush boycott and, 62–63; gender gap and, 173, 181–88; on illegal

immigration, 137; immigration and, 200; income of, 206; Japanese Americans and, 19, 27, 55–56; Korean Americans and, 61–63, 123, 285, 288–89, 293–94, 296–99, 301, 305n. 11; Latinos and, 298, 384; location of, 204; Los Angeles civil unrest of 1992 and, 289; media and, 62–63, 76n. 89; model minority myth and, 55–58; other ethnic groups and, 136, 138; partisan politics of, 148, 161; perceptions of, by whites, 45–46, 56–58, 60, 62–63, 71n. 44, 83–84, 91; political concerns of, 46, 392; political participation of, 18–19, 27, 55–58, 62–63, 60, 378; poverty and, 206; Proposition 187 and, 137, 143; Proposition 209 and, 141, 145; racial gap and, 178–88; racial retrenchment and, 55–57; racism and, 40–46, 53–63, 81–84, 139–40, 385–86; segregation of, 385; sexism and, 176–77; underclass myth and, 57–58, 75n. 76

Akaka, Daniel, 327

Alien Land Act, 263–64

American Association of Physicians of Indian Origin (AAPI), 278

American Federation of Labor, 261, 265

APPPCON (Asian Pacific Policy and Planning Council), 160